To Repair t
Reparation and Reconstruction in South Africa

Edited by Erik Doxtader and Charles Villa-Vicencio

Institute for Justice
and Reconciliation

The financial assistance of the Swiss Agency for Development and Co-operation is gratefully acknowledged

First published in 2004 in southern Africa by
David Philip Publishers, an imprint of New Africa Books (Pty) Ltd 99 Garfield Road,
Claremont 7700, South Africa

Second Impression 2006

ISBN 13: 978-0-86486-618-9
ISBN 10: 0-86486-618-6

Cover and text design: Fresh Identity
Project manager: Karen van Eden
Editor: Linda le Roux
Proofreader: Tessa Kennedy
Typeset in 11 on 13 pt Bembo by Peter Stuckey
Cover illustration: Velile Soha
Printed and bound by Mega Digital

Contents

Preface vi
Archbishop Desmond Tutu

Contributors ix

Introduction: Repairing a Damaged Future xiii
Erik Doxtader and Charles Villa-Vicencio

Section One
The Controversial Terms of Reparations Policy in South Africa

1   Truth and Reconciliation Commission of South Africa:
    Excerpts from the Report of the Reparation and
    Rehabilitation Committee 1
2   Statement to the National Houses of Parliament and the
    Nation at the Tabling of the Report of the Truth and
    Reconciliation Commission, 15 April 2003 15
    Thabo Mbeki
3   Reparations – It Is Still Not Too Late
    Mary Burton 29
4   The Joint Sitting of Parliament, 15 April 2003:
    A Rhetorical View of the Reparation Debate 44
    Philippe-Joseph Salazar

Section Two
Reparation, Restoration, and Reconciliation:
An 'Agonising Balancing Act'

5   A Difficult Justice: Reparation, Restoration and Rights 66
    Charles Villa-Vicencio
6   Legal Norms, Moral Imperatives and Pragmatic Duties:
    Reparation as a Dilemma of Transitional Governance 88
    Stef Vandeginste

7   Voices Not Heard: Small Histories and the Work of Repair 106
      Fiona C. Ross and Pamela Reynolds
8   The Matter of Words in the Midst of Beginnings: Unravelling
      the 'Relationship' between Reparation and Reconciliation..... 115
      Erik Doxtader
9   Out of the Crooked Timber of Humanity: Humanising Rights
      in South Africa 149
      Mieke Holkeboer
10   Doing Justice in South Africa: Restorative Justice and
      Reparation 166
      Jennifer J. Llewellyn

Section Three
Progress in the Face of History: The Ongoing Work of
Reparations and Reconstruction in South Africa

11   Across the Divides of Perception: The Strategic and Moral
      Demands of Reparation at the End of the TRC 184
      Karin Lombard
12   Reconciliation, Reparation and Reconstruction in Post-1994
      South Africa: What Role for Land? 197
      Lungisile Ntsebeza
13   For the Next Generations: Remaking South Africa's
      Juvenile Justice System 211
      Ann Skelton
14   Amnesty, Reparation and the Object of Reconciliation in the Context
      of South Africa's Truth and Reconciliation Commission 224
      Ilan Lax
15   The Promise and Pitfalls of Apology 242
      Trudy Govier and Wilhelm Verwoerd
16   The Rupture of Necklace Murders: A Need for Psychological and
      Broader Strategies of Reparation 256
      Pumla Gobodo-Madikizela
17   Building Sites of Repair: Freedom Park and its Objectives 265
      Revel Fox

Section Four
Precedents, Lessons and Hopes: International
Perspectives on Reparations

18   Pursuing Private Actors for Reparations for Human Rights
     Abuses Committed in Africa in the Courts of the
     United States of America 271
     Jeremy Sarkin
19   Reparation Efforts in International Perspective: What
     Compensation Contributes to the Achievement of
     Imperfect Justice 321
     Pablo de Greiff
20   On Monuments, Memorials and Memory: Some Precedent
     Towards a South African Option 359
     Neville Dubow
21   Ritual, Reparation and Reintegration: The Challenge of
     Reconciliation in Post-Conflict African Societies 379
     Tyrone Savage and Zola Sonkosi
22   A Plan of Integral Reparations 393
     Truth and Reconciliation Commission of Peru
23   Reparation Policy in Nigeria 401
     Sonny C. Onyegbula

Preface

Desmond M. Tutu
Archbishop Emeritus of Cape Town

The Truth and Reconciliation Commission (TRC) has completed its work and made a range of recommendations, suggesting how we as a nation might continue to endeavour to heal ourselves. Included in these recommendations are proposals on reparations. The government has responded – not seeing fit to accept the recommendation we made on individual reparations to those who the Commission found to be victims of gross violations of human rights. Yes, I am disappointed that victims will not receive more. When we consider the total cost of these reparations in relation to other forms of expenditure, including the purchase of military equipment, victims have a right to feel aggrieved.

The oppressed people of this nation showed unbelievable magnanimity at the time of our political settlement. They could have demanded a lot more than they did. The TRC's recommendations on reparations were always never intended to be more than a symbolic acknowledgment of the price paid by many South Africans in the long struggle against apartheid. These recommendations provided government, the people and the nation as a whole with an opportunity to do just that. Generosity, kindness and hope for a better future, those characteristics of our transition to democracy in 1994, need to be reaffirmed at every opportunity. They must be made the abiding spirit of our nation.

So where do we go from here? We as a nation need to continue to engage one another around questions of how to deal with our past – not least with regard to providing restorative measures for those who have suffered most. The aim of reparation is to empower individuals and communities to take control of their own lives. It is to restore the human dignity of victims and acknowledge the price they have paid in reclaiming their dignity. Restitution demands that all that has been taken from victims needs to be returned to them. We have never asked for that in South Africa. The need is to find balance that empowers, acknowledges and provides a dignified opportunity for all South Africans – victims, perpetrators and beneficiaries of apartheid – to share in the creation of a nation that affirms the dignity of all its citizens. This requires serious debate, social engagement between people who have been historically separated from one another and a willingness to show spiritual and material generosity towards one another.

Such debate can in itself be part of the healing. It is here that we meet one another as people, trying to see the problem from the perspective of the other, finding the necessary middle ground that enables us to go forward. There are no simple solutions to the challenge we face. Justice and reparation can, and need to take, many different forms. There will always be trade-offs, not everybody will always be happy with the outcome, but solutions in the sense of finding the next logical step forward that links reconciliation, reparation and justice *are* there. We have found them before and we need to find them again and again and again. That is what nation-building is all about.

Reparation is ultimately about transcending both the material and social divide, recognising that the one is dependent on the other. This is where the reparation debate needs to go. Government has a specific obligation in this regard. It is answerable to a huge majority of largely poor people. It has the power to make things happen and a constitutional mandate to create a united nation – to which poverty remains the biggest and most demanding threat. The president has, in his response to recommendations of the TRC, promised communal reparations in the form of housing, health care and education aimed at the upliftment of all who have suffered under apartheid. Government further speaks of incentives to business to invest in job creation, poverty relief and skills development. It is part of the democratic responsibility of all South Africans to monitor the outcome of these developments.

There may well be legal grounds for compensation claims against business. One would, however, hope that court proceedings are a last resort, to be implemented perhaps only if business fails to respond adequately to the challenge of repairing past wrongs. Archbishop Njongonkulu Ndungane has called on business to engage reparations claimant groups as an alternative to lawsuits which he attributes to 'sheer frustration' in the face of indifference to their demands. A simple acknowledgement of having benefited from apartheid would be a good place to begin.

The SA *Reconciliation Barometer* shows that most South Africans, black and white, feel they cannot personally influence the reconciliation process.

This malaise needs to be redressed. I suggested, at the handing over of the Final Report of the Commission earlier this year, that every family, black and white, who can afford to do so adopt an indigent family, giving them R100 or R200 a month. Others have skills to offer. This could make a huge difference to the lives of the poor. The impact could be massive if every church, mosque, synagogue, board meeting, social club and dinner party in the country took time out to promote the idea.

We pride ourselves at having pulled off a negotiated political settlement, celebrate the miracle of the new South Africa and continue to talk about the importance of nation-building. The president reminded us on a previous occasion that if 'we handle the transformation in a way that doesn't change a good part of the status quo, those who are disadvantaged will rebel, and then goodbye reconciliation'. The question is how to enable government, business and individuals to rise to the challenge of economic compromise. Whatever we may think of the government's response to the TRC's proposals on reparations, this is where the future of reconciliation is likely to be located. It is time to tackle the challenge head-on.

I hope this book will be widely read and debated. This collection of essays sets out the reparation debate in a balanced and creative way. In many ways the real debate, a sense of deep engagement, still needs to happen. I am delighted to associate myself with this publication that comes from an institute of which I am proud to be patron.

Cape Town
November 2003

Contributors

Mary Burton served as a commissioner on the Truth and Reconciliation Commission, and on its Human Rights Violations Committee. Prior to that, she was active in various non-governmental organisations campaigning for human rights and against apartheid, in particular the Black Sash. In 1994 she was appointed as the provincial electoral officer in the Western Cape Province, for South Africa's first fully democratic national elections. She is at present the deputy chairperson of the governing Council of the University of Cape Town.

Pablo de Greiff is the director of research at the International center for Transitional Justice in New York. Born in Colombia, he graduated from Yale University (B.A.) and from Northwestern University (Ph.D.). Recently, he was Associate Professor in the Philosophy Department at the State University of New York at Buffalo, where he taught ethics and political theory. He has published articles on transitions to democracy, democratic theory, and the relationship between morality, politics and law. He is the editor of five books, most recently, *Global Justice and Transnational Politics* (MIT Press, 2002). At the ICTJ, among other projects, he directs a large scale project on reparations, which will be published under the title *Repairing the Past: Compensation for Victims of Human Abuse*. He is also working on a book entitled *Redeeming the Claims of Justice in Transitions to Democracy*.

Erik Doxtader is an Assistant Professor of Rhetoric at the University of Wisconsin-Madison, USA and a Senior Research Fellow at the Institute for Justice and Reconciliation. A former Social Science Research Council-MacArthur fellow, he has co-edited two books and published a number of essays on the South African transition and the dynamics of reconciliation. At present, he is completing a book that investigates the history and practice of reconciliation in South Africa.

Neville Dubow is Emeritus Professor of Fine Art, University of Cape Town. A multi-disciplinarian in art and architecture, he has lectured extensively in these fields, and has written on their relationship to memory. His recent publications include *Imaging the Unimaginable: Holocaust memory in art and architecture*.

Revel Fox is the founder and senior partner of Revel Fox and Partners, Architects and Planners, a firm which has been in existence since 1966. He was a delegate to the IDASA/ANC conference held in Dakar, Senegal in 1987. He was a Cape Town city councillor from 1996 to 1999, representing the ANC, and serving on the Planning Committee and the Cape Peninsula National Park Committee. In recognition of his lifelong contribution to excellence in architectural practice, education and professional affairs, and the advancement of architecture in South Africa, he has had the degree of D. Arch *(honoris causa)* conferred on him by the University of Natal in 1993, and the University of Cape Town in 2001.

Pumla Gobodo-Madikizela is a clinical psychologist and former member of the Truth and Reconciliation Commission. She is Associate Professor of Psychology at the University of Cape Town and adjunct professor in the Unilever Ethics Centre at Natal University. Her book *A Human Being Died that Night: A South African Story of Forgiveness* was published in 2003.

Trudy Govier PhD, is an independent philosopher, based in Calgary, Canada.

Mieke Holkeboer has a PhD in Theology from the University of Chicago, USA. She has served as Research Fellow at the Institute for Justice and Reconciliation. Her research focuses on the development and practice of international human rights law.

Ilan Lax is a qualified practising attorney. He joined the TRC as a member of the Human Rights Violations Committee (HRVC) on 1 March 1996. Although he was based at the Durban regional office of the TRC, he served throughout the country. He also served on the legal working group of the Commission. After serving on the HRVC for about two years, in March 1998 he was appointed as a member of the Amnesty Committee and served there until June 2001. He has recently served as policy advisor to the TRC in Sierra Leone.

Jennifer J. Llewellyn is an Assistant Professor, Dalhousie Law School, Nova Scotia, Canada.

Karin Lombard is project leader of the SA Reconciliation Barometer of the Institute for Justice and Reconciliation.

Lungisile Ntsebeza is a Senior Researcher in the Programme for Land and Agrarian Studies (PLAAS) at the University of the Western Cape, South Africa.

Sonny C. Onyegbula is a member of the Faculty of Law at the University of the Western Cape, South Africa.

Pamela Reynolds is Professor of Anthropology at Johns Hopkins University, Baltimore, USA. She has written many books on children in southern Africa and has published widely on aspects of children's experiences of violence and political activism. She is co-editor of *Violence and Subjectivity* and *Remaking A World*.

Fiona C. Ross teaches social anthropology at the University of Cape Town. She lives on a smallholding near Stellenbosch with Andy and their sometimes belligerent cat, Bovril, and likes to listen to the booming of the ostriches on the neighbouring farm.

Philippe-Joseph Salazar is Distinguished Professor, Centre for Rhetoric Studies, University of Cape Town, and Director, Rhetoric and Democracy, Collège International de Philosophie, Paris.

Jeremy Sarkin is Senior Professor of Law and Deputy Dean, Law Faculty, University of the Western Cape, South Africa, and legal advisor to Chief Riruako, paramount chief of the Hereros of Namibia; BA LLB (Natal), LLM (Harvard), LLD (UWC); attorney of the High Court of South Africa, attorney at law in the State of New York, USA. He can be contacted at jsarkin@global.co.za.

Tyrone Savage is currently Africa Programme Co-ordinator at the Institute for Justice and Reconciliation. Following studies at the University of Cape Town, he was awarded a Fulbright Fellowship for graduate studies in conflict mediation. He is a graduate of Syracuse University's Maxwell School of Citizenship and Public Affairs. His publications include *Rwanda and South Africa in Dialogue: Addressing the Legacy of Genocide and a Crime Against Humanity*.

Ann Skelton is a human rights lawyer who has specialised in the rights of children in the criminal justice system. In 1997, she was appointed by the South African Minister of Justice to lead a project of the South African Law Commission to develop a comprehensive new statute regarding children accused of crimes. The Child Justice Bill, which emanated from this process, embodies restorative justice principles. Currently, Skelton is the national co-ordinator of the Child Justice Project, a UN technical assistance project based in the Department of Justice in Pretoria. The main objective of the project is to assist both government and civil society to prepare for effective implementation of the new child justice system.

Zola Sonkosi leads the Institute for Justice and Reconciliation's Africa Programme. He taught African politics and political economy for many years at the universities of Frankfurt, Leipzig, Zurich and the Technical University, Berlin. He has served as an advisor to the Green Party in the State Parliament of Lower Saxony on issues concerning immigrants and refugees in Europe, African conflicts and North-South conflicts.

Stef Vandeginste holds an MA in law from the Catholic University of Leuven, Belgium (1990). He did research on the human rights situation in the Central African Great Lakes Region for Amnesty International and worked for the United Nations Development Programme in Rwanda. He is currently doing research on the international right to reparation for victims of gross and systematic human rights violations at the Law Faculty of the University of Antwerp.

Wilhelm Verwoerd is a programme co-ordinator at the Glencree Centre for Reconciliation, Co. Wicklow, Ireland and a research fellow of the Centre for Applied Ethics, Department of Philosophy, University of Stellenbosch, South Africa.

Charles Villa-Vicencio is Executive Director of the Institute for Justice and Reconciliation. He served as the research director for the South African Truth and Reconciliation Commission. He is a former professor of religion and society at the University of Cape Town. He was appointed a fellow of that university in 1994. He has published widely in the area of South African reconciliation and transitional justice.

Introduction:
Repairing a Damaged Future

Erik Doxtader and Charles Villa-Vicencio

Reparation is difficult work for the present. In the face of a history that will not 'end', it holds the question of how to craft a present for the future. Much more than an ideal to be achieved in some vague time yet to come, its hope for transformation is a call to act right now. The fact that reparation can neither erase history's pain nor fully compensate for its losses is not a reason to conclude that what's past is past or that legacies imply an inevitability which defies correction. But this is not to say that there are ready-made solutions. Much more than a policy that culminates in a one-time payout or fleeting acknowledgement, the power of the reparative may reside in an attitude, a willingness to see historical deprivation and inequality as a common problem that demands struggle for a future in which things are made otherwise.

For South Africa, ten years has brought profound if not miraculous change. In the midst of incredible bloodshed and despair, the negotiated end of statutory apartheid brought with it one of the world's most progressive constitutions and the election of Nelson Mandela, a man celebrated globally as the very embodiment of democracy's spirit; an economy in its death throes has not only been resuscitated but grown; the work of the Truth and Reconciliation Commission (TRC) has helped uncover the legacy of apartheid, recognise the experiences of those who suffered under its rule, and teach something about how citizens might continue the task of learning to live together in ways that are both peaceful and productive.

At the beginning of democracy's second decade, there is much to celebrate and much left to do. It is too soon to tell whether the South African transition will produce the kind of society most hoped for in the heady days of 1994 elections. Neville Alexander offers a salutary warning in this regard, suggesting that the signal characterisation of South Africa as a 'society in transition' carries within it both the potential for real change and the risk of becoming what he so aptly calls an 'ordinary country', a nation driven by a 'normal, bourgeois, democratic polity' that simply provides a new set of beneficiaries to replace the old. Contending that there is very little danger of left-wing evolutionary upsurge in the short to medium term, Alexander suggests that in the long run, entrenched inequality can only result in significant instability rooted in a 'movement of desperation'.[1] In the light of history, the gross discrepancy between rich and poor constitutes a fundamental threat to both citizens and the nation. The urgent need to bridge this gap is the fundamental problem of how to undertake repair and muster the capacity for reconstruction.

With uncertain outcome, the transition continues. Measures of reparation for those who were exploited and victimised by apartheid were always going to be controversial and contested. The South African government's response to the recommendations presented by the TRC in mid-2003 has been greeted with both relief and disappointment. Business and most whites are relieved at the government's apparent reluctance to impose targeted taxes and unwillingness to support the legal actions that have been initiated against companies which benefited from apartheid. However, the government's reparation package has left some feeling betrayed. Even as a symbolic acknowledgement of their suffering, the announced payment of R30,000 is seen by them as grossly inadequate. The declared government intention to augment this sum with communal or collective reparation, in the form of housing, health care, and education aimed at the upliftment of all who suffered under apartheid, is dismissed as a responsibility of government that is unrelated to the duty to make repairs for the crimes of apartheid. Others disagree, contending that a democratically elected government needs to serve all citizens and that it cannot single out or devote itself to one specific group of victims. In light of the debate, it appears that the present phase of the South African transition turns partly on the ability of policy-makers, institutions, and citizens to find a meaningful middle ground that will facilitate the redress of a vast material inequality which contains the seeds of deep (re)division.

Debate over reparation is likely to grow substantially in the next months and years. In some sense, the controversy is just coming into its full form. With the stage set by the release of the TRC's final reparations recommendations and government's response, the stakes of the controversy will be heightened both by the 2004 election and the significant national and international reflection that will occur around the tenth anniversary of democratisation. In any case, the dispute will circle around a number of important problems. Has the form of South Africa's transition served all

South African citizens equally? Did the negotiations give too much away? Did the need for political stability come at the expense of material redistribution? How well did the TRC do with its charge to formulate proposals for reparation? Were too many expectations placed on the Commission? Has dissatisfaction with reparation policy risked the project of reconciliation? Will it? Does restorative justice depend on a broad-based reparation programme? What are the moral, legal and political obligations to pay reparation? What exactly is the difference between reparation and reconstruction? Do they trade off? If so, how are the coming choices to be made? Who can, will and ought to pay? What happens if they do not?

Reparation matters. The essays that compose this volume leave no doubt about their significance. They also demonstrate that the standing questions about reparation form a constellation of linked problems, not all of which are fully understood. Indeed, recalling Kader Asmal's important 1992 appeal, the contributions indicate that controversy over how to 'make good' has much to do with the fact that there are many ways to define both the means and ends of reparations.[2] From money and land to symbolic exchanges that bring recognition and opportunities for remembrance, the reparative takes a variety of forms. Its need can be justified on a number of grounds, including legal obligation, moral duty, the public good, and a concern for the restoration of human dignity. Moreover, the essays here underscore that reparation takes time and force difficult choices about who and who will not benefit. Citing finite resources, standing mistrust, and the sheer enormity of the problem, many of the authors argue that the future of reparation depends on the creation of a deliberate debate that is infused with a significant dose of civic virtue. Frequently tied to a spirit of ubuntu, many of the essays contend that the possibility for meaningful reparation rests on the emergence of an *ethos*, a form of individual and collective character that can motivate individuals and institutions to strive not just for the 'minimally decent' but for a practical sense of ethical care, a commitment that entails reaching across historical divisions and transcending self-interest in the name of building a common future.

A great deal is on the table and not much has been settled. In the name of both understanding and promoting debate, this volume gathers the problem of reparation around four specific questions: What are the current terms of South African reparation policy? In the midst of transition, how is it possible to strike a productive balance between the demands of reparation, reconciliation and justice? What challenges have appeared during an(

after the work of the TRC? How does the South African experience both
benefit from and contribute to international reparation efforts? In the end,
the essays here suggest that these issues cannot be separated. They are problems that delineate the work to come, the difficult task of rendering the
irreparable as it is not.

Debating Reparation Policy

There is both ambiguity and controversy around the announced terms of
South Africa's reparation policy. Here, we begin this volume by reprint-
ing several texts that document the contemporary history of reparation in
South Africa. The first is a selection from the TRC's 2003 Final Report in
which the Commission explains its mandate and details its recommendations for reparations. The second is a transcript of the address delivered by
President Thabo Mbeki to Parliament on the occasion of the tabling of
the Commission's report. In it, the president announces that government
will pay individuals reparations but will do so with 'some apprehension'
about their value in building 'a better life for all'. Read together, these
two policy documents reveal an important set of uncertainties and tensions about how to define and implement reparation strategies in the wake
of apartheid. The texts are important precisely as they expose the problem
of how South Africa can balance the redress of individual need and
collective development. Too, the texts betray a sense of frustration, a
lingering dispute between the TRC and the state executive over when
and how to take up and resolve the reparation question.

Disagreement about reparation is not new. Its complex history is well
documented by Mary Burton in her essay on the development of the TRC
and the evolving work of its Reparation and Rehabilitation Committee.
Centrally, Burton's essay raises important questions about how the
Commission's final recommendations have been received and asks whether
the debate to come will advance or undermine the TRC's goals and credibility. In his reflection on Parliament's debate about the TRC's Report,
Philippe Salazar wonders whether there has been any debate at all. The
question is a vital one, particularly as it speaks to the issues of how the term
'reparation' has been entered into the South African political lexicon and
the ways in which elected officials shape the contours of public deliberation.

Reparation policy is not easy to make. Viewed at once, the institutional
statements and critical commentaries over the development of reparation

legislation indicate that dispute over the matter is likely to linger, if not intensify. About much more than money, the reparative involves significant questions about how to define the dynamics of nation-building and spur collective action in the midst of dire need and a legacy of deep division.

The Difficult Balance of Transition

From the perpetration of gross violations of human rights to the everyday indignities of life under apartheid, the need for reparation is often set on the grounds of justice. However, as Charles Villa-Vicencio notes in his essay, 'justice is not self-defining' and it has many forms, some of which may do more harm than good in the context of transition. As well, many different kinds of action can have reparative effects and there are many reasons to undertake reparation initiatives. Not all of these means and ends are consistent. Some may trade off, provoking disputes about who is being served and who is being left behind. When coupled to perceptions as to how justice has not been done, such disagreement can complicate if not confound the promotion of reconciliation. Today, South Africa faces the question of how to sustain and co-ordinate programmes that heal individual and collective wounds, restore dignity, build unity, create political-economic equality, and foster a culture of human rights.

In the difficult time of transition, much hangs in the balance. The essays in the second section of the volume consider the problem of how this balance is best made and set into practice. In his contribution, Villa-Vicencio charts the individual, communal, and national dimensions of reparation. The result is a theory of 'difficult justice', one that is addressed to both the material and subjective elements of restoration. Drawing from the tenets of international law, Stef Vandeginste's essay details the legal case for reparation. Observing that the legal aim of reparation is to 'wipe out the consequences of an illegal act and reestablish the situation that would have existed if that act had not been committed', he finds that this work is not easy, especially in the context of transitional situations which complicate the demands of the law and place tremendous emphasis on creating policies that do not (re)divide young democracies. In their essay on the voices heard and not heard at the TRC, Fiona Ross and Pamela Reynolds explore this problem in a different way. Emphasising that 'suffering and healing in South Africa are particular', they expose rifts in the Commission's work and question the degree to which repair can proceed through testimony. At base, their subtle study indicates that the meaning of reparation is highly contextual and that institutional efforts to promote repair are not without individual and collective risk. In his essay, Erik Doxtader asks how controversy over the meaning of reparation is linked to the potential for reconciliation. Concerned with the question of how the reconciliatory and the reparative were set into relation during the development of the TRC, the essay is both a historical survey and critical reflection on the importance of remembering that the tension between these two goods may well help support the work of democratic transition. Looking both inside and outside, Mieke Holkeboer's essay speaks to the ways in which the South African experience may demand a rethinking of international human rights norms, particularly in terms of how they do and do not take account of local variation and contextual difference. Jennifer Llewellyn underscores the point, arguing that restorative justice is not a weak justice but one that finds strength in the ability of human beings to enter into and sustain relationships.

Reparation neither undoes the past nor comes with assurances of success. Inside and outside the laws of state and morality, the reparative does not always mean the same thing and can have both additive and deleterious effects on other initiatives that are designed to support transition and promote democratisation. Both an opportunity and a risk, the essays here suggest that reparations are vital and that they must be carefully related to programmes that strive for reconciliation, restoration, and reconstruction. The balance is a delicate one, a question of how to create anew with care.

The Work that Remains

Reparations take time. Their success demands sensitivity to both individual need and collective interest. They also require an ongoing and frequently frustrating commitment to change in the face of scarce resources. Once-off payments matter little if they are not accompanied by measures that allow recipients to build a better future; symbolic forms of acknowledgement may have little meaning if they do not involve citizens and open opportunities for participation. In 1994, the TRC was heralded as one initiative among many designed to repair and heal the wounds of the past. With its close, there is now an important opportunity to reflect on what the Commission and its counterparts have accomplished and what tasks remain unfinished.

The essays that compose the third section of this volume detail some of the work that lies ahead. Is there popular support for reparations in the wake of the TRC? This question is central to Karin Lombard's analysis of recent South African public opinion. In her essay, Lombard demonstrates that many citizens remain divided – often along racial lines – about the need for reparations and the question of who should foot the bill. Set against the backdrop of dramatic economic inequality, these differences portend both complacency and conflict, a situation in which the powerful turn a blind eye while the weak grow increasingly frustrated. According to Lungisile Ntsebeza, land is a crucial element of the problem and one that has not been fully factored into the reparation equation. Detailing the slow pace of the land reform process and the entrenched legacy of colonial dispossession and forced removal, Ntsebeza shows how the land question is tied to the historical exploitation of black labour, a form of victimisation that fell outside the TRC's narrow definition but which may well demand constitutional remedy. Also concerned with the effects of colonialism, Ann Skelton wonders about the coming generations in her essay on juvenile justice. Drawing from the lessons of the TRC, especially its claims as to how ubuntu can serve as a basis for restorative justice, Skelton details the terms of the Child Justice Bill, legislation that may both enhance the rights of youth and contribute to the strengthening of South Africa's social fabric.

The work of the TRC is a central concern of Ilan Lax's essay. In it, he charts the development and difficulties of the amnesty process and asks whether the Commission's truth-seeking efforts constituted a form of reparation. The question is difficult to answer. For Lax, the hope of re-conciliation rests heavily on reconstruction and reparation initiatives that demonstrate why amnesty for perpetrators was not just another sacrifice for those who suffered under apartheid. In their essay, Trudy Govier and Wilhelm Verwoerd confront a central aspect of the TRC process in order to understand better the reparative promise and limits of the apology. Isolating the relationship between apologies and those forms of acknow-ledgement that help make amends, the essay underscores that restoration is an ongoing and often fraught process. In her essay, Pumla Gobodo-Madikizela offers a different but congruent perspective, arguing that the faultlines that run within many communities demand new forms and strategies for reparation. One of the essay's central lessons is that reparation policy may founder if it is not tailored to specific situations, historical experiences and contexts. At the same time, Revel Fox's discussion of the Freedom Park suggests that reparation also needs to entail the creation of shared spaces that can fund collective remembrance and provide symbolic resources for nation-building. In short, there is much left to build. A vital step, the TRC did not and indeed could not do it all. The work that remains requires both imagination and dedication, a commitment that will need to extend well into democracy's second decade.

International Precedents and Lessons

Reparation is an international concern. This is true in several senses. For one, the evident unhappiness with the South African government's approach has led a number of individuals to file lawsuits against several multinational corporations in US courts. Too, the problem of how to design effective reparation programmes is a concern in a number of countries, each of which is struggling to overcome and redress the costs of deep division and atrocity.

The final section of the volume is addressed to the international dimensions of the reparation debate. In his essay, Jeremy Sarkin offers a detailed investigation of the precedents and problems that attend international lawsuits for reparation, many of which are being filed under the American Alien Torts Claims Act. A key aspect of Sarkin's analysis is that these suits are not a 'panacea', even as they underscore the role played by corporations in the perpetration of human rights violations. In his contribution, Pablo de Greiff offers both an empirical survey and normative critique of international reparation programmes. Considering efforts undertaken in places such as Germany, Chile and Argentina, de Grieff asks how reparation programmes might be best designed. For Neville Dubow, this problem has much to do with the matter of memory. Troubling the difference between the monumental and memorial, Dubow draws from his work in Germany to raise questions about the better and worse ways of remembering in the name of reparation. Tyrone Savage and Zola Sonkosi's examination of post-conflict reintegration and healing underscores a different facet of the problem, especially as it details how ex-combatants are often left to the side, forgotten and without concrete means to move beyond the personal and collective wounds of war. At this level, international experience demonstrates that effective reparation needs to be both comprehensive and tied to the local efforts of non-governmental organisations. Detailing the 'Plan of Integral Reparations', an extract from the Final Report of the Peruvian Truth and Reconciliation Commission provides important insights about how to create such integrated programmes. Finally, Sonny Onyegbula's essay on reparation policy in Nigeria lends important complexity to the debate, especially as he details how calls for reparation can be complicated by governmental claims about why independence struggles are demeaned by calls for monetary compensation.

In the end, things cannot simply *be*. Read together, the essays in this volume counsel that matters ought not to remain consigned to the state they that *are* in. The irreparable, a condition in which there *is* literally and metaphorically 'no shelter possible' for human beings, cannot continue.[3] Somehow, in a moment less given than created, it must *become* something else. To undertake reparation is to enter into a struggle with the irreparable, that which appears to defy alteration or transformation. Such efforts are not flights of fancy but committed engagements that demand a mixture of realism, imagination, and collective (inter)action. The reparative may yet work to render things otherwise. Its work may well make a difference that matters.

Acknowledgements

Following a volume on reconciliation in Africa and one on the South African amnesty process, this is the third book that we have co-edited. At some level, these books may constitute a kind a trilogy dedicated to the questions and problems that appear within the South African transition and in other efforts to heal deep division. Over a year in the making, the present volume has taken shape in a period that has seen the close of the TRC and renewed questioning about the form and future of reconciliation and reconstruction. The discussions that led to the decision to undertake the book involved a number of individuals. We are grateful to all of these participants for their insights and generous spirit of inquiry. In particular, we owe a great debt to our colleagues at the Institute for Justice and Reconciliation, all of whom have supported the work and contributed much to its design and its development. Deborah Gordon and Moira Levy played key roles in the production phases of the volume. Their tireless efforts have been indispensable. For both of us, the volume has afforded an important learning experience, a chance to think anew about the contours and demands of transitional politics and reconciliation. In some sense, such work is never finished but only begun.

Notes

1   Neville Alexander, *An Ordinary Country: Issues in the Transition from Apartheid to Democracy in South Africa* (Pietermaritzburg: University of Natal Press, 2002), 167–8.

2   Kader Asmal, 'Victims, Survivors and Citizens – Human Rights, Reparations, and Reconciliation,' Inaugural Lecture, University of the Western Cape, 25 May 1992.

3   Giorgio Agamben, *The Coming Community*, trans. Michael Hardt (Minneapolis: University of Minnesota Press, 1993), 38.

1
Truth and Reconciliation Commission of South Africa

Excerpts from the Report of the
Reparation and Rehabilitation Committee

Introduction*

1 In 1998, the Reparation and Rehabilitation Committee (RRC) reported on its work and presented its policy recommendations to the President.[1] This formed part of the Final Report of the Truth and Reconciliation Commission (the Commission), which was handed to the President of South Africa on 28 October 1998. In that chapter, the RRC discussed the need for reparation and the moral and legal obligation to meet the needs of victims of gross human rights violations. The RRC also outlined the nature and progress of the urgent interim reparation (UIR) programme and submitted a comprehensive set of proposals for final reparation. The present chapter needs to be read in conjunction with that earlier chapter.

Mandate of the Reparation and Rehabilitation Committee

2 The RRC received its mandate from the Promotion of National Unity and Reconciliation Act No. 34 of 1995 (the Act),[2] which made

---

* Excerpt from *Truth and Reconciliation Commission of South Africa Report*, Volume Six, Section Two, Chapter One, 2003. All excerpts were taken from the Commission's Report, as published on its website URL: <http://www.doj.gov.za/trc/report/index.htm>. While endnote numbers in these excerpts do not match those found in the Report, their content and location remain unaltered.

provision for measures of reparation for those who had suffered human rights violations.

3 As stated in the Final Report of the Commission, the Preamble to the Act stipulates that one of the objectives of the Commission was to provide for:

the taking of measures aimed at the granting of reparation to, and the rehabilitation and the restoration of the human and civil dignity of, victims of violations of human rights; ...

4 As an integral part of the Commission, the RRC was required to draw up a set of recommendations to the President with regard to:

(i) the policy which should be followed or measures which should be taken with regard to the granting of reparation to victims or the taking of other measures aimed at rehabilitating and restoring the human and civil dignity of victims;

(ii) measures which should be taken to grant urgent interim reparation to victims; ...[3]

5 Furthermore, section 25(b)(i) of the Act stipulates that the RRC may: *make recommendations which may include urgent interim measures as contemplated in section 4(f)(ii), as to appropriate measures of reparation to victims; ...*

6 The Act also provides for referral to the RRC by the other Committees of the Commission. Thus:

When the Committee [on Human Rights Violations] finds that a gross violation of human rights has been committed and if the Committee is of the opinion that a person is a victim of such violation, it shall refer the matter to the Committee on Reparation and Rehabilitation for its consideration in terms of section 26.[4]

7 Similarly:

(1) Where amnesty is granted to any person in respect of any act, omission

or offence and the [Amnesty] Committee is of the opinion that a person is a victim in relation to that act, omission or offence, it shall refer the matter to the Committee on Reparation and Rehabilitation for its consideration in terms of section 26.[5]

(2) *Where amnesty is refused by the Committee and if it is of the opinion that − (a) the act, omission or offence concerned constitutes a gross violation of human rights; and (b) a person is a victim in the matter, it shall refer the matter to the Committee on Reparation and Rehabilitation for consideration in terms of section 26.*

The Commission's Reparation and Rehabilitation Policy

8   The policy recommendations submitted to the President by the Commission consisted of five basic components. Following internationally accepted approaches to reparation and rehabilitation, the RRC stressed the following principles: a) Redress: the right to fair and adequate compensation; b) Restitution: the right to the restoration, where possible, of the situation existing prior to the violation; c) Rehabilitation: the right to medical and psychological care, as well as such other services and/or interventions at both individual and community level that would facilitate full rehabilitation; d) Restoration of dignity: the right of the individual/community to an acknowledgement of the violation committed and the right to a sense of worth, and e) Reassurance of non-repetition: the right to a guarantee, by means of appropriate legislative and/or institutional intervention and reform, that the violation will not be repeated.

9   These principles provided a basic framework from which to elaborate the specific proposals outlined below:[6]

Urgent interim reparation
10   UIR is defined as assistance for people in urgent need, with a view to providing them with access to appropriate services and facilities. In this regard, the Commission recommended that limited financial resources be made available to facilitate such access where necessary.

Individual reparation grants

11 This is an individual financial grant scheme. The Commission recommended that each victim of a gross human rights violation receive a financial grant, based on various criteria, to be paid over a period of six years.

12 It was proposed that individual reparation grants be paid to victims (if alive) or relatives/dependants (where victims were deceased). The amount to be paid should be calculated according to three criteria: an amount that acknowledges the suffering caused by the violation; an amount that enables access to requisite services and facilities; and an amount that subsidises daily living costs according to socio-economic circumstances. As the cost of living is higher in rural than in urban areas, it was recommended that victims living in the rural areas should receive a slightly higher grant. The amount also varied according to the number of dependants (up to a maximum of R23 023 per annum). It was recommended that the annual amount be paid twice a year for a period of six years and be administered by the President's Fund, which is located within the Department of Justice and Constitutional Development.

Symbolic reparation and legal and administrative measures

13 Symbolic reparation encompasses measures that facilitate the communal process of remembering and commemorating the pain and victories of the past. Such measures aim to restore the dignity of victims and survivors.

14 Commemorative aspects include exhumations, tombstones, memorials or monuments, and the renaming of streets or public facilities.

15 Legal and administrative measures include matters such as the issuing of death certificates or declarations of death in the case of people who have disappeared, expunging criminal records where people were sentenced for politically related offences, and expediting outstanding legal matters.

Community rehabilitation programmes

16 The establishment of government-led community-based services and activities is aimed at promoting the healing and recovery of individuals and communities affected by human rights violations. As many victims

were based in communities that were subjected to systemic abuse, the RRC identified possible rehabilitation programmes and recommended a series of interventions at both community and national level. These included programmes to demilitarise youth who had been involved in or witnessed political violence over decades; programmes to resettle the many thousands displaced by political violence; mental health and trauma counselling, as well as programmes to rehabilitate and reintegrate perpetrators of gross violations of human rights into normal community life.

Institutional reform

17 Institutional reform included legal, administrative and institutional measures designed to prevent the recurrence of abuses of human rights. The Commission drew up a fairly substantial set of recommendations aimed at the creation and maintenance of a stable society – a society that would never again allow the kind of violations experienced during the Commission's mandate period. These included recommendations relating to the judiciary, security forces and correctional services as well as other sectors in society such as education, business and media.

18 The RRC, focusing on the need to implement these recommendations, proposed that a structure or body be set up in the office of the State President or Deputy President and headed by a national director of Reparation and Rehabilitation. Further, the RRC recommended that reparation desks be established at provincial and municipal levels to ensure effective delivery and monitoring.

Delays in the Implementation of Reparation Thus Far

19 Since the submission of the Final Report of the Commission with its proposals for reparation, there has been a considerable delay on the part of government in setting forth its vision for the Reparation and Rehabilitation Programme. Indeed, government's only response thus far has been to challenge the individual reparation grant component of the Commission's recommendations.

20 This delay has led to ongoing public debate and widespread criticism. Much of this criticism has been directed at the Commission, as public

perception, frequently fuelled by the media, has continued to see reparation as the responsibility of the Commission rather than of the government.

21 The fact that this delay has taken place against the background of the amnesty process is also unfortunate. The fact that victims continue to wait for measures of reparation while perpetrators receive amnesty has fuelled the debate about justice for victims[7] within the Commission process.

22 It needs to be strongly emphasised that giving victim evidence before the Commission was not simply a question of reporting on the past. It was intended to change people's views and experiences of their own pain and suffering. It was intended, moreover, to play an important role in reconciling the nation. This exposure and exploration of past experiences – this reconciliation – needed to be accompanied by reparation and rehabilitation – related services and the meeting of financial and other needs. Without this important component, the work of the Commission remains essentially unbalanced.

23 It should be noted further that, while the public debate has tended to focus on individual financial grants, the reparation policy proposed by the RRC was much broader in intent. In other words, it did not focus simply on financial compensation. It catered not only for the individual needs of those who suffered from past abuses, but had implications for communities that had been targeted for abuse as well as those requiring fundamental institutional transformation.

The Case for Reparation and Rehabilitation: Domestic and International Law[†]

1 In its broadest sense, the mandate of the Reparation and Rehabilitation Committee (RRC) was to affirm, acknowledge and consider the impact and consequences of gross violations of human

†   Excerpt from *Truth and Reconciliation Commission of South Africa Report*, Volume Six, Section Two, Chapter Two, 2003.

rights[8] on victims, and to make recommendations accordingly. In doing so, the RRC had access to a rich source of information about measures of reparation, drawn from domestic and international law and opinion.

Domestic Law and Democratic Accountability

Domestic Law

2   The obligation to institute measures of reparation is enshrined in South African law itself.

3   The Constitution of the Republic of South Africa Act No. 200 of 1993[9] (the Interim Constitution) recognised the principle that the conflicts of the past had caused immeasurable injury and suffering to the people of South Africa and that, because of the country's legacy of hatred, fear, guilt and revenge: 'there is a need for understanding but not for vengeance, a need for reparation but not for retaliation, a need for *ubuntu* but not for victimisation'.[10] This view was given concrete expression in the Promotion of National Unity and Reconciliation Act No. 34 of 1995 (the Act), which mandated the Commission to develop measures for the provision of reparation to those found to have been victims of gross violations of human rights.

4   Through the Act and in unambiguous language, the legislature made clear its intention that 'reparations' of some kind or form should be awarded to victims. This reaffirms the belief that the Act created rights in favour of victims. For example:

[T]he Commission shall – ...

(f)   make recommendations to the President with regard to –

(i)   the policy which should be followed or measures which should be taken with regard to the granting of reparation to victims or the taking of other measures aimed at rehabilitating and restoring the human and civil dignity of victims [section 4];

Any person who is of the opinion that he or she has suffered harm as a

*result of a gross violation of human rights may apply to the Committee for
reparation in the prescribed form ... [section 26(1)].*

*The recommendations referred to in section 4(f)(i) shall be considered by the
President with a view to making recommendations to Parliament and making regulations [section 27(1)].*

5   Entitlement to reparation therefore arises from the provisions of the Act
itself. The only qualification is that the recipient must be a victim of a
gross violation of human rights as defined in section 1 of the Act,[11] and
as further elaborated in subsequent promulgated regulations.

Legitimate expectation

6   The general statutory obligations imposed upon the Truth and
Reconciliation Commission (the Commission) created a legitimate
expectation on the part of victims of gross violations of human rights
that the Commission would fulfil this part of its mandate. This legitimate expectation gave rise to legally enforceable rights in terms of
section 26 of the Act. According to this section, persons are entitled
to apply for measures of reparation by virtue of having been referred
as a victim to the RRC either by the Amnesty Committee[12] (the
Committee) or the Human Rights Violations Committee[13] (HRVC).

7   The principle of legitimate expectation has been accepted in our law[14]
and has since been enshrined in the South African Constitution.
Victims, therefore, have a legitimate expectation that they are entitled
to measures of reparation once the RRC has considered their applications for reparation and referred them to the President's Fund and/or
relevant government department in the proper manner.

Implications and Concluding Comments[††]

1   The issue of reparation and rehabilitation is real for every victim,
though to varying degrees. As history takes the country further and
further away from the historical moment of the negotiated settlement

---

†† Excerpt from *Truth and Reconciliation Commission of South Africa Report*, Volume Six,
Section Two, Chapter Seven, 2003.

in South Africa, and as other challenges, especially that of HIV/AIDS, press ever more insistently on the national consciousness, it may become more and more tempting to deal dismissively with the issue of reparation and rehabilitation. There may be those who feel that there are things that cannot be repaired or rehabilitated. This too may discourage further consideration of the issue. Moreover, it may be argued that there is something very positive about a country that wishes to move forward.

2   Although we may currently be experiencing fatigue about the consequences of the past, it remains true that if we do not deal with the past it will haunt and may indeed jeopardise the future. We need to remember that the Truth and Reconciliation Commission (the Commission) was established in large part because of the dangers of inappropriate forgetting. We acknowledged then and must remember now that moving forward requires acknowledgement of the past, rather than denial. To ignore the suffering of those found by the Commission to be victims would be a particular kind of cruelty. After all, it was the testimony of these victims that gave us a window onto how others saw the past and allowed us to construct an image of the future.

3   There has been a tendency to dismiss those declared as victims by the Commission as an 'elite victim group'. It needs to be borne in mind that, given the systemic abuse committed during the apartheid era, virtually every black South African can be said to be a victim of human rights abuse. By using the fact that they testified as evidence of their 'elite' character, these critics are in essence propounding the astounding argument that these victims should be punished (denied legitimate expectations) for having come forward.

4   There were very many victims of apartheid and, certainly, those who came before the Commission are only a subset of a much larger group. This is why, when balancing individual and socially oriented reparation, the Commission sought to address the specific needs of those who came before it in order to contribute to the wider truth about the nation's history, while at the same time addressing the broader consequences of apartheid. It is almost impossible to design a reparation programme without leaving some gaps. Nevertheless, the fact that not all victims

will receive individual financial grants cannot be allowed to prevent at least some clearly deserving victims from getting such awards.

5   The reality is that a specific group of victims was identified via a legislated and broadly accepted process. While their circumstances are possibly more representative than otherwise, their uniqueness lies in the fact that they chose to engage in the process.

6   There are major challenges for the reparation and rehabilitation process. As indicated in earlier chapters, it is often difficult to distinguish victims from non-victims and even to isolate key events that caused subsequent problems in people's lives. It is not always possible to draw a clear line between a gross violation of human rights and the more general features of oppression. It is difficult to know where, in the ongoing development of individuals, families and communities, one could measure the effects of human rights abuses, even if such measurement were theoretically possible. Given the very limited resources in South Africa, very little of this work can be done.

7   Besides, even if South Africa had unlimited resources at its disposal, much of the damage that has taken place is irreparable. Human development in the context of abuse and violation is not infinitely reparable, and part of the task for healing in South Africa lies in accepting what cannot be done.

8   The acceptance of limitations, however, does not mean the abdication of responsibility, but rather a sober assessment of what can and cannot be achieved.

9   It is this assessment that must form the basis of our future growth as a nation. Poverty and the economic implications of the AIDS epidemic make economic considerations important in the rehabilitation process. The line between victims and non-victims is often obscure; hence it may be ethically problematic to provide victims with preferential access to services such as education, housing and employment. It is, moreover, common knowledge that many public sector services – such as health, welfare and education – are woefully under-resourced in South Africa. Wishing that things were different will not make

these problems go away. Again, attempts to give preference to victims in these services could potentially meet with resistance because there is not, in any case, enough to go around.

10 Despite this, preferential opportunities on the basis of need for victims across the political spectrum may be important symbolic acts: they would communicate that the current leadership takes seriously what South Africans have endured, and signal a commitment to establishing a just and humane society in which human rights are respected.

11 Given resource constraints, creative ways of generating funds earmarked for rehabilitation services should be considered. These could include tax incentives to encourage private sector businesses to contribute to a specific post-Truth and Reconciliation Commission Fund. The economic and social implications of a time-limited taxation levy on wealthier South Africans' earnings also need to be considered.

12 However funds are generated or redirected from other budgets, it is important that we do not forget the high levels of emotional pain in our country and the fact that we need to build up services to deal specifically with these. Public sector mental health provision is inadequately resourced at present and there is insufficient training and ongoing support for frontline helpers across a range of sectors including education, labour, safety and security, defence, health, and welfare. Resourcing is an issue, and there is a lack of creative thinking about making services physically, linguistically and culturally acceptable to communities. Professional mental health and welfare organisations should be encouraged to share information on successful projects, on methods of assessing impact and on improving the cost-effectiveness of such endeavours. Professional services should act in concert with community-based services. The combination of professional expertise and community-driven support is likely to provide the most cost-effective, helpful and culture-friendly mix.

13 Within the public health sector, dedicated posts for working on reparation and rehabilitation issues need to be established countrywide. The reparation and rehabilitation aspects need to be emphasised for a limited period, after which time these posts could become part

of the general public mental health pool. It is important to attract talented and energetic people to such posts. In this respect, the secondment of personnel from other sectors (the health system, the nongovernmental organisation (NGO) sector, higher education and the private sector) should be considered.

14 Symbolic measures of reparation such as monuments and museums are important but should ideally be linked with endeavours that improve the everyday lives of victims and their communities. One way of combining the two aims is to involve victims prominently in the design and/or manufacture of monuments and in the running of museums. There are already good examples of this in the country.

15 There is much to do, and not all our ideals can be realised. But the Promotion of National Unity and Reconciliation Act No. 34 of 1995 (the Act) gave an undertaking that something would be done and, for the sake of the future, steps must be taken to take the process forward. Furthermore, much of the current order's legitimacy rests on a fair and appropriate response. The issues, problematic though they are, cannot be ignored.

16 It cannot and must not be forgotten that the Act allowed for reparation for those who testified before the Commission and were subsequently identified as victims. While the recommended measures of reparation are not and cannot ever be proportionate to the harm suffered, reparations may be understood at least as an act of good faith and a serious attempt to alleviate some of the material and psychological trauma that victims endured. Today, when the government is spending so substantial a portion of its budget on submarines and other military equipment, it is unconvincing to argue that it is too financially strapped to meet at least this minimal commitment.

17 In this context, the argument that individual reparations come at the cost of social reparations is hardly persuasive; the two are not mutually exclusive within the context of broader budgetary priorities.

18 As we showed earlier in this section, the legal and normative arguments are unassailable. It may be recalled, too, that the overarching

goal of reconciliation and national unity, as expressed in the Constitution and the founding Act, was born of a fragile balance with consequences that go far beyond the Commission itself.

19 The challenge to decision makers is how to acknowledge those who actively engaged with the legal framework of the Act and were found to be victims of gross human rights violations. They must honour the social contract in which these victims engaged, while at the same time adequately acknowledging those who did not or were not able to engage in the process, without overvaluing or under-valuing either party.

20 The Reparation and Rehabilitation Committee (the RRC) believes that its recommendations – which emphasise both individual and collective reparations – represent a blueprint for a workable solution to this pervasive tension.

21 The challenge to us all is to honour the process and to take responsibility for shaping our future. If we ignore the implications of the stories of many ordinary South Africans, we become complicit in contributing to an impoverished social fabric – to a society that may not be worth the pain the country has endured.

Notes

1 See Volume Five, Chapter Five.
2 Sections 25 and 26 of the Act.
3 Section 4(f) of the Act.
4 Section 15(1).
5 Section 22.
6 See Volume Five, Chapter Five.
7 The Commission's use of the term 'victim' was explained in its Final Report on the grounds of the original wording of the Act. The RRC acknowledges the connotations associated with the term as a multiplicity of experiences, or engendering notions of the 'victim' having being vanquished or conquered in some way. The alternative, 'survivor', is open to a more fluid interpretation, but still fails to represent the variations of that survival. In the context of the Commission, it is a definition based on the specific violation experienced by the individual – that is, killing, abduction, torture or severe ill-treatment. It is not a term based on the individual's current state or understanding of himself or herself. This 'violation-based' definition is unsatisfactory to the Commission in that it promotes a homogeneous grouping of those who approached

the Commission and has the potential to stifle creative approaches to the issue of reparative interventions.

8   Killings, torture, severe ill-treatment and abduction. A number of violations were reported to the Commission which did not fall into these categories. These were described as 'associated violations'.

9   Constitution of the Republic of South Africa Act No. 200 of 1993, 'National Unity and Reconciliation', Chapter Fifteen.

10   Constitution of the Republic of South Africa Act No. 200 of 1993.

11   Section 1(xix) of the Act defines 'victims' as – (a) persons who, individually or together with one or more persons, suffered harm in the form of physical or mental injury, emotional suffering, pecuniary loss or a substantial impairment of human rights – (i) as a result of a gross violation of human rights; or (ii) as a result of an act associated with a political objective for which amnesty has been granted; (b) persons who, individually or together with one or more persons, suffered harm in the form of physical or mental injury, emotional suffering, pecuniary loss or a substantial impairment of human rights, as a result of such person intervening to assist persons contemplated in paragraph (a) who were in distress or to prevent victimisation of such persons; and (c) such relatives or dependants of victims as may be prescribed.

12   Section 22 of the Act.

13   Section 15(1).

14   Administrator of the Transvaal and Others v. Traub and Others 1989 (4) SA 731 (A) at 761 D.

2

Statement to the National Houses of Parliament and the Nation at the Tabling of the Report of the Truth and Reconciliation Commission[*]

President Thabo Mbeki – 15 April 2003

Madame Speaker and Deputy Speaker;
Chairperson and Deputy Chairperson of the Council of Provinces;
Deputy President;
Chief Justice and Members of the Judiciary;
Former Members of the Truth and Reconciliation Commission;
Ministers and Deputy Ministers;
Distinguished Premiers;
Honoured Traditional Leaders;
Leaders of the Chapter Nine Institutions;
Honourable Leaders of our Political Parties;
Your Excellencies, Ambassadors and High Commissioners;
Honourable Members;
Distinguished Guests;
Fellow South Africans:

We have convened today as the elected representatives of the people of South Africa to reflect on the work of the Truth and Reconciliation Commission, to examine its Recommendations and to find answers, in practical terms, to the question – where to from here!

We wish to acknowledge the presence of Commissioners of the erstwhile

---

[*] The transcript of this address is taken from the website maintained by the African National Congress <URL: anc.org.za>

TRC, who took time off their busy schedules to join us in commending the Report to our national Parliament.

I am confident that I speak on behalf of all Honourable Members when I say to these Commissioners, and through them, to Archbishop Desmond Tutu and the other Commissioners not present here today, that South Africa sincerely appreciates the work that they have done. Our thanks also go to the staff of the Commission and all who contributed to the success of the work of the TRC, which we are justified to celebrate today.

They did everything humanly possible to realise the objectives of a process novel in its conception, harrowing in its execution and, in many respects, thankless in balancing expectation and reality.

Our assessment of the TRC's success cannot therefore be based on whether it has brought contrition and forgiveness, or whether at the end of its work, it handed us a united and reconciled society. For this was not its mandate. What the TRC set out to do, and has undoubtedly achieved, is to offer us the signposts in the Long March to these ideals.

What it was required to do, and has accomplished, was to flag the dangers that can beset a state not premised on popular legitimacy and the confidence of its citizens, and the ills that would befall any society founded on prejudice and a belief in a 'master race'.

The extent to which the TRC could identify and pursue priority cases; its ability to bring to its hearings all relevant actors; the attention that it could pay to civil society's role in buttressing an illegitimate and illegal state; and the TRC's investigative capacity to pursue difficult issues with regard to which the actors had decided to spurn its call for co-operation – all these weaknesses were those of society and not the TRC as such.

And, we make bold to say that all these complexities make the product of the work of the TRC that much more outstanding and impressive.

The pain and the agony that characterised the conflict among South Africans over the decades, so vividly relived in many hearings of the Commission, planted the seed of hope – of a future bright in its humanity and its sense of caring.

It is a future whose realisation gave life to the passion for the liberation of our people, of Oliver Tambo and Chris Hani, the tenth anniversary of whose passing away we mark this month. This includes others such as Robert Mangaliso Sobukwe and Steve Bantu Biko, who passed away 25 years ago this year and last year respectively. They joined and have since been joined by many other patriots to whom freedom meant life itself.

We are indebted to all of them; and we shall work to ensure that their memory lives on in the minds of generations to come, inspired by our common determination that never again should one South African oppress another!

At a critical moment in our history, as a people, we came to the conclusion that we must, together, end the killing. We took a deliberate decision that a violent conflict was neither in the interest of our country nor would it solve our problems.

Together, we decided that in the search for a solution to our problems, nobody should be demonised or excluded. We agreed that everybody should become part of the solution, whatever they might have done and represented in the past. This related both to negotiating the future of our country and working to build the new South Africa we had all negotiated.

We agreed that we would not have any war crimes tribunals or take to the road of revenge and retribution.

When Chris Hani, a great hero of our people, was murdered, even as our country was still governed by a white minority regime, we who represented the oppressed majority, said let those who remained in positions of authority in our country carry out their responsibility to bring those who had murdered him to book. We called on our people neither to take the law into their hands nor to mete out blind vengeance against those they knew as the beneficiaries of apartheid oppression.

We imposed a heavy burden, particularly on the millions who had been the victims of this oppression, to let bygones be bygones. We said to them – do not covet the material wealth of those who benefited from your oppression and exploitation, even as you remain poor.

We walked among their ranks saying that none among them should predicate a better future for themselves on the basis of the impoverishment of those who had prospered at their expense. We said to them that on the day of liberation, there would be no looting. There would be celebrations and no chaos.

We said that as the majority, we had a responsibility to make our day of liberation an unforgettable moment of joy, with none condemned to remember it forever as a day of bitter tears.

We said to our people that they should honour the traditions they had built and entrenched over centuries, never to hate people because of their colour or race, always to value all human beings, and never to turn their backs on the deeply entrenched sentiment informed by the spirit of ubuntu, to forgive, understanding that the harm done yesterday cannot be undone today by a resolve to harm another.

We reminded the masses of our people of the values their movement for national liberation had upheld throughout a turbulent century, of everything they had done to defend both this movement and its values, of their obligation never to betray this noble heritage. Our people heeded all these calls.

By reason of the generosity and the big hearts of the masses of our people, all of us have been able to sleep in peace, knowing that there will be no riots in our streets. Because these conscious masses know what they are about, the Truth and Reconciliation Commission was able to do its work enjoying the co-operation of those who for ages had upheld the vision of a united humanity, in which each would be one's brother or sister. These are an heroic people whose greatest reward is the liberation of their country.

Of them, the TRC says:

> *Others did not wish to be portrayed as a 'victim'. Indeed, many said expressly that they regarded themselves instead as soldiers who had voluntarily paid the price of their struggle ... Many have expressed reservations about the very notion of a 'victim', a term which is felt to denote a certain passivity and helplessness ... Military operatives of the liberation movements generally did not report violations they experienced to the Commission, although many who were arrested experienced severe torture. This is in all likelihood a result of their reluctance to be seen as 'victims', as opposed to combatants fighting for a moral cause for which they were prepared to suffer such violations. The same can be said for most prominent political activists and leadership figures ... The Commission did not, for example, receive a single Human Rights Violation statement from any of the Rivonia trialists.*

Some of these, who had to go through the torture chambers of the apartheid regime to bring us our liberty, are with us in this chamber today. There are others who sit on the balcony as visitors, who lost their loved ones whom they pride as liberators, and others who also suffered from repression.

Surely, all of us must feel a sense of humility in the face of such selfless heroism and attachment to principle and morality, the assertion of the nobility of the human spirit that would be demeaned, denied and degraded by any suggestion that these heroes and heroines are but mere 'victims', who must receive a cash reward for being simply and deeply human.

I know there are some in this House who do not understand the meaning of what I have just said. They think I have said what I have said to avoid the payment of reparations to those whom the TRC has identified as 'victims', within the meaning of the law.

Indeed, the TRC itself makes the gratuitous comment (para. 16, p. 163, Vol. 6) that:

Today, when the government is spending so substantial a portion of its budget on submarines and other military equipment, it is unconvincing to argue that it is too financially strapped to meet this minimal (reparations) commitment.

Apart from anything else, the government has never presented such an argument. It is difficult to understand why the Commission decided to make such a statement.

Elsewhere in Volume 6, the Rev. Frank Chikane, Director General in the Presidency and former General Secretary of the South African Council of Churches, is falsely reported as having made a presentation to the Amnesty Committee, which he never did.

He is then said to have told this Committee that he had participated in killing people. We do not understand how this grave and insulting falsification found its way into the Report of the TRC. We are pleased to report that Archbishop Tutu has written to Rev. Chikane to apologise for this inexplicable account.

The poet Mongane Wally Serote teaches us: 'to every birth its blood'. And so, today we acknowledge the pain that attended the struggle to give birth to the new life that South Africa has started to enjoy.

In this era of increased geopolitical tension, we dare celebrate as South Africans that we found home-grown solutions that set us on a course of reconstruction and development, nation-building, reconciliation and peace among ourselves.

At this time, when great uncertainty about the future of our common world envelops the globe, we dare stand on mountain-tops to proclaim our humble contribution to the efforts of humanity to build a stable, humane and safer South Africa, and by extension, a more stable, more humane and safer world.

Honourable Members,

If we should find correct answers to the question, where to from here, we would need to remind ourselves of the objectives of the TRC from its very inception, so aptly captured in the preamble to the Promotion of National Unity and Reconciliation Act:

> ... *the Constitution of the Republic of South Africa, 1993 provides a historic bridge between the past of a deeply divided society characterised by strife, conflict, untold suffering and injustice, and a future founded on the recognition of human rights, democracy and peaceful co-existence for all South Africans, irrespective of colour, race, class, belief or sex;*

> ... *the Constitution states that the pursuit of national unity, the well-being of all South African citizens and peace require reconciliation between the people of South Africa and the reconstruction of society;*

> ... *it is deemed necessary to establish the truth in relation to past events as well as the motives for and circumstances in which gross violations of human rights have occurred, and to make the findings known in order to prevent a repetition of such acts in future;*

> ... *the Constitution states that there is a need for understanding but not for vengeance, a need for reparation but not for retaliation, a need for ubuntu but not for victimisation.*

I am certain that we are all at one that the pursuit of national unity, the wellbeing of all South African citizens and peace require reconciliation among the people of South Africa and the reconstruction of our society.

These are the larger and fundamental objectives that should inform all of us as we work to give birth to the new South Africa. The occasion of the receipt of the Report of the TRC should give us an opportunity to reflect on these matters.

Both singly and collectively, we should answer the question how far we have progressed in the last nine years towards the achievement of the goals of national unity, national reconciliation and national reconstruction. Both singly and collectively, we have to answer the question: what have we contributed to the realisation of these goals?

These larger questions, which stand at the heart of what our country will be, did not fall within the mandate of the Truth and Reconciliation Commission. The TRC was therefore but an important contributor to the achievement of the larger whole, occupying an important sector within the larger process of the building of a new South Africa.

As stated in the Act, the TRC had to help us to establish the truth in relation to past events as well as the motives for and circumstances in which gross violations of human rights occurred, and to make the findings known in order to prevent a repetition of such acts in future.

It had to help us to promote understanding and avoid vengeance, to extend reparation to those who had been harmed and discourage retaliation, to rely on the spirit of ubuntu as a deterrent against victimisation.

The TRC has done its work as was required. As stipulated in the TRC Act, we are here to make various recommendations to our national Parliament, arising out of the work of the TRC.

As the Honourable Members are aware, there is a specific requirement in the law that parliament should consider and take decisions on matters relating particularly to reparations. It would then be the task of the Executive to implement these decisions.

The law also provides that the national legislature may also make recommendations to the Executive on other matters arising out of the TRC process, as it may deem fit.

Let us now turn to some of the major specific details that the TRC enjoins us to address.

The first of these is the matter of reparations.

First of all, an integrated and comprehensive response to the TRC Report should be about the continuing challenge of reconstruction and development: deepening democracy and the culture of human rights, ensuring good governance and transparency, intensifying economic growth and social programmes, improving citizens' safety and security and contributing to the building of a humane and just world order.

The TRC also argues for systematic programmes to project the symbolism of struggle and the ideal of freedom. This relates to such matters as academic and informal records of history, remaking of cultural and art forms, erecting symbols and monuments that exalt the freedom struggle, including new geographic and place names. The government accepts these recommendations.

Special emphasis will continue to be paid to rehabilitation of communities that were subjected to intense acts of violence and destruction. Experience gained with the projects in Katorus in Gauteng and

Mpumalanga in KwaZulu/Natal demonstrates that great progress can be made in partnership between communities and government.

Further, with regard to specific cases of individual victims identified by the TRC Act, government has put in place and will intensify programmes pertaining to medical benefits, educational assistance and provision of housing and so on. From time to time, Ministers have elaborated and will continue to expatiate on the implementation of these and other related programmes.

The TRC has reported that about 22 000 individuals or surviving families appeared before the Commission. Of these, about 19 000 required urgent reparations, and virtually all of them, where the necessary information was available, were attended to as proposed by the TRC with regard to interim reparations.

With regard to final reparations, government will provide a once-off grant of R30 000 to those individuals or survivors designated by the TRC. This is over and above other material commitments that we have already mentioned.

We intend to process these payments as a matter of urgency, during the current financial year. Combined with community reparations, and assistance through opportunities and services we have referred to earlier, we hope that these disbursements will help acknowledge the suffering that these individuals experienced, and offer some relief.

We do so with some apprehension, for as the TRC itself has underlined, no one can attach monetary value to life and suffering. Nor can an argument be sustained that the efforts of millions of South Africans to liberate themselves were for monetary gain. We are convinced that, to the millions who spared neither life nor limb in struggle, there is no bigger prize than freedom itself, and a continuing struggle to build a better life for all.

The second of the specific details in the TRC recommendations pertains to the issue of amnesty.

A critical trade-off contained in the TRC process was between 'normal' judicial processes on the one hand, and establishment of the truth, reparations and amnesty on the other.

Besides the imperatives of managing the transition, an important consideration that had to be addressed when the TRC was set up was the extent to which the new democratic state could pursue legal cases against perpetrators of human rights violations, given the resources that would have to be allocated to this, the complexities of establishing the facts beyond reasonable doubt, the time it would take to deal with all the cases, as well as the bitterness and instability that such a process would wreak on society.

The balance that the TRC Act struck among these competing demands was reflected in the national consensus around provision of amnesty – in instances where perpetrators had provided the true facts about particular incidents – and restorative justice which would be effected in the form of reparations.

Given that a significant number of people did not apply for amnesty, what approach does government place before the national legislature and the nation on this matter?

Let us start off by reiterating that there shall be no general amnesty. Any such approach, whether applied to specific categories of people or regions of the country, would fly in the face of the TRC process and subtract from the principle of accountability, which is vital not only in dealing with the past, but also in the creation of a new ethos within our society.

Yet we also have to deal with the reality that many of the participants in the conflict of the past did not take part in the TRC process. Among these are individuals who were misled by their leadership to treat the process with disdain. Others themselves calculated that they would not be found out, either due to poor TRC investigations or what they believed and still believe is too complex a web of concealment for anyone to unravel. Yet other operatives expected the political leadership of the state institutions to which they belonged to provide the overall context against which they could present their cases: and this was not to be.

This reality cannot be avoided.

Government is of the firm conviction that we cannot resolve this matter by setting up yet another amnesty process, which in effect would mean suspending constitutional rights of those who were at the receiving end of gross human rights violations.

We have therefore left this matter in the hands of the National Directorate of Public Prosecutions (NDPP), for it to pursue any cases that, as is normal practice, it believes deserve prosecution and can be prosecuted. This work is continuing.

However, as part of this process and in the national interest, the National Directorate of Public Prosecutions, working with our intelligence agencies, will leave its doors open for those who are prepared to divulge information at their disposal and to co-operate in unearthing the truth, for them to enter into arrangements that are standard in the normal execution of justice, and which are accommodated in our legislation.

This is not a desire for vengeance; nor would it compromise the rights of citizens who may wish to seek justice in our courts.

It is critically important that, as a government, we should continue to establish the truth about networks that operated against the people. This is an obligation that attaches to the nation's security today, for some of these networks still pose a real or latent danger against our democracy. In some instances, caches of arms have been retained which lend themselves to employment in criminal activity.

This approach leaves open the possibility for individual citizens to take up any grievance related to human rights violations with the courts.

Thirdly, in each instance where any legal arrangements are entered into between the NDPP and particular perpetrators as proposed above, the involvement of the victims will be crucial in determining the appropriate course of action.

Relevant Departments are examining the practical modalities of dealing with this matter; and they will also establish whether specific legislation is required in this regard.

We shall also endeavour to explain South Africa's approach on these matters to sister-governments across the world. Our response to any judicial matters from these countries will be handled in this spirit and through the legal system. In this regard, we wish to reiterate our call to governments that continue to do so, that the maltreatment of former anti-apartheid fighters, based on the legal definitions of an illegal regime characterised by the United Nations as a crime against humanity, should cease.

In the recent past, the issue of litigation and civil suits against corporations that benefited from the apartheid system has sharply risen. In this regard, we wish to reiterate that the South African government is not and will not be party to such litigation.

In addition, we consider it completely unacceptable that matters that are central to the future of our country should be adjudicated in foreign courts which bear no responsibility for the well-being of our country and the observance of the perspective contained in our constitution of the promotion of national reconciliation.

While government recognises the right of citizens to institute legal action, its own approach is informed by the desire to involve all South Africans, including corporate citizens, in a co-operative and voluntary partnership to reconstruct and develop South African society. Accordingly, we do not believe that it would be correct for us to impose the once-off wealth tax on corporations proposed by the TRC.

Consultations are continuing with the business community to examine additional ways in which they can contribute to the task of the reconstruction and development of our society, proceeding from the premise that this is in their own self-interest. In addition to intensifying work with regard to such tasks as poverty eradication, and programmes such as Black Economic Empowerment, encouraging better individual corporate social responsibility projects, implementation of equity legislation and the Skills Training Levy, we intend to improve the work of the Business Trust.

In this context, we must emphasise that our response to the TRC has to be integrated within the totality of the enormous effort in which we are engaged, to ensure the fundamental social transformation of our country. This requires that at all times, we attain the necessary balance among the various goals we have to pursue.

The TRC also recommends that what it describes as the beneficiaries of apartheid should also make contributions to a reparation fund. The government believes that all South Africans should make such contributions. In the pursuit of the goal of a non-racial society, in which all South Africans would be inspired by a common patriotism, we believe that we should begin to learn to work together, uniting to address the common national challenges, such as responding to the consequences of the gross violations of human rights of which the TRC was seized.

In this regard, I am certain that members of our government will be among the first to make their contributions to the reparation fund, despite the fact that they stood on one side of the barricades as we engaged in struggle to end the apartheid system.

Many in our country have called for a National Day of Prayer and Traditional Sacrifice to pay tribute to those who sacrificed their lives and suffered during the difficult period of oppression and repression whose legacy remains with us. The government accepts this suggestion and will consult as widely as possible to determine the date and form of such prayer and traditional sacrifice. This is consistent with and would be an appropriate response to the proposals made by the TRC for conferences to heal the memory and honour those who were executed.

We shall also continue to work in partnership with countries of the subcontinent, jointly to take part in the massive reconstruction and development effort that SADC has identified as critical to building a better life for all. The peoples of southern Africa, including the majority in South Africa, endured untold privations and were subjected to destabilisation and destruction of property and infrastructure. They all deserve the speeding up of programmes of integration, reconstruction and development that governments of the region have agreed upon.

Madame Speaker,

The Truth and Reconciliation Commission has made many detailed observations and recommendations on structures and systems, which will be dealt with by relevant Ministers and Departments.

For the purpose of reparations, the government has already established the President's Fund, which is now operational, and has, as we earlier indicated, successfully dealt with the matter of urgent reparations. Like the TRC, we do hope that citizens from all sectors will find it within themselves to make a contribution to this Fund. Most of the resources that have been allocated for individual and community reparations that we referred to above will be sourced from this Fund, over and above the normal work of the relevant Departments.

We concur with the TRC that intensive work should be undertaken on the matter of monuments as well as geographic and place names. A Trust with the requisite infrastructure, headed by Mongane Wally Serote, has been set up to implement the main project in this regard, which is the construction of the Freedom Park whose constituent parts are the Memorial, the Garden of Remembrance and the Museum. This should start by the tenth anniversary of freedom in 2004.

The National Directorate of Public Prosecutions and relevant Departments will be requested to deal with matters relating to people who were unaccounted for, post mortem records and policy with regard to burials of unidentified persons. We would like to encourage all persons who might have any knowledge of people still unaccounted for to approach the National Directorate of Public Prosecutions, the South African Police Service and other relevant departments.

The Department of Justice and Constitutional Development will monitor the implementation of all these programmes, and it will report to Cabinet on an on-going basis.

What we have identified today, arising out of the report of the TRC, forms part of the panoply of programmes that define the first steps in a journey that has truly begun. South African society is changing for the better. The tide has turned and the people's contract for a better tomorrow is taking shape.

The goals we defined for ourselves a decade ago, as we adopted the Interim Constitution, to pursue national unity, to secure peace and the well-being of all South African citizens, to achieve national reconciliation and the reconstruction of our society, have not fully been realised, despite the progress we have made.

The situation we face demands that none of us should succumb to the false comfort that now we live in a normal society that has overcome the legacy of the past, and which permits us to consider our social tasks as mere business as usual.

Rather, it demands that we continue to be inspired by the determination and vision that enabled us to achieve the transition from apartheid rule to a democratic order in the manner that we did. It demands that we act together as one people to address what are truly national tasks.

We have to ask ourselves and honestly answer simple questions.

Have we succeeded to create a non-racial society! The answer to this question is no!

Have we succeeded to build a non-sexist society! The answer to that question is no!

Have we succeeded to eradicate poverty! Once more the answer to that question is no!

Have we succeeded fully to address the needs of the most vulnerable in our society, the children, the youth, people with disabilities and the elderly! Once again the answer to this question is no!

Without all this, it is impossible for us to claim that we have met our goals of national reconciliation and reconstruction and development. It is not possible for us to make the assertion that we have secured the well-being of all South African citizens.

The road we have travelled and the advances we have made convey the firm message that we are moving towards the accomplishment of the objectives we set ourselves. They tell us that, in the end, however long the road we still have to travel, we will win.

In the larger sense, we were all victims of the system of apartheid, both black and white. Some among us suffered because of oppression, exploitation, repression and exclusion. Others among us suffered because we were imprisoned behind prison walls of fear, paralysed by inhuman beliefs in our racial superiority, and called upon to despise and abuse other human beings. Those who do such things cannot but diminish their own humanity.

To be true to ourselves as human beings demands that we act together to overcome the legacy of this common and terrible past. It demands that we do indeed enter into a people's contract for a better tomorrow.

Together we must confront the challenge of steering through a complex transition that demands that we manage the historical fault-lines, without papering over the cracks, moved by a new and common patriotism.

It says to all of us that we must honour those who shed their blood so that we can sit together in this Chamber by doing all the things that will make it possible for us to say, this South Africa that we have rebuilt together, truly belongs to all who live in it.

I am honoured to commend the Report of the Truth and Reconciliation Commission to our National Houses of Parliament and the nation.

Thank you.

3
Reparations – It Is Still Not Too Late

Mary Burton

It was 11 April 1996, less than four months after the establishment of the Truth and Reconciliation Commission (TRC). The occasion was a public information meeting in the hall of the Hewat College in Athlone, Cape Town. Similar meetings were being held in other parts of the country, but this was only the second one in the Western Cape, the first having taken place two days earlier in Guguletu.

The atmosphere was distinctly tense. At the meeting in Guguletu, hard questions had been put to the TRC panel, and this evening was expected to be much the same. Many members of the public were hostile to the concept of granting amnesty to perpetrators of abuses of the past, and this was after all an area which had seen much strife and many young people injured and killed.

The objectives of these meetings were to make information available about the TRC's mandate and its plans, and to provide an opportunity for precisely such questions. The speakers on the panel outlined the historical context and the legislation that had brought about the Commission, and expressed the need for people to come forward to testify about their experience. In the preceding weeks many statements had already been gathered, and public hearings of the testimonies of victims of gross violations of human rights would begin in various parts of the country within days.

On that evening the questions and debate were evidence of the interest and depth of feeling which the TRC aroused. There was anger at the prospect of amnesty, but there was also understanding of the need to overcome the bitterness of the past. There was some mistrust, but there was also a willingness to face harsh truths and to find a way to deal with them. There was a remarkable absence of any demand for compensation, or for any financial gain to be derived from making a statement. When commissioners spoke about the need to gather the stories to contribute to a truly balanced history of events, people accepted this as a worthwhile goal. As the meeting dispersed, the TRC representatives felt that there had been a considerable degree of acceptance of the Commission's role.

At all such meetings TRC spokespersons were at pains to make it clear that its Reparation and Rehabilitation (R&R) Committee had power only to make recommendations to the government. They would undertake widespread discussions and investigations before doing so. No indications were given that there might be financial compensation, and this was never an inducement to testify.

Over the next few months, a great deal of the TRC work was directed towards taking statements, carrying out the necessary corroborative work and organising the public hearings at which victims of gross violations of human rights would testify. At the same time, however, the R&R Committee was beginning to address its mandate to make recommendations to the president on reparations. As early as May 1996, the R&R Committee was reporting to the Commission on its preliminary thinking towards a policy:

As the first round of hearings has unfolded, it has become evident that most requests for reparation fall into the long-term category of Reparations and Rehabilitation, rather than the Urgent Interim Assistance category. Witnesses have asked for assistance and intervention ranging from payment for a funeral to bursaries for education, from health care to memorials and from tombstones to community centres. Some witnesses did ask for financial assistance. Very few witnesses asked for counselling, but it was evident that there are people still significantly burdened by the pain of their experiences, who would benefit from counselling or emotional support of some type.[1]

In evaluations carried out after the first round of public hearings in the various centres, commissioners pointed out that the question frequently put to witnesses by panel members – 'What can the TRC do for you?' – could lead to unrealistic expectations, and should be modified to minimise this possibility.

It was clear that there was neither a widespread expectation of monetary compensation, nor any indication from the TRC that such compensation might be forthcoming. A later and much-quoted comment from then-Deputy President Thabo Mbeki, that 'our people did not join the struggle for money', can be substantiated by the thousands of statements made by victims who did not make large demands. Nevertheless, Dr Wendy Orr, who was deputy chairperson of the R&R Committee, has said:

> *Much has been made, both in South Africa and internationally, of the apparently modest requests for reparation made by testifiers at TRC public hearings. This has been overstated. Analysis of TRC data shows that when deponents are making a statement in private, they most commonly ask for money or compensation. This is not to say that their requests are extravagant or unreasonable ... The fact that very modest requests were made in public should not mask the reality that impoverished victims also asked for and need money. It is impossible to meet the mandate of restoring human and civil dignity when dignity is undermined by the daily struggle to survive ... The most common requests were for money and/or compensation. In addition, many victims asked for services that money can purchase, such as housing, education and health care.[2]*

Over the next few months, discussions in the TRC referred to:

- The need for support structures, especially in the rural areas, for people struggling to come to terms with past violations;
- Proposals for facilitating a symbolic re-burial as a form of Urgent Interim Assistance and also a long-term reparation policy;
- Emotional support;
- Medical assistance;
- Educational assistance; and
- Symbolic reparation.

The R&R Committee continued to study the existing models in other parts of the world, and to enter into discussions with government and non-governmental bodies. This was a lengthy process, and it was not until the TRC meeting in July 1997 that, after various earlier drafts, the Committee tabled its policy proposal. It made a strong argument for a comprehensive policy, which would include the payment of financial reparations. It cited the legislation that had established the TRC, moral and legal arguments, and international law and precedents.

Legislation: The Promotion of National Unity and Reconciliation Act

The Preamble to the Act stipulates that one of the objectives is to provide for the 'taking of measures aimed at the granting of reparation to, and the rehabilitation and the restoration of, the human and civil dignity, of victims of violations of human rights'. Section 4(f) states that one of the functions of the TRC shall be 'to make recommendations to the president with regard to:

- The policy which should be followed or the measures which should be taken with regard to the granting of reparation to victims or the taking of other measures aimed at rehabilitating and restoring the human and civil dignity of victims;
- Measures which should be taken to grant Urgent Interim Reparation to victims'.

Further, section 25(b)(i) of the Act notes that the Committee 'may make recommendations which may include urgent interim measures as contemplated in section 4(f)(ii), as to appropriate measures of reparation to victims'. In terms of section 42, 'the President, in consultation with the Ministers of Justice and Finance, will establish a President's Fund. All money payable to victims in terms of regulations promulgated by the President shall be disbursed from this fund'. In sum, it is evident that in establishing the TRC, the legislators contemplated the possibility of the payment of individual reparations.

Moral and Legal Basis

The Committee stated that the moral argument for reparation for the victims of the conflict of the past was a very strong one. Its report reads:

> It is generally accepted that victims and survivors of terrible atrocities of the past deserve reparation and rehabilitation. The state, as well as the community, owes it to them that adequate measures should be taken to restore their dignity and self-respect. Comprehensive forms of reparation should also be implemented to restore their physical and mental well-being. Without adequate reparation and rehabilitation measures, there

can be no reconciliation, either on an individual or community level.

Rehabilitation and rehabilitation measures are necessary to counterbalance the amnesty process in South Africa. The granting of amnesty to perpetrators of gross human rights violations is so generous and comprehensive that, without equally generous and comprehensive reparation measures to alleviate the plight of victims, the process will prove to be extremely one-sided and unfair. Furthermore, victims who are losing the opportunity of benefiting from civil claims against the perpetrators for their suffering, need to be compensated.

The responsibility for reparation is with the present government, which is morally obliged to carry the debt of its predecessors and has accepted this. It is however equally imperative that the whole community – especially those sections of the community who benefited most from the unjust systems of the past – should accept its co-responsibility for the reparation and rehabilitation of the victims of the conflicts of the past.[3]

In terms of South African law, the report refers to the case of *Azapo and Others v the President of the Republic of South Africa and Others*, in which the applicants sought an order declaring Section 20(7) unconstitutional. (Section 20(7) states that a person who has been granted amnesty for an act shall not be criminally or civilly liable in respect of that act.) The court held that the section was not unconstitutional, and Justice Didcott explained:

Reparations are usually payable by states, and there is no reason to doubt that the postscript envisages our own state shouldering the national responsibility for those. It therefore does not contemplate that the state will go scot free. On the contrary, I believe, an actual commitment on the point is implicit in its terms, a commitment in principle to the assumption by the state of the burden.

The Statute does not, it is true, grant any legally enforceable rights in lieu of those lost by claimants whom the amnesties hit. It nevertheless offers some quid pro quo for the loss and establishes the machinery for determining such alternative redress. I cannot see what else it might have achieved immediately once, in the light of the painful choices described by Mahomed DP and in the exercise of the legislative judgement brought to bear on them, the basic

*decision had been taken to substitute the indeterminate prospect of repara-
tions for the concrete reality of legal claims wherever those were enjoyed. For
nothing more definite, detailed and efficacious could feasibly have been
promised at that stage, and with no prior investigations, recommendations
and decisions of the very sort for which provision is now made.*

The late Justice Ismael Mahomed, then Deputy President of the
Constitutional Court, had spelt out the 'painful choices' which the Act
had sought to address, and judged that the potential for exposing the truth
of the past through the process of amnesty was an essential part of the
process, and that this was balanced with 'the election made by the makers
of the Constitution … to permit Parliament to favour "the reconstruction
of society" involving in the process a wider concept of "reparation",
which would allow the state to take into account the competing claims on
its resources but, at the same time, to have regard to the "untold suffering"
of individuals and families whose fundamental human rights had been
invaded during the conflict of the past'.[4]

International Instruments

The R&R Committee pointed out that the right of victims of human
rights abuses to fair and adequate compensation was well established in
international law, and that South Africa had signed a number of international instruments which placed it under an obligation to provide victims
with such fair and adequate compensation. It argued that these instruments, as well as rulings made by bodies established to ensure compliance
with their provisions, indicated that it is not sufficient to award 'token' or
nominal compensation to victims. It stressed that the quantum of reparation awarded to victims should be sufficient to make a meaningful and
substantial impact on the quality of their lives.

The R&R Committee referred to the Universal Declaration of Human
Rights (and its use of the term 'effective remedy') and to the International
Covenant on Civil and Political Rights, which had established a Human
Rights Committee to consider a number of cases where the Covenant had
been breached. In all the cases cited it had held that where the state or any
of its agents are responsible for killings, torture, abductions or disappearances, it is under a legal obligation to pay compensation to the victims or
their families. The fact that in the majority of instances the Human Rights

Committee had used the term 'compensation' indicated that the award to victims should be meaningful and substantial.

The R&R Committee further referred to the Convention against Torture and Other Cruel, Inhuman or Degrading Treatment of Punishment (also signed by South Africa) and the Inter-American Convention on Human Rights. It concluded that there is a well-established right of victims of human rights abuse to compensation for their losses and suffering. It argued that the policy recommended by the TRC to the government should be in accordance with South Africa's international obligations, and that the reparations awarded to victims should therefore be significant and substantial.

The Discussion Within the TRC

During the 18 months of thought and discussion, considerable stress and anxiety had been felt within the Commission itself on the matter of reparation, and also by victims who were increasingly upset by the lack of response they received after their original deposition.

There was a sense among members and staff of the Commission that the R&R Committee had taken on too many wider issues of rehabilitation, instead of clarifying and finalising the reparation policy to be recommended to the president. On the other hand, the Committee found itself hampered by delays from government, which was slow to follow up on joint discussions and to respond by drafting the necessary regulations and approving a 'Reparation Application Form'. At the same time, the Committee was waiting for the Human Rights Violations Committee to speed up the process of making findings in the case of the victims. Until this was done, and the R&R Committee received lists of names and addresses, it could not send out the Reparation Application Forms.

The Commission had several urgent decisions to make before matters could proceed:

- Should there be an open or closed list of victims?
- What constituted 'severe' in the category of 'severe ill-treatment'?
- Could armed combatants be considered victims of gross violations of human rights?
- Most difficult of all, what amount would be appropriate for the individual grant? And should it be the same for all?

For the commissioners, these were agonising decisions. How could they recommend a closed list, which would consist only of those people who were found by the TRC to have been victims of gross human rights violations, when it was evident that there were thousands of people who had not made statements, for a variety of reasons? And yet it was the task of the Commission to bring closure to this process. Eventually, the argument prevailed that those people who *had* come forward had made a brave decision to do so and they had ensured the success of the very process itself. Without their participation there could have been no TRC. They deserved to be acknowledged for this, as well as for the nature of their suffering itself. It was agreed that a closed list would be submitted to the government for reparation.

This decision opened the debate over the amount: if the list was to be closed would it not be a further injustice to those excluded from it if the reparation payment was to comprise a large sum? Would it not create conflict and resentment in communities? Those who raised these questions were accused of paternalism and racism, but there were real concerns about the potential consequences. Finally the R&R Committee, citing international precedents and the rights of victims to compensation, convinced the Commission to adopt its recommendation for a cash grant to be paid to individual victims, spread over a six-year period.

The category of 'severe ill-treatment' then became particularly important. Was the Commission to decide whether the loss of a limb could be equated with suffering from exposure to teargas? Was detention without trial a gross violation, and if so, for how long? How could the TRC calculate the loss to a family of a child, a parent, a spouse? A clear decision emerged: the grant must be the same for all, as neither a means test nor a calculation of damage suffered was a possibility.

One of the most painful debates concerned the status of armed combatants. In accordance with international agreements, it became evident that a soldier, in the service of either the state or its opponents, could not be classified as a victim of a gross violation of human rights if he or she was injured or killed in a combat situation. This was a necessary decision, but one which was extremely hard for families to accept, given the history of the South African conflict, and also the consequence of being thus excluded from the possibility of reparation.

Public Announcement of Reparation Policy

With these decisions reached, the policy proposals could be finalised. In October 1997 they were publicly launched in Cape Town by the TRC chairperson, Archbishop Desmond Tutu, and the Committee. The R&R Committee reported that: 'On reflection the proposals were generally well received. The African National Congress, Democratic Party and National Party in principle supported the policy proposals immediately.'⁵ The essence of the reparation policy was as follows:

- An annual payment to victims (or their dependants if the victim is dead) for a period of six years of an amount of between R21 000 and R23 000 according to various criteria; it was estimated that this would cost the state approximately R3 billion in total, since it appeared that the number of victims on the list would not exceed 22 000;
- An 'Urgent Interim Reparation' payment of R2 000 (or more in exceptional circumstances) to those on the list who had suffered hardship as a result of the violation;
- Symbolic reparations, such as days of remembrance, monuments and places of memory;
- Practical assistance, such as issuing death certificates or official declarations of deaths, also concerning outstanding legal matters related to reported violations;
- Community rehabilitation in the form of improved service delivery in the fields of health, education and housing.

The full recommendations are to be found in Volume 5 of the TRC Report.

Further Delays

By the end of 1997, the TRC was expected to be in the last phases of its work before closing down. It had been in existence for two years instead of the originally contemplated 12-18 months, but a great deal of work remained to be done. While its life had been extended for a few more months, there remained urgent tasks to complete. Yet the Human Rights Violations Committee was reporting that it was still 'in the process of finalizing the first batch of national findings. These would consist of some 3 200 findings, involving 5 374 victims'. The R&R Committee was still waiting for the Reparation Application Form and the Urgent Interim Reparation regulations to be promulgated. The draft Reparation Application Form was being field tested by the Community Agency for Social Enquiry (CASE).[6]

The January 1998 meeting of the Commission was faced with a major difficulty. The R&R Committee tabled an urgent report that reflected the issues it confronted in finalising the process of distributing Urgent Interim Reparations. First, the Department of Finance had asked for responses on a number of issues concerning cash flow implications, quantified hidden costs, administration costs and control mechanisms. Second, the promulgation of the necessary form and regulations was consequently delayed, although they had been drafted and were with the Minister of Justice awaiting promulgation. CASE had recommended changes to the application form (which had been made, so the form was ready).

The R&R Committee therefore proposed a 'refinement' to its earlier policy, in order to allow for quicker and more efficient implementation. It would depend on a more inclusive notion of urgency, where every victim would benefit from an urgent interim payment, for those in severe need (according to the Urgent Interim Reparations criteria) as well as those who were not. This would ensure that the largest possible proportion of the available resources would be delivered to the victims and minimise administrative structures and processes.

All people found to be victims still had to fill out an application form, which was a simplified version of the original – giving basic demographic details and banking information. This would reduce the need for field workers as there would not be a need for assistance for people to fill out sections of information on which 'urgency findings' would be made. However, the Committee still saw the application form as an important instrument for eliciting critical information. The Commission debated these proposals at length, and finally agreed:

- There would still be a two-track reparation policy, i.e. urgent interim relief and final reparation. Urgent Interim Reparations would be implemented through presidential decree; the final reparation policy would be approved by Parliament;
- All people found to be victims would be eligible for urgent interim relief of R2 000 each;
- The form would be simplified to facilitate the process;

- The Minister of Justice would be asked to fast-track the process and the promulgation of the regulations and the form so that payments could be made as soon as possible.

This decision encountered obstacles at government level. At the February 1998 meeting, it was reported that the Ministry of Justice insisted that there were no blanket Urgent Interim Reparations. 'They maintain that not everyone would receive R2 000; some may receive less, some more. The Commission had agreed in January that it would be desirable for everyone found to be a victim to receive R2 000, but the policy had to be amended.' Criteria had to be drawn up which every victim must meet before receiving assistance, but only need and hardship would need to be demonstrated.

At the same meeting, the Human Rights Violations Committee said that by 23 February at least 2 000 findings would be ready to hand over to the R&R Committee. Plans were made to send out the letter from the Human Rights Violations Committee informing each victim of the finding, together with the Reparation Application Form.

By the March meeting of the Commission, the R&R Committee report sounded increasingly desperate. Committee members and some staff were leaving, and the work was falling on the shoulders of too few people. In August 1998, the senior staff member responsible for the R&R Committee, Thulani Grenville Grey, told the Commission that he was very concerned about the slow rate at which formal notifications were being sent out, and that this stage of the process was under-resourced. However, the President's Fund was ready to pay 450 persons for whom recommendations had been made. Each payment would have a signed letter from the president. There was, however, a delay because of the president's heavy schedule.

Commissioner Yasmin Sooka was concerned that despite 20 000 findings being made, only 1 600 notifications had gone out. She anticipated that this process would have to continue beyond the life of the Commission. By the September meeting it was reported that no payments had been made, although 7 533 application forms had been sent out, 1 600 forms had been received, and 700 were ready for payment, but were awaiting the president's signature and a launch. The Commission decided to make a formal request that the payments be made without waiting for the signed letters and the launch.

Reports were also tabled about angry meetings with organised victim support groups. The offices were inundated with enquiries about payment, and there was general frustration within the Commission. Wendy Orr said: 'The concept of urgent reparation became a complete farce when its delivery only started shortly before the end of the TRC in October 1998.'[7]

The TRC Final Report and the Government's Response

In October 1998 the TRC presented its five-volume Report to then President Nelson Mandela, and Parliament. The greater part of the Commission was placed in suspension, while the Amnesty Committee was obliged to continue until it had completed its task. A small staff, and two commissioners (Yasmin Sooka and Hlengiwe Mkhize), remained responsible for the ratification of the victim findings and the process of handing over to the President's Fund the names and addresses of those qualifying for Urgent Interim Reparations.

The parliamentary debate on the Report was eagerly awaited, but the discussions during that debate (on 25 February 1999) brought no further comfort to victims. Many of the speeches suggested that individual reparation grants might not be adopted, and that the focus might be on community reparations in the form of redistribution, reconstruction and development. Final decisions were held over until the completion of the Amnesty Committee's work, and the last additional codicils to the Report were handed to the president.

In any event, this did not take place until 21 March 2003, when the two final volumes were handed over to President Mbeki. The volumes contained the Amnesty Committee's report, a number of reports assessing whether any adjustments should be made to previous findings in the earlier volumes, a complete list of the names of those found to have been victims of gross violations of human rights, with a summary of their experience, and an updated list of recommendations.

The new recommendations repeated the previous Report's proposed policy of final reparation to be paid by the state over a six-year period. It also went further and advocated the payment of additional reparation by corporations, banks and parastatals which had benefited in some way from apartheid policies. Five years earlier, the TRC had accepted indications from the private sector that it was willing to make a voluntary contribution to reparation and rehabilitation. Now the TRC noted that victims had been made to wait a long period, without receiving any answer from the government about its intentions, and without deriving much benefit from business initiatives. It therefore recommended to the government that business either make a far more substantial commitment to reconstruction or be forced to do so by means of a wealth tax or specific levy.

The Report was discussed in Parliament on 15 April 2003, and subsequently by an ad hoc committee of Parliament. President Mbeki rejected the suggestion of a wealth tax, to the great relief of business representatives and potential investors in South Africa. He criticised efforts by various organisations and foreign lawyers to bring suits against mining companies, international banks and parastatals.[8] He did, however, urge all South Africans to contribute voluntarily to funds for reparations. He also announced that there would be a once-off payment of R30 000 as a reparation grant to each victim identified by the TRC. These decisions were subsequently supported by the ad hoc committee, despite representations by civil society.

Predictably, this decision evoked a bitterly disappointed and angry response. Perhaps if the government had made known its intentions five years earlier there might have been a greater degree of acceptance. It would have been possible to make an announcement at that stage – the number of victim findings made by the Human Rights Violations Committee was known, and only a small number of additional victims were identified through the amnesty process.

Now the long silence and period of waiting had eaten away at positive feelings towards the TRC process. During that period, too, unemployment and poverty had worsened and people's faith in a transformation that would improve their living conditions had been eroded. Press reports quoted victims as saying, 'I feel bad, bad. It is peanuts'; 'I am not happy, I am sick and I have six children and no food'; 'It is like a hand-out.'[9]

The situation at the end of August 2003 was that Urgent Interim Reparation of between R2 000 and R3 000 had been paid out to about 17 000 applicants by the end of November 2001. This presupposed that the President's Fund had the necessary names and addresses to pay the final R30 000 as soon as the legal procedures had been put in place. Several spokespersons indicated that the government would act as speedily as possible and this would indeed be welcomed.

One of the demands made by organisations representing victims, including those who had not accessed the TRC, was the re-opening of the list. This would be a serious difficulty for the government, and it seemed that some other mechanism would have to be found to deal with those who suffered. On the other hand, there should be some structure established to deal with genuine errors on the part of the TRC and to which queries and applications for review could be addressed. However, a different way of dealing with the broader issue of those who suffered will have to be sought. It is generally acknowledged not only that there were many victims who did not go through the TRC process, but also that there were thousands of people who suffered under apartheid (and indeed under previous discrimination) in ways which were not provided for in the TRC's mandate.

So far the government's response in this regard has been to speak of community reparations, although these have not been clearly defined. It is of course true that many of the government's successful strategies, such as the provision of housing, health services, social benefits, electricity, water and the elimination of racial injustices in the area of education and employment opportunities, can be seen as redressing the wrongs of the past. However, something much more immediately tangible is required if those people who remain the poorest and most disadvantaged in our society are to feel any benefits.

There is a strong lobby among civil society organisations for the introduction of a Basic Income Grant. This could form a logical counterbalance to the payment of reparation to a limited number of victims. The universal payment to all South Africans would have an immediate impact on the very poorest and most excluded families, would enable them to have better access to educational and employment (even self-employment) opportunities, and give them a sense that they are not totally excluded from such benefits.

Examples in other countries sound a warning about difficulties in the future if these issues are not dealt with wisely. In both Chile and Argentina, for example, after decades the governments are having to deal with renewed public pressure for just mechanisms to redress the past. It is not too late for the South African government to enter into discussions with a broad range of organisations and to reconsider the amount of reparation offered, as well as other issues. The churches and other faith organisations have an important part to play. Large corporations and individual citizens could do a great deal to indicate their willingness to contribute to making up for the wrongs of the past.

The TRC has been widely praised as South Africa's special way of facilitating transition. It has been fairly successful in exposing much of what happened, and in using the amnesty mechanism to deal with some of the perpetrators. But it will be seen to have failed if thousands of people continue to have a sense of grievance and injustice. The government and all South Africans should take serious note of the need to work towards reconciliation through creating better lives for all.

Notes

1   TRC, Working document tabled at Commission meeting, 15–16 May 1996.
2   Wendy Orr, 'Reparation Delayed is Healing Retarded', in *Looking Back, Reaching Forward: Reflections on the Truth and Reconciliation Commission of South Africa*, eds. Charles Villa-Vicencio and Wilhem Verwoerd (Cape Town: UCT Press, 2000), 241-242.
3   R&R Committee Report, tabled at TRC meeting, 17 July 1997, p 4.
4   Quoted in TRC, Final Report, Vol. 1, (Pretoria: RSA, 1998), 177-178.
5   R&R Committee Report to TRC, December 1997.
6   Reports to the December 1997 meeting of the Commission. It should be noted that at the same meeting there were discussions on a funding strategy to raise additional contributions to the President's Fund. It was planned that there would be a meeting, or a 'breakfast', to which the heads of 20 major companies would be invited. Preliminary discussions had been held with some leaders of the private sector who had indicated a measure of support, and with the President's Office.
7   Orr, 'Reparation Delayed', 247.
8   Litigation is being pursued in a New York court by lawyers (American and South African) representing apartheid victims and several organisations against major corporations, accusing them of making unjust profits as a result of apartheid policies. Several South African government spokespersons have condemned this action. Discussions in South Africa are continuing, with support from civil society and religious organisations, seeking a mediated solution.
9   Christelle Terreblanche, 'Victims of Apartheid Disappointed at "Hand-Out",' *Cape Times*, 16 April 2003.

4

The Joint Sitting of Parliament, 15 April 2003:

A Rhetorical View of the Reparation Debate

*Philippe-Joseph Salazar**

The cursory remarks that follow are meant to be a rhetorician's response to the joint sitting of Parliament, on 15 April 2003, upon the remittance of the Final Report of the Truth and Reconciliation Commission (TRC).

These remarks are, however, prompted by an enduring sense of the TRC's topicality, which manifested itself at a conference held at the French Academy, in June 2003.[1] Its theme was reconciliation and sovereignty. Paul Ricœur gave a momentous address. So did Pierre Truche, past president of the French Court of Cassation (the equivalent of a judge president of a supreme court of appeal or first Lord of Appeal) and a philosopher of law in his own right. Truche concluded his address with a celebration of the TRC, and with an intimation that the end of justice (the law) was to end justice (trials and sentencing) and, in a sort of Hegelian *Aufhebung*, to sublimate justice by/in/through restoration. He saw in the TRC, and so did most of the constitutionalists present at the symposium, a process by which popular sovereignty affirms itself beyond the constitutional intent itself, frames justice beyond justice, and therefore presents the traditional view of political sovereignty with a considerable challenge: reparation, restoration.

With that in mind, I awaited with great expectations, after the remittance of the Final Report of the TRC on 21 March 2003, the ensuing

* The author thanks Miss Nathalie Bucher for having provided source material; her final year thesis in the MPhil programme in Rhetoric Studies (University of Cape Town, 2003) analyses the rhetorical structures of this joint sitting of Parliament (also to be presented at an OSSREA workshop, October 2003, Cape Town).

debate in Parliament on 15 April 2003. My hopes were to witness a lively public debate together with a more vigorous debate, in Parliament, on reparation and the interlinking of sovereignty and restorative justice. None of these expectations were met. The reason why public debate has hardly taken any shape is the remit of my colleagues in communication and media studies. Thoughtful studies on the public sphere in South Africa are still missing.[2] As a mere rhetorician, concerned with political deliberation and argumentation, my take on the issue is different. My un-expectations, as I would call them, outstripped my expectations, as the joint sitting of Parliament did cast a somewhat harsh light on some rhetor-ical aspects of our new republic.

Concerning Rhetorical Traditions

The remittance of the TRC's Final Report was, on the face of it, the sort of ritual of commemoration and oratorical display the 2nd republic, the democratic one, has inherited from the 1st, the oligarchic.

In rhetoric studies, we consider that rhetorical traditions endure sur-reptitiously.[3] No need here to have read Pareto, to know that elites have an understandable, in some respect healthy, propensity to borrow forms of deliberation from one another, even after sharp revolutionary ruptures. Human societies are not absolutes. Rhetorically speaking, the problem is that such borrowings are often hidden ones and shape deliberative styles, even though users themselves are often reluctant to admit it.[4] For one United States Supreme Court judge, and a former senator, who declares to a junior colleague, 'There is one book which is by far better than anything published before and after: Aristotle's *Rhetoric*,'[5] how many politicians deny the most obvious? that the business of politics is to convince others, and to this end rhetoric is called. Modern democratic politics are supported by a variety of rhetorical traditions[6] that form sets of 'taken-for-granted' and which are no longer recognised as rhetorical tools,[7] while they provide 'power' with its structuring, persuasive 'art'.[8]

With regard to South Africa, owing to the legal, constitutional and political continuity that marked, against all odds and the greatest odd of all – the definition of apartheid as a crime against humanity, hence the previous republic as a criminal government (elected *cum* electors) – the passage from oligarchy to democracy and the transition from liberationist activism to elective office, the permanence of ceremonial rhetoric on the side of apartheid's supporters, as well as on that of the new ruling class, should not surprise us. Apartheid, like most Fascist regimes it emulated, being the last born of that breed, needed an æsthetics to impress and to endure. On the other hand, the ANC's iconology and visual rhetoric bear witness, still today, to an indelible attachment to Soviet or East German Social Realism. Both iconological and rhetorical traditions are very much part of the South African political landscape, and it is not the misguided call for 'monumental parks' or just 'monumentality' that will help assuage my concern that South African political æsthetics, in its persuasive dimension, remains locked in repetitive patterns seen as global rhetorical standards.

However, to deal only with words,[9] the debate which took place in Parliament on 15 April 2003 raised different rhetorical questions from those I anticipated. I would like to sketch some of the issues regarding the rhetorical dimension of the 'joint sitting', as it is formally called.

What is a Joint Sitting Debate?

The very first question that arises concerns the rhetorical form given to the debate. The Act creating the TRC makes it mandatory that: 'The President shall, in such manner as he or she may deem fit, bring the final report of the Commission to the notice of the Nation, among others, by laying such report, within two months after having received it, upon the Table in Parliament.'[10] The Act does not provide for a debate in Parliament, by either or both houses, let alone a joint sitting; it simply uses a time-honoured, if somewhat obscure, expression, 'laying upon the Table of Parliament'. What does 'tabling' actually imply? The expression partly reflects the customs of debate and proceedings in the British tradition which, one hopes, would no longer be part of the 2nd republic's functioning. I am not certain the average South African knows what it means.[11]

More profoundly, the permanence of this deliberative glossary illustrates an unseen tension between the requisites of a written constitution, albeit not approved by popular referendum, and customs embedded in having a non-written one. This Republic has a written Constitution, yet the members of the constituent assembly did not see fit to promulgate a set of rules for debate that would reflect the unprecedented conditions upon which the Constitution is founded – a civil war arrested and the absence of either executions or blanket amnesty, in short, reconciliation, together with the oddest legal/constitutional continuity seen in recent times – or to organise directly the working of Parliament. Leaving it to committees is, again, taken for granted. However, in terms of Parliamentary rhetoric, this failure to further organise the deliberative functioning of the Constitution resulted in the 2nd republic's having at its disposal a set of rules, with regard to debate in the chambers, that is, by and large, inherited from tradition. Debate and tabling follow customs of address (not to mention ceremonial trappings) that are inherited from the apartheid republic and, ultimately, from the British Parliament. In particular, it was left to a committee to establish the Joint Rules and Regulations, which have a direct bearing on this joint sitting.

What is at stake here is not the expediency of such rules but their appropriateness to a new democratic culture, or even their ingenuity. Indeed, in other republican regimes, like the French republican system, a new constitution nullifies the previous one both in terms of its inherent value (the constitution 'constitutes' the nation) and in terms of how it organises government because sovereignty, the people, is indeed 'represented', deliberatively, by deputies. It provides clear-cut frames for deliberation.[12] Assemblies vote, as soon as the constitution is approved by popular ballot, their own rules for debate.[13] One tends to forget that Parliament is that institution which makes the sovereign deliberate, by delegation, since the concept of direct democracy is deemed unworkable in large polities.[14] Interestingly, what is called, in South Africa, Parliamentary 'privilege' is a mere rewording of Article 9 of the English Bill of Rights of 1689 (concerning the inviolability of MPs' freedom of speech within the house).[15] South Africa, in this respect, has not cast aside a pre-modern, colonial conception of Parliamentary debate. That South Africans do not own the basis for determining occasions for deliberation is a singular feature, and a shortcoming.[16] It is most surprising that none of the deliberative modes fostered by the liberation struggle, now and again paid homage to by Nelson Mandela as 'collective leadership', are to be found in current practice.

The direct implication of this state of affairs is that the turn of phrase 'joint sitting' belongs to the Joint Rules and Regulations,[17] although it is implied in sections of the Constitution relating to the president's arbitrarily summoning an 'extraordinary sitting of Parliament' to consider 'special business'[18] or, compulsorily, to approve a 'state of national defence' (this is a figure of speech, redolent of the French Revolution, to signify a state of emergency, a feature of apartheid).[19] In addition, it is in the Procedure section of the Joint Rules and Regulations that one finds another key element: 'No vote or decision may be taken by or in a joint sitting.'[20] The immediate, rhetorical consequence of this rule is self-evident. The joint sitting is not a debate. It is not named so in Parliamentary order papers, although most MPs and Parliamentary civil servants will call it a debate.[21] And anyone who attended the joint sitting, or saw it on television, could see that it was made of a series of pronouncements or statements by selected speakers,[22] including 'maiden speeches' by MPs who had not yet addressed Parliament.[23] What we, as a spill-over audience, witnessed on our television screens on 15 April 2003 was a puzzling throwback to pre-democratic rhetoric, when stultified rhetoric was the hallmark of the apartheid republic. It was not a debate such as a Parliamentary democracy would have been expected to hold on so momentous an occasion, the TRC Final Report: speeches, questions, motions, vote.

The joint sitting of 15 April 2003 is a rhetorical conundrum. It is, however, not the only one. To gauge Parliamentary rhetoric, of which joint sittings are just an instance, it is worth considering first its correlate, presidential rhetoric. The formal link between the two is provided by the Constitution itself since an 'extraordinary sitting [of Parliament]' may be summoned by the president 'to conduct special business', as already quoted. The Report and the question of reparation were, indeed, special business.

What is Presidential Rhetoric?

I have explained elsewhere what I call the 'two rhetorics of the presidency' in South Africa.[24] Suffice it here to underline three key points for the purpose of defining what is more broadly labelled 'rhetorical presidency'.[25]

At face value, the 2nd republic is a Parliamentary democracy. Within Parliament the National Assembly alone is the result of direct, universal suffrage. The president is elected by one of the two houses, the National Assembly, among its members.[26] In other words, the National Assembly alone enjoys direct popular legitimacy. By contrast, the president's legitimacy, as president (not as a member, the president ceases to be a member upon election to the presidency), is derivative.

Political scientists are aware of the reasons why this arrangement was a necessary tool in the smooth passage from oligarchy to democracy, why the framers thought it unwise to have a president elected directly by the people, a choice related to that of not putting this Constitution to the test of a popular referendum. An aside: These choices seemed expedient enough, at the time. Not having sought the People's approval for the Constitution may come back to haunt South Africans if there is ever a severe political crisis. The members of the constituent assembly found a way to deal with this constitutive anomaly: The so-called Public Participation Programme offered a semblance of popular legitimacy by transferring the latter from assent to conception, and by proposing that which, in rhetoric, we call a 'plasmatical' solution, in terms of which each citizen-to-be was deemed to have been 'involved' in writing the fundamental law.[27]

In addition, constitutionalists know what sort of constitutional entailments usually follow from shared popular legitimacy (when both president and Parliament hold in such case power from the ballot box). It often results in a prime minister seeking, in a variety of ways, Parliament's approval, often through a vote of confidence; and conversely in powers of dissolution being vested in the president. Under this Constitution, just as the president collapses both roles of president and 'head of the cabinet,'[28] he cannot dissolve Parliament;[29] the National Assembly can, however, pass a vote of no confidence, resulting in the dismissal of the president or his cabinet, but a newly elected president does not need a vote of confidence to be able to proceed.[30]

The neat result of this balanced construction, that may well lead one day to such blockage of the system that violence alone, by a coup d'état or a revolution, will prise it apart, is self-evident. The president does not hold his legitimacy directly from the sovereign, the People, but from the National Assembly, within Parliament. The presidency has to construct popular legitimacy by other means. There has been, in consequence, a tendency, supported by state communication services and the ANC, accepted uncritically by the press who should know better, and taken as granted by public opinion who should be told better, to market or even merchandise the 2nd republic as a presidential regime. The presidency has, for the past ten years, and more markedly for the past five years, deployed a skilful rhetorical strategy to buttress a belief in direct legitimacy and to impress on the public the concept of a president as the first arm of government, possibly above Parliament.

Whether it enhances or usurps democracy is a matter I leave to political scientists. From a rhetorician's angle, the consolidation of a rhetorical presidency in South Africa bears the marks of 'evocation of interpretation', as it aims at mobilising the public around an intended meaning,[31] the persuasive prevalence of the presidency.[32] The rhetorical cornerstone of this mobilisation is the so-called 'state of the nation address'. Addresses such as the one with which the president opened the 15 April joint sitting have to be read within such persuasive mobilisation.[33]

What is, rhetorically, the 'state of the nation' address? The epithet 'so-called' or even 'self-styled' is fitting and just, insofar as the Constitution does not provide for the president to address Parliament at its opening, or for any speech at all when the legislature holds its inaugural session – except the Speaker calling the Assembly to order. It can only be found in the Joint Rules and Regulations where we read of an 'annual or special address' necessitating that extraordinary rhetorical event, a joint sitting.[34] The mention of an *annual* address is nowhere in the Constitution itself. What are at work are a rhetorical global taken-for-granted and a rhetorical tradition.

Traditionally, under apartheid, the head of state or government would open Parliament; traditionally, in a British-style democracy, the monarch reads a speech of general policy, written by the prime minister, followed by a debate. Both aspects are represented in the so-called state of the nation address, however with a major difference: the responsibility of cabinet is not put to the test for the simple reason that such responsibility is not written in the Constitution. Still, rhetorical traditions creep up unnoticed.[35] It would have been inconceivable for the first democratically elected, albeit indirectly elected, president not to have addressed the first democratically elected, albeit by a list ballot, Parliament. Nelson Mandela's speech in Parliament, in 1994, was a taken-for-granted. It is likely that, even if the founding president had not been a statesman of Nelson Mandela's stature, the tradition would have been as peremptory. So, when Nelson Mandela gave his second, by then already tagged 'state of the nation', address the tradition was appropriated, taken for granted, orchestrated and firmly entrenched, as if it had been conceived for that purpose, opening Parliament, which it was not. The speech Mandela delivered at the second opening of the First Parliament was no longer attached to the justifiable ceremonial of a new democracy being installed. It was now linked to routine politics. This move should have been questioned. It was not. Repetition carries strong evidential powers.

The rhetorician remains in fact puzzled at the media's ready acceptance of this rhetorical act, at their uncritical use of the odd titulature 'state of the nation', borrowed from what is perceived to be an American tradition. I cannot dwell here on the chequered history of this tradition in the USA – beyond the fact that the expression has a nice ring and makes for neat headlines. The media, who are so vigilant in asserting independence, have bought into the rhetorical presidency and its very first persuasive act, the invention of a form of address that alters the shape of politics.

In this context, the duty vested on the president 'to commend' the TRC Report to the nation has led to a re-enforcing of the rhetorical presidency. As the TRC Act mandates the president on how best to propagate the Report, quite naturally the presidency saw in a tabling at an 'extraordinary sitting' the right occasion to develop further the rhetorical presidency, and further mobilise effects of popular legitimacy. 'To commend', yet another quaint expression inherited from the British tradition (no definition exists, in the Constitution, as to what 'to commend' means), rhetorically functions as 'a command'. It is to be expected that the presidency will rely systematically or opportunistically (depending upon the president's office strategy, or lack thereof) on the 'tabling of important reports' as a tool for presidential intervention within Parliament, tools for 'commendation'.

This in itself is not a bad thing, so long as the rhetorical presidency nurtures debate and does not supplant Parliamentary deliberation. Recent studies of Parliament have shown that deliberation is at a low ebb.[36] What is of concern is how the transformation of the presidency into a form of rhetorical agency may lead to an arrogation of deliberation. By way of comparison, and to summarise scholarship in the field of (American) presidential rhetoric studies, a signal change has been noted by which the American presidency has been using the state of the nation address not as a means to communicate to Congress important messages,[37] but as a means to shape politics and affect the definition itself of the American republic.[38] The American presidency uses this form of address to appeal directly to the nation, and to comfort the idea, foreign to the framers, that the president is also an interpreter of the Constitution. Direct address is not simply playing politics, putting pressure on Congress when needed, it transforms the presidency in ways that are echoed in the South African case. As both presidents are not directly elected by the People (the systems are different but the bottom line is that, unlike the French president, they are not), their rhetorical effort is a constant attempt at gaining, retaining or increasing the *èthos* of their office and, by implication, personal power.

Èthos qualifies, in rhetoric, the authority an audience accords a speaker to address a debatable issue. (It does not mean the audience, or parts of it, agrees with the speaker or even has trust, it simply recognises the latter's competence, defined itself in a variety of ways.) The founding president had no such need for *èthos*, even with his adversaries. The inheritor does, even with his partisans. As a consequence, any direct address, either to Parliament or to the People is an assertion of popular legitimacy (interestingly enough, the presidency has not yet grasped fully the range of possibilities direct address offers). More importantly, it casts the president as a privileged voice for phrasing, performing, embodying the Constitution.

These features are to be found in the joint sitting address by Thabo Mbeki. The president spoke first and tried to give the authoritative reading, on behalf of the nation, of the TRC Report. The stultified structure of the debate and the sequencing of ANC speakers, whom we should consider as surrogate speakers,[39] afforded the presidential *èthos* to appear under different guises, at regular intervals, indeed with variations, but casting over dissenting voices a pervasive presence. Every third speaker or so was an ANC orator.[40] For the rhetorician, in Perelmanian terminology,[41] such strategy of surrogacy is called proof (of *èthos*) by presence. The Joint Rules and Regulations may function on a sophism, yet, as the public belief is that the president must address the nation, in and from Parliament, the sophism in which it is grounded is rhetorically performative. The next stage, indeed, will be for the presidency to appropriate direct forms of address, above and outside Parliament, and replace the state of the nation-in-Parliament address by new forms, as necessity arises (such as, at the time of a referendum, a state of national defence, or a vote of no confidence). In sum, the notion of a joint sitting to hear the president draws on the taken-for-granted of a presidential annual speech. Parliament is an echo chamber for persuasive mobilisation. This is the heart of the rhetorical presidency.

Levels of Rhetoric and the Question of Expediency

The third aspect worth considering pertains therefore to the rhetorical end of the joint sitting itself (not its status, not the opportunity it affords presidential rhetoric). In rhetoric, a distinction is often drawn between an external and internal end.[42] The external end is to persuade, the internal end is to put into action the best available means. In turn, the regulated determination of means allows persuasion to become a transaction between orator and audience, a form of social link, and not merely an effect (that is, the achievement of the external end). Setting aside this rather complex question, what matters here, in this instance, is how a rhetorical set-up, such as a joint sitting, provides for a multiplicity of internal ends.

To begin with, an interplay exists between the three canonical genres any speech or set of speeches may adopt. Bearing in mind the already mentioned uncertainties as to the nature of the joint sitting, the fact is that the so-called debate did take place. Rhetorically speaking, a political speech, or a set of speeches in a given situation, can be approached from three, mutually non-exclusive, angles. A public speech is either forensic, deliberative or epideictic (ceremonial).

Forensic rhetoric deals with a case, something which, like in a court of law, is subject to a contention of evidences regarding its cause (who did it? did she do it?); what is incontrovertible is that 'it happened'. The rest is debatable. The exchange of opposing parties revolves around the attribution of cause, not on its reality (this is the reason why rhetoric holds that forensic debate is always past-oriented). Truth is always a matter of evidence provided and argued. No more, no less.

By contrast, deliberative rhetoric is future-oriented: a decision must be taken in response to a problem, that engages the future of the community, and arguments are exchanged. A proposal has no reality, except in the arguments proffered; it is a 'scenario' (a translation of the Greek word *plasma*). The best argued scenario wins and, one hopes, provides for the most expedient policy.

Finally, epideictic rhetoric deals in values. Epideictic speeches extol what makes a social link, a community, a polity stand together, and this is the reason why they are, in practice, ritualistic or, at the very least, ceremonial or festive. They have a sort of transcendental or uplifting quality, they place the community in the presence of its core values (hence, epideictic rhetoric is present-bound: it arrests time to help contemplation).

Each genre has its own finality: a forensic speech purports to establish justice (if we establish 'who did it' we can restore the law's integrity); a deliberative speech aims at expediency (if we find the most useful, expedient, policy, we can move forward); an epideictic speech reinforces values (the Ancients called it 'beauty' – this is what I term elsewhere the 'cosmetics' of democracy: democracy needs to be felt as 'beautiful'). Rhetorically, that is in the process of persuasion, which is why speeches are given by politicians in the first place, this triple distinction between justice, expediency, beauty is far from facile. For instance, it may be 'expedient' to use unjust arguments, or just to use un-expedient arguments (the strict application of law can lead to political unrest). In other terms, arguments do not operate similarly.

Turning to the joint sitting of Parliament, it is possible to fit this grid of reading onto it. Without being asked to do so, but impelled by a pre-constitutional tradition that allows or even makes it mandatory that analogous reports be tabled, Parliament passes judgement. It looks at the Report of the TRC, it examines it, from a variety of angles and it sees whether the proceedings and recommendations tally with the brief, as given in the Act. Parliament judges the TRC. But, because Parliament has not been called to accept or reject the Report by way of a vote, this forensic examination has not achieved its internal end (a judgement by censure or approval). So long as Parliament cannot censure the Commission, these remarks are made in vain. The natural movement, in a democratic Parliament, to close a crucial policy debate by a vote has not taken place. The natural form, in a democratic assembly, for an exchange of arguments to resolve itself in a judgement has not happened. As it stands, the debate is a movement arrested, a form un-achieved. The question then arises as to the function of criticisms passed on the Commission. Constitutionalists will argue that the Constitution does not provide for a vote, that ensuing debates and formulations of policy will provide for such forums. Rhetoricians will reply that this particular rhetorical event had all the elements, if not the cohesion, of a judgement being passed on the TRC, and that, under this light, the outcome is still unclear. Both would agree, however, that the speeches served some purpose.

Which brings us to the second level, that the joint sitting adopted a deliberative dimension. Whereas, at its most obvious, a political speech is a deliberative move, hinging essentially on the articulation of a 'what next', a far less apparent confusion exists, within the expediency of such a deliberative set-up, between justice and expediency. In this particular instance, the president formulated the expediency question of reparations in a fitting formula ('where to from here!').[43] However, the fit of the formula, as it were, rested on the correlation between justice and expediency or, to rephrase it in terms of finality of arguments, between judging a case and proposing a scenario, an essential tension. To adjudicate entails passing judgement on people, to envision a solution is to attribute agency. Both arguments do attribute responsibility, but the first is based on evidence produced, while the second is on evidence adduced.

The president's speech was, in that respect, well constructed. It provided a critical review of the Report, by way of citations showing how the TRC has acted in accordance with the requirements of the Act, how and when it was mistaken in (1) passing policy judgements, (2) asserting the course of criminal justice (for new cases of amnesty) and (3) questioning constitutional standards (in the case of international litigation). In this respect, the presidential speech was forensic in style, purpose and conclusion. The president fulfilled, 'as he [saw] fit' says the Act, the burden of commendation placed on him. However, what the Act did not envisage was for the president to engage in such a review of the Report. The commendation was a political commendation, not a forensic one. It went unnoticed, by the press namely, that the president acted doubly on that day. He passed judgement and he used it to formulate a policy concerning, in particular, reparation.

These are two different rhetorical moves. By vesting on himself a duty to evaluate, the president reinforced the impact, the *èthos* of the rhetorical presidency, in short he demonstrated his better ability to read the Constitution, to correlate the Constitution to the twin commandment of the TRC Act, as we must not forget that the TRC Act is grounded in the Epilogue of the Interim Constitution, that it precedes the Constitution just as reconciliation is the grounding for the nation.[44] The president acts 'presidentially' by correlating the TRC with the Constitution. In doing so he does 'defend' the Constitution.[45] The president's only rhetorical duty as president is to present the Report without passing judgement, and to remind Parliament of its duties. Rhetorically, the finality of this correlation is 'justice'. The fundamental law and the 'law' that subsumes it, the grounding in reconciliation, are beyond expediency. They are just.

On the other hand, he has indeed the duty to defend his party's and his cabinet's take on the Report, and in that case, to develop a deliberative argument, based on expediency, no longer on justice. What his speech illustrates is simply the confusion that presently exists regarding the exact rhetorical nature of the presidency. But, the act of reviewing the Report in political terms pertains to expediency. And, as leader of the ANC, he has indeed to fulfil that rhetorical function. The inability of most media to distinguish the two levels is noteworthy.

In fact, the last speaker, the Minister for Justice and Constitutional Development (who gave, in terms of delivery, the best performance of that five-hour long 'debate'),[46] brought to a forceful summation the rhetorical stance made by the president in his initial speech. Having defined the logic of the joint sitting ('the president has performed his task under section 44 of the Act [it] is for Parliament to then perform its function under section 27(2) of the Act'),[47] the minister proceeded, in fact, to provide a peroration to the government's, and the ANC's, argument. He tied up the themes articulated (at times dis-articulated) by the sequence of nine speeches,[48] and ended on a strong ethical as well as emotional appeal (he resorted to the presidential *èthos* and to patriotism) – which is exactly how a peroration must function. He was aware that his audience, whose attention was somewhat taxed after more than four hours of listening, needed to be stirred, and he found the correct, lively, congenial delivery just to achieve that effect. His statements were, at the time, effective in pulling together the audience and serving the press with sound bites, although in retrospect, they raised more problems than they actually solved – bearing in mind that rhetorical evidence is 'on the spot'.[49] For instance, he asserted that it had been 'a very good debate'[50] (in such circumstances, it would have been self-defeating not to celebrate Parliament's skills, yet, what took place was not a debate, just a listing of positions, statements indeed); he added that it had been a 'wonderful discussion'[51] (when no discussion took place, except perhaps between the benches);[52] his remark that 'all of us had a moment to reflect'[53] was, however, rhetorically fitting, and I will return to its rhetorical meaning, the epideictic moment. The speech was deftly conceived, and delivered. His and Mbeki's framed the 'debate'.

On the one hand, the minister whose portfolio it is to direct government policy in terms of constitutional matters (the TRC is insolubly married to the Constitution) and justice (which does relate to reparation on specific issues such as the Land Court,[54] and to 'justice' in more general, let us say political, terms) spoke last and performed his ministerial duty, to remind Parliament of two key aspects of the Act in relation to the implementation of recommendations: the commendation to the nation by the president, the commendation by the president to Parliament with ensuing action by the latter.[55] It 'empowers' Parliament to do what the Act requires, that is the furtherance of justice, from amnesty to reparation.

On the other hand, the speech was nonetheless a partisan speech, lively and at times bellicose,[56] that collapsed, via the minister's surrogate voice, the two persons of the president, the President-in-Parliament, as the Constitution provides, and the president-leader of the nation, as an ANC member. In this respect, far from 'not [going] over the debate', as the minister enjoined Parliament, the speech itself re-iterated the massive ambiguity I have delineated between rhetorical personas, and, for that reason, did 'go over the debate', by recasting it, one more, final time, within parameters that are, quite simply, non-evident, problematic, except if we now turn our attention to three rhetorical notions: the rhetorical situation, homonymy and the epideictic moment.

These three notions are, in rhetoric, not necessarily closely related but, for the sake of clarity, given that rhetorical analysis is not yet the stock-in-trade of South African studies of public deliberation, I shall keep them together by way of conclusion.

Rhetorical Situation and Homonymy

What sort of 'event' was the joint sitting? One fundamental condition for deliberation to take place, that is, have efficiency, is the existence of a 'rhetorical situation'. What is a rhetorical situation?[57] It 'may be defined as a complex of persons, events, objects, and relations presenting an actual or potential exigence which can be completely or partially removed if discourse, introduced into the situation, can so constrain human decision or action as to bring about the significant modification of the exigence'.[58] In short, any audience is not a rhetorical audience unless the orator(s) can, in view of an exigence, modify or remove it by persuasion, taking into account constraints. As Bitzer says, advocacy often fails when speakers are unable to identify the constraint and/or the exigence of a local situation.

Now, in the case of the joint sitting, are we in the presence of just a collection of hearers and listeners, or in the presence of an audience? Put differently, what is the exigence that can be modified or removed through persuasion? Phrased in a third way, what are the constraints? The answer is far from self-evident.

At a plain level, the 27 orators had no one to convince as no vote or no decision were to sanction their efforts, even though a vote in favour of the Report would have been a foregone conclusion. Persuasion that does not effectuate action is not persuasion. That, later on, Parliament would meet and debate and take resolutions is a different matter. On 15 April, in spite of massive media attention trained on Parliament, and instant coverage by the international press, the audience made of Parliamentarians was not a rhetorical audience, it was merely a collection of listeners who needed not to be convinced of anything. A close scrutiny of the main speeches reveals a tiresome reiteration, party by party, hackneyed party lines, all *pro domo* apologies. However, beyond Parliament, there were possibly several rhetorical audiences, the South African citizens, the press, national and international lobbying groups and news watchers. These were, potentially at least, global rhetorical audiences.

If there was an exigence of magnitude, that day, it was the question of reparation. The ANC and the Democratic Alliance did little to remove or modify the exigence; they, in fact, denied there was an exigence, by offering a literal reading of the TRC Act. And they could do so, because they were addressing Parliament, which was not a rhetorical audience. Diplomatic and international agencies with specific exigences and under constraints of their own, were also not rhetorical audiences. To have them so, the government would have had to determine the exigence of each major outside audience, the constraints of each and every one of them, and formulate adequate arguments that, on the face of it, would have collided with each other. Wisely, government stuck to reading the Act and amplifying it with largely ethical and emotional appeals. A few dissenting parties, by contrast, opted not for reading the Report in light of the Act, but for questioning the premises of the Act itself,[59] if not the transitional safeguards themselves, which, in a normal debate, would have led to points of orders and challenges and possibly legal recourses.[60] What dissenting vituperations tried to evoke was, precisely, an exigence and a rhetorical audience, as if the democratic transition had not taken place and the game could be played all over again. But, as Bitzer shows, an exigence is a given, it cannot be constructed by orators for their own purposes.

What was left to most orators, in this strangest of 'debate', was therefore to re-assert values. Rhetorically speaking, the affirmation of values belongs to the epideictic moment. Speakers used the joint sitting to articulate thoughts that were presented as the 'philosophy' of their party or ideology, as if, the contention of debate removed, solemnity thus adduced would lend more weight to them.[61] However, because there was no rhetorical situation, no rhetorical audience, no exigence, just an epideictic moment bent solely on celebration of values, orators could indulge in homonymy.

Homonymy is fundamental to persuasion. Or, to sum up a question that has traversed, and animated, the tension between rhetoric and philosophy since the Sophists,[62] democratic deliberation relies on words more than ideas, formulated arguments more than logical abstractions. It is in the human and civic nature of democratic deliberation that words, expressions, even sentences are used that sound the same but mean different things to different people. In public deliberation (by contrast with rational exchange, if it ever exists) persuasive transactions are rarely based on pre-established meanings and the apportioning of words and arguments to these meanings; hence the traditional Liberal reluctance to accommodate rhetoric within democracy;[63] and the germane fabrication of fixed glossaries by totalitarian ideologies. Good debate often relies on uncertain terminology, as the *travaux préparatoires* to CODESA cogently showed in the South African transition. People deliberate better when, out of the persuasive transaction, and from it alone, meanings take shape and expedient policies are formulated. Strikingly, in the 15 April joint sitting, each speaker tried to define, in their own words, what 'reconciliation, reparation, compensation' means. Definitions ranged from the trivial to the lofty, from the mundane to the sacred, from the technical to the humanistic.[64] They will not satisfy rationalists. Their homonymy did not help define restorative justice and reparation, but it helped secure a place for 'reparation' in our political vocabulary. What homonymy achieved was, in an epideictic, celebratory moment, inserting 'reparation' as a value worth contemplating in the South African stock of rhetorical commonplaces, in the same manner as the founders' insistence on 'reconciliation' made this word – however homonymous, however used and abused, especially by those who resented the advent of democracy yet were, nonetheless, led to confess and to repent and to use expressions that made their mouths bleed – an incontrovertible *topos*.

In sum, the 15 April 2003 joint sitting served a three-fold rhetorical purpose: it underscored the development of a rhetorical presidency, it opened a questioning of Parliamentary deliberative traditions and it made argumentative material out of the word 'reparation'.

Notes

1   The symposium, *Rhétoriques et droits*, was held at the French Academy and the Ecole normale supérieure, sponsored by the Fondation Singer-Polignac, on 11-13 June 2003, under the high patronage of Academician Jacqueline de Romilly and Chancellor Edouard Bonnefous. The proceedings will appear, in March 2004, as a special issue of *Le Genre Humain*, B. Cassin, O. Cayla, Ph-J. Salazar eds, Paris, Le Seuil, with essays by Paul Ricoeur and Jacques Derrida.
2   Readers interested in a full rhetorical treatment of South Africa's passage to democracy are invited to look at my *An African Athens. Rhetoric and the Shaping of Democracy in South Africa* (Mahwah, NJ/London: Lawrence Erlbaum Associates, 2002), Series: Rhetoric, Knowledge and Society.

3   A South African-Polish project on 'Public Deliberation and Strong Democracy in Poland and South Africa: Two Rhetorical Models for Participatory Citizenship in Post-Totalitarian Cultures' is currently investigating patterns of deliberation after a transition to democracy (SA National Research Foundation and Polish Foundation for Research, at the Centre for Rhetoric Studies, University of Cape Town).

4   A study of the rhetorical tradition feeding into this Constitution has not yet been attempted. Neither was it until recently that American scholarship, in fact, came to grips with hidden rhetorical patterns that have, in turn, impacted on similar texts, this Constitution included. See Stephen E. Lucas, 'The Rhetorical Ancestry of the Declaration of Independence', *Rhetoric and Public Affairs* 1(2), 1998: 143-184.

5   Justice Hugo Black to Justice Earl Warren, quoted in Martin Carcasson and James Arnt Aune, 'Klansman of the Court: Justice Hugo Black's 1937 Radio Address to the Nation', *Quarterly Journal of Speech* 89(2), 2003: 161 (themselves quoting Roger K. Newman, *Hugo Black. A Biography* (New York: Pantheon Books, 1994), 427).

6   See John M. Murphy, 'Inventing Authority: Bill Clinton, Martin Luther King Jr, and the Orchestration of Rhetorical Traditions', *Quarterly Journal of Speech* 83(1), 1997: 71-89.

7   The notion of 'taken-for-granted' has been developed by Thomas B. Farrell, *Norms of Rhetorical Culture* (New Haven: Yale University Press, 1993).

8   I refer to Robert Hariman, *Political Style. The Artistry of Power* (Chicago and London: The University of Chicago Press, 1995).

9   However, as I am not a Boeotian, I refer readers to a treatment of visual rhetoric in my *African Athens*, section 3 of Chapter 4, 'Troping the People', and the whole of Chapter 7, 'The Rhetorical Cosmetics of Peace'.

10 Act 34 of 1995, section 7 (44).

11 At the time of the writing of the Constitution, during the public participation programme, repeated calls were made to have the fundamental law written in 'plain English'. The 'table' referred to here is, originally at least in Britain, the Table of the Clerk of the House, upon which is placed the mace, symbol of the sovereignty of Parliament. Notably, the notion of a 'chairperson', so common today in the constitution of Parliamentary committees, also stems from the British tradition: an early mechanism appeared at the Commons by which the house would debate more freely a matter of importance by constituting itself as a Committee of the whole house that was no longer presided over by the Speaker but a 'chairman'. In that case, the mace went under the table.

12 See the last excerpt of my *L'art de parler. Anthologie de manuels d'éloquence* (Paris: Klincksieck, Series: Cadratin, 1, 2003).

13 It is worth noting that, in spite of the early keeping of *Rolls* and research into precedents that began in the 17th century, of a collation in 1781, of W. Blackstone's hallowed *Commentaries on the Laws of England* (1768) and later work by John Hatsell, who was Clerk of the House, a systematic analysis of the Commons' order of proceedings only began after a French scholar (Samuel Romilly) had edited them – in preparation for the meeting of the 1789 General States that led to the establishment of a constitutional assembly in France. This work on British deliberative practice culminated in J. Redlich's *The Procedure of the House of Commons*, first published in German (Vienna, 1905). By contrast, the French Republicans wanted, at the outset, written down rules

for deliberation, whereas in Britain the spirit of customary law made them unnecessary. Jeremy Bentham's momentous work (in French) on *Tactique des assemblées législatives par E. Dumont* (1816) remains crucial in any debate on Parliamentary deliberative practices.

14 I must mention here that, as the European Union is enlarging, a debate is growing, among rhetoricians, about the possible value of direct democracy in smaller countries, of which there are many, with an even smaller electoral population.

15 Constitution of the Republic of South Africa, Act 108 of 1996, Section 58 (1).

16 The Constitution simply states that the National Assembly and the National Council of Provinces must have rules 'consistent with democracy' (Sections 57(2)b and 70(2)c). Rhetoricians would provide a range of answers on what such consistency can be made of, in terms of debate at the very least.

17 Joint Rules and Regulations: '7(1) The President may call a joint sitting of the Houses when it is necessary for (a) the President to deliver the annual or special address to Parliament or (b) a purpose mentioned in section 42(5) or 203 of the Constitution. (2) The Speaker and the Chairperson of the Council, acting jointly, may call a joint sitting of the Houses when necessary (source: Parliamentary press office, ref. December 10, 1999/12:25/JOINTRUL.DOC/jn, revised:17/03/2000/11:15; obtained by N. Bucher).' 'Joint sitting' is implied in sections of the Constitution relating to the president's summoning an 'extraordinary sitting of Parliament', as mentioned earlier, either for 'special business' or to approve a 'state of national defence' (notes 18 and 19 below).

18 Constitution, Section 42(5), reiterated in 84(2)d.

19 Constitution, Section 203(2).

20 Joint Rules and Regulations, Section 13(2).

21 Interviews conducted by Nathalie Bucher. Notably, one major Opposition MP, when challenged on naming it a debate, relented, accepted the notion that it was not, in fact, a debate, and remarked on the lesser degree of 'real debate' in the second legislature (1999–2004), by contrast with the first legislature (1994–1999). Remarks that tally with surveys conducted in 2001 and 2002 by my students, Bridget Young and Connie Mpokhoto, as part of the MPhil programme in Rhetoric Studies and with focus area grants by the National Research Foundation (Centre for Rhetoric Studies, University of Cape Town).

22 The procedure of selection is itself difficult to trace, let alone codify. One of the speakers confided that the list of speakers was unavailable ahead of time, at least to her, although MPs had been given ample notice for the joint sitting (see Bucher's thesis for a detailed description of time allocation, speaker selection, order of proceedings). The overall sentiment one draws from it is that of a 'courtly style', in Hariman's typology.

23 The inclusion of 'maiden speeches' is commendable, in a sitting of such importance. But, whereas it expresses, perhaps, a wish by the Whips to balance veterans with novices, backbenchers with ministers or prominent opposition orators, it also means that some new members had to wait four years, and barely a year prior to the end of their mandate, before being able to address the House. Either Parliament is far too numerous or rules and customs of address have to be revisited.

24 In addition to two chapters in my *African Athens*, refer to my 'Joining Religion and Politics. The South African Rhetorical Presidency', *Journal for the Study of Religion* 14(1), 2001: 35-45.

25 The expression has not gained currency in South African English. It is however commonly used by American scholars to qualify the ascendancy of their presidency as a rhetorical agency. I refer to M. Medhurst (ed.), *Beyond the Rhetorical Presidency* (College Station, Texas: A&M Press, 1996). Since then, the debate has known some developments but, by and large, the parameters described are still valid and transferable to other Western-style republican democracies.

26 Constitution, Section 86.

27 On *plasma* and the simulacra of Constitution-writing, see my *African Athens*, Chapter 4. I say 'citizens-to-be' in so far as South Africans were, at that stage, in an interesting, and tense, intermediary phase: citizens under the Interim Constitution and in virtue of the 1994 elections, yet not citizens under the Constitution. As the treason trial of the Boeremag has underscored, the legitimacy of the interim disposition, which was not put to popular vote (specifically white, and, perhaps, coloured and Indian, in the old cast of things), is subject to challenge. The case can be made that F. W. de Klerk violated the Constitution of the apartheid republic by not calling a referendum in November 1993 (in view of precedents). Agamben's argument regarding 'states of exception' is extremely topical here. The Interim Constitution was the last act of the state of emergency, yet an act of 'justice' in the fundamental meaning *justitium* possesses. I will return to this point in my forthcoming *Le Grand Serment* (Paris: Le Seuil). See Giorgio Agamben, *Etat d'exception* (Paris: Le Seuil, 2003) (translation of *Homo Sacer*).

28 Official terminology (Section 91(1)).

29 Or not in the manner dissolution is construed in most Western-style democracies. Dissolution is, under this Constitution, initiated by the Assembly itself or in the case of its own failing to elect a president (Section 50 of the Constitution).

30 Motions of no confidence are envisaged by sections 102(1) and (2). Removal is also envisaged, although the epithet 'serious' that gives performative value to 'serious violation of the Constitution and the law' and 'serious misconduct' (Section 89(1)a, b) is odd. One would also think any violation of the Constitution should be deemed 'serious' on the premise that the president 'must uphold, defend and respect the Constitution' (Section (83)b). Constitutional logic can be 'rhetorical'.

31 The expression, and concept, belong to Murray Edelman, *Constructing the Political Spectacle* (Chicago: The University of Chicago Press, 1988).

32 An excellent booklet aimed at visitors and investors, *SA at a glance SA 2003–4* (Craighall: Editors Inc., 2003), seemingly supported by a number of international organisations and partly edited by former US ambassador George Trail, although replete with substantiated information offers a flow-chart of Governance and Politics in which the president and cabinet are shown as the source of all power (p. 36). No mention is made of the fact the president is not elected by popular ballot (p. 38). The booklet shoots itself in the proverbial foot: it extols South African democracy, but gives a picture of a top-down regime.

33 In the Official Report of Debates (Hansard) it is styled 'address' (tape 94-95-96, disk 353, take A-C. 1). The ANC website says 'statement' (http://www.anc.org.za/anc-docs/history/mbeki/2003/tm0415.html). The unstable terminology mundanely reflects the indeterminate nature of the speech.

34 Section 7(1)a. See note 16 above.

35 See John M. Murphy, 'Inventing Authority'.

36 Surveys done by my students B. Young and C. Mpokhoto, as mentioned in note 21 above.

37 Firstly the American president is the 'national' element of a 'federal' mixed régime; secondly, in the *Federalist Papers* the address is dealt with summarily as a secondary executive's power, *The Federalist*, 77, which the Constitution of the United States in turn defines so: 'He shall from time to time give to the Congress information of the state of the Union,' Article Two, Section 3, (my emphases indicate the semantic issues). The joint sitting is also therein: 'He may, on extraordinary occasions, convene both houses ...' By contrast, the French republican tradition, which is the other global model at work in most republican democracies, forbids the president to even enter the parliamentary precinct (regardless of the form, parliamentary or presidential, of the constitution).

38 On this debate, see Medhurst (ed.), *Beyond the Rhetorical Presidency*.

39 A good description of surrogacy in political rhetoric can be found in Judith S. Trent and Robert V. Friedenberg, *Political Campaign Communication* (Westport and London, Praeger, 2000) (4th ed.), 198-202.

40 There were 27 speakers (ANC underlined): President Thabo Mbeki, ANC, Premier of Gauteng, Mbhazima Shilowa, ANC, Tony Leon, DA, Minister of Education, Prof. Kader Asmal, ANC, Mangaqa A. Mncwango, IFP, Minister of Trade and Industry, Alec Erwin, ANC, Premier of the Western Cape, Marthinus van Schalkwyk, NNP, Semamanyane D. Motubatse-Hounkpatin, ANC, Rev. Kenneth R. Meshoe, ACDP, Maj. Gen. Bantu Holomisa, UDM, Premier of Limpopo, Adv. Ngoako Ramatlhodi, ANC, Dr Pieter W. A. Mulder, FF, Isaac S. Mfundisi, UCDP, Dr. Motsoko S. Pheko, PAC, Malesane P. Themba, ANC, Celia-Sandra Botha, DA, Pandelani J. Nefolovhodwe, Azapo, M. P. Mentor, ANC, T. E. Millin, IFP, Mudene Smuts, DA, Derek A. Hanekom, ANC, Sunklavathy Rajbally, MF, Casperus Aucamp, AEB, Adv. Johnny H. de Lange, ANC, Mahomed F. Cassim, IFP, Wetshotsile J. Seremane, DA, Minister for Justice and Constitutional Development, Penuell M. Maduna, ANC. In Hansard the speakers who hold elected offices are listed under their title alone (for example: The President of the Republic).

41 Chaim Perelman, *L'Empire rhétorique. Rhétorique et argumentation* (Paris: Vrin, 1997), Chapter 4.

42 The clearest exponent is Eugene Garver, *Aristotle's Rhetoric* (Chicago: The University of Chicago Press, 1994).

43 The President of the Republic (Hansard, unrevised copy, tape 94-96, disk 353, take A-C. 2).

44 I refer to the Paris conference mentioned at the beginning of this essay, and its forthcoming proceedings.

45 Constitution, Section 83 b.

46 The joint-sitting began at 14.00 and was adjourned at 19.03 (Hansard).

47 P. Maduna, lines 1-13 (Hansard, unrevised copy, tape 117, disk 374, take V.1).

48 Interview by N. Bucher reveals that the Democratic Alliance (DA) devised a strategy by dividing their allocated time between four speakers and, as reported, decided not to step on each other's toes by tackling the same issue, or the same issue from the same

angle. I am not convinced W. K. Seremane provided the best peroration to the DA's suite of arguments, but I refer here, for a more detailed analysis, to Bucher's thesis.

49 Speeches are rhetorically evaluated in two ways, the impact at the time and the impact after delivery. A speech may be largely unimpressive at the time, but have a lasting effect, and vice versa. This is because a speech is always audience-related. The construction of argument, the delivery, the emotional appeals have a specific target, always known by the orator or approximated. The audience is part of the proof. Once a speech becomes a matter of record, different tools are applied.

50 P. Maduna, line 3 (Hansard unrevised copy, tape 117, disk 274, take V.1).

51 P. Maduna, lines 5-6 (Hansard unrevised copy, tape 117, disk 274, take V.1).

52 During Ms T. E. Millin's maiden speech, the presiding officer, Deputy Chairperson of the NCOP, J. Mahlangu, called the Houses to order: 'We are rather conversing too loud.' (Hansard unrevised copy, tape 110, disk 268, take P.11, lines 3-6.)

53 P. Maduna, line 6 (Hansard unrevised copy, tape 117, disk 274, take V.1).

54 On the Land Claims Court's rhetorical status, I refer to my forthcoming 'Compromise and Deliberation. A Rhetorical View of South Africa's Democratic Transformation', in Mohamed Nachi (guest ed.), *Le Compromis, Social Science Information/Information sur les sciences sociales* 43(2), 2004, 145-166.

55 The whole section 27 is worth quoting: 27(1) The recommendations referred to in Section 4(f)(i) shall be considered by the President with a view to making recommendations to Parliament and making regulations. (2) The recommendations referred to in Subsection (1) shall be considered by the joint committee and the decisions of the said joint committee shall, when approved by Parliament, be implemented by the President by making regulations. (3) The regulations referred to in Subsection (2) (a) shall – (i) determine the basis and conditions upon which reparation shall be granted; (ii) determine the authority responsible for the application of the regulations; and (b) may – (i) provide for the revision and, in appropriate cases, the discontinuance or reduction of any reparation; (ii) prohibit the cession, assignment or attachment of any reparation in terms of the regulations, or the right to any such reparation; (iii) determine that any reparation received in terms of the regulations shall not form part of the estate of the recipient should such estate be sequestrated; and (iv) provide for any other matter which the President may deem fit to prescribe in order to ensure an efficient application of the regulations. (4) The joint committee may also advise the President in respect of measures that should be taken to grant urgent interim reparation to victims.

56 P. Maduna: 'Maybe like Tony Leon you might have been neither fish nor foul, etc [Interjections]', lines 1-3, Hansard (unrevised copy, tape 117, disk 374, take V.10). I guess the transcript should read 'fowl' not 'foul'.

57 The notion was developed in a seminal article by Lloyd F. Bitzer, 'The Rhetorical Situation', *Rhetoric and Philosophy* 1(1), 1968: 1-14.

58 Bitzer, 'Rhetorical Situation', 6.

59 For instance the somewhat arduous argument about amnesty made by M. A. Mncwango (Hansard unrevised copy, tape 100, disk 359, take G.1, line 12).

60 P. J. Nefolovhodwe, in the AZAPO line, recalled the momentous challenge brought by his party and the subsequent decision (25 July 1996) by the Constitutional Court to uphold the constitutionality of section 20(7) of the TRC Act, and qualified the

Presiding Judge as a DP member – indirect accusation of bias, under the cover of Parliamentary privilege?

61 For instance, by resorting to the device of 'saluting heroes' (Ms M. P. Mentor, Hansard unrevised copy, tape 110, disk 368, take P.1).

62 I refer, aware of my brevity, to Jaakko Hintikka, *Tine and Necessity* (Oxford: Clarendon, 1973) and Barbara Cassin, *L'Effet Sophistique* (Paris: Le Seuil, 1995), in particular her rebuttal in the long note 8, 586-588.

63 See the incisive review article by Robert L. Ivie, 'Democratic Deliberation in a Rhetorical Republic', *Quarterly Journal of Speech* 84(4), 1998: 491-530; Joseph M. Bessette, *The Mild Voice of Reason. Deliberative Democracy and American Government* (Chicago: The University of Chicago Press, 1994); Amy Gutman and Dennis Thompson, *Democracy and Disagreement* (Cambridge, Mass.: The Belknap Press of Harvard University Press, 1996).

64 For a glossary, I refer to Nathalie Bucher's thesis. The author acknowledges support by the National Research Foundation, South Africa.

5

A Difficult Justice:

Reparation, Restoration and Rights

Charles Villa-Vicencio

Reparation is not primarily about compensation, in the sense of payment for loss suffered. No payment is ever sufficient for the loss of a child, a spouse or a friend. 'To say someone can pay me for the loss of my son is terrible,' says Cynthia Ngewu, mother of Christopher Piet, killed by the security police in Guguletu in 1986. 'I just want some help to deal with my pain.'[1] Christopher Ribeiro, son of Florence and Fabian Ribeiro who were murdered in Mamelodi, Pretoria in 1986, demands more: 'I want justice. That is my right. The killers must pay for what they did to my parents. I want reparations, the government must pay.'[2] Nyameka Goniwe, widow of Matthew Goniwe, one of the Cradock Four, who was murdered with Sparrow Mkonto, Fort Calata and Sicelo Mhlauli by the security police outside Port Elizabeth in 1985, talks of the importance of material reparation, while insisting that 'no monetary payment can ever be sufficient to repair my loss'. 'I want to feel we as a nation are dealing with the underlying forces that drove people to do what they did in the 1980s,' she tells us. 'That would be the beginning of reconciliation and healing for me.'[3]

The political complexities of an emerging society are deep and threatening. When does prosecution become victor's justice? What forms should reparation take? What should reconstruction budgetary priorities look like? These kinds of concerns render concepts of *justice, reparation, restoration, and rights* – all crucial ingredients in reconciliation – troublesome. The immediate goal of political transition is less than the ultimate manifestation of *Summum Bonum*. It is to rise above the Hobbesian sense of the *Summum Malum*, the threat of ultimate evil, as a basis for establishing the essential principles from which the *Commune Bonum* can emerge. The primary objective of transitional justice is the emergence of a 'minimally decent society,'[4] within which there is sufficient justice to prevent a resort to the kind of abuse from which the nation is seeking to save itself. It involves a conception of the rule of law in which minimalist versions of justice may be all that is possible in the given circumstances and the beginning of a restorative process within which the dignity, reintegration and reparation of victims are prioritised.

Justice is not self-defining. It is contextual. It is about what is required and what is possible in a given situation. It has many layers, addressing different needs. Sometimes they are complementary. Sometimes they are contradictory. *Retributive justice, deterrent justice, compensatory justice, rehabilitative justice, exonerative justice, restorative justice* – each has a time and a place in a given situation. No one model of justice covers all the stops. Not least in a situation of political transition, justice is about *not* neglecting those 'stops' that prepare the way for victims and perpetrators, their respective families, their communities and the nation as a whole *to learn to live together* after years of enmity. This is a *difficult justice*.[5] Justice, suggests Richard Rorty, has to do with 'larger loyalty'.[6] It has to do with taking into account the rights, the demands and the needs of all those on whom a policy impacts and who have the capacity to disrupt or sustain it. 'There is no such thing as pure justice in the real world,' suggests the late Dullah Omar, former South African Minister of Justice. 'It is about fairplay and the need to do what can be done to balance the books as best we can. I'd like to add, with a preference for victims and the poor.'[7]

Different forms of *reparation* compete. The inherent tension between individual demands for justice and reparations, communal needs for economic development and growth, and the political needs of the nation leaves an indelible mark on the transitional justice debate. As legitimate and understandable as the demands of victim organisations may be for a full and adequate slate of reparation, there are other demands on the government that limit its capacity to respond positively to all that some victims demand.

Restoration comes to different people in different ways. To some, it never comes. Some demand criminal prosecutions. Some claim the right to litigate for civil claims. Many want the payment of monetary reparations.[8] Most want to know *why* they were made to suffer. They want to know *who* killed their spouse, child or parent.[9] Others want *acknowledgement* and an apology by the persons concerned.[10]

Rights clash. They sometimes contradict one another. They need to be balanced. Judge Richard Goldstone, former justice of the Constitutional

Court and prosecutor of the International Criminal Tribunal for the former Yugoslavia and later for Rwanda, reminds us that South Africa's willingness to compromise on normal justice was a key ingredient to the political settlement in 1994: 'If the ANC had insisted on Nuremberg-style trials for the leaders of the former apartheid government there would have been no peaceful transition to democracy, and if the former government had insisted on a blanket amnesty then, similarly, the negotiations would have broken down. A bloody revolution sooner rather than later would have been inevitable.'[11] Not everyone was happy with the resultant compromise. Some resented the need to surrender their right to prosecution and litigation. The late Chief Justice, Ismael Mahomed, deputy president of the Constitutional Court at the time, spoke of an 'agonising balancing act' between the right of victims to obtain legal redress and the need for reconciliation and a rapid transition to a new political future. It involves balancing what is required for the 'correction of the old' and the 'creation of the new'.[12] June O'Connor writes of the need to broaden the reconciling lens in the realm of the political, from '*me* and *my* future' to '*we* and *our* future'.[13] Donald Shriver argues that, 'vengeance, however understandable from the perspective of the victim, ultimately kills politics, if by politics we mean negotiations between groups that permit people to realise their mutual interests without destroying those very interests in acts of violence'.[14] In a democratic order, suggests G. H. Mead, a responsible citizen is required, in stepping into the voting booth, to vote for someone else's interests in addition to his or her own.[15] 'If former victims,' writes Rajeev Bhargava, 'don the mantle of victors and seek comprehensive retributive justice in either its no–nonsense revolutionary or its liberal democratic form, then they may instantly turn all former perpetrators and beneficiaries into victims. And, if the distinction between victims and perpetrators is obliterated, South Africa is likely to be in the same state as former Yugoslavia or like India during its partition. *This would be a disaster.*'[16]

   This *difficult justice*, imbedded as it is in the reparation debate, is the focus of what follows. The inevitable tensions within and between *individual*, *communal* and *national* demands need to be acknowledged and accepted. This chapter is an attempt to do so. Reparation, at best, is an exercise in facilitating this. To suggest homogeneity at the individual, communal or national level would, of course, be wrong. Attention is given here to what are conceivably the most troublesome characteristics of these different levels, recognising that each level impinges on the other and that these and other tensions are unlikely ever to be resolved to the satisfaction of everyone concerned. Politics is ultimately the art of the possible, even where the possible can be stretched to reach new levels of possibility – and reparation can only be an approximation and symbolic signal of what in a perfect world should be offered to victims.

Personal Anger, Revenge and Compromise

Promoters of truth commissions, peacemaking and conflict resolution understandably stress the negative side of revenge. With justification, Martha Minow warns, 'the fantasy of revenge simply reverses the role of perpetrator and victim, continuing to imprison the victim in horror and degradation'.[17] Hannah Arendt takes a stronger position. She writes of the importance of forgiveness as a mechanism to break the cycle of violence because it is 'the only reaction which does not merely react, but acts anew and unexpected, unconditioned by the act which provoked it'.[18] 'The question that all victims must answer,' suggests Kole Omotoso, '[is] at which point do we become what we are fighting against?'[19]

This said, the desire for retaliatory action by victims and survivors of gross violations of human rights is as understandable as it is difficult to curtail. For many, retribution is the most obvious (for some the *only*) way of discharging resentment and anger. It is seen to provide immediate satisfaction, even though it may provide no solution to the underlying cause of the conflict or offer any form of social or economic restoration. Focusing on present gratification, often in a context where there is no fulfilment of past promises, it is difficult to convince those who demand satisfaction of the virtue of delayed gratification.

Wise statecraft includes the need to recognise that many within a nation are *not* prepared or ready to put the past behind them. The point is well made by José Zalaquett, who served on the Chilean National Truth and Reconciliation Commission. 'Leaders,' he suggests, 'should never forget that the lack of political pressure to put these issues on the agenda does not mean they are not boiling underground, waiting to erupt.'[20] The demand by many Chileans, almost ten years after the establishment of the Chilean Commission, that General Augusto Pinochet stand trial, following his arrest in the United Kingdom, underlines Zalaquett's point. Some are not prepared to settle for less than retribution. Some demand revenge.

Jeffrie Murphy and Jean Hampton write thoughtfully of the need to deal with the desire for revenge in the wake of moral wrong, posing the question of *how to deal* with this anger to the benefit and healing of the individual or community concerned and the nation as a whole.[21] The sheer weight of the emotions of those who suffered gross violations of human rights, feelings that no atonement, compensation or any other form of human balm can easily appease, lends credence to a defence of organised (state) retributive justice as an exercise in taming, balancing and recasting the personal animus involved in vengeance. By institutionalising feelings of anger, resentment and even hatred, the state exercises procedural controls over individual and group anarchy. In Susan Jacoby's words, it is an alternative to the 'wild justice' that emerges where 'normal justice' is absent.[22] And yet Jacoby argues that naked revenge and aggression are but one manifestation of this anger. Other manifestations include *self-effacing behaviour* where the victim entrenches his or her sense of victimhood, consciously or subconsciously burdening society with guilt and the need to respond to their dependency. *Social detachment*, in the form of refusing to engage others or to respond to opportunities for restoration, is another manifestation of victimhood. Revenge and open aggression undermine any society, not least those in the fragile process of transition. Other responses of vindictive anger imprison both the victim and society, inducing a paralysis that hinders society from reaching beyond the past towards a different kind of future.

It is in the interests of society as a whole as much as it is in the interests of victims themselves, to the extent that it is possible, to facilitate the management and healing of victim anger and its exclusion from the nation-building process. The peace and stability of the new order is dependent on the willingness and ability of victims to share in that order and to make it work. 'In a society in transition, unable to use history and public trust as ballast, the goal for public safety, happiness and reconciliation is inextricably linked to the healthy psyche of victims.'[23] This is the ultimate purpose of reparation.

The Promotion of National Unity and Reconciliation Act, No. 34 of 1995 provides guidelines for this. It mandates the South African Truth and Reconciliation Commission (TRC) to 'promote national unity and reconciliation … by … restoring the human and civil dignity of … victims … by recommending reparation measures in respect of them'. It goes further to define reparation as 'any form of compensation, *ex gratia* payment, restitution, rehabilitation or recognition'. The Act does not talk of *healing* per sé. It talks of *'national unity'* and the *'restoring of human and civil dignity'*.

The late Chief Justice Mahomed writes meaningfully of the sacrifice and emotions of the victims, before calling on victims and perpetrators alike to 'become active, full and creative members of the new order'. They need 'to cross the historic bridge from the past to the future, not with heavy dragged steps delaying and impeding a rapid and enthusiastic transition to the new society at the end of the bridge'.[24]

In seeking to facilitate the crossing of the bridge, the intent of the TRC was, inter alia, to create a safe space within which victims and survivors could give cathartic expression to emotions of anger and grief. In *practice*, however, it was sometimes seen as an attempt to impose categories of reconciliation and forgiveness onto the prevailing emotions of anger. Richard Wilson suggests that the Commission was formulaic in its endeavour to move victims beyond anger to closure and forgiveness. He suggests that 'the virtue of forgiveness and reconciliation were so loudly and roundly applauded that emotions of revenge, hatred and bitterness were rendered unacceptable, an ugly intrusion on a peaceful, healing process'.[25] Generalisations about the TRC hearings aside, the containment, if not the suppression, of anger is a two-edged sword. It could have wrecked the South African settlement. It could, on the other hand, paper over a level of resentment yet to impact on the long-term peace process.

Anger demands satisfaction, often in the form of retribution – with access to the courts being affirmed as a fundamental human right. It is this that has made some question the moral and legal legitimacy of amnesty. The most celebrated case in this regard is the Constitutional Court's ruling in response to the application brought by the Azanian People's Organisation (Azapo) and others concerning the validity of the Promotion of National Unity and Reconciliation Act. Briefly stated, the court upheld both the criminal and civil clauses of the Act, while affirming reparation as a quid pro quo for the surrender of the right to prosecution. In so doing, it ruled that Parliament was justified in adopting a *wide* concept of reparation, which needs to be communally balanced against other state obligations for reconstruction.[26]

The relationship between amnesty and reparation continues to be a contentious issue. This aside, a national survey shows that South Africans are ready to find compromise solutions on such divisive issues as amnesty and reparation. Black and white South Africans indicated that amnesty for perpetrators of gross violations of human rights in the apartheid context is morally unjust, and yet 72% of black South Africans conceded that amnesty was a price that needed to be paid to secure a peaceful transition to democratic rule in South Africa. Interestingly, only 39% of whites saw it as such.[27] Black South Africans, in particular, were also ready to accept that the inherent injustice of amnesty can be compensated for in different ways. The payment of compensation was seen as one such palliative, while a sincere apology and an opportunity for victims and survivors to relate the stories of their suffering in public were cited as important alternatives to normative forms of retribution and even reparation.[28]

These results suggest that most South Africans, including victims, who have not made peace with the past, at least to the extent that they continue to experience periodic grief and anger, are seeking ways of dealing with the past without demanding retribution. Emotional healing defies neat chronological progress. Where it happens at all, it is a circular process that includes regression and progress, healing and relapse. It suggests a willingness and ability to move forward, to share in the reconciliation process, rather than to engage in the kind of self-effacing social detachment of which Jacoby writes.[29] The affirmation and restoration of the dignity of victims, at the same time, requires that their suffering and loss be *acknowledged, accounted for* and in some way *compensated* – recognising that the latter can take different forms. It is this that demands that the recommendations of the TRC on reparation, as well as the government's response to these recommendations, be placed under the spotlight of critique and enquiry.

The stated willingness of the government (see President Mbeki's address elsewhere in this anthology) to grant indemnity from criminal prosecution, although not civil prosecution, to perpetrators willing to disclose their culpability for past gross violations of human rights is crucial. This compromise needs to be negotiated with careful regard to the threat that prosecutions (on either side of the political divide) may present to the political stability of the nation – *as well as the needs, sensitivities and rights of victims and survivors of gross violations of human rights.* The danger is that political pressure from all sides of the political spectrum could lead to a flood of criminal indemnities that fail to do justice to the concerns and needs of the victims. Such insensitivity could unleash the unappeased anger that continues to be present beneath the surface of an apparent willingness to accept and, in some instances, support the non-prosecution of perpetrators. Left unattended and unappeased, under certain circumstances, these emotions could be politically mobilised to the detriment of the nation-building project. Latent personal anger can only be ignored at the peril of communal and national stability. The rule of law, at least in the sense of the particular level of justice that any society can afford at a particular stage of its transition, is in and of itself an important ingredient of reconciliation.[30] It is a form of reparation that provides a level of security that few societies can afford to neglect. The president's clear insistence that there shall be no blanket amnesty is an important step in this direction.

The flipside of the prosecutions/amnesty case is reparation. The unhappiness of many victims with the government's offer of a R30 000 payment to individuals found by the TRC to be victims of gross violations of human rights can, to some extent, be ameliorated by the nature and extent of the president's promise that this will be augmented with communal reparations in the form of housing, health care and education aimed at the upliftment of all who suffered under apartheid. The government further speaks of incentives to business to invest in job creation, poverty relief and skills development. The payment of monetary reparations and paid services is an important part of restoration. Yael Danieli suggests 'money concretises for the victim' society's responsibility for the violation of his or her rights, the wrongness of the deed, the innocence of the victim and the fact that society cares. 'It is at least a token. It does have a meaning ... In our system of justice, of government, when damage occurs money is paid.'[31] Payments and paid services can go a long way to acknowledgement. For a poor family, a limited payment can also make a significant difference to their quality of life.

Individual anger, continuing grief, human rights, augmented by a willingness to find compromises for insoluble problems, make personal reparations politically important. They need to allow for the many, varied and often conflicting emotions of those who have suffered most. Reparation focusing on the individual is important for the individuals themselves. It also impacts on the wellbeing of the community and nation. Reparations of a communal and national kind can, in turn, have a decisive impact on the emotions of individuals. There needs to be 'a wide concept of reparations'[32] that addresses the nuances of all levels of society – personal, communal and national.

Communal Needs, Expectations and Patience

The strongest argument against individual reparation has always been that the 22 000 victims of gross violations of human rights named by the TRC are but a small percentage of those who suffered violations under apartheid. There is a sense in which all black South Africans are victims of apartheid abuse. 'Sort out the poverty, unemployment, crime and lack of self-esteem, which are the direct consequences of apartheid, and reconciliation will follow.' 'No matter how generous reparation payments may be, they cannot redress such fundamental problems facing the nation,' is the common refrain of those who do not support the payment of individual reparation.

Recognising that the South African settlement was characterised by a political trade-off, involving moral compromises, economic concessions and the inevitable contradictions associated with such settlements, Neville Alexander suggests that South African society inevitably carries within it both the potential for real change and the possibility of becoming what he describes as 'an ordinary country' driven by a '"normal", bourgeois, democratic polity' – resulting in the replacement of one set of beneficiaries with another.[33] Granting that there is little danger of a left-wing revolutionary upsurge in the short to medium term, he suggests that in the long run entrenched inequality will result in new forms of struggle. He writes of a 'movement of desperation that can only rebel against the emerging new order'.[34] Ironically, the very economic policy of the new order of which Alexander is most critical is essentially in agreement that the focus of restoration ought to be on broad-based economic restructuring rather than individual reparation. The question concerns the kind of restructuring required for this to happen.

Critics of present South African economic policy sometimes forget the disastrous state that the economy was in when the new government came to power in 1994.[35] 'We were scarcely in a position to consider significant development projects, let alone reparations. The economy was on its knees. Our first priority and only hope for a successful transition was economic growth. Whatever the failures of subsequent budgetary priorities – and there are many – it needs to be understood against this background.'[36] Foreign exchange reserves were down to less than three weeks of imports, the budget deficit had reached record heights, there was double-digit inflation and interest rates were at 24%. The economy has been stabilised, but the economic growth that is required – projected at approximately 6-7% over a sustained period – has not been realised. Herein lies the rub. Census 2001 figures released by Statistics South Africa put the growth rate since 1996 at 3.1%, while Econometrix figures show the gross domestic product per capita in real terms to have risen by only 1.3% over the period. The census found that 33.7% of the population had jobs when the census was completed in October 2001. At least 24% were unemployed and 42.3% were not economically active.

Expectations by those black South Africans in 1994 who had borne the brunt of apartheid oppression and exploitation were, at the same time, fiscally quite unrealistic by the standards of any nation. Demands for economic redress continue to be made, with very good reason. The question is how to meet these demands. The only realistic option for meeting even the most modest and realistic needs of the victims of apartheid is to grow the economy or plunge the nation into significant debt – a fate that South Africa has to date, unlike Turkey, Argentina and a host of other developing countries, managed to avoid.

The government has been severely criticised for its spending priorities, corruption, overly tight monetary policy and failure to tax foreign and South African corporations and others who benefited from apartheid at a higher rate to generate the funds needed for a more generous reparation package for the poor. This said, the South African economy has not simply been resuscitated. It has been structurally transformed. Protective tariffs, blocked rands, many exchange controls and other fiscal restraints of the apartheid era have been removed, making the country more competitive in the given world of globalisation – and few but its most zealous opponents recognise that globalisation, in one form or another, is here to stay. 'It is not whether you globalise … it is how you globalise,' suggests the Minister of Finance, Trevor Manuel.[37] The essential criticism of government fiscal policy is not that it has not benefited the economy per sé; it is that it has not benefited the poor.[38] If a country is to be taken seriously by the major powers, it is expected to have a robust, healthy economy. A strong economy is a source of influence in global politics. Such influence frequently, however, fails to feed the hungry child in Khayelitsha or provide the job that an unemployed person requires in Soweto. The challenge facing the nation is to reconcile its long-term geo-economic/strategic objectives with the pressing, immediate issues of domestic economic and social delivery. The failure to address the latter tangibly can only have the most negative long-term impact on the political stability of the nation – to the detriment of the economy as a whole.

Sampie Terreblanche reminds us that in 1970 the per capita income of whites was almost 15 times higher than that of Africans. From 1970 to 1994, the income of the poorest half of the population, or 60% of the black population, fell another 50%, and it has fallen a further 10% since 1994.[39] Socio-economic transformation has not taken place on a broad scale. Debate on fiscal policy is beyond the scope of this chapter. Whatever the appropriate economic vehicle may be, few people would disagree that the most urgent need facing South Africa is the need to increase the rate of economic growth and create jobs. In the language of the reparations debate, an essential ingredient of the kind of socio-economic transformation needed 'to restore human and civil dignity' to the victims of apartheid is job creation.

The Africa Report of the Commission of Human Security, chaired by Sadaka Ogata, former head of the United Nations' refugee agency, and Amartya Sen, internationally renowned development economist, is important in this regard. Based on a broad-based field study that incorporates 14 African countries, it stresses the importance of economic stability, not least for emerging nations. The study asks what it is that makes people insecure and what kinds of interventions are needed to address people's concerns in this regard. Topping the list is poverty and lack of basic services. Next come violent conflict, refugees, poor governance, and political instability and human rights abuse.[40] The findings merge broadly with the essential argument that human security, dignity and political stability occur when basic material needs are met. A simple assessment of the hierarchy of needs is enough to confirm this. Bluntly put, a simple payment of reparations to victims of apartheid, as important as this is, is not sufficient to restore the human and civil dignity of apartheid's victims. Reparation demands more.

Hope that there would be injections of foreign aid to rebuild the country, creating the necessary economic infrastructure to underpin human security, has not resulted in the kind of material support necessary to rebuild the nation in the wake of the collapse of apartheid. The peaceful political transition in South Africa evoked euphoria among Western nations, but this did not extend to their wallets. Long-term foreign investment is slow and cautious. Even support for the African Union (AU) or New Partnership for Africa's Development (Nepad) cannot be taken for granted. This will require serious nation-building, democratic reform and economic development by African nations. There is no quick or easy solution to economic growth – and it clearly needs to come from within. It will require education, skills training, economic growth, delivery of goods and services, job creation and good governance. At the level of restoring human and civil dignity, it needs to be driven by a national commitment to bridging the gap between the rich and poor, drawing the poor and unemployed into the economy and encouraging participation in the democratic structures that exist to enable citizens to shape government and national policy. The ruthless pursuit of personal and corporate wealth by the few is, needless to say, to the detriment of the national project.

Again the question emerges: *how* to engender this commitment? It will take more than government coercion, although persuasion and incentive will help. The government has a huge majority of largely poor voters. It has the power to make things happen and a constitutional mandate to create a united nation – to which poverty remains the biggest and most demanding threat. And yet to do so, it requires the support of the corporate sector, including the new black elite and foreign investors. It needs to demonstrate that its policies are to the ultimate benefit of all South Africans in a climate where the majority of people continue to live in abject poverty that is, in many instances, worse than it was prior to 1994.

Viable communal reparations, which focus on economic growth and the restoration of human dignity, are not easy to realise. People of different races, political persuasions and economic standing will need to find one another in a common commitment to a future characterised by inclusivity, mutual trust and co-operation, with a view to the promotion of greater equality. Given past memories, present disparities and future fears that undermine the kind of trust-building, risk-taking and creative partnership that is required for viable reconciliation, the task promises to be a difficult one. Finite resources and limited economic growth pose the question whether equitable redistribution of resources is simply not too daunting for the established wealthy classes, as well as the nouveaux riches, to make the necessary adjustments. Questions continue to emerge concerning individual freedoms and national interests. Tough decisions need to be made regarding the national budget. The balance between market-driven realities and community needs will need to be negotiated. Issues of corporate responsibility challenge established business practices.

It took a sense of cataclysmic national disaster, with the nation facing total collapse, for political enemies to reach a political settlement in 1994. A sense of economic crisis of equal proportions does not presently exist, which makes it much more difficult to enable the nation to summon the emotional, subjective and spiritual energy needed to face the economic challenge inherent in communal reparations. Evidence, at the same time, suggests that this energy is latently present. It needs to be correctly tapped. South Africans are learning to live together, not least when the present situation is compared with the level of conflict that prevailed prior to 1994. In the national survey referred to earlier, despite concerns expressed on a range of issues that continue to divide the nation, South Africans across the colour line indicated that they thought the country would be a poorer place if there were no other racial groups in the country.[41] There is no desire, expectation or anticipation of ever returning to the apartheid era, except among the most zealous racists. What is needed is a new sense of the need for South Africans to face the reality of what level of economic justice is required to enable the new order to hold. What is clear is that the level of poverty that presently prevails is a threat to the wellbeing of those South Africans whose quality of life is both adequate and in many cases above that of many in first world countries. This reality ought to be enough to provide the incentive to contribute voluntarily to the transformation of the existing economic order that reflects the highest disparity between the rich and poor anywhere in the word except Brazil.

The tragedy is that most South Africans are not obviously ready to respond materially to the challenge. While indications are that the majority of South Africans of all races support the payment of reparation to apartheid's victims – only 10% of whites indicate that they are personally ready to contribute to such payments.[42] It is, at the same time, clear that black empowerment rarely reaches the poorest of the poor. There is simply no obvious commitment among those who *have* to uplift the poor at the cost of their own wellbeing.

This said, government policy is not to coerce economic equality. It has distanced itself from the class action lawsuits against companies which have benefited from apartheid in American courts, and rejected the TRC's proposed tax surcharge on corporations. The government's focus is on voluntarism. If this works, it can deliver more than coercion. The question is whether it will work. There may well be legal grounds for reparation claims against business. Such action, however, if successful at all, will provide recompense only after an extended court battle. And there is no clear indication of what the outcome of such action may be. In the meantime, the economic demands of the broader community of the poor continue.

The question is not essentially what needs to be done. It is how to kindle within the South African soul the willingness to grasp the nettle and make the kind of compromise that characterised the 1994 political settlement – this time to face the economic challenge. If not addressed with rational and immediate urgency, coexistence – the hallmark of the South African settlement – is likely to unravel. The problems involved are huge. There are no easy answers. Indeed, if they are to be resolved at all, a new social contract involving all South Africans is required – designed to at least change the nature of the conflict surrounding these problems, recognising that the problems themselves are not likely to be resolved in the near future. It is a classic case of the chicken and the egg. There cannot be reconciliation without development and reconstruction, and yet there cannot be the latter without reconciliation. Social harmony makes for economic growth and economic growth makes for social harmony. The two belong together. In the words of President Mbeki: 'It's a very delicate thing to handle the relationship between these two elements [transformation and reconciliation]. It's not a mathematical thing; it's an art … If you handle the transformation in a way that doesn't change a good part of the status quo, those who are disadvantaged will rebel, and then goodbye reconciliation.'[43] It is here that the litmus test of communal reparation will occur.

National Vision, Belonging and Hope

Individual and communal reparations obviously impact on the national political milieu. A national vision of how to engage the conflicting demands of the individual person or sector on the one hand and broader communal needs on the other lies at the heart of national politics. Politics is about negotiations. Democracy is about compromise. An economy that generates adequate employment creates space for stakeholders to feel they have a share in the outcome. National leadership is about the projection of this vision, enabling the emergence of a nation characterised by inclusivity. Bluntly put, people who feel alienated or excluded from mainstream society are unlikely to feel any sense of compulsion to share in the nation-building project. The role of political leadership in this regard is crucial. Leadership, along with what John Paul Lederach calls 'moral imagination' is, at the same time, not the exclusive responsibility of leaders.[44] It is an imagination that is made possible where people 'feel they still have a voice'. It emerges where individuals and local communities see themselves as part of the 'bigger picture of relationships' – able to contribute to the larger scheme of things, as well as to benefit from relations being forged at this level. The participation of civil society is crucial for a national vision to take root and grow in the broader community. It is a vision that must ultimately be generated and sustained within the public square.

The vision of the 'new' South Africa is, of course, enshrined in the South African Constitution. Said to be the most progressive and morally substantial in the world, it contains a vision that emerged from the long struggle against oppression that preceded it. Home-grown, in the sense of responding to the special needs and circumstances of the South African situation, it is written in accordance with international norms and standards, affirming South Africa's re-entry into the international community.[45] It combines the celebration of past successes and the commemoration of past failures. In order to ensure that a constitution does not degenerate into a mere 'piece of paper', it is necessary that legislators translate the constitutional vision into functional legislation and that ordinary South Africans turn vision into reality. The challenge encapsulated in the contradiction between constitutional vision and present reality is huge. It is also important. It is a lure that draws us beyond who we are to whom we should become.

A nation committed to reconciliation is a nation bound by a common commitment to a vision of what it can become. It is a vision that must permeate and sustain every layer of a nation's identity from arts, culture and religion to education, business and entertainment. Leaders, citizens, young, old, women, men and youth need to both shape and promote the vision. National pride, self-confidence and expectation are essential in seeking to transcend past and present divisions. For this to occur, respect and understanding between citizens is necessary. This involves a commitment to inclusivity – to learn to live together.

President Mbeki's 'I am an African' speech stressed inclusivity, unleashing an important debate on identity, belonging and national inclusivity. Some jostled to be the self-appointed gatekeepers of 'African' and 'South African' identity. The debate has been a heated one. An important contribution came from South African author, Zakes Mda. Noting the irony that it had recently become respectable for whites to be seen as African, he says:

African identity is a very novel phenomenon. It is, in fact, an identity-in-the-making. Until a hundred years ago the inhabitants of the continent did not

*generally refer to themselves as Africans – either as a racial or a continental
identity. They recognised and celebrated various identities that were based on
ethnicity, clan, family, gender and class – and later on nation and religion.*

*In South Africa the first people to collectively call themselves Africans
were the descendants of the Dutch and French Huguenot settlers who were
known as the Boers because of their agrarian culture.*

*Although most Africans are black, not all black people are Africans.
Most importantly, not all Africans are black.*[46]

The notion that South Africa belongs to all those who choose to live
within it is a vision of both invitation and challenge. The invitation is to
transcend race, culture and past identity as well as class, health status and
immediate social needs. The challenge involves the full implications of living in a country that continues to be ravaged by the injustices of the past.
'Invitation' and 'challenge' are the flip sides of the same coin, which
involves the affirmation of the inherent link between reconciliation and
economic development. Reflecting on these challenges, South Africa
author Njabulo Ndebele powerfully and yet simply suggests that reconciliation has not so much to do with present realities as with 'who we can
become'.[47]

'Reconciliation,' suggests Archbishop Desmond Tutu, 'is not about
being cosy; it is not about pretending that things were other than they
were. Reconciliation based on falsehood, on not facing up to reality, is not
true reconciliation and will not last.'[48] A vision that unites must necessarily
face the truth about the past. It must, at the same time, seek ways to deal
realistically with the heritage of the past to the benefit of the victims of that
past and the wellbeing of the nation as a whole. It involves facing the
implications of the nation's past inhumanity with uncompromising hon-
esty, while envisaging the possibility of the new. Most agree on the ideals
involved in the latter. The question is how to deal with the heritage of the
past, a past that lingers in the present, a past that for many is still present.
The pertinent question is *how* to move to who and what we can become.

Debate on the mechanisms best suited to facilitate this transition must
continue. Military tribunals, trials, lustration, amnesty, apologies, truth
commissions and the International Criminal Court (ICC) are all under the
spotlight. Madeleine Alingue, speaking at a conference in Bogota,
Colombia on peace-making in Latin America, referred to the South
African TRC as a 'global footprint', offering a way of dealing with the

kind of problems that haunt countries in the Andean region – Colombia, Peru, Ecuador and Guatemala. Responding to the South African initiative with more enthusiasm than most South Africans would share, she identified the importance of a 'moment in time' which presents itself as a 'mystique' that we 'banalise' at our own peril. 'It is a moment in time. It is the opening of a process,' she argued, 'which rarely offers itself to a nation … It must be cherished and protected. Critique it, analyse it, assess it, but don't despise it. Nurture it.'[49] Mary Robinson, speaking at the torn and fragmented World Conference against Racism, Racial Discrimination, Xenophobia and Related Intolerances held in Durban in 2001, paraphrased Martin Luther King in urging the divided peoples of an array of assembled nations 'not to lose sight of the goal'. 'It is within our grasp,' she suggested, 'to attain a ringing respect for human dignity.'[50] Alingue and Robinson give insight into the courage that is needed to learn to live together. It involves material change. It also involves subjective engagement.

The work of the TRC is over. It must be over. It is time to move on. The vision that initially gave it birth, a vision only partly realised through the work of the Commission, now needs to be taken forward. At the level of reparation, the national demand is for the leadership to facilitate and encourage the kind of inclusivity and participation to which reference has already been made. National leadership style and the invitation to participate in the national debate are crucial in this regard.

Participation and feeling comfortable enough to participate vigorously in the political process is an essential ingredient of democracy. Not least in transitional societies, deeply divided by the past, this kind of participation is essential for dealing with issues that continue to divide the nation. It involves the creation of space within which the material and subjective dimensions of estrangement can be addressed – at the heart of which is a relationship-centric approach to political problem-solving. It is here that the will and the courage to embrace the kind of change that facilitates reconciliation can happen. It involves the creation of new mental maps, the projection of new possibilities and a willingness to risk failure as an alternative to waiting for the inevitable to crush any possibility of renewal. It requires 'deep conversation' where former enemies and adversaries can seek common ground despite their historic and actual differences. It is a vision that also transcends the spoken word.

Symbolism, monuments, memorials and the arts have a significant contribution to make in pursuit of national reconciliation. Sue Williamson, the Cape Town-based artist who documented the transition to democracy, reflects on the possibility of the arts contributing to the creation of this vision. 'By mediating through art the myriad images and information offered for public consumption in the mass media, I try to give dispassionate readings and offer a focus of new opportunities for engagement. Art can provide a distance and a space for such considerations.'[51] Artists, musicians, architects, poets and novelists have much to contribute to the emerging spirit of the nation. Within the artist's space for reflection, the nation is invited to rediscover the past in different ways, to encounter the other and to contemplate a new future.

The president's commitment to the building of a Freedom Park, discussed elsewhere in this volume by Revel Fox, can provide an important place within which reflection, discovery and contemplation can happen. It can go a long way to assist in the creation of a climate of acknowledgement and memory of the victims of gross violations of human rights. For this to happen, the nature and integrity of the Park is crucial. It needs to provide negative judgement on South Africa's racist past. Past atrocities cannot be minimised or glossed over. 'To describe the [Holocaust] concentration camps *sine ira* [without outrage] is not to be "objective", but to condone them,'[52] writes Hannah Arendt. The same needs to be said of apartheid. 'Shoah', 'genocide', 'apartheid', 'ethnic cleansing'. These are words that must evoke anger. There must be time and space for this. The nation needs to mourn. It needs a place to mourn, to enable those who mourn to come and go as they remember in grief and by engaging life.

Traditional and religious rituals, symbols of suffering and places of memory have an important role to play in moving beyond mourning and anger. Mourning and its adjacent emotions cannot be bypassed in the process of so doing. White South Africans, often in a hurry for blacks to forget about apartheid and move on, fail to remember this. The Freedom Park also needs to celebrate victory over the past – and to enable all South Africans to be drawn into that celebration. This is presumably what the president had in mind when, in addressing the Centenary Congress of the South African Institution of Civil Engineering, he said:

[W]e will never ask you, whose vocation is to build, in order to expand the life opportunities of humanity, to create new monuments that diminish our humanity.

As our country's pledge to celebrate our common humanity forever, we will build our Freedom Park. When it is done, it should be like no other in the world. When it is done, it should touch the souls of the humble people who expected nothing, and those who, in the past, were blind to the terrible harm that was done to those among them by a society that showed small justice, and still less pity. On Freedom Park, they must together say, here we are fulfilled.

We want our visitors from other lands who will come to Freedom Park themselves to say — we came to this great monument built by the people of South Africa to see, and left renewed in our humanity.

It will be your task to give form to these dreams, to work with the historians and archaeologists, the poets and the architects, the landscape gardeners and the musicians and those with broken nails on dirty hands, to build a monument that will both speak of our past and serve as a lodestar pointing our way into the future, itself the product of a prophesy and the trumpet of a prophesy.

The question I must ask, perhaps only in the rhetoric, is — will you, the civil engineers, the creators of the new Africa, will you respond to this historic challenge and leave all future generations with a statement in rock and steel on Freedom Park that says, here stands a living thing that constitutes the tribute of the civil engineers to their people and the peoples of the world?[53]

Justice, not least in a situation of political transition, is necessarily a *difficult justice*. The balance between individual, communal and national demands needs constant attention. Although the different levels of restoration are inherently linked, they often happen in different ways. One, in turn, often feeds off the other. To integrate the demands of each of these levels, while facilitating a process that enables the necessary balance between them to be maintained, is the essence of *real politik*. A viable society cannot afford to elevate one set of needs to the exclusion or neglect of others — and still have the centre hold. In this balanced sense, reconciliation is not some idealistic dream. It is good politics. To realise this is the beginning of the maturing of the South African democracy — born, as it inevitably was, in fierce competitiveness and fragility. Political maturity acknowledges different levels of human security. For a nation to prosper, it requires citizens to recognise that this fine balance must necessarily be maintained.

Notes

1 Reparations and Memorialisation: The Unfinished Business of the TRC. A conference organised by the Institute for Justice and Reconciliation, October 2000.

2 Christopher Ribeiro, son of Florence and Fabian Ribeiro, speaking at the Prime Minister's Forum: Truth, Justice and Reconciliation, Stockholm, Sweden, April 2002.

3 Cape Town, April 2003.

4 Rejeev Bhargava, 'The Moral Justification of Truth Commissions', in *Looking Back, Reaching Forward: Reflections on the Truth and Reconciliation Commission of South Africa*, eds Charles Villa-Vicencio and Wilhelm Verwoerd (Cape Town: University of Cape Town Press, 2000), 60.

5 See Donna Pankhurst, 'Issues of Justice and Reconciliation in Complex Political Emergencies: Conceptualising Reconciliation, Justice and Peace', *Third World Quarterly*, No. 1, Vol. 20, (1999): 239–256.

6 Richard Rorty, 'Justice as a Larger Loyalty', in *Cosmopolitics: Thinking and Feeling Beyond the Nation*, eds P. Cheah and B. Robbis (Minneapolis: University of Minnesota Press, 1998), 54–55.

7 Interview, Cape Town, February 2000.

8 Centre for the Study of Violence and Reconciliation, 1997/98. See www.csvr.org.za

9 Truth and Reconcilation Survey, 2001. See http://www.ijr.org.za

10 Research into the TRC amnesty process shows that acceptance of the process increased significantly where the victim or family received acknowledgement and a legitimate apology. Those who found the process acceptable increased further, by an almost equal percentage, where the victims or their families were also afforded an opportunity to tell their story. See J. L. Gibson, 'Truth, Justice and Reconciliation: Judging Amnesty in South Africa.' Paper delivered at the 59th Annual Meeting of the Midwest Political Science Association, 19–21 April 2001, Chicago, Illinois. See www.ijr.org.za

11 Richard Goldstone, The Hauser Lecture, New York University, 22 January 1997.

12 Ismael Mahomed DP, Judgement in Constitutional Court of South Africa. Case CCT 17/96, 25 July 1996.

13 June O'Connor, 'Fostering Forgiveness in the Public Square: How Realistic a Goal?' *Journal of the Society of Christian Ethics*, 22 (2002): 179.

14 Donald Shriver, 'Long Road to Reconciliation: Some Moral Steppingstones.' Paper delivered at Oxford University, Burying the Past: Justice, Forgiveness and Reconciliation in the Politics of South Africa, Guatemala, East Germany and Northern Ireland, 14–16 September 1998.

15 Ibid.

16 Quoted in Villa-Vicencio and Verwoerd, *Looking Back, Reaching Forward*, 65.

17 Martha Minow, *Between Vengeance and Forgiveness: Facing History After Genocide and Mass Violence* (Boston: Beacon Press, 1998), 13.

18 Quoted in Marcia Byrom Hartwell, 'The Role of Forgiveness in Reconstructing Society After Conflict.' Reprinted at www.jha.ac/articles/9048.htm

19 *Cape Times*, 16 February 1999.

20 Quoted in Alex Boraine et al., *Dealing with the Past* (Cape Town: Idasa, 1994), 15.

21 J. G. Murphy and J. Hampton, *Forgiveness and Mercy* (New York: Cambridge University Press, 1998), 18.

22 Susan Jacoby, *Wild Justice: The Evolution of Revenge* (New York: Harper and Row, 1983), 10.
23 Gabriel O'Malley, 'Respecting Revenge: The Road to Reconciliation', *Law, Democracy and Development*, Vol. 3 (1999): 188.
24 Mahomed DP, Judgement in Constitutional Court of South Africa. Case CCT 17/96, 25 July 1996.
25 Richard Wilson, 'Reconciliation and Revenge in Post-Apartheid South Africa: Rethinking Legal Pluralism and Human Rights', *Current Anthropology*, 41 (2000): 89.
26 Section 2, 32 (4) of the Interim Constitution allows that no section of the Constitution, including the postscript on amnesty, should be regarded as having less validity than any other part of the Constitution. Of the nine judges, Judge Didcott provided a separate concurring judgment, suggesting there is no way for the court to assess the cost involved or whether it is impossible to compensate all victims of apartheid. Arguing that the Act allows for 'some quid pro quo for the loss' suffered as a result of gross human rights violations, he concedes that nothing 'more definite, detailed and efficacious could feasibly have been promised at this stage'. His substantial argument is, however, that Section 33 (2) of the Interim Constitution allows for amnesty for vicarious liability.
27 Survey results: http://www.ijr.org.za. See 'Truth – Yes, Reconciliation – Maybe: South Africans Judge the Truth and Reconciliation Process', 2001. See http://www.ijr.org.za
28 James L. Gibson, 'Truth, Justice and Reconciliation: Judging Amnesty in South Africa.' Reprinted at http://www.ijr.org.za
29 Jacoby, *Wild Justice*, 10.
30 Pankhurst, 'Issues of Justice and Reconciliation', 250.
31 Quoted in N. J. Kritz (ed.), *Transitional Justice: How Emerging Democracies Reckon with Former Regimes* (Washington DC, US Institute for Peace, 1995) Vol. 1, 572-582.
32 Mahomed DP in CCT 17/96, 25 July 1996.
33 Neville Alexander, *An Ordinary Country: Issues in the Transition from Apartheid to Democracy in South Africa* (Pietermaritzburg: University of Natal Press, 2002), 167-168.
34 Ibid, 171.
35 Allister Sparks, *Beyond the Miracle: Inside the new South Africa* (Cape Town: Jonathan Ball, 2003).
36 Phillip Dexter, at the inaugural conference of the Institute for Justice and Reconciliation, Transcending a Century of Injustice, 11 May 2000.
37 Human Sciences' Research Council Conference, Kleinmond, 4 May 2003. http://www.treasury.gov.za
38 Hein Marais, *South Africa: Limits of Change. The Political Economy of Transformation* (London: Zed Books, 1998); Patrick Bond, *Elite Transition: From Apartheid to Neoliberalism in South Africa* (Pietermaritzburg: Natal University Press, 2000); Neville Alexander, *An Ordinary Country*; Sampie Terreblanche, *A History of Inequality in South Africa, 1652–2002* (Pietermaritzburg: University of Natal Press, 2002).
39 Sampie Terreblanche, Ibid, 392.
40 Quoted in John Battersby, 'Insecurity Rules as Nations Grapple with New Realities of a Changed World', *Sunday Independent*, 25 May 2003.
41 62% of blacks, 64% of whites, 79% of coloureds and 76% of people of Asian origin

indicated their preference for a country of racial diversity. See http://www.ijr.org.za
42 91% of blacks, 54% of whites, 64% of coloureds and 90% of South Africans of Asian origin support the payment of direct compensation to victims by government. Ibid.
43 Quoted in an interview with Ingrid Uys in *Millennium Magazine*, May 1996.
44 John Paul Lederach, 'The Horizon of Peacemaking: The Strategic Challenges of Post Agreement Change.' Keynote address, Research Initiative for the Resolution of Ethnic Conflict (RIREC) conference, University of Notre Dame, South Bends Indiana, September 2002.
45 See articles by Lourens du Plessis and Jeremy Sarkin in 'The South African Constitution as Memory and Promise', in *Transcending a Century of Injustice*, ed. C. Villa-Vicencio (Cape Town: Institute for Justice and Reconciliation, 2000), 63-84.
46 In his address at the Culture, Identity and Citizenship conference organised by the Institute for Justice and Reconciliation, December 2001. See http://www.ijr.org.za
47 In his address at the Institute for Justice and Reconciliation's award ceremony of the Reconciliation Award given to Tim Modise, 8 March 2000.
48 TRC, 'Foreword', in TRC Report (Pretoria: RSA, 1998).
49 At Seminario Internacional: Reconciliacion Y Justicia en la Construccion, De La Paz, Bogota, 2-3 April 2002.
50 Durban, 31 August – 7 September 2001.
51 Sue Williamson, 'Artist's Statement' in the brochure for the 'Truth Games', a series of interactive pieces based on the hearings of the TRC.
52 Hannah Arendt, 'A Reply', *The Review of Politics* 15 (January 1953): 79.
53 8 May 2003.

6

Legal Norms, Moral Imperatives and Pragmatic Duties:

Reparation as a Dilemma of Transitional Governance

Stef Vandeginste

There is a long-standing legal principle that responsibility for a wrongful act entails a duty to make up for the damages caused by such an act. It is a rule that seems to belong to the body of natural justice.[1] It was known in ancient Roman tort law and it has also been recognised as governing the responsibility of states. The Permanent Court of International Justice, in 1928, ruled that the obligation to make reparation for a breach of an obligation is 'a principle of international law, and even a general conception of law'.[2]

Equally undisputed in public international law is the object of such a duty to make reparation: 'Reparation must, as far as possible, wipe out all the consequences of the illegal act and re-establish the situation which would, in all probability, have existed if that act had not been committed.'[3] Therefore, restitution in kind is considered the preferential form of reparation. For instance, unlawfully occupied territories must be returned, illegally detained people must be released, internationally wrongful legislation must be repealed. If restitution is materially impossible, reparation usually consists of the payment of an amount of compensation.

We may conclude that, in legal theory, reparation is a relatively straightforward issue: responsibility for a wrongful act entails a legal duty to make reparation and reparation aims at wiping out all consequences of the wrongful act. In addition to its straightforwardness, this legal theory also seems to correspond to basic moral imperatives and to reflect what is generally felt to be just.

However, despite these characteristics, the issue of reparation has always turned out to be highly problematic in the context of transitional governance following a period of large-scale serious human rights violations. This chapter seeks to clarify why and to what extent, in situations after prolonged political repression, legal norms, moral imperatives and pragmatic duties may point in various directions on the roadmap of reparation. In the next section, some specific features of reparation for human rights violations are dealt with. In addition, reference is made to specificities, linked to a context of transitional governance, that may help to further clarify the issue.

Particularities of Reparation for Human Rights Violations in Political Transitions

The nature of human rights obligations

Outside the human rights sphere, most international treaties give rise to reciprocal obligations, with partner states accepting equal duties and conferring equal benefits on each other.[4] As a result, acts committed in breach of a treaty result in a direct injury of the partner state, which will logically claim reparation. Even outside the conventional context, customary international law, for instance concerning the lawfulness of war and the use of force by states, generally gives rise to obligations of a reciprocal nature.[5]

The nature of human rights obligations clearly differs from the above. As the Inter-American Court of Human Rights has noted, human rights obligations have 'the purpose of guaranteeing the enjoyment of individual human beings of those rights and freedoms rather than to establish reciprocal relations between States'.[6] As a result, holding states accountable for breaches of human rights obligations and enforcing their duty to repair is conceptually notably different than in the traditional reparation regime designed by public international law.[7] In addition, although specific human rights conventions, including the International Covenant on Civil and Political Rights (ICCPR), the African Charter on Human and Peoples' Rights, the European Convention on Human Rights (ECHR) and the UN Convention against Torture and Other Cruel, Inhuman or Degrading Treatment or Punishment, include provisions with regard to victims' rights to compensation (see e.g. art. 9 ICCPR), rehabilitation (see e.g. art. 14 Torture Convention), just satisfaction (see e.g. art. 41 ECHR), etcetera, 'there exists no general rule of customary international law to the effect that any grave violation of human rights creates an individual reparation claim under international law'.[8]

Who should be held responsible for the suffering and/or responsible for reparation?

As noted above, reparation is intrinsically linked to responsibility for wrongful acts. Establishing responsibility can be done in various degrees:

First, awarding reparation may go hand-in-hand with finding criminal responsibility of individual suspects. Recent developments, notably the jurisprudence of the two ad hoc International Criminal Tribunals for Rwanda and for the former Yugoslavia and the establishment of the International Criminal Court,[9] have importantly elaborated the notion of individual criminal responsibility for a 'hard core' of serious human rights violations, namely acts of genocide, crimes against humanity and war crimes. In practice, notwithstanding the important achievements of the ad hoc Tribunals in the international fight against impunity of perpetrators, victims have been largely neglected and their right to reparation non-existent.[10] At the national level, systematic criminal prosecution of perpetrators during transitional governance is in itself rare and, for a variety of reasons, highly problematic.[11] In Rwanda, since the end of 1996, criminal trials have taken place against around 7 000 genocide suspects.[12] Although victims have in several cases taken part in the proceedings as civil claimants[13] and obtained important awards of compensation, not a single actual payment of compensation has been made (as of May 2003). We may conclude that, in practice, the organisation of criminal trials of perpetrators, which is very often problematic in itself, has so far not been a successful avenue leading towards reparation for victims.

A second option is to hold individually responsible perpetrators civilly liable for reparation. In other words, the claim is not based on the criminal responsibility of torturers, death squads and the like, but on their civil responsibility for tort.[14] Currently, however, there is no international mechanism for bringing an international civil action against an individual perpetrator. At the national level, home country legislation – such as the South African amnesty legislation[15] – and procedural complexities may create significant hurdles, strongly limiting victims' capacity to initiate civil reparation claims against individuals. More importantly even, in a large majority of cases, perpetrators are likely to be insolvent or render themselves insolvent or their assets may be outside the reach of successful litigants.

In an exceptional case against the estate of Ferdinand Marcos, former president of the Philippines, damages were awarded by US courts as a result of a successful class action on behalf of an estimated 10 000 victims of torture, disappearance and summary execution.[16]

One increasingly popular instrument is to use civil human rights litigation in US courts on the basis of the Alien Tort Claims Act[17] against (wealthy) corporations. A recent example is the claims by the Namibian Herero People's Reparations Corporation against Deutsche Bank and other German companies.[18] This raises the more general issue of legal responsibility of corporations as a result of direct, indirect (or beneficial) or silent complicity in human rights abuses.[19] In conclusion, it should be noted that using civil claims against individual perpetrators (individuals or corporations) is unlikely, in particular in the event of mass victimisation, to offer the solution for the general reparation challenge in a transitional context, despite the important precedent value and policy impact that specific cases may have (see below).

Third, states can be held responsible for human rights violations, insofar as these acts are unlawful acts that are legally attributable to the state.[20] There are two specific issues that are particularly relevant in the context of transitional governance. First, the conduct of an insurrectional movement which becomes the new government of the state is attributable to the state. In other words, victims of human rights abuses committed by, for instance, the Rwandan Patriotic Front (RPF) rebellion in Rwanda or by the ANC in South Africa, can hold the state legally accountable and claim reparation for damages suffered. While this may be legally correct, the political reality in transitional societies in most cases renders this impossible. Nevertheless, it can rightly be argued that this constitutes a major credibility test of a new regime's stated policy of reconciliation and reconstruction. Does the new regime genuinely want to deal with its own dark past? Does it create a forum where accountability for its own violations is established? And does it treat the call for reparation by 'its own victims' equally? It goes without saying that the ANC has scored much better on this test than the RPF. Second, the responsibility of a successor government for abuses committed in the past under a previous regime is beyond any doubt. However, in the words of the Independent Expert of the UN Commission on Human Rights, C. Bassiouni, this 'may create an unfair burden',[21] in particular in transitional situations where the available resources for the new regime, in the light of the enormous reconstruction and development challenges, are likely to already be very limited. As a final remark, it should be noted that, insofar as the responsibility of the state is challenged in court, the above-mentioned limitations of a judicial approach apply equally (see also below).

The above deals with strictly legal responsibility, either criminal or civil. When it comes to nation-building and reparation as an instrument of reconciliation between groups in society, this is an overly narrow approach. Politically and morally speaking, there may be reason for individuals, corporations and groups in society to take responsibility for reparation, without being strictly responsible for the victims' suffering.[22] This is partly, but not solely, true for financial reasons: funding a reparation programme may well go beyond the normal budget of the state. Unless alternative sources of funding are found, advocating a reparation programme may mean advocating a reparation tax, which in turn may cause victims to suffer a second time. Voluntary contribution schemes, inviting people who benefited – whether they liked it or not! – from past, structural repression, also send a strong signal of genuine willingness to reconcile and to bridge the divisions of the past. Taking the same examples of Rwanda and South Africa, reference can be made to the 'Confession of Detmold'[23] and to the 'Home for All Campaign' and 'Declaration of Commitment by White South Africans'.[24]

A final but fundamental issue deals with the very notion of responsibility in situations of transition following an era of structural violence and institutionalised injustice. Structural violence is often 'invisible', almost perceived as 'normal' and embedded in social structures. It is reflected, for instance, in unequal access to resources, to health care, to political power, etcetera. It is maintained by longstanding policies of discrimination and inequality and, whenever necessary, eruptions of directly visible violence.[25] By its very nature, responsibility for structural violence is hard to attribute, in particular in formal court proceedings. The institutional and thematic hearings before the Truth and Reconciliation Commissions of South Africa, Sierra Leone and Peru are highly laudable attempts to shed light on this kind of responsibility. Translating these findings from responsibility for structural violence to responsibility for reparation is obviously no easy task.

Who are the victims and who should benefit from reparation?

UN Commission on Human Rights independent expert C. Bassiouni proposes the following definition of a victim: 'A person is a "victim" where, as a result of acts or omissions that constitute a violation of international human rights and humanitarian law norms, that person, individually or collectively, suffered harm, including physical or mental injury, emotional suffering, economic loss, or impairment of that person's fundamental legal rights. A "victim" may also be a dependant or a member of the immediate family or household of the direct victim as well as a person who, in intervening to assist a victim or prevent the occurrence of further violations, has suffered physical, mental or economic harm.'[26]

Several relevant, and sometimes highly problematic, aspects should be noted: First, the use of the term 'victim' is not neutral. It is disliked by some, abused by others. On the one hand, the qualification of human beings as victims seems to be a necessary step towards official recognition of victims' rights and needs, including reparation. But at the same time, as R. Mani notes, 'in practice this appellation disempowers victims by emphasizing their denial of and need for rights. It strips victims of choice and reduces their capacity for regaining agency ... The term victim defines individuals in terms of their past, and ignores the desire many might have to move beyond the past, inhabit the present and look to the future'.[27] Many victims, therefore, see themselves as heroes or survivors rather than as victims. On the other hand, people may invoke their victimisation to claim – rightfully or not – preferential treatment or even to justify their recourse to violent revenge and human rights violations. Referring to Northern Ireland and the reference by both loyalist and republican paramilitaries to their status of victims, M. Smyth notes: 'The acquisition of the status of victim becomes an institutionalised way of escaping guilt, shame or responsibility.'[28]

It is important to recognise both direct and indirect victims. Indirect victims are those who are linked to direct victims in such a way that they also suffer as a result of that link.[29] As a result, relatives of killed victims will – at least theoretically! – be entitled to claim reparation for their own damage (mental suffering, loss of a breadwinner, etcetera) and to claim compensation on behalf of their deceased spouse, father, daughter, etcetera. In the case of Chile, a monthly compensation programme was established for victims who disappeared or were executed, for the benefit of the surviving spouse, the mother (or, in her absence, the father), the mother or father of any natural children of the person, and children of the direct victim up to 25 years of age.[30]

Equally important is the distinction between individual victims and collective victims. Especially in transitional situations, after prolonged periods of political repression, specific groups in society (indigenous peoples, regions, ethnic groups, etcetera) may have been systematically victimised, and individuals targeted merely because they belonged to such a collectivity. As we will return to below, an appropriate reparations policy needs to include both individual and collective measures to be able to respond to both types of repression. It should also be noted that both notions (of indirect victims and of collective victims) are to some extent culturally determined. For instance, in *Aloeboetoe v. Suriname*, the Inter-American Court of Human Rights recognised multiple wives and children of a deceased victim, as well as the Saramaca tribe as a whole, as being entitled to compensation.[31]

Given the above, in a transitional context, the range of people and groups who, for legal and moral reasons, can rightfully claim the status of victim and, as a result, claim reparation is likely to be very wide. On the other hand, the practical realities of a post-conflict society are likely to impose a real dilemma on any transitional government. Insufficient resources and lack of institutional and logistical capacity to deal with all reparation claims will necessitate both creative thinking on behalf of policy-makers and a sense of realism among victims. The above has shown that ranking different levels of responsibility or guilt is an extremely sensitive issue. This is even more true when it comes to defining and selecting the group of victims who qualify as beneficiaries of a reparation policy, and, in doing so, indirectly ranking their suffering and qualifying it as more or less important. Moreover, selecting victims also means excluding other victims, which in itself may be a source of re-victimisation.[32]

Two additional elements are worth mentioning with regard to the criteria of selecting victims. First, not only criminal prosecution, but also the choice of who is recognised as victim, has an impact on what is perceived as a 'serious' wrong, an 'important' violation and a 'real' crime. In other words, selecting victims may indirectly also be perceived as ranking violations in terms of seriousness. The mandate of the South African Truth and Reconciliation Commission was criticised for 'embracing the legal fetishism of apartheid', focusing primarily on the victims of those violations that were illegal even under apartheid (for instance torture) and implicitly qualifying other injustices (for instance forced removals) as a 'lesser wrong'.[33] As far as the latter example is concerned, it should be noted that the reparation offered by the Land Claims Commission and Court obviously constitutes an important correction of such possible perception. Second, in some cases, the selection of victims and the decision on their entitlement to reparations is determined in the light of their current needs rather than on the basis of the harm that was inflicted on them. If so, this demonstrates a conceptual shift from reparation as a human right of victims to a more humanitarian or developmental approach. For instance, the Rwandan National Assistance Fund for Needy Victims of Genocide and Massacres, which was launched in June 1998, specifically targets the economically most disadvantaged victims of the 1994 genocide and massacres; its activities are centred on housing, education, health and social reintegration.[34] Differently, the aforementioned draft UN Basic Principles and Guidelines on the Right to a Remedy and Reparation for Victims of Violations of International Human Rights and Humanitarian Law provided 'reparation should be proportional to the gravity of the violations and the harm suffered' (Principle 15).

What is reparation after (gross and systematic) human rights violations?

In the event of gross human rights violations, the normal goal of reparation (see above, to 'wipe out all the consequences of the illegal act and re-establish the situation which would, in all probability, have existed if that act had not been committed') can seldom or never be attained. What can reparation then usefully mean as an objective of transitional justice?

As mentioned above, restitution in kind is considered the preferential form of reparation under public international law. However meaningless and irrelevant this may seem at first sight, it remains a useful component. All too often, reparation is nearly automatically translated into financial compensation, as if it were possible to ever undo the harm and suffering by making payments into a bank account. A clear example of this one-sided monetary approach to reparation is the United Nations Compensation Commission, established in 1991 after the unlawful invasion and occupation of Kuwait by Iraq.[35] Restitution as a form of reparation can be meaningful both at individual and at collective levels. As far as individual victims and individual forms of reparation are concerned, restitution means, for instance, that those who are illegally detained should be given back their liberty. Criminal records of those who were wrongfully convicted should be expunged. Property should be returned to those who were chased from their land and houses. For torture victims, restitution means that their dignity is returned, which requires in the first place an acknowledgement of their suffering. In the case of killings or disappearances, restitution means that the bodies of the victims are searched for and that they are returned to their relatives who can rebury their loved ones, in accordance with the cultural practices of the community and family. Obviously, these measures of restitution will have to be supplemented by other forms of reparation (see below). As far as collective measures are concerned, restitution means, for instance, that citizenship is returned to those minorities who were deprived of this legal right. For those groups in society who were systematically excluded from education or discriminated against as far as health care is concerned, restitution means that their access to such services is restored.

In addition to restitution, the draft UN Basic Principles and Guidelines distinguishes four other types of reparation: compensation, rehabilitation, satisfaction and guarantees of non-repetition.

Compensating severe suffering and, *a fortiori* the loss of life, is simply impossible. But the payment of compensation nevertheless remains a useful and necessary form of reparation. Amounts awarded for the loss of a father or the loss of a finger or for mental pain and anguish, etcetera, may and do vary enormously in international and national case law and policy.[36] But, in all these cases, compensation is at the same time a symbolic act. In the words of Y. Danieli, 'the money concretises for the victim the confirmation of responsibility and wrongfulness'.[37] It is a tangible acknowledgement that wrong was done and that it is taken seriously. In order to serve the latter purpose, one should avoid adding insult to injury by paying ridiculously low amounts. And above all, it is important to maintain a link between the financial compensation awarded to victims and the acknowledgement of wrongdoing and responsibility. In Argentina, the Mothers of the Plaza de Mayo refused the compensation offered by the government in the absence of an official political and historical recognition of the disappearance of their children. Japan's establishment of the Asian Women's Fund to pay compensation to the Comfort Women was strongly criticised for being a welfare-oriented system based on gender and development needs rather than on acceptance and acknowledgement of responsibility for wrongdoing.

Rehabilitation refers to the restoration of a victim's physical and psychological health. It includes access to medical and psychological care as well as to legal and social services (Principle 24). Under satisfaction are included: cessation of continuing violations, verification of the fact and public disclosure of the truth, search for bodies and reburials, official declarations or judicial decisions to restore the dignity and reputation of the victims, apologies, judicial or administrative sanctions against people responsible for the violations, commemorations and tributes to the victims and inclusion of an accurate account of the violations in educational materials (Principle 25). Guarantees of non-repetition are structural measures and institutional reforms that are specifically oriented towards the prevention of a recurrence of the violations (regarding the independence of the judiciary, civilian control of the army, protection of human rights defenders, etcetera).

Probably the best way to define what reparation should look like in a specific transitional context is to ask victims themselves and to involve them as much as possible in the process. This process may not only lead towards the most appropriate solution, reform or standard of compensation. It also has the major advantage of empowering and revalorising victims, whose needs and thoughts are, possibly for the first time ever, taken seriously. On the basis of interviews taken from Holocaust survivors and Argentinean, Chilean and Japanese American victims, Danieli finds three general goals and recommendations: re-establish the victims' equality of value, power and dignity; relieve their stigmatisation and separation from society; repair the nation's ability to provide and maintain equal value under the law and the provision of justice.[38]

How to claim and/or deliver reparation

A final particularity about reparations for gross and systematic human rights violations, which cuts across much of the above, has to do with the enforcement of reparation rights and the actual delivery of reparation. This overarching question relates to the choice between, and the merits of, respectively judicial (formal court proceedings at national or international level) and non-judicial approaches (specific administrative bodies, truth commissions, compensation funds, etcetera).

The major limitations of a judicial approach can be summarised as follows. Even when legal remedies are available for victims, a judicial procedure may in any case be no more than a theoretical option for a large majority of victims who lack the most basic information, the necessary legal assistance and the minimal financial resources. Secondly, a judicial approach presupposes the existence of a properly functioning justice system, while in many transitional societies human and material resources are highly inadequate. Thirdly, in a judicial approach, procedural guarantees and conditions of legitimacy need to be carefully taken into consideration to ensure sanctions or reparative payments are not imposed on suspected perpetrators in an arbitrary and unsubstantiated manner. Before a compensation fund, claiming and awarding reparation is not linked to the establishment of guilt or responsibility and can therefore be procedurally more flexible. Finally, most judicial processes are designed to deal with individual responsibility, individual harm and individual reparation rights. In a transitional context, a judicial approach is therefore unlikely to be able to respond fully to reparation needs that inherently have a strong collective dimension. Nevertheless, the judicial enforcement of reparation as an individual and justiciable right remains an important option, despite the above-mentioned limitations. Even one single successful claim in court can be a most convincing argument for a government to acknowledge the suffering of the victims, adopt a reparations policy and establish a non-judicial reparation mechanism. Also, a judicial decision sends a strong signal of the wrongfulness of the acts and of the rightfulness of the victims' aspirations.[39]

Judicial and non-judicial approaches are obviously not mutually exclusive. The example of Guatemala may clarify this. The Inter-American Commission on Human Rights, in its fifth report on the situation of human rights in Guatemala,[40] values the important steps taken by the government in 2001 to recognise the responsibility of the state of Guatemala for the violations denounced in cases pending before the Commission and to compensate the relatives of the victims in six cases. Obviously, formal procedures before the Inter-American Commission, even under the friendly settlement mechanism, or before the Inter-American Court will never be able to deal with reparation for all of the estimated 200 000 victims who lost their lives during the 34-year civil war.[41] However, by stressing that 'the Commission considers that full compliance with the recommendations of the Commission for Historical Clarification is one essential requisite for discharging the international responsibility incurred in relation to the violations of the conflict', the Inter-American Commission adds to the general public pressure and may also strengthen the position of those members of the government who are committed to implementing the National Reparation Programme[42] as recommended by the Commission for Historical Clarification.[43]

Reparation on the transitional agenda

Reparation deserves a firm place on the agenda of transitional governance. Ideally, this agenda item at the same time abides by the national and international normative framework of reparation, responds to its underlying moral imperatives, and takes into account the pragmatic realities of reconstruction after conflict in a society where needs exceed means. If a balance is found between these determining factors, reparation can constitute the ultimate bridge between the past and the future and connect objectives of justice (primarily oriented towards the past) with objectives of reconciliation (primarily oriented towards the future). In fact, providing reparation for past abuses is an indication of the state's commitment to upholding the rule of law and to rendering justice in the future: 'Reparatory measures appear most definitional or the liberalizing move, as these responses instantiate recognition of individual rights.'[44] Also, for reconciliation to be able genuinely to prevent the use of a divided past as a source of renewed conflict, a recognition of the past suffering and a serious public effort to repair the harm done, at least symbolically, is essential.

There is no perfect answer to the challenge of reparation after violent conflict. Fully meeting all expectations is not realistic. Mendez stresses the need to see the state's obligation of providing reparation as an 'obligation of means', not of 'results'. In other words, the process is as important as the outcome; a government may fulfil its obligations 'by conducting a process, even if in the end, the whole truth cannot be established or the known perpetrators are themselves acquitted'[45] or no full reparation is provided for. Considering reparation as a process rather than as an outcome or a result also seems more responsive to the different psychological impact of reparation for victims, by taking into account the important dimension of time. In fact, for some, receiving reparation may be the start of a personal healing process, while for others, it may mean the end of it.[46] Also, at the macro-level of society, official acknowledgement and apologies may, for the authorities, constitute the end of the transitional process, while, for the victims, it may be the mere start of it.[47] In any case, however, looking at reparation as an obligation of means and as a process does obviously not mean that any attempt whatsoever at providing reparation, irrespective of its outcome, is fine. Also, measures that qualify as reparation do not automatically serve the purpose of reconciliation and justice and do not automatically bridge the gap between the past and the future either. Some may even be counterproductive. Attention needs to be paid, *inter alia,* to the following aspects:

- Reparation programmes should avoid strengthening existing or creating new discriminatory practices. Reparation can easily be perceived as an instrument of revenge in the hands of the new regime. Therefore, politically biased or one-sided reparation policies and practices may be detrimental to overall reconciliation objectives. A selection of reparation beneficiaries on the basis of the type of repression suffered may be necessary and justified (see below), but not if this is done on purely political grounds: in other words, victims of torture, whether at the hands of agents of the past regime or of former rebels, should in principle be given access to the same reparation regime.
- However debatable, a definition and, as a result, a selection of victims qualifying as beneficiaries of a specific reparation policy seems unavoidable in a transitional context.[48] Even if done on objective grounds, for capacity-related reasons, and in a politically balanced manner (see above), this selection risks creating anger and a perception of exclusion, or may even lead to 're-victimisation'. By excluding certain categories from reparation benefits, these victims may feel neglected and non-recognised as victims. As an example, reference can be made to the mandate of the National Commission for Truth and Reconciliation in Chile and of the Chilean National Corporation for Reparation and Reconciliation (which was established in response to the report of the Commission). In both cases, only victims of disappearance or death were considered, and victims of torture (except when leading to death), arbitrary arrest, illegal detention and exile were excluded. On the other hand, looking at Latin American practice, Lean finds a clear advantage in selecting and (significantly) reducing the number of beneficiaries: 'Where claims are limited, this may actually make it much more likely that states will meet reparation demands, for economic reasons. The cases of Brazil, Honduras and Suriname, where payments have been made to a small number of claimants, and the cases of Guatemala and El Salvador, where large numbers of claims have been documented but no reparations have been undertaken, certainly support this hypothesis.'[49]

- Due attention needs to be paid to the phenomenon of victim competition. Victims do not necessarily speak from one mouth. On the contrary, when it comes to recognition, compensation and positive discrimination, they may even be opponents. The degree of self-organisation among victims of a specific ethnic, regional, indigenous, religious or other group may have a strong influence on their access to decision-making processes and on the responsiveness of policy-makers to their reparation claims. Different groups of victims may want to demonstrate how 'unique' and much more severe their suffering, and, in doing so, 'monopolize the symbolic capital that such a unique fate brings and to convert it into political and economic opportunities that might begin to compensate for the massive injustice'.[50] A reparation programme should take into account this phenomenon to prevent deepening existing divisions in society.

- The moral imperatives and the pragmatic duties a transitional government faces may be difficult to reconcile when it comes to setting standards for lump sum compensation amounts. On the one hand, excessively limiting the number of beneficiaries may be perceived as biased and unfair (see above). On the other hand, strongly reducing compensation to the payment of a largely symbolic amount of money may – in particular when not explained properly and unless supplemented by other, possibly collective, measures – add insult to injury. This may also mean that the hunger for reparation remains (possibly unspoken for a while) on the political agenda. But most of all, awareness should be raised that other needs also necessitate the allocation of public resources, that establishing and implementing reparation policies requires time. In other words, it is important not to create false expectations. Any transitional government will face other important challenges of reconstruction – including that of the physical infrastructure of the country – and other essential (economic and human) development goals. Resources are limited and their allocation requires a highly unpopular exercise of priority setting. Ideally, some objectives of reparation and sustainable human development can be combined: for instance, investments in the health sector may be combined with free medical services for torture victims. The example illustrates how reparation in some cases even depends on reconstruction and development policies. Rehabilitation for torture victims may be virtually meaningless if the health sector is not an overall priority of transitional governance.

Even when additional financial resources for reparation are raised by means of a specific reparation tax, the latter should be designed in a way that does not chase investors out of the country, hindering economic development.

- An important future-oriented element of reparation, which can be qualified as a 'guarantee against non-repetition' and which is indicative of the new regime's commitment towards upholding the rule of law and the protection of human rights, relates to the rights of victims of future human rights violations in the post-transition era. Victims and their representatives should have the right to file complaints and have them promptly and impartially investigated. Victims and their dependants should be entitled to obtain reparation, and, in order to enforce their rights, have access to the appropriate judicial forum. Legal and administrative reforms may be needed to achieve this, as well as awareness-raising campaigns for the general public and specifically for magistrates, police and military authorities, prison administrators, etcetera.

Conclusion

Reparation is an important item on any transitional agenda. As a long-standing notion under international law, it responds to basic moral imperatives of fairness and hunger for justice. In the specific context of transitional justice after violent conflict, reparation rights and needs have a number of specific characteristics that have reshaped the traditional notion. The above has shown the importance of maintaining a connection between, on the one hand, reparation and, on the other, responsibility and acknowledgement: reparation should never be a mere instrument of buying oblivion and silence. The above has also clarified how reparation balances on the edge between sometimes confronting reconstruction duties and challenges and how, when carefully conceived, it can operate as a bridge between the past and the future, and as an instrument to better integrate objectives of justice and reconciliation.

Notes

1   C. Tomuschat, 'Reparation for Victims of Gross Human Rights Violations', *Tulane Journal of International and Comparative Law*, Vol. 10 (2002): 157.
2   Case concerning the factory at Chorzow (Merits), *P.C.I.J. Series A*, No. 17, 13 September 1928, 29.
3   Ibid., 47.

4   D. Shelton, *Remedies in International Human Rights Law* (Oxford: Oxford University Press, 1999), 47.

5   For a detailed study of the notion of reparation in relation to wars, see P. d'Argent, *Les Reparations de Guerre en Droit International Public. La Responsabilité Internationale des Etats à l'Epreuve de la Guerre* (Brussels: Bruylant, 2002).

6   'Other Treaties' subject to the consultative jurisdiction of the Court (Art. 64 ACHR), Advisory Opinion OC-1/82, Series A No. 1, 24 September 1982, http://www.corteidh.or.cr/Serie_A_ing/Serie_A_01_ing.doc

7   It would lead us too far to analyse the legal notion of 'injured State' which the International Law Commission has laid down in its draft Articles on Responsibility of States for Internationally Wrongful Acts to respond to this issue. See UN General Assembly Resolution A/RES/56/83 of 28 January 2002 and its Annex.

8   C. Tomuschat, 'Reparations for Victims', 183.

9   See Rome Statute of the International Criminal Court, 17 July 1998. The statute entered into force on 1 July 2002, following the 60th ratification.

10 The status of the victim and the possibilities of seeking reparation are clearly more appropriately addressed in the statute of the ICC. See C. Jorda and J. de Hemptinne, 'The Status and Role of the Victim', in *The Rome Statute of the International Criminal Court. A Commentary*, Vol. 2, ed. A. Cassesse et al. (Oxford: Oxford University Press, 2002), 1387-1419.

11 'Review of transitional periods reveals that successor criminal justice raises profoundly agonizing questions for the affected societies, so that its exercise is often eschewed.' R. Teitel, *Transitional Justice* (Oxford: Oxford University Press, 2000), 27.

12 République Rwandaise, Cour Suprême, *Fonctionnement Général des Juridictions Gacaca dans le Contexte Judiciaire et Socio-Politique*, Kigali, 18 April 2003, 3.

13 Through the typically Roman-Dutch law procedure of *constitution de partie civile*.

14 See C. Scott, ed., *Torture as Tort. Comparative Perspectives on the Development of Transnational Human Rights Litigation* (Oxford: Hart, 2001).

15 On the effect of granting an amnesty, section 20 (7)a of the 1995 Truth and Reconciliation Act provides: 'No person who has been granted amnesty in respect of an act, omission or offence shall be criminally or *civilly liable* in respect of such act, omission or offence and no body or organisation or the State shall be liable, and no person shall be vicariously liable, for any such act, omission or offence.' (emphasis added) See also A. O'Shea, *Amnesty for Crime in International Law and Practice* (The Hague: Kluwer Law International, 2002), 267-293.

16 Shelton, *Remedies*, 86-87.

17 The Alien Tort Claims Act awards universal jurisdiction to US federal courts for human rights violations committed abroad. For more detail about the attractiveness of US courts for this type of claim see B. Stephens, 'Translating *Filartiga*: A Comparative and International Law Analysis of Domestic Remedies For International Human Rights Violations', *Yale Journal of International Law*, Vol. 27, No. 1 (2002): 1-57.

18 See J. Sarkin, 'Holding Multinational Corporations Accountable for Reparations for Human Rights and Humanitarian Law Violations Committed during Colonialism and Apartheid: An Evaluation of the Prospects of Such Cases in Light of the Herero of Namibia's Genocide Cases and South African Apartheid Cases Being Brought in the

United States under the Alien Tort Claims Act', in *Bedrijven en Mensenrechten. Verantwoordelijkheid en Aansprakelijkheid*, eds E. Brems and P. Van den Heede (Antwerp: Maklu, 2003), 209-252.

19 See A. Clapham and S. Jerbi, 'Categories of Corporate Complicity in Human Rights Abuses', *Hastings International and Comparative Law Review*, Vol. 24 (2001): 339-349.

20 See H. Dipla, *La Responsabilité de l'Etat pour Violation des droits de l'Homme. Problèmes d'Imputation* (Paris: Pedone, 1994).

21 UN Commission on Human Rights, Report of the Independent Expert on the Right to Restitution, Compensation and Rehabilitation for Victims of Grave Violations of Human Rights and Fundamental Freedoms, Mr C. Bassiouni, submitted pursuant to Commission on Human Rights resolution 1998/43, UN Doc. E/CN.4/1999/65, 8 February 1999, para. 87. At the request of the UN Commission and Sub-Commission, Special Rapporteur Theo van Boven and Independent Expert Cherif Bassiouni have drafted the Basic Principles and Guidelines on the Right to a Remedy and Reparation for Victims of Violations of International Human Rights and Humanitarian Law (see the Annex to UN Doc. E/CN.4/2000/62 of 18 January 2000). This draft has been on the agenda of the Commission for several years now, without being formally adopted. See G. Echeverria, 'The Draft Basic Principles and Guidelines on the Right to a Remedy and Reparation: An Effort to Develop a Coherent Theory and Consistent Practice of Reparation for Victims', Article 2, Vol. 1, No. 6 (December 2002): 6-19.

22 'For while beneficiaries do not bear moral responsibility for gross violations of apartheid, they do bear moral responsibility to redress its consequences.' M. Mamdani, 'The Truth According to the TRC', in *The Politics of Memory: Truth, Healing and Social Justice*, eds I. Amadiume and A. An-Na'im (London: Zed Books, 2000), 183.

23 See http://www.theo.kuleuven.ac.be/clt/advoc_laurien_detmold.htm

24 See http://www.homeforall.org.za

25 The notion of structural violence is a key concept in the work of Johan Galtung. See, inter alia, J. Galtung, *A Structural Theory of Revolutions* (Rotterdam: University Press, 1974).

26 UN Commission on Human Rights, *The Right to Restitution, Compensation and Rehabilitation for Victims of Gross Violations of Human Rights and Fundamental Freedoms*. Final Report of the Special Rapporteur, Mr M. Cherif Bassiouni, submitted in accordance with Commission resolution 1999/33, UN Doc. E/CN.4/2000/62, 18 January 2000, para. 8.

27 R. Mani, *Beyond Retribution. Seeking Justice in the Shadows of War* (Cambridge: Polity Press, 2002), 120.

28 M. Smyth, 'Putting the Past in Its Place: Issues of Victimhood and Reconciliation in Northern Ireland's Peace Process', in *Burying the Past: Making Peace and Doing Justice after Civil Conflict*, ed. N. Biggar (Washington: Georgetown University Press, 2001), 108-109.

29 L. Huyse, 'Chapter 4. Victims', in *Reconciliation After Violent Conflict: A Handbook*, eds D. Bloomfield et al. (Stockholm: International IDEA, 2003), 54.

30 See the case study on Chile in *Transitional Justice. How Emerging Democracies Reckon With Former Regimes*, ed. N. Kritz (Washington: USIP, 1995), Vol. 111, 505.

31 Aloeboetoe y otros v. Suriname, Series C No. 15, 10 September 1993. See D. Shelton,

o.c., 187-188 and W. M. Reisman, 'Compensation for Human Rights Violations: The Practice of the Past Decade in the Americas', in *State Responsibility and the Individual. Reparation in Instances of Grave Violations of Human Rights*, eds A. Randelzhofer and C. Tomuschat (The Hague: Kluwer Law International, 1999), 63-108.

32 Huyse, 'Chapter 4', 61.

33 Mamdani, 'The Truth', 181.

34 For some critical comments see S. Vandeginste, 'Victims of Genocide, Crimes against Humanity and War Crimes in Rwanda. The Legal and Institutional Framework of Their Right to Reparation', in *Politics and the Past. On Repairing Historical Injustices*, ed. J. Torpey (Lanham: Rowman and Littlefield, 2003), 264-265.

35 For a detailed analysis of the UNCC mandate and operations see, inter alia, M. Frigessi di Rattalma and T. Treves, *The United Nations Compensation Commission. A Handbook* (The Hague: Kluwer Law International, 1999).

36 For an excellent analysis of international practice, see Shelton, *Remedies*, 214-291.

37 Y. Danieli, 'Preliminary Reflections from a Psychological Perspective', in *Seminar on the Right to Restitution, Compensation and Rehabilitation for Victims of Gross Violations of Human Rights and Fundamental Freedoms*, eds T. van Boven et al. (Maastricht: Netherlands Institute of Human Rights, 1992), 206.

38 Ibid., 211-212.

39 This paragraph is a summary of section 9.5.1 in S. Vandeginste, 'Chapter 9. Reparation', in *Reconciliation after Violent Conflict*, eds Bloomfield et al., 145-162.

40 Inter-American Commission on Human Rights, *Fifth Report on the Situation of Human Rights in Guatemala*, OAE/Ser.L/V/II.111, 6 April 2001.

41 This is the number of victims reported by the Guatemalan truth commission, the Commission for Historical Clarification, in 1999 in its report, *Memory of Silence*.

42 See http://shr.aaas.org/guatemala/ceh/report/english/recs3.html

43 For more details about the Guatemalan transitional justice process see R. Sieder, 'War, Peace and the Politics of Memory in Guatemala', in ed. Biggar, *Burying the Past*, (Washington DC: Georgetown UP, 2001) 2001, 184-206.

44 R. Teitel, *Transitional Justice*, 8.

45 J. Mendez, 'In Defense of Transitional Justice', in *Transitional Justice and the Rule of Law in New Democracies*, ed. J. McAdams (University of Notre Dame Press, 1997), 12.

46 See also Redress, *Torture Survivors' Perceptions of Reparations. Preliminary Survey* (London, Redress 2001), 32.

47 See also M. Gibney and E. Roxstrom, 'The Status of State Apologies', *Human Rights Quarterly*, Vol. 23, No. 4 (2001): 911-939; M. Cunningham, 'Saying Sorry: The Politics of Apology', *The Political Quarterly* (1999): 285-293.

48 In order to avoid any misunderstanding, it is important to note that this does not mean that other victims may lose, in legal terms, their right to a remedy for the violation of their human rights. It means that more easily accessible and specific appropriate non-judicial reparation programmes are established for the benefit of some categories of victims.

49 S.F. Lean, 'Is Truth Enough? Reparations and Reconciliation in Latin America', in ed. Torpey, *On Repairing*, 179.

50 L. Huyse, 'Chapter 4', 64.

7

Voices Not Heard: Small Histories and the Work of Repair[1]

Fiona C. Ross and Pamela Reynolds

In April 1998, a meeting took place between victims of apartheid living in Zwelethemba, the community in which we have been working,[2] and an international expert on trauma. The meeting had been facilitated by a member of the South African Truth and Reconciliation Commission (TRC). The expert had come to ask about the forms of reparation victims expected. A community leader introduced people who had been involved in opposition to the previous regime. She said, '... this is a victim; this lady lost her children; this lady lost her brother, she is also a victim ...' The expert, seeking to devise a proposal for action to be implemented after the Commission's end, said to the group:

> *I would like to hear from you. That will be part of my recommendation to the TRC and to the United States Government. So go ahead. We have to have a dialogue.*

The community leader replied:

> *They wrap themselves around our soreness and then go away. Why does the TRC say they want to heal us? ... You come in, in a hurry. Come in, out again. That is the way it's been, and we are the victims. We don't think that is the way we are going to heal.*

Our chapter considers the implications of telling stories of pain and loss before the South African TRC. We focus on the vexed relationships of reciprocity and intimacy that arise when people are asked to talk about pain in the context of a project of national reconciliation. If truth is, as Seremetakis would have it, extra-linguistic, a 'condition of embodiment', then what are the processes and experiences of translating felt truth into 'stories' for public consumption?[3] Stories, once public, circulate beyond the confines of the intimate, raising questions about the relation of speech to repair, and about the weight of words. The chapter is tentative in tracing the workings and dissonance of the process of truth-finding and reconciliation set in motion by the TRC.

Since its inception in 1995 and the commencement of its public work in 1996, the Commission has engaged in transactions around pain. Established to document the nature, extent and patterns of gross violations of human rights committed between 1960 and 1994, it has involved the trading of stories of pain inflicted or received. Its task was to promote national reconciliation through the revelation of truth, found and narrated through a reciprocal process of talking about pain and registering its effects. Our discussion draws on the Commission's process as a whole, and raises questions about its effects on society, particularly among those who stood against the apartheid state. Here we do not wish to emphasise the material nature of pain, its infliction, its experience and its effects, but to draw attention towards the dislocations in the telling and receiving of stories of pain. We ask about the nature and consequences of such interactions, about the ways in which stories are told, the silences that hold them, and implicit dangers attendant on a public telling.

The Weight of Words

We characterise the Commission's undertaking in terms of reciprocity: stories of pain were told in partial exchange for healing, reparations, amnesty, a new narrative of reconciliation. Words have been made central to a process in which experiences of pain were translated into stories of human rights violations. These have circulated beyond the confines of the intimate through the media (print, audio and electronic broadcasts of the Commission's work took place daily), through public hearings and through discourses of human rights violation.[4] Personal control over the contexts of telling, the recipients of stories and the uses to which stories are put has been relinquished in the process of telling 'to the fullest extent' those experiences of loss and pain that the Commission defined as gross violations of human rights. Pain has been imbued with measurable weight by converting experiences of violence into narratives of violation that form the grounds for reparation. Through the process of the Commission's public hearings then, specific kinds of experience become a medium of exchange. They mark particular moralities that, generated in a given context, spread beyond the immediacies of present-time and the context of local placement. And they mark also transformations in the intimate nature of the experience of pain.

The Pull of Listening

If to talk about one's past is to give of oneself then the manner of receipt is important. Listening is, ideally, not passive. It may be demanding in requiring another to talk. It may be intrusive in probing behind the formulated tale, that is, the story we tell ourselves to explain ourselves and protect ourselves. It may matter what the motive is in asking for others' stories.

Stories of the infliction or reception of pain are told for many reasons. In the case of testimonies given before the Commission by amnesty applicants, the explanations of how violations were committed appeared motivated primarily to avoid the consequences of criminal and civil prosecution. The Promotion of National Unity and Reconciliation Act that brought the TRC into being did not require of those seeking amnesty that they express contrition, nor did it require reciprocity between individuals. In some, few, instances, contrition and remorse were expressed alongside. Associated with forgiveness are conditions and limitations. Susan Jacoby holds that without contrition, forgiveness has no significance as a social bond for restoring civilised relations between the injured and the injurer.[5] She stresses the absolute importance of reciprocity. Avishai Margalit argues that remorse offers 'a non-magical way of undoing the past' by allowing us to change our interpretation of the past.[6] She traces forgiveness's path and finds its end point in overcoming resentment. She argues that if forgiveness is a duty, it is a duty not to the other but to the self.[7] Yet, when translated, the Commission's names in Xhosa, *Ikhomishani yenyaniso noxolelwaniso*, and in Afrikaans, *Die Waarheids en Versoenings Kommissie*, suggest different meanings to the English title. Instead of the Truth and Reconciliation Commission, our respondents say the words translate as 'The Commission on Truth and Forgiveness'. Here, the weight of words implies a greater moral responsibility for those who suffered than for those who inflicted suffering.

Victims of human rights violations told of their pain and loss for a variety of reasons. Some sought public acknowledgement. Some sought to under-

stand their experiences, to make sense of the reasons and actions of perpetrators, while some spoke out in order to clear names besmirched. Many
sought assistance for a younger generation. Some testified to be recognised
and gain access to reparations. Others came forward because their pain
required urgent attention. Some spoke willingly, others less so. Some people
spoke out courageously, beautifully, poetically and angrily before the TRC.
Diverse styles of telling quickly became reified, crystallising into formulaic
narratives that could lack the capacity to hold the attention.

Some people were resentful of the pressure brought to bear on them
by members of the Commission to tell their stories of loss and suffering.
This was especially so among some women whose husbands had been
killed and whose deaths had become central tropes in the struggle against
apartheid. They felt the pull of others' listening. Some, who for a variety
of reasons, did not testify or make statements, are bitter now. They feel
themselves excluded from acknowledgement and from the legal consequences that flowed from the Commission's work.

Others who have suffered deeply seek to carry their pain in silence.
Their silence excludes, often hurts, those with whom they live, but it may
be a strategy of survival. It may be an attempt to protect others from the
knowledge of suffering caused; to protect organisations; or even to protect the self against the recognition of harm. The cost of such silence may
be high: individuals may consciously exclude themselves from institutionalised forms of assistance; unaware of the extent of harm, families and
communities may fail to support. And in some instances communities may
attempt to hold in silence events of the past – to protect the innocent, to
hold awareness of the social effects of violence at bay, to create a seamless
narrative of suffering or resistance in the past.

It is not only the sufferers who are silent in the face of pain. Those
working on or near the TRC have found that others' stories weighed
heavily. Some people who have testified have found the costs of public
speech to be high. Others have found in the public domain a form of
recognition and acknowledgement that offsets the complexities of speech
that may deviate from prescribed form and standardised narratives. It is
dangerous to assume that narratives are inert. Events may return them to
social life, reactivating and redirecting their force. We must now ask who
bears the weight of recall, and with what consequences over time.

It can be easier not to listen. Families of those who have been greatly
harmed find it hard to pay attention to an individual's pain when it seems

not to abate over time. One young man we know was tortured in prison every day for four months then held in solitary confinement for three years and, once released, took refuge in drink. He is struggling now to study and to hold himself together but his kin have lost sympathy. 'You are old now,' they say, 'and should be contributing money to the family, not asking for support.' Their assumptions that pain has a finite lifespan, that adulthood brings responsibilities for others beyond responsibility for self, that listening to pain, too, is of finite duration, reflect in some part the rhetoric of the TRC, which asserted that speaking and healing would follow one another closely in time.

For some, talking does not ease the pain, notwithstanding assumptions that speech is cathartic. Anne Michaels, writing about grief, says: 'Some stones are so heavy only silence helps you carry them.'[8] Yet, silence may not be innocent. Many people did not make testimonies or give statements. In the small town in which we work, relationships of distrust and anger, built up over the years of apartheid and in the intervening period, have rendered opaque the process of soliciting testimonies. Local power dynamics have altered the potential to gain access to redress and public acknowledgement. Memory is stirred by some in the face of others' longing to forget.

Recording and Recovery

Early in the Commission's process, a colleague at a workshop held to discuss the relationship between the Commission and mental health practitioners in the Western Cape commented that the Commission was 'the full stop at the end of apartheid'. The idea that the Commission was a form of punctuation in time was widespread, facilitated in some ways by the language of catharsis and closure that accompanied its work and by the emphasis on reparation as an event.

It is dangerous to think that the truth has been excavated and achieved and that therefore we can close the discussion on the past and, thus remembering, move forward. The vignette with which we open the paper describes the sense of fragility that is a consequence of testifying about pain. Healing is not automatic when mediated by words. The Commission, drawing from its Latin American counterparts, held that it was important to remember in order to ensure that the past could not be repeated. A popular conception, this is not the only position on the past.

Anne Michaels expresses perhaps the most extreme opposite perspective when she writes:

It is not the unknown past we are doomed to repeat, but the past we know. Every recorded event is a brick of potential, of precedent, thrown into the future ... This is the duplicity of history: an idea recorded will become an idea resurrected. Out of fertile ground, the compost of history.[9]

We do not hold to her position, but it is clear that the manner of recording matters. Adrienne Rich calls for attention to the limits of what can be heard if '... the secret is spoken yet not received because it is dissonant with the harmonies we like to hear'.[10] She urges that pain be kept vocal so it cannot become normalised and acceptable. Yet, sometimes the commissioners seemed to ask for too much when they said, 'Tell us more about your pain, your torture, your feelings.' It may be important to recognise 'thresholds of secrecy',[11] such as humiliations that do not diminish in memory if described in words.

To wrap oneself in the 'soreness' of another may reflect Wittgenstein's injunction to feel another's pain in one's own body.[12] It may also reflect a simulation of the suffering of victims in voices that appropriate it in order to create legitimacy for the appropriators.[13] Perhaps an epistemological practice, grounded, as Arjun Appaduari suggests, in an ethics and politics of intimacy, may say something important about how to write or record loss without subverting it.[14] In her analysis of materials presented in *Social Suffering*, Veena Das concludes that ownership of pain rests in the self and that there is no right of appropriation. Her suggestion that anthropology serve as a body of writing which lets the pain of the other happen to it may provide a pointer for other writings of pain.[15] The kinds of work undertaken by the Commission and others like it run the risk of too simple a translation of the memory of pain from the intimate to the public, the risk of generating fixed positions. We fear that the Commission failed to recognise the intimacy of recording pain. There is a danger that the range of reasons for which people testified or did not, the complexity of decisions to testify about pain or loss, and the consequences of these are ignored or erased. Already, silences are being overwritten with voices that do not take account of the particularity of the local.

A deep understanding of the past and its influence on the present can only come from intensive work at the micro-level. Even then, truths are not transparent. The Commission's work was predicated on memory, and memory is complex, closely tied to power, seldom innocent. Take an example: We worked alongside each other in one town and sometimes we gathered different sets of stories about somebody's activities in the past. The truth seems to slip behind set attitudes, long-held suspicions, old power dynamics and current wariness. Members of the community in which we worked know one another, and the activities of those involved in times of conflict are remembered in the face of events in the present. In these contexts, neither memory nor forgetting is innocent, and encounters may revitalise old tensions, reinvigorate distrust or rekindle comradeship. The effects are not easily predictable. For example: one man we know recently went to a party and danced with a girl who danced exquisitely. She had just returned home from the US and, as they danced, she turned to him and said, 'Why did you necklace my brother?'[16] The same man works on a community forum as does the policeman who tortured him. He asked the policeman if he remembered him and the policeman said, 'Yes, I do.' Another man went to the hospital for treatment and passed the doctor who had declared him fit enough to continue being tortured. In these stories, it is hard to know what truths need excavation, what talk will heal and what tensions will exacerbate hidden resentments.

The Work of Repair

Suffering and healing in South Africa are particular. Comparisons with pain caused in other places may obscure the specific character of that experienced here. In the absence of a careful accounting of harm and of the local registers of success against which to weigh damage, the extent and duration of harm may be underestimated. Yet, there is also the danger of anticipating trauma for survivors or their children. Anticipation can lead to prescription. Individual and social recovery may take the sustained attention of a variety of institutions – the family, community, healers, friends, state institutions – over an extended period of time, sometimes generations. Where, as in South Africa, these institutions have been eroded, it is important to take note of the resources – personal and social – that are brought to bear in recognising pain, and in intervening to ameliorate it. After the Commission's work has ended, we have still to learn what forms of expression pain or trauma have taken and may yet take, and by whom it is heard, attended to and healed. We know little of forms of damage, the routines of coping, the strategies of recovery, the contexts in which efforts to recover fail, the limitations of institutions in relation to healing.

In our work, we have been struck by the work of recovery and repair; by the ongoing effort of forging the ordinary in conditions marked by and shaped in contingency. E. Valentine Daniel suggests that:

> *To recover is not the same as to uncover or discover. Recovery ... is more akin to regaining one's balance, albeit in a new place and time; it is a coming to terms with the contemporary forces that buffet without allowing these forces to overwhelm. Recoveries often do entail radical rearrangement of meanings and forms, but they do not necessarily presume radical ruptures, nor do they deny all continuity, all memory – whether real or imagined – and all familiarity.*[17]

In thinking about violence's aftermath, Deepak Mehta and Roma Chatterji argue that the recovery of the everyday involves 'coming to terms with the fragility of the "normal"'.[18] Veena Das and Arthur Kleinman note that: 'While everyday life may be seen as the site of the ordinary, this ordinariness is itself recovered in the face of the most recalcitrant of tragedies: it is the site of many buried memories and experiences.'[19] They continue, 'The recovery of the everyday, resuming the task of living (and not only surviving), asks for a renewed capability to address the future,' and asks for a record of 'the small local stories in which ... communities are experimenting with ways of inhabiting the world together'. Rather than understanding repair in terms of reconciliation and reparation, here it is linked with inhabitation and the work of time. Taken together, these formulations lead in a direction that recognises the contingency of the present. They allow us to consider the effort of (re)making the everyday, without necessarily imputing a cathartic aspect to language, assuming healing, or presuming that social institutions are sufficiently robust to undertake the work of recovery over time. We need to take seriously the ways in which people labour to create desired forms of life, especially where, as in the instances we've described above, encounters are burdened, where histories of conflict and violence saturate interactions, where language is fraught and where social institutions remain fragile.

Notes

1   An earlier version of this chapter was published under the title 'Wrapped in Pain: Moral Economies and the South African Truth and Reconciliation Commission in South Africa', *Context*, Vol. 3 1999 (1): 1-9. We are grateful to the editors for permission to reproduce the material.

2   It was documented by a colleague, Susan Levine, who kindly allowed us to use the notes she took.

3   N. C. Seremetakis, *The Senses Still* (Chicago: Chicago University Press, 1994), 6.

4   C. Colvin, 'Limiting Memory: The Routes and Roots of Story Telling in Post-Apartheid, Post-TRC South Africa', in eds C. van der Merwe and R. Wolfswinkel, *Telling Wounds*. Published proceedings of the conference on Narrative, Trauma and Memory, Cape Town, 2002, 234-44; F. Ross, *Bearing Witness: Women and the Truth and Reconciliation Commission in South Africa* (London: Pluto Press, 2003).

5   Susan Jacoby, *Wild Justice: The Evolution of Revenge* (London: Collins, 1985), 347.

6   Avishai Margalit, *The Ethics of Memory* (Cambridge, Mass.: Harvard University Press, 2003), 199.

7   Ibid, 207.

8   Anne Michaels, *Fugitive Pieces* (London: Bloomsbury, 1998), 77.

9   Ibid, 161.

10   Adrienne Rich, *What is Found There. Notebooks on Poetry and Politics* (London: Virago, 1995), 147. 1st publication New York: WA Norton, 1993.

11   A. Feldman, *Formations of Violence: The Narrative of the Body and Political Terror in Northern Ireland* (Chicago: University of Chicago Press, 1991), 11.

12   Quoted in Veena Das, 'Language and Body: Transactions in the Construction of Pain', *Daedelus* Vol. 125 1996 (1): 69-70.

13   Veena Das, *Critical Events: An Anthropological Perspective on Contemporary India* (Delhi: Oxford University Press, 1995), 191.

14   Arjun Appaduari, 'Fieldwork in the Era of Globalisation', *Anthropology and Humanism* 22 1998 (1): 115-118.

15   V. Das, 'Sufferings, Theodicies, Disciplinary Practices, Appropriations', *International Social Science Journal* Vol. 154 1997: 572.

16   Necklacing: a tyre filled with paraffin was placed around the neck of a suspected informer and set alight, burning the person to death.

17   E. Valentine Daniel, *Charred Lullabies: An Anthropography of Violence* (Princeton: Princeton University Press, 1996), 73.

18   Deepak Mehta and Roma Chatterji, 'Boundaries, Names, Alterities: A Case Study of a "Communal Riot" in Dharavi, Bombay,' in eds. V. Das, A. Kleinman, M. Lock, M. Ramphele and P. Reynolds, *Remaking a World* (Berkeley: University of California Press, 2001), 157–200.

19   Veena Das and Arthur Kleinman, 'Introduction', in eds. V. Das, A. Kleinman, M. Lock, M. Ramphele and P. Reynolds, Remaking a World (Berkeley: University of California Press, 2001), 4.

8

The Matter of Words in the Midst of Beginnings:

Unravelling the 'Relationship' between Reparation and Reconciliation

Erik Doxtader

A word does not rot unless it is buried in the mouth for too long. A word buried in the ground only grows roots.

Yvonne Vera

I don't believe reconciliation can only come through Mandela or Thabo Mbeki's speeches.

Xolile Dyabooi

Beginnings (be)come with words. Transitions move with speech, (inter)(ex)change that abides in, makes with, and challenges the contingency of its founding expression. Between old and new, concepts for the present grow meaning slowly, spreading across time's horizon and burrowing deep into the layers of moments. If mistaken for imprecision or delay, this work prompts the desire for 'consolidation', a motion that stealthily overwrites the potential for speech/action with an abstract possibility of closure. Beginnings open to middles not endings. If the terms of this 'between' are forgotten, if either the past or future is deemed definitive in isolation, the 'middle time' of transition is emptied of its energy, the capacity to make anew.[1] Words for beginning, reconciliation and reparation both perform and explain this creativity. They hold (between them) the constitutive question of how to stand in a present and craft the ground for history-making. For *now*, the question is as important as its answer.

A testament to its remarkable potential, the South African transition continues. Over the last 14 years, the move from apartheid has taken form and substance within words that matter. Many believe that this 'negotiated revolution' could not have been otherwise, that the alternative to words was only and forever devastation. If so, the onset of transition marked a beginning of significant complexity, a moment that brought the need for 'ceaseless debate' about how to 'make good again'.[2] This effort required the creation of common ground, a shared vocabulary that emerged through 'talk about talk', the (productively) failed words of a first constitutional convention (CODESA) and the (extra-legal) success of a second's 'sufficient consensus'. At the multi-party negotiating process, the god-terms of this constitutive power were plentiful and rarely with singular meaning. The ambiguity was both a virtue and risk of the transition that they were intended to perform.[3] In a post-amble that recalled Rousseau, the play between them was profound and daunting, an enactment of what had been made and an explanation of what remained in the making. The words of an actual reconciliation (re)presented the question of what was (yet) to be done with the potential of reconciliation's words.

A potential is not a guarantee. In the midst of transition, words are neither definitive power nor sufficient solace. For far too many, they are in excess of needs, desires and pain. There is much that cannot be told, captured or coerced into language, let alone set into a book that costs a week's income or worse. Words matter. But it seems that they do not always matter in a material way. The speech needed to fashion and sustain the commons, the lexicons that have to be forged in the name of civic participation and politics, require at least time, energy and place. These goods remain in terribly short supply. The faith of reconciliation's words runs thin at the moment one pauses to consider the statistics that document poverty, add up the figures that betray the tenacity of apartheid's legacy, see the shacks that line the N2 highway on the way to those brisk airport departures, and listen to the struggles for food, water, health care and employment that occur daily in (horrifically understated) 'historically disadvantaged communities'.[4]

Reconciliation changes what exactly? What are its words *doing* to repair the damage? In the minds of some, reconciliation is not simply specious but the lever for a pernicious trade-off that leaves the material to lag behind the symbolic.[5] But this objection may itself be evidence of a frustration that comes with treading water. At the end of the day, the econometrics offered by social democrats do not always leave us so much to go on. The undeniable need for material change remains fantastical if calls for redistribution account for neither structure nor attitude.

Reconciliation and reparation are two vital and contested ways of explaining and performing the work of beginning. Each is a relational term, a concept addressed to the invention, development and maintenance of relationships between people, things and ideas (norms). Each has a long and ambiguous history, legacies concerned with how human beings undertake the work of understanding and making history. By definition, each makes a promise that it cannot keep. Yet, for all that they have in common, reconciliation and reparation stand together awkwardly. The tension is readily evident in the South African transition, especially as it appears in the design, work and results of the Truth and Reconciliation Commission (TRC). In her journo-poetic chronicle of the Commission, Antjie Krog observes the difficulty: 'If people don't get reparation they won't forgive. If people are not forgiven, they won't offer reparation.'[6] Today, the ambiguity is a source of ongoing and frequently bitter controversy.

The architects and shepherds of the TRC process are unlikely to be remembered for their elegant or efficient approach to the matter of reparation. Having waited and waited some more, recognised victims are now set to receive sums that disappoint if not provoke feelings of betrayal, resentments that appear to threaten the spirit and promotion of reconciliation. Frustrated, a few have turned the law's debatable assurance of a *quid pro quo* in a different direction, launching international suits that have been condemned by the government on the grounds that they may impede foreign investment's role in reconstruction and undermine South Africa's ability to direct its own reconciliation process.[7] Surrounding the dispute, evident in the tense and ongoing exchanges between President Thabo Mbeki and opposition leader Tony Leon, there is the problem of whether it is time to identify and call on the 'beneficiaries' of apartheid to make repairs or if such a demand risks the very reconciliation to which it aspires.

Between words that matter and the matter of words, we are left firmly and uncomfortably between. In the midst of transition, there is significant struggle over the question of whether the reconciling action of speech can *actually* redress history's material-criminal deprivations or if such discursive power matters only in the wake of work that repairs that which has (or might have) been. At a moment when the duties of justice – ever the third term – are both yet in the making and altogether (painfully) clear, what is the appropriate relationship between the reconciliatory and the reparative? Is reconciliation the road to repair or must the road first be paved?

As debated in South Africa, these questions turn on a problem of priority. In the discourse produced by and surrounding the TRC, there is now something of a presumption that reparation is necessary for reconciliation. However, this claim has more than one meaning. For some, necessity is a marker of temporal or conceptual priority; the conditions for reconciliation exist only after reparation has occurred. For others, the issue is defined by the obligations of duty and its laws. Wounds demand strict redress; the sacrifice entailed in reconciliation can be justified (just) only as it occurs on a level playing field. Wary that such distinctions mark quibbling, pragmatists offer an attractive third perspective: reconciliation and reparation are best conceived as counterparts. The difficulty, however, is that this package deal neither escapes nor resolves the question of relation, the problem of *how* these goods inform, bear on and perhaps unravel one another.

The South African transition contains the question of how reconciliation and reparation are actually and ideally related. With no aspiration to fashion a conclusive reply, this chapter is addressed to the question itself. Concerned with the puzzles created by the answers that are presently on the table, it contends that it is time to pose the question anew. This argument for the priority of inquiry rests on two basic contentions. On one side, the transitional power of both reconciliation and reparation has been degraded by standing and popular explanations of how they are (best) related. Specifically, the case for the priority of reparation presupposes a generative power that appears only as it stands in productive opposition *with* reconciliation. On the other, efforts to link reconciliation and reparation have obscured the point that the *question* of their relationship matters. If recovered and held open as a question, the problem of what sits between these goods is a provocation to reflect on the unexpected consequences of beginning and an opportunity to invent practical ways of (be)coming into a transition that continues.

Timeless answers do not serve. The relationship between reconciliation and reparation is the abiding question of how to invent the potential for beginning in relation. Here I will develop this idea through three lines of inquiry. From a brief recollection of the ambiguity that appeared between reconciliation and reparation in the transition's early days, the chapter's first section considers how the question of their relationship involves a problem of definition. Both reparation and reconciliation are difficult to define. Lacking fixed object or prototypical form, each contains the potential to invent and support human relationships, modes of interaction and exchange that move and fluctuate over time. From an illustration of how these two relational concepts gather their power from very different conceptions of law's *status* in the work of transition, the second section turns to the question of how the relationship between reconciliation and reparation has been explained and justified. Examining both policy debates and criticisms of the TRC's development, I detail three puzzles that follow from the common case that reparation has (necessary) priority over reconciliation. In different ways, these puzzles highlight but then obscure the problem of how reconciliation and reparations enact and help support transition. Accordingly, it is useful to reformulate the question 'what is the relationship between reconciliation and reparations' to 'how are relationships constituted and performed between these two relation-making concepts?' The benefit of this turn is some purchase on the ways in which the reparative and the reconciliatory stand in a shared and perhaps constitutive opposition. In the final section, I suggest that what sits and moves between the reparative and the reconciliatory are questions about whether and how transitions need to define the history with which they 'deal', blur the line between material and discursive exchange and create incentives for people to undertake that work of beginning which often appears to violate principles of self-interest. While these concerns are present in the development of the TRC and may help to explain some of the controversy provoked by its work, the larger concern is how these questions bear on the problems that sit on the horizon of democracy's second decade.

Terms of Transition

Where does one begin? With a negotiated revolution that left an instruction which was fulfilled by the creation of a Commission of Truth and Reconciliation charged to *deal* with its (non)revolutionary effect, the matter of the new that could not be constitutionalised. In fact, the word 'deal' is everywhere in the conception, design and development of the TRC.[8] In late 1993 and early 1994, it was time to deal. Sometimes it was with the generals and sometimes with a larger past. Always, the dealing needed to be done in a 'morally acceptable way'. Everyone agreed on that, at least until it was time to talk about what the moral meant and how it related and did not relate to the political. And thus, the lexical swirl began. Among a long list of others, 'dealing' became an evolving (usually) short-hand for: healing wounds; forging national unity; restoring humanity; preventing denial; creating moral accountability; finding truth; creating a model for the world; hearing confession; transforming perceptions; opening up discourse; risking a witch hunt; building a culture of human rights.[9]

This beginning, it's a big deal. Tied closely to a remarkable process of negotiations, the TRC begins with words about South Africa's need for words that might penetrate the fog of history's violence and lift the veil of its silence. This speech about the value of speech did not always have and did not always need to have clear meaning. The rhetorical architecture of the Commission – the invention of a 'juristic person' dedicated to hearing, disclosure, reporting, articulating full pictures and recommending – required policy-makers to link (bridge) an ambiguous set of foundational terms that would help carry the country from old to new. As 'dealing with the past' was both (simultaneously) a recovery project and a means of tran-scendence, the precise nature of these conceptual relationships was still to be *known*. Paradoxically, the moment was one in which the normative was both in the making and evidence that there was *necessary* work to be done.

What was this necessity? What was its precise referent and what was happening within it? This too was a problem, an indication that all was not (yet) new. More precisely, the transition was seen to harbour threats, historical animosities and fears that appeared poised to disrupt the consti-tution of beginning. Most evident in security force demands for indemnity, the problem could not be pigeonholed. Thus, not quite simultaneously, the risks of the past were used to justify both an amnesty and a 'victim-centred' process of truth-seeking.

This solution did not satisfy those who worried that impunity would deepen old wounds and foster the desire for revenge. However, the deal to link amnesty and voice was rendered virtuous and lent significant momentum by a post-amble, written late one night at Kempton Park, which held that the 'secure foundations' to 'transcend' could '*now* be *addressed* on the basis that there is a need for understanding but not for vengeance, a need for reparation but not for retaliation, a need for ubuntu but not for victimisation'.[10] This call for a rhetorical invention of the new contained the political theory that provoked, informed and troubled the TRC. It also confirmed the miraculous quality of the transition, especially if one recalls Hume's reflections as to how miracles push if not exceed the meaning of words and our understanding of how they work to break and bring us into relations.[11] This is not an idealisation. Far too many have criticised the South African transition and the TRC without first pausing to consider the immense pressure involved in the work of having to 'make-it-up-as-one-goes-along'. Transitions do not have blueprints and they don't consolidate to schedule. This is part of their virtue and the energy of their risk.

In the transition's early days, the post-amble was seen to hold and announce a tension between reconciliation and reparation. In its 298 words, the terms stood in ambiguous relation and were constellated with a third – reconstruction – in a way that was not easy to explain.[12] As it appeared, the reparative seemed more of an attitude for change than a concrete process akin to the reconciliation that was to be undertaken through amnesty. Before, during and after the TRC's tenure, uncertainty turned to dispute. Helped by the terms of the 1996 AZAPO judgment, especially Justice Didcott's partial dissent, the post-amble was held up as evidence that reparation was a necessary condition for reconciliation.[13] While contested and disputable, some have claimed, and continue to claim, that this relation is a matter of contract, a potential irony given the Transvaal Provincial Court's 1994 finding about the extra-legal status of the negotiations at the multi-party negotiating process.[14]

Early debates over the TRC raise questions about how to (best) relate reconciliation and reparation. They also underscore that the problem rests heavily on the meaning of these two terms. Exactly what is it that exists or needs to be set into relation? While necessary to avoid working in a vacuum, this definitional work is notoriously difficult. It requires striking a balance between Andre du Toit's good advice to 'use words such as re-conciliation, amnesty and amnesia in their serious sense or not at all', and a critical scrutiny of concepts that does not rule out the serious possibility of their play.[15] Along this middle course, the need is thus not so much singular definition as a consideration of the connotations and discursive operations that are contained and moving within the concepts of recon-ciliation and reparation. With respect to the problem at hand, these 'ostensive definitions' are useful as they illustrate that the relationship between the reconciliatory and the reparative is a double problematic, a matter of how to relate two terms that hold very different senses of what is involved in the task of beginning and sustaining human relationships.[16]

The contingency of language contains a precision capable of invention, one that has the potential to interrupt, create and stabilise the time and ground of action. With respect to reconciliation, this ought not to be forgotten. When they defined reconciliation through amnesty, the framers of South Africa's Interim Constitution recalled if not recollected a problem of definition that runs back to at least 403 BCE.[17] What is reconciliation? In an early and influential discussion about reconciliation in South Africa, Tina Rosenberg proposed a 'definition of true reconciliation' arguing that: 'People are only ready for reconciliation if they are ready to live a normal life in a normal country.'[18] A bit of a hedge, this interpretation leaves us to struggle with the problem of what counts as (making) 'ready'. More precisely, it skirts the paradox that attends the question of reconciliation's definition, the problem of how to define a good which appears at precisely that time (*kairos*) when the grounds of definition are not only unstable but suspect, when the logic and law of identity that backs the power to define what 'is' represents a source of endless violence. Normality is as much reconciliation's provocation as its hope.[19]

Reconciliation opposes the danger of the Word's creation and strives to find within it the basis for a (re)turn to the creativity of words. This challenge to law is fundamental, an attempt to turn the 'causality of fate', the power of law to render life hostile to itself, towards the potential for self-formation in abiding relation to Other.[20] It begins in the experience of *stasis*, a time of 'word-trouble', a moment when the designs of speech conspire only towards identitarian relationships of (mutual) negation.[21] Thus, the potentially least helpful definition of reconciliation is that which holds it out as an 'essentially contented concept'. Reconciliation is precisely otherwise.[22] A good that contests essentialism, it is 'a concept that means beyond itself' and likely 'bars its [own] affirmation in a concept'.[23] This is simply to say that reconciliation endeavours to render things as they are not. Between relationships of (mutual) exclusivity, it attempts to craft a middle ground, a space that does not negate (history's) violence but which gathers it into a shared opposition. In this turn, from enmity to (civic) friendship, reconciliation entails both movement and exchange, a shifting that crafts the common ground needed to tarry. Thus, the most distracting definition of reconciliation is that it is a process. Of course it is. The crucial issue is what constitutes and performs the potential of this process, the capacity of reconciliation to trouble and provide the words needed to interrupt time in the name of a beginning, turn law's justifications of violence towards the grounds of understanding, and open spaces for critical dialogue about the power of dialogue.

Written for the occasion of Nelson Mandela's 85th birthday, Jakes Gerwel's tribute is instructive in this regard. Reflecting on the 'expanding circles of identification' that appear in the 'truthful reliability' of Mandela's stories, Gerwel hints that the fabric of reconciliation is woven partly with threads of speech that are imbued with 'characteristic humility' and textured by the guiding value of 'human solidarity'.[24] In both form and content, the tapestry embodies and performs character, an *ethos* that is not credibility but the undertaking of speech infused with a sense of self-risk, a willingness to relax the certainty of one's own historical commitments and identity in the name of recognising the Other.[25] One of many, Mandela's speech at the start of Parliament's debate over the Promotion of National Unity and Reconciliation Act is a significant example, an address that both subtly directs attention to the importance of 'how' one speaks and contends that the 'majority party (ANC) must have the understanding and humility' to not only hear the 'fears and concerns of minorities' but to go a remarkable step further, and acknowledge the 'sacrifices' that they made during the work of ending apartheid.[26]

In reconciliation's meaning, the line between politics and faith is very thin. This ambiguity is evident in the TRC's Final Report, a text that underscores the difficulties involved in coming to *know* what reconciliation *is*. Its defining hope is that things and relationships might be otherwise in a different way. The practical benefit of its study is thus some understanding of what it means to begin (again). Between the possibilities of memory and the debts of history, what can happen *now*? Such moments are long overdue and anxious. The exhilaration that attends the 'birth of something new on earth' is equally a dire risk: 'A new beginning at an alleged zero point is the mask of strenuous forgetfulness – an effort to which sympathy with barbarism is not extraneous.'[27] In reconciliation, this hope and danger are placed and remain in close relation. With revolutionary ideals, the character of its invention 'remains small'.[28] This is to say that reconciliation abides in the cost of its 'necessary' transgression; the sacrifice of law's identity and identity's laws does not necessarily occur on the altar of justice or rigour. Reconciliation remains open to the need for its own revision. It strives to make something good of contingency while also holding out the possibility that the contingent is itself good for something.

The concept of reparation also sits and moves between past and future.

The term's meaning is perhaps somewhat easier to grasp, especially to the degree that its constitutive operation tends towards an exchange of things more than performances of recognition. However, this distinction is extremely tenuous.[29] It fades altogether if Soyinka is correct when he claims that the reparative contains within it the very problem of the human, the ontological question of how to grasp and redress the denial of humanity.[30] Thus, the call to restore and renew contained in the Latin root *reparo* is not simply the need to roll back the clock but the problem of how to return Being to being. In the midst of reparation, the times must *be* and be *made* otherwise. This simultaneous giving and going (back) is recalled in the Greek *apodosis*, a term that connotes both repair and a rendering by definition. With(in) reparation, there is a presumption for the capacity and need to define. The reparative represents the 'founding' harm, the original referent that marks both the need for redress and delineates the condition to which the repaired are to be returned.[31]

Does this moment exist? Can it? Imaginary or otherwise, it is a hinge of justice, a view or perhaps a haunting of potential deprived, the difference between what might have been and what is. The wound is real, of this there is no question. It is an experience, object and event to which the law's precedent can be gathered and directed.[32] Whereas reconciliation opposes the law in order to fashion the exception to its violence, reparation calls the law out, depending on it to close and mend the violence of its (past) exception.

The TRC recommended reparation through this call to law, setting its need on the grounds of domestic and international jurisprudence and a basic moral obligation. In the Commission's expressed view, reparation marks 'government's obligation to ensure justice to the victims of the past. Stated differently, amnesty without an effective reparation and rehabilitation programme would be a gross injustice and betrayal of the spirit of the Act, the Constitution and the country'.[33] In the name of (re)making what could have been, this claim to reparation has the standing of law and constitutes a (law of) duty to annul harm, return that which has been lost and deter the repetition of criminality. This work is not a move to the 'hazy zone of remorse' but a 'move to the material', a shift from the question of whether apologies for atrocity can ever *be* sincere to the matter of causality, the acknowledgement that harm done necessitates its concrete repair. But then the caveat within the concept appears: (no)thing can make up for the loss; no life can be returned; time will not run backwards; potential cannot be re-realised. Within the promise of repair is the (ontological) certainty of its own breakage.[34] Inevitably, the real must be (re)dressed with the symbolic, of which money, land and shelter are the most material. In reparation, the idea of justice is thus not so much denied as left to stand between these two awkwardly related realms, the symbolic and the material. The flux of *satisfactio* defines reparations. Far from absolute, their value is conditioned by the contingency and limit of human experience in time.[35]

Transitional Terms

In the differences of definition, there are some hints as to how the concepts of reconciliation and reparation are related. Both promise and endeavour to perform a turn, a form of (inter)change, between people and things that are otherwise held to be exclusive. With respect to historical animosity and histories of atrocity, both attempt to undo, to reach through and beyond contradiction in the name of becoming and beginning (again). In this work, each approaches the law from a different stance and attitude. However, such features do not reveal the full picture. In South Africa, the problem is an old one, evident quite clearly, for instance, in the 1985 *Kairos Document*'s questions about whether reconciliation was justifiable if it was not preceded by the justice of reparative atonement.[36] More on our minds, the design and extended debate over the TRC has featured substantial discussion of how these two relational terms can and ought to be related. This discourse is significant both in terms of how it sets reparation before reconciliation and the way in which this prioritisation yields puzzles about the constitution, operation and power of each concept.

In May 1995, Parliament convened its second reading debate on the Promotion of National Unity and Reconciliation Act. Held several months after an extensive public hearings process, then Minister of Justice, Dullah Omar, opened the debate with a speech in which he argued that South Africa needed 'genuine reconciliation' and defined the work of the proposed TRC through a set of goals which did not explicitly include reparation.[37] The omission is surprising and perhaps not given that the legislation on the floor only authorised the Commission to make recommendations about reparation with respect to victims of gross human rights violations. Performing this conditionality to some degree, Omar claimed towards the end of the speech that the Commission's proposed Reparations & Rehabilitation Committee could be 'one of the most important' in the 'overall process of trying to bring about maximum justice for victims, subject to the Constitution and also to national unity and reconciliation'. In short, reparation and reconciliation were related but the terms of this relationship appeared to be mediated by something yet unspoken.[38]

In his contribution to the same debate, Johnny de Lange seemed to draw a relation of distinction between reparation and reconciliation, suggesting that the TRC would be one of several nation-building exercises. According to De Lange, the latter would focus more on the material elements of the transition while the Commission would be geared to redressing the 'psychological devastation of the legacy of apartheid'.[39] For his part, Kader Asmal's speech did not feature discussion of reparation, a noted departure from his previous writings on the matter. For instance, in his highly influential inaugural address at the University of the Western Cape, Asmal argued that the crimes of apartheid demanded 'restitution', and that international law codified the 'duty to pay reparation'. Of many possible forms, the need for such restitution (*Weidergutmachung* – to 'make good again'), he contended, was a crucial lesson of the German experience, a guard against 'collective amnesia' and 'vital to the process of rehabilitation'.[40] Several weeks after Asmal's inaugural address, a condensed and more direct version of the position appeared in South African newspapers. Here, the main contention was that reconciliation could not occur through a declaration of law which did not alter the 'Prospero and Caliban relationship' that sits between 'victim-survivor and the overlord'.[41]

At crucial points in the debate over the TRC's founding law and its mandated work, it is precisely the law that appears between reparation and reconciliation. The tension is subtle, a question of how to relate the standing of the legal obligation to provide reparation and the status of the law in the moment given to reconciliation. The problem is present at creation. In August of 1994, not long after the first draft of the Promotion of National Unity and Reconciliation Act was tabled, Omar addressed Parliament, arguing that apartheid had not only severed the relationship between law, justice and morality but had left in its wake a legitimacy crisis for the law, a deficit that required and justified the work of reconciliation.[42] Momentarily setting aside the argument from international law, Omar's position suggests that the law's standing in transition follows from reconciliation. Echoed in the post-amble of the Interim Constitution, reconciliation is the basis through which to (re)make the power of law, a (meaningful) rule that is implicitly assumed to be present in the call and warrant for reparations. At least publicly, however, there is not significant discussion of this dilemma in the early days of transition, an absence that both reflects the ambiguous legal status of the constitutional negotiations process and counsels caution in drawing too bright a line between events at the Kempton Park negotiations and the TRC.

In the policy-making debate over the TRC, the most common claim about the relationship between reparation and reconciliation is that the former is a prerequisite for the latter. If not first, reparation must certainly appear *with*. Recalling something of Asmal's seminal argument, Father Smangaliso Mkhatshwa made a concise case for this relationship in an address to Parliament on 22 September 1994. Following from an argument about the 'liberal neo-Kantian contract theory on which our new constitution is based', he turned to the matter and conditions of reconciliation, arguing that: 'The question of reconciliation is very important. It is important for us to realise that it is not just a question of bear-hugging, kissing and the shedding of tears. There can be no genuine reconciliation without justice, restoration, and reparation. These are the essential ingredients.'[43]

Echoed frequently in Parliament over the course of the debate on the TRC, this position was both affirmed and amplified somewhat by the Commission when it argued that the 'road to reconciliation' had to run across the terrain of justice. 'Essential to counterbalance amnesty', the TRC claimed that victims had a 'right to reparation' and that 'without adequate reparation and rehabilitation measures, there can be no healing or reconciliation'.[44] In the TRC Report issued in 2003, the Commission also advanced a somewhat broader formula, one in which reconciliation hinged on forms of material reconstruction that would make a 'home for all South Africans'.[45]

Outside the TRC, critics have challenged these positions and questioned whether the Promotion of National Unity and Reconciliation Act and the Commission itself had an adequate approach to reparation. Soyinka, for instance, wonders whether the project overlooked and discounted the 'missing link between Truth and Reconciliation'. Making a strong case, Soyinka argues that reparation is a 'condition of co-existence', a 'memory structure' that must precede reconciliation for the simple reason that the former constitutes the ground, referent and meaning of the latter. Reasoning from an event outside South Africa, he contends, '[R]estitution must first be made. This was the bedrock.'[46] As it feels the past echo in the body, the poetic muse of forgiveness abides in a hope that does not forsake a sense of presumption.

Words hold concepts and enable their (inter)action. Over time, these relationships are heard, become familiar, and make their way towards presumption. The history of this process is the power of common sense, a gathering of meaning that is neither happenstance nor devoid of rules that have a kind of precedential power. In South Africa, the concept of reparations appears to have a certain but also variable priority over reconciliation. In time, process and morality, reparation is *said* repeatedly (by both advocates and critics of the TRC) to come before reconciliation. The form of this relationship is encouraged by a body of international law that delineates the right to repair, calls for the redress of wounds inflicted onto subjected bodies and urges recovery of the dignity lost in the subjections of atrocity. Only then, reconciliation. Viewed rhetorically, this formula constitutes the basis for a claim as to how transitional societies can and should deal with the past. In South Africa, the stakes of this path are heightened both by the connection between reconciliation and a 'forgetting' amnesty in the Interim Constitution's post-amble and by controversy over whether forgiveness is an appropriate trope of the 'new'. Ultimately, however, what is interesting about the case for prioritising reparation over reconciliation is how it yields a theory of *justice* in transition that sometimes overwrites the question of *transitional* justice. Puzzling, the movement held in the adjectival may well matter.

The presumption that reparation should or must precede reconciliation is both comfortable and with significant merit. The work of reparation is not simply a payout but the task of identifying harm and devising avenues for its redress. International law provides a useful set of benchmarks for this work even as some forms of reparation may fulfil its call to duty without the undertaking of trials that may or may not be successful.[47] However, the move to set reparation prior to reconciliation is not without puzzles. In the significant debate that surrounds and follows the creation of the TRC, three of these puzzles appear readily. Alone and together, they prefigure questions about whether the desire to set the reparative first does damage to both its own aspiration for inventiveness and the transformative operations of reconciliation.

First, the claimed priority of reparation may be rooted in an obligation to moral and legal precedent that reconciliation interrupts if not opposes in the name of its (re)making. In the midst of transition, the provision of reparation depends on establishing a case for those obligations that can and must necessarily be fulfilled. In some contrast, the concept of reconciliation appears to open the grounds of transition by calling just this historical necessity into question, asking whether the time for change depends on setting aside the edicts of the timeless – the rules, contents, precedents and duties of law that have been used to sustain the 'causes' which justify violence. While discomforting, this interpretation of reconciliation was evident and important in the start of the 1990 talks-about-talks. Caught in a spiral of conflict, both the ANC and the National Party government agreed to set aside the announced obligations of their own historical commitments and laws in the name of finding common ground. Indeed, each was criticised for this effort, accused of immorality and treachery by some of their own members and constituents. However, the choice was arguably not a flight into raw pragmatism. It was a decision reached at the limit of choice, at a moment when the promise of the moral was the fate of its reduction to physics, the action–reaction of an endless battle that renders moral agency into a hopeless abstraction.

With claims about the necessity of reparation there appear similar problems, ones that are compounded by the severe legitimacy crisis that faces law at the end of apartheid. If it is to do more than invoke law that may or may not be trusted, the provision of reparation in a moment of transition sits in tension with the question of how to resolve what law can be carried forward to the new. More than a matter of 'stability', the issue is how individual human beings stand in time, moving between the law's reparative promise of closure and reconciliation's hope for creativity beyond its fold.[48]

Second, the a priori subject of reparation appears to overwrite something of reconciliation's (relational) object. Linked to the first, the puzzle here revolves partly around how to determine who deserves reparation and what good it might do. In South Africa, this question of desert has been answered partly through the tenets of international human rights law: reparations are available to the victims and immediate 'relatives and dependents' of those who have suffered gross violations of human rights.[49] With this criterion, an individual (or set of individuals) is named, constituted as a subject that has standing for if not a right to reparation. Leaving aside the question of how it relies on doctrines of natural law that have substantial blood on their hands, this international formula sits in significant tension with reconciliation.[50] At some level, the concept of reconciliation is one that opposes and endeavours to turn the constitution of the self-certain subject towards a contingent and constitutive inter-dependence with an Other. For liberalism, this turn marks a sacrifice, a degradation of precisely the sovereign that reconciliation names as an impediment to the formation of human relationships. Classically conceived, reparation tends towards the liberal, embracing a prior 'subject' that does not readily sit with cultural-political discourses of collective subjectivity which, by setting identification over identity, help generate and sustain calls for reconciliation, as opposed to other modes of conflict resolution. If so, the demand for prior reparation leaves the post-amble's call for ubuntu with a deeply uncertain status. Evident in the present dispute between the government and those who have filed suit against inter-national companies who are alleged to have supported the apartheid regime or undertaken 'sanction-busting', the right to repair may narrow debate over the kinds of reparation that are needed in particular contexts. In short, the prior and potentially adversarial logic of reparation may fore-close opportunities in which reconciliation undertakes the recovery, expression and understanding of human interest.[51]

Third, isolated calls for reparation may presuppose the means and meaning of material exchange designed to heal the wounds of the past. At issue: the law's urging of reparation does not always extend to questions of how they can be made (over time). One cost of this gap may be a con-flation of the subsistent and the reparative. Reparations involve more, an ongoing commitment to both recover and cultivate potential beyond the lowest common denominator. If so, they depend on the ability of citizens to express their needs, be heard, and enter into networks that create and support capacity-building. While this expression also may blur the rela-tionship between the individual and the communal, the puzzle here is whether and how reconciliation plays a constitutive role in this work. Atrocity and sustained oppression deter and distort the capacities of expression. The voice is rendered uncertain; meaning comes to embody untruth. The result is that the determination of what counts as reparative may hinge partly on a process of reconciliation in which the capacity to be heard is recovered and the choice to not be heard respected. The prob-lem is particularly evident in controversy over certain types of 'symbolic' reparation, disputes that appear when communities are confronted with the erection of monuments and memorials that have little, exclusive or contrary meaning. In such situations, something is missing, the question of how to facilitate interactions that address and move between the expression of self (interest) and the redress of material need.

The puzzles of priority are neither abstractions nor concrete criticisms. Rather, they underscore that reparation and reconciliation are each directed to the problem of how to 'make good' in the midst of transition. In this effort, Soyinka claims that 'Truth alone is never enough to guarantee reconciliation. It has little to do with crime and punishment but with inventiveness – devising a social formula that would minister to the wrongs of dispossession on the one hand, chasten those who deviate from the human communal order on the other, serve as a criterion for the future conduct of that society, even in time of stress and only then, heal'.[52] It is here that the puzzles interlock. With its hope for inventiveness, the prior reparation is able to 'make' only as it (silently) depends on that which it wants to defer. In a deeply divided society, the 'devising of a social formula' is the question of reconciliation. If more than edict of law, the generative capacity of the reparative comes before the *condition* of reconciliation at the cost of the latter's process, a turn that interrupts the violent time of necessity, constitutes a subject able to stand in relation to history, and supports a system of human exchange that is more meaningful than mechanical. Invention is not fate and (immanent) critique does not root its architecture after the fact.[53] This is to say that the puzzles which follow from the reparative's priority do not call for analytic resolution. They are the calling of a prior question, an invitation, interest and warrant to ask after what stands and moves between reparation and reconciliation. This is the priority, the problem of how their relation of opposition contains the potential of constitutive power.

Terminological Transitions

Reversal is not the answer. The dilemmas at hand are not resolved by putting reconciliation first in the queue. Such a solution risks unearthing reconciliation, setting it on that very groundless ground which was used to warrant apartheid's endless 'promise'.[54] The gesture would also (further) condone turning dialectic into a shouting match; the claim to priority is sometimes a way of avoiding listening. In partial distinction to revolution and incremental reform, the work of transition does not come with a banister. It asks for the faith needed to think and act from an excluded middle in which much more is unsettled than not. Reparation and reconciliation are both ways of reasoning in such moments. They are guides for under-standing the tensions, bridging the divides and moving on the terrain of the between. The reparative and the reconciliatory are not simply goals of transition but contingent expressions and fragile embodiments of its practice. They are themselves transitional concepts, goods that resist *being* pre-thought in isolation and which strive for *becoming* through thought-ful relation. Thus, the resolution of their relative priority may be less important than seeing and asking after the question that sets them into a difficult but also productive relation.

What is the potential for beginning (again)? Held in common, this question stands between reparation and reconciliation. However, each is provoked to a different reply. Sometimes read as contradiction, this incon-gruity is a motive to prioritise, to erect an order that promises to smooth the way forward but which leaves significant puzzles behind. This reaction haunts, making it difficult to approach, let alone plot how reconciliation and reparation make or invent the new. If so, there may be some benefit to holding the tension open, abiding *between* these two concepts in order to grasp better how their relationship appears around particular questions that attend the work of beginning and the ways in which their mutual opposition helps each to constitute the other.

In closing, my aim is to isolate three such questions, problems that demand less of an answer than ongoing practical reflection, a considera-tion of what *happens* during transition and how this work carries on after its alleged conclusion. In short, as echoes of the puzzles that appear with the claimed priority of reparation, the questions at hand ask whether and in what ways transition constitutes a recurring potential to begin.

What is to be made with the power of the past? Reconciliation and repara-tion are related by their opposed conceptions (making) of time, memory and history. For reconciliation, the task is to fashion a present moment in which to stand between past and future. This now–time challenges the terms of (historical) law, naming its promise as *self* defeating. Against the 'causes' of violence, reconciliation is thus a struggle for the memory of contingency, the faith needed to make without the certainty of control or the precedents that sustain states of exception. The suspension of this normality, the creation of an exception to the law's exception, is a begin-ning with a synchronic texture. Deep but not long, the moment of reconciliation turns the *stasis* of law to the *status* needed to oppose and reconstitute its power with that memory which its precedent cannot contain. In the call for reparation, however, the work at hand is to stand between past and future in the name of constituting a movement in the present. In this moment, the struggle is not to interrupt law's endless promise (of continuity) but to realise its declared end. The memory of historical harm is not simply the betrayal of law but the need for its invocation, a cause to (re)implement its (retro)action such that law comes to reverse the effects of its own historical outcome. As precedent thus matters, the time of reparation has a distinctly diachronic quality. It is a beginning in which citizens are (re)turned to the *status* that they deserved before the appearance of *stasis*.

In the midst of transition, the inhumanity of history's law is the justification (by faith) for its release and a (causal) warrant for the exercise of its necessity. For now, reconciliation brackets this past but does so in a manner that reveals its loss(es) as the object of a reparation which must face the question of whether and to what degree the force of law can be assumed and applied without replicating the form of its historical violence. Put differently, reconciliation and reparation each reflect the risk of the other, the dangerous moments of redemptive (sacrificial) action that rise above the grounds of judgement and the judgements of precedent which supplant and sometime deter the constitution of collective action.[55] This double ontological problem is the fraught question of whether 'coming to terms' with the past entails what Christian Lenhardt has called 'anamnestic solidarity'. In its most basic form, the problem posed by Lenhardt is whether the generation which achieves liberation cannot but stand on the backs of those who have suffered previously, reducing them to the raw instruments or means of happiness. The question has provoked substantial debate, much of it appearing over the course of the German *Historikerstreit*.[56] A significant part of the discussion is tied to Walter Benjamin's theory of materialist history, a position which holds that the past is unfinished and that the dead, forgotten in the name of progress, both remain and await redemption. For Benjamin, morality is not enough; history must proceed as a political act of solidarity, one that does fate redemption but struggles to open the past in the name of finding what is '"truly new" in the present'.[57]

The issue is not whether to remember or to forget. Rather, the problem is whether the tension between the reparative and the reconciliatory is a space for asking questions about how best to read history in the name of constituting memory's manifold power. In South Africa, this is a practical problem. Recall how the case for reparation and reconciliation emerged from the need to 'deal with the past'. While both were justified with this idea, each came to place significant pressure on what it meant. In particular, early discussions held that undealt with history was a threat – a wound that would fester, a power that would haunt and a legacy that would encourage vengeance. But, the particular 'force' that sat within and behind these characterisations was left largely unexplained.[58] By design or default, the question of how to deal with the past was framed apart from the issue of whether those called to reconcile and undertake reparation had congruent understandings of how time passes, the ways in which history's laws 'work', what they mean with respect to the present, and what force memory plays in the formation of morality and the practice of justice. In transition, perceived differences regarding the power of the past may well matter.

What different interpretations of history are at play within South Africa's deep division? Broadly speaking, do various forms of African and Afrikaner communalism endow the past, present and future with the same meaning? Do individuals make history or do groups? If both, how? In what ways do damages and wounds carry across time and how does this movement bear on the creation of effective remedies? What lies behind the 1960 cut-off date inscribed by the Promotion of National Unity and Reconciliation Act? While the list can be extended, these questions sit between reparation and reconciliation, basic to the subject and object of each. In some sense, they are prior to decisions about which can and ought to have priority. If the new is given to a 'restored immediateness' that can fund the future through the past, the power of reconciliation and reparation may develop only as they sit together in the name of grappling with what lies in the middle, a potential that moves between history's universal legislations and the energy of its particular manifestations. In short, the tensions between the reparative and the reconciliatory may be resolved at the cost of an opposition which gathers the (ontological) 'explosiveness' of a beginning.[59]

What is the potential of (ex)change? Between reconciliation and reparation there is a shared and difficult promise, a hope for (retro)action, a (re)turn to/of the past that helps make a present for the future. This event is neither an abstract possibility nor a concrete reality. It is rather a form of potential, a making within contingency.[60] This has two implications. First, it means that reconciliation and reparation do not have fixed objects. The power of each to turn one state (of relations or affairs) to another may be variously addressed to alienated individuals, groups, communities and a nation. Thus, the potential of each depends on decisions as to who is in 'need' and what this need entails. Second, potentials are not self-actualising. With respect to reconciliation and reparation, they depend on choices about how to forge relationships and systems of exchange that contain opportunities for (inter)action. As these 'ends' are themselves contingent, the potential of both goods is in some sense the constitution of potentiality.

While these are obvious points, the potential of the reconciliatory and the reparative is frequently explained through accounts that obscure their interdependence. On one side, reconciliation is held out as a creature of the symbolic and the dialogic. Its potential is thought to be actualised in words that give voice to experience, garner acknowledgement and direct animosity towards shared oppositions that allow estranged parties to find common ground. A Word for words, reconciliation turns the power of creation towards the return(s) of creativity. On the other side, reparation is typically held to turn on the exchange of goods that return capacity. The debt paid is not simply a recognition of desert but a way to (re)create the work of life. When set into the context of transition, however, the relationships undertaken through reconciliation appear to constitute the referent for material exchange and the materiality of reparation underpins and supports the capacity for expression. More than truth-finding, reconciliation entails speech that opens and teaches ways of seeing that which requires repair. On the other side of the coin, the provision of material goods may provide the time, energy and resources needed to speak and be heard (more than once).

While the TRC frequently did well to blur the difference between reconciliation and reparation, the results have left many unhappy. Potentials are difficult to fulfil. Their promise beckons expectation that cannot always be realised. With the Commission's *Final Report* now tabled and Parliament resolved to pay a small individual reparation package, the question now is not whether reparation has actually produced reconciliation but whether the potential that sits between them might be relevant to the ongoing work of political-economic development. In this regard, the position offered by Amartya Sen is suggestive. In his work on the controversial connection between material equality, justice and liberty, Sen takes issue with John Rawls' influential view that the provision of a so-called set of primary goods can underpin a just system of resource distribution, one that holds the potential for material equality. In reply, Sen wants to ask 'the equality of what?' and wonders if this conception of justice does not come at the cost of a certain sort of liberty, a concern for the 'constitutive elements of living' that differ between individuals with different capabilities and ways of life.[61] Put otherwise, Sen claims that resource distribution needs to and often does not take into account 'variations in our ability to convert resources into actual freedoms'.[62] Potential matters. In the context of the problem of how to relate reconciliation and reparation, Sen's position highlights that their conceptual interplay may be more important than their relative priority, especially after the former's institutional 'process' has closed up shop and the latter have been 'paid'. Reconciliation is a means of hearing and diagnosing the relative capabilities and conditions that influence what can and cannot be done with reparative goods at the same time that the distribution of such goods allows for assessments as to how and how well reconciliation supports meaningful political-economic engagement. In short, a transition dedicated to 'unity in difference' demands concerted struggle with what remains and moves between people, words and things.[63]

What is the calling of recognition? Reconciliation and reparation appear in the name of both the individual and common good. Reconciliation affords opportunities to fashion the self in relation to Other and to remake the terms of collective-political life. Reparation can give back a sense of self and provide materials needed to rebuild the social-economic fabric of a deeply unequal society. In transition, the work of both is intertwined and ongoing. The relationships developed through the conciliatory do not so much culminate as grow over time, just as the repair of lost opportunity and agency does not occur all at once. However, this open-ended quality contains risk. Reconciliation's promise of harmony may grow less credible as friction endures and as those who have suffered are asked to accept additional burdens. Similarly, the offences that warrant reparation may fade from view, a discounting that can prompt blame and bitter disputes over who owes what to whom and for how long. In both cases, these problems are heightened to the degree that reconciliation and reparation operate outside the state's law, to the extent that 'real' reconciliation cannot be demanded and legally authorised payments bring less than full satisfaction.

The reparative and reconciliatory depend on a sense of obligation that cannot be mandated or legislated. In practice, as calls to duty do not always or even readily translate into action, this means that both goods struggle with the problem of voluntarism. In the midst of conflict without definitive end, individuals may perceive reconciliation and reparation projects as unreasonable and they may abstain from participating on the grounds that such initiatives run contrary to their own (self) interest. To turn the exclusive to the inclusive, reconciliation asks for a sacrifice, an unwarranted gift in which the causes of history have to be set aside, the force of law relaxed and the certainty of identity rendered contingent. For its part, the reparative may request that those in the greatest need accept something less than full recovery. Much more importantly, it depends on a contentious category of people, the 'beneficiaries' of the past system, to accept responsibility for and undertake the redress of wounds that they did not – strictly speaking – inflict.[64] In the minds of this constituency, such work may appear unjustified and thus easily dismissed. In South Africa, the dramatic unwillingness of the business community to return at least something of what has been made on the backs of black labour and the bitter dispute that followed the launch of the 'Home for All' campaign underscore that, as the motive for reparation and reconciliation does not occur 'naturally', strong appeals to duty may both fail to overcome 'rational' interest and provoke (re)balkanisation.

The promise of reconciliation and reparation programmes hinges on their ability to create compelling incentives and sustained motivation for the (ex)change of exclusivity.[65] Such work may benefit as the tension between reconciliation and reparation is not resolved but used to support a 'struggle for recognition'. However, while popular to the point where it connotes nearly all manner and mode of post-traumatic remedy, recognition is not a cure-all. The concept implies a difficult process, the terms of which may not always be helpful in understanding the situation in South Africa.[66] Accordingly, my suggestion here is not that recognition is a means of transcendence or healing (in isolation) but that it may develop from the tension between reconciliation and reparation in order to constitute and centre a struggle over what these concepts mean, who is and ought to be implicated in their operation, and what good they might serve.

Struggles for recognition can begin when social or public goods are prioritised in a manner that produces structural alienation and perceptions of exclusion. Between reconciliation and reparation, this tension is compound: the announced priority of reparation has left eligible individuals to wonder why its necessity is not reflected in policy and rendered those who have the capacity to pay defensive about whether they have a place in the new order. The racial dimension of the problem heightens the stakes. Read together, this dissatisfaction constitutes a potentially shared opposition, a basis for asking whether and how expressions of self-interest comport with announced views of collective life. Proceeding within contradiction, recognition struggles are events that reveal tensions between what people claim to value and what they say that they are willing to do. Thus, they offer less outright agreement than a space in which to dispute and (re)make socio-political norms. Outside the law, this work has a significant precedent in South Africa: the talk about talks. After the TRC, this benchmark is worth remembering, a moment when struggle immanently turned interests that contained the potential for (endless) violence towards the question of how to create (inter)action that would bridge the transitional demands of identity (re)formation and the creation of (re)formative identifications. A key element of recognition struggles, this capacity to create, ask, reply to and sometimes refuse questions may be a crucial element of beginning. Mixing up things and people, questions have the potential to set meaning into movement. Their expression can constitute a willingness to listen and demonstrate a desire to hear an Other's truth. Apartheid thus deterred them, fearful of their outcome – metaphor. This is a legacy that continues. At the end of the day, there is no satisfactory answer to the problem of how to motivate reconciliation and reparations. But this needs to be put explicitly on the table in a way that does not replicate identitarian debates of old and which does not use the 'legitimacy' of governance to deter the practice and accounting of constitutive power.[67] Between reconciliation and reparation, the struggle for recognition has more to do with the appearance of relational questions than definitive answers to the question of their relationship.

Coda

In the midst of questions, the terms of closure are somewhat elusive. Or perhaps, illusive. The line is a fine one, a marker of the difference between a potential that supports beginning and one that promises endlessly. With reparation and reconciliation, this tension may well be definitive. Certainly, it is a problem that is found and held between them. The relationship between reparation and reconciliation appears in the question of how to make the relational, the gestures, ideas and structures that join and bind, that afford understanding but which exceed the terms of knowledge. What *is* a relationship? Our inability to answer this question conclusively is the impetus to prioritise. The vulnerability felt in ambiguity is a reason to undertake the deterrence of its exploitation. But the risk is also an opportunity, a moment in which to make things otherwise in a different way. In short, reparation and reconciliation contain the ambivalence of beginning. Between them, as the work of law stays behind and the hope of faith looks beyond, there is both a need to pursue that transitional justice which can lend form to change and a call to abide in the time of the transitional, a duration of power that questions, upsets and (re)constitutes the meaning of the just.

What do reconciliation and reparation mean? What do they mean in relation? Now, the question presented by these questions is what they might yet reveal about the movement and potential of a transition that continues. As they intersect, diverge and constitute one another, the ongoing work of reconciliation and reparation may require a relational *perspective* that resists the vacuum of critique in isolation and a *relational* perspective which affords time and space to question, to ask after the decisive in a non-definitive way. This work is particularly important given that the reparative and the reconciliatory are not the only tropes at work on the South African landscape. The constellation continues to shift and complicate itself. The lights of reparation and reconciliation cross those of reconstruction, amnesty and truth. There are (still) more questions than answers. Not (yet) a cause for despair, it is worth recalling Gadamer's view of such moments:

> *The voice that speaks to us from the past — whether text, work, trace — itself poses a question and places our meaning in openness. In order to answer the question put to us, we the interrogated must ourselves begin to ask questions.*[68]

With the question, there is a potential for history-making. In this beginning, words of transition matter and they may well have matter. This is true for reconciliation and reparation, even as the formulas that swirl around and link them do not add up. A motive to question, the disparity is a priority and a limit of the same: the imperative implied in 'what is to be done?' cannot be severed from the problem of how to make and agree on norms of 'doing'. What can be(come) between us? Whether new or old, democracy consolidates (excludes) this question of the middle at the cost of precisely those relationships that contain the potential to begin (again).

Notes

1   The phrase 'middle time' is Piet Meiring's. See Piet Meiring, 'The *Baruti* versus the Lawyers: The Role of Religion in the TRC Process', in *Looking Back, Reaching Forward: Reflections on the Truth and Reconciliation Commission of South Africa*, eds. C. Villa-Vicencio and W. Verwoerd (Cape Town: UCT Press, 2000), 123-133. For a more expansive discussion of the temporal operations of transition see Hannah Arendt, *On Revolution* (New York: Viking Press, 1965).

2   Kader Asmal, 'Victims, Survivors and Citizens – Human Rights, Reparations, and Reconciliation', inaugural lecture, University of the Western Cape, 25 May 1992. Carried into the TRC and evident in the Commission's call for South Africans to create and sustain 'cultures of debate', the call for engaged speech was evident and explicit in the early days of transition.

3   The point of becoming is to escape the fate of the sovereign. Too many have presumed that 'mere speech' is best stripped from the realm of politics and placed too much faith in law's assurance that the ambiguities of language do not cloud the certainty of its justice. In transition, if at all, neither view will suffice. In the tense now–time that marks transition, the words that forge the moral and political relationships which join and stand between human beings must be invented, frequently by salvaging the capacity to speak and the truth of expression from the lies and distortions of what has (not) been said before. This problem of relearning how to undertake the speech of truth has been well and elegantly treated by Vaclav Havel in 'The Power of the Powerless', in *Without Force or Lies: Voices from the Revolution of Central Europe in 1989–1990*, ed. W. Brinton, trans. P. Wilson (San Francisco: Mercury House, 1990), 43-127. In the context of South Africa, see Deborah Posel, 'The Language of Domination, 1978-1983', in *The Politics of Race, Class and Nationalism in Twentieth Century South Africa*, eds. Shula Marks and Stanley Trapido (London: Longman, 1987), 439.

4   Desai treats these issues in stark and revealing terms. See Ashwin Desai, *We Are the Poor: Community Struggles in Post-Apartheid South Africa* (New York: Monthly Review Press, 2002). A broader discussion appears in Neville Alexander's recent work. See Neville Alexander, *An Ordinary Country* (Pietermaritzburg: University of Natal Press, 2003).

5   This argument has been made in a variety of contexts, including the debate over reparation. Several analysts have argued that the political economy of the transition was such that far more attention was paid to its symbolic dimensions than the need to remake systems and lines of resources distribution. Ingrid Woolard thus claims that the transition was such that the coming of 'black rule' did little to offset 'white power'. See Ingrid Woolard, 'The Extent of Poverty and Inequality', in *Creating Action Space:*

The Challenge of Poverty and Democracy in South Africa, ed. Conrad Barberton (Cape Town: Institute for Democracy in South Africa, 1998), 13-39. Hein Marais' work marks an extended and more nuanced consideration of these problems, one that has been supplemented recently by Sampie Terreblanche's expansive work on income inequality in South Africa. See Hein Marais, *South Africa: Limits to Change – The Political Economy of Transition* (London: Zed Books, 1998); Sampie Terreblanche, *A History of Inequality in South Africa, 1652–2002* (Durban: Natal University Press, 2003).

6 Quoted in Lyn Graybill, *Truth and Reconciliation in South Africa: Miracle or Model?* (Boulder: Lynne Rienner, 2002), 154.

7 SAPA, 'Government Opposed to Apartheid Lawsuits', *Mail and Guardian*, 27 August 2003, electronic edition <URL:www.mg.co.za>. NA, 'Mandela Criticises Apartheid Lawsuits', *Mail and Guardian*, 25 August 2003, electronic edition.

8 Most notably, the idea plays a central role in the conference held by Justice in Transition in February 1994. See Alex Boraine, Janet Levy, Ronel Scheffer, eds., *Dealing with the Past: Truth and Reconciliation in South Africa* (Cape Town: Institute for Democracy in South Africa, 1994).

9 Essential reading, these are only a handful of the functions and outcomes that were attributed to the TRC during Parliament's second reading debate over the Promotion of National Unity and Reconciliation Bill. A gloss of the debate reveals that there are over 50 different explanations of what the Commission could and would do (see *Debates of the National Assembly, Second Session – First Parliament, Republic of South Africa*, 17 May 1995, 1339-1442). The list grows if one includes statements and testimony heard in the public hearings convened by the Portfolio Committee on Justice. In Parliament, while some heralded the Commission as a unique experiment that would make good on the post-amble's call to bridge past and future, others contended that the legislation was 'conceived and born in sin', created behind closed doors in Cape Town's southern suburbs and promised only division. For the latter position, see J. W. Maree, *Debates of the National Assembly, Second Session – First Parliament, Republic of South Africa*, 17 May 1995, 1394-6.

10 With the emphases added, these words are found in the post-amble or epilogue of the 1993 Interim Constitution (Constitution of the Republic of South Africa, Act 200 of 1993, Chapter 15, following 251), a text that closed with a call for reconciliation that required Parliament to legislate the 'mechanisms, criteria and procedures, including tribunals, if any', of an amnesty. The post-amble is thus one key factor in the development of the TRC. However, it is interesting to note that 'truth' does not appear in the text, an omission that speaks to a debate after its writing and which also suggests that Soyinka may be overreading the underlying justification for the Commission when he reduces the effort to 'Truth as prelude to reconciliation'. See Wole Soyinka, *The Burden of Memory, The Muse of Forgiveness* (New York: Oxford University Press, 1999), 13.

11 David Hume, *Of Miracles* (London: Open Court Press, 1985). There is work that remains on whether and how the South African transition marked a miracle. The term is often used in a cursory way or confined to theological discussions. Emmanuel Levinas's observation that the miracle is the 'beginning of thought or experience' underscores the potentially larger stakes of the issue. See Emmanuel Levinas, 'The *I*

and the Totality,' in *Entre Nous* (New York: Columbia University Press, 1998), 16.

12 The distinction between reconstruction and reparation is not one that I am able to address here in detail. On both a cursory and close reading, the post-amble appears to lay greater stress on reconstruction, coupling the term to reconciliation. By contrast, the term 'reparation' plays a somewhat lesser role in the text, a counterpart to 'retaliation'. The matter is debatable and has been important in the controversy over the government's approach to reparation, especially as it has appeared to favour collective reconstruction projects over individual reparation. At a larger level, the question may be whether reconstruction was intended as the economic correlate of reconciliation.

13 Justice Didcott's opinion is both a concurrence and a slight dissent, one that appears to suggest that an amnesty which relieves victims of their constitutional rights to pursue remedies in the courts is justifiable to the degree that it offers 'some *quid pro quo* for the loss'. However, this finding is prefaced by an acknowledgement that no such guarantee is present in the Promotion of National Unity and Reconciliation Act. See *AZAPO et al. v. President of the Republic, et al.*, 25 July 1996, par. 60-66. Reprinted at: <http://www.doj.gov.za/trc/legal/azapo.htm>. For additional commentary on the challenge see Jeremy Sarkin, 'The Trials and Tribulations of South Africa's Truth and Reconciliation Commission', *South African Journal on Human Rights* 12 (1996): 617-640; Peter Parker, 'The Politics of Indemnities, Truth Telling and Reconciliation: Ending Apartheid without Forgetting', *Human Rights Law Journal* 17 (30 April 1996): 1-13.

14 See the decision in *Government of the Self-Governing Territory of KwaZulu v. Mahlangu and Another*, Transvaal Provincial Division, 1994 (1) South Africa 626.

15 Andre du Toit, 'South African Response', in Boraine, Levy, Scheffer, *Dealing with the Past*, 133.

16 Ludwig Wittgenstein, *Philosophical Investigations*, trans. G. E. Anscombe (no publication data available), *14–43;* Ludwig Wittgenstein, *The Blue and the Brown Books* (New York: Harper Torchbooks, 1960), 25-30.

17 Following the rule of the so-called Thirty Tyrants in 403 BCE, the citizens of Athens undertook a process of reconciliation that included an amnesty. In the context of the situation in South Africa, I have examined this event elsewhere. See Erik Doxtader, 'Easy to Forget or Never (Again) Hard To Remember? History, Memory and the "Publicity" of Amnesty', in *The Provocations of Amnesty: Memory, Justice and Impunity*, eds. C. Villa-Vicencio and E. Doxtader (Cape Town: David Philip, 2003), 126-131. The larger question, however, has not been examined in significant detail; that is, how the dominant interpretations of reconciliation in South Africa build and deviate from the concept's historical meaning in the fields of philosophy, theology and politics. For one brief but important treatment of the issue, see Itumeleng Mosala, 'The Meaning of Reconciliation: A Black Perspective', *Journal of Theology for Southern Africa* 59 (1987): 19-25.

18 Tina Rosenberg, 'Latin America', in Boraine, Levy, Scheffer, *Dealing with the Past*, 67.

19 A more detailed consideration of the difficulties that attend the definition of reconciliation can be found in Erik Doxtader, 'Reconciliation: A Rhetorical Concept/ion', *Quarterly Journal of Speech* 89 (2003): 267-292.

20 This notion is developed by the young Hegel. The central point is that reconciliation proceeds against the law (of identity) in the name of its (re)constitution on the grounds of identification. See G. W. F. Hegel, 'The Spirit of Christianity and Its Fate', in *On*

Christianity: Early Theological Writings, trans. T. M. Knox (New York: Harper, 1948).

21 This interpretation of *stasis* is developed in Barbara Cassin, 'Politics of Memory: On Treatments of Hate', *The Public-Javnost: Journal of the European Institute for Communication and Culture* VIII (2001): 9-22.

22 For the original position, see W. B. Gallie, 'Essentially Contested Concepts', *Proceedings of the Meeting of the Aristotelian Society* 56 (1956): 167-198. There are a number of important commentaries on Gallie's argument. For two that are relevant to the matter at hand, see Eugene Garver, 'Rhetoric and Essentially Contested Arguments', *Philosophy and Rhetoric* 11 (1978): 156-172; Andrew Mason, 'On Explaining Political Disagreement: The Notion of an Essentially Contested Concept', *Inquiry* 33 (1990): 81-98.

23 Adorno is relentless on this point. See Theodor Adorno, *Negative Dialectics*, trans. E. B. Ashton (Continuum: New York, 1973), 145, 160.

24 Jakes Gerwel, 'The Leader Who Held It All Together', *Madiba at 85: A Celebration, Cape Times* 18 July 2003, 10.

25 With respect to the rhetorical practice of reconciliation, I have developed this sense of character elsewhere. See Erik Doxtader, 'Making History in a Time of Transition: The Rhetorical Occasion, Constitution, and Representation of South African Reconciliation', *Rhetoric and Public Affairs* 4 (2001): 223-260; for a more general view see Patchen Markell, 'Tragic Recognition: Action and Identity in Antigone and Aristotle', *Political Theory* 31 (2003): 6-38.

26 In this respect, the speech is both a performance and advocacy of reconciliation. See Nelson Mandela, *Debates of the National Assembly*, Second Session – First Parliament, 17 May 1995, 1349-50. In theology, the idea of *kenosis* is sometimes used to address this operation. With respect to reconciliation, it connotes an outpouring (of self) – for no good reason – and the announcement of a Word that beckons words. Rendered secular, the gift is not necessarily forgiveness or even love, except as the latter is understood as a dialogic event in which the self stands against law in the name of speaking *to* an Other with whom they are deeply alienated. A number of critics have claimed that the TRC itself introduced a discourse of forgiveness into the transition. This claim is dubious. See Dullah Omar, 'Introduction', in *Truth and Reconciliation Commission* (Rondebosch: Justice in Transition on behalf of the Ministry of Justice, 1995), 3. In this volume, Fiona Ross and Pamela Reynolds make an important observation on this point as it relates to different ways of translating 'reconciliation'.

27 Respectively, see Arendt, *On Revolution*, 207-13; Adorno, *Negative Dialectics*, 71.

28 The phrase is Heidegger's, one that is developed richly in George Steiner, *Grammars of Creation* (New Haven: Yale University Press, 2002).

29 One issue that appears at this juncture is the way in which the meaning of reparation is audience-dependent, contingent on expressions from individuals or groups as to what they believe would serve to repair the harm done. In the context of the TRC, this is evident in the testimony of some individuals who claim that symbolic forms of recognition are desired and appropriate. The extent to which the law deems this a 'valid' reparation is difficult to assess and outside the bounds of the present essay.

30 Soyinka finds the problem in slavery, asking 'What is slave? And to *begin* with, what humanity is it?' (emphasis added). Reflected also in the wake of the Shoah, the question

of how to begin in the (continuing) midst of inhumanity – the cessation of 'force' is not the end of the violence – this raises fundamental questions regarding how being can stand, come to standing in relation to truth. See Giorgio Agamben, *Remnants of Auschwitz: The Witness and the Archive,* trans. Daniel Heller-Roazen (New York: Zone Books, 1999).

31 For the law, this definitional work is conceived as the assessment of 'desert', an indication both of harm done and the necessity of punishment or at least restitution. The issue is central in the debate over whether and how to grant reparations for slavery. See, for instance, Jill Frank, 'Democracy and Distribution: Aristotle on Just Desert', *Political Theory* 26 (1998): 784–802; Human Rights Watch, 'An Approach to Reparations', 19 July 2001.

32 Others in this volume have detailed the legal definitions and forms of reparation. I will not rehearse them here.

33 TRC, TRC Report, Vol. 6, (Pretoria: RSA, 2003), 110.

34 This raises the question of whether certain kinds of revolution might constitute the capacity for a self-reparation that would actually 'reoccupy' the past. Perhaps more important, there is the problem of whether reparation thus (re)subjects the victim to their own wounds, an issue that has been raised with respect to the prolonged wait that South African victims have had to endure for anything but short-term compensation.

35 Paul Griseri's discussion is useful on this point, a consideration of the reparative as something that entails the restoration of rules for collective behaviour and development that command 'assent'. See Paul Griseri, 'Punishment and Reparation', *The Philosophical Quarterly* 35: 141, 408.

36 The Kairos Theologians, *The Kairos Document: Challenge to the Church,* 2nd ed. (Grand Rapids: Eerdmans, 1986).

37 Precisely, Dullah Omar contended, 'The commission is designed to realize the following goals: Firstly, it should obtain an account of the methods, policies, and causes of human rights violations. Second, it must attempt to explain the causes of such violations and their consequences for the victims, their relatives, and society. Thirdly, it must facilitate the granting of amnesty to persons who make a full disclosure of offences associated with political objectives, and to restore the human and civil dignity of victims by granting them an opportunity to relate their own accounts of the violations of which they are the victims. Fourthly, it must recommend legal and administrative measures in order to prevent the future commission of human rights violations. Fifthly, a report must be compiled which will provide as comprehensive an account as possible of the events and circumstances of past human rights violations.' See Dullah Omar, *Debates of the National Assembly,* Second Session – First Parliament, Republic of South Africa, 17 May 1995, 1344.

38 Similarly, Antjie Krog writes, 'The Reparation and Rehabilitation Committee could make or break the Truth Commission. It will help little if the transgressors walk away with amnesty, but the victims, who bear the appalling costs of human rights abuses, experience no restitution. No gesture of recognition or compensation.' See Antjie Krog, *Country of My Skull: Guilt, Sorrow, and the Limits of Forgiveness in the New South Africa* (New York: Random House, 1998), 250. It is interesting how this claim appears in the midst of Krog's chapter on how the Truth Commission 'gets to all of us', an

expression of the stress and unravelling induced by its proceedings and the pressure to get the formulas right.

39 Johnny de Lange, *Debates of the National Assembly*, Second Session – First Parliament, Republic of South Africa, 17 May 1995, 1431. The speech is a further illustration of the difficulties involved in crafting a meaningful connection between the ideas of reconciliation, reconstruction and reparation.

40 Asmal, 'Victims, Survivors and Citizens', 16-17.

41 Kader Asmal, 'Sins of Apartheid Cannot be Ignored', *Evening Post*, 8 June 1992, n.p. In the April 2003 debate over the *TRC Final Report*, Asmal brought the matter explicitly to reconciliation, arguing that 'true reconciliation needs to recognize the necessity for redress', a corrective action that requires 'reparations for individuals to be communally balanced against other state obligations for reconstruction'.

42 This argument appears repeatedly over the course of the debate over whether and how to create a TRC. Parts of it are present in Asmal's early claims about the need to avoid 'Nuremberg-style' trials in favour of a reconciliation process that would bring both acknowledgement and accountability. In the second reading debate, Mac Maharaj makes an explicit case for reconciliation as a way of (re)making and (re)legitimising law. See Mac Maharaj, *Debates of the National Assembly*, Second Session – First Parliament, Republic of South Africa, 17 May 1995, 1431.

43 Father Smangaliso Mkhatshwa, *Debates of the National Assembly*, 22 September 1994, 3077.

44 TRC, *Final Report, Vol. 5*, 170. With respect to reparation, the Promotion of National Unity and Reconciliation Act called for the TRC to formulate recommendations with 'regard to the granting of reparation to victims or the taking of other measures aimed at rehabilitating and restoring the human and civil dignity of victims'.

45 TRC, *Final Report, Vol. 1*, 110.

46 Soyinka, *Burden*, 35, 81-2. In this sense, Soyinka's view that reparation is a structure of memory deserves serious consideration: 'Reparations, then, as a structure of memory and critique, may be regarded as a necessity for the credibility of Eurocentric historicism, and a corrective for its exclusionist worldview' (*Burden*, 39). The argumentation about the memory structure of reparations is also present in the TRC's *Final Report, Vol. 6*, 139.

47 This argumentation forms an important element of Ismail Mahomed's finding in the AZAPO case (see esp. paragraphs 22-32). As well, during the development of the Promotion of National Unity and Reconciliation Act, Dullah Omar noted on a number of occasions that South Africa would not be beholden to the edicts of international law but would take their lessons in relation to the situation within the country.

48 Recalling Didcott's findings in the AZAPO case, the *quid pro quo* solution to this problem may be only partially convincing. In it, the law's dependence on the contract remains and goes unscrutinised. For Walter Benjamin, this remnant stood as precedent for that legal and extra-legal violence which deterred the development of conciliatory speech. See Walter Benjamin, *Critique of Violence. Reflections: Essays, Aphorisms, Autobiographical Writings*, trans. Edmund Jephcott (New York: Schocken Books, 1986). The distinctions drawn by Benjamin have been subject to significant debate, particularly as they bear on the problem of how to undertake the transition

work of constitution-building. For a respective objection and extension of Benjamin's position see Jacques Derrida, 'Force of Law', *Cardozo Law Review* 11 (1990) and Giorgio Agamben, *Homo Sacer: Sovereign Power and Bare Life*, trans. Daniel Heller-Roazen (Palo Alto: Stanford University Press, 1990).

49   TRC, *Final Report, Vol. 5*, 176.

50   For an important and elegant gloss of international law's history see Sven Lindqvist, *Exterminate All the Brutes* (New York: Granta, 1997).

51   This intersects the problem of what ubuntu means in the context of the post-amble and the degree to which it shapes both the transition and the cultures within it. The matter is the subject of a heated and ongoing debate. However, it is interesting to see how Kader Asmal's early 1992 definition of reparation, one that stressed the need to tack between the individual and the collective, did not get fully or clearly carried through the writing of the Promotion of National Unity and Reconciliation Act. Additionally, there is the question of whether a liberal and adversarial framework for reparation could cope with harm done before 1960, a period in which the problem of the colonial and a 'colonialism of a special type' occupies a more central position on the political stage and in popular memory.

52   Soyinka, *Burden*, 44.

53   This is a significant source of puzzlement in Soyinka's account of the TRC, the fact that much of his analysis proceeds largely at the level of the impressionistic and forgoes a close consideration of the actual arguments that were made during the development of the Commission. There is some irony to this given the stress he places on the need to undertake reparation that pays detailed attention to the harms of history.

54   This refers to the fact the Dutch Reformed Church repeatedly defended 'separate development' on the grounds that it would lead to reconciliation in the next life. See, for instance, NGK – General Synod, *Human Relations and the South African Scene in Light of the Scripture* (Cape Town, 1974).

55   For a detailed discussion of the problems that come with acting and judging in transition see J. B. Bernstein, 'Confession and Forgiveness: Hegel's Poetics of Action', in *Beyond Representation: Philosophy and Poetic Imagination*, ed. R. Eldridge (Cambridge: Cambridge University Press, 1996), 34–65.

56   Christian Lenhardt, 'Anamnestic Solidarity: The Proletariat and its Manes', *Telos* No. 25 (Fall, 1975), 136. For a discussion of the idea in the context of South Africa, see Pieter Duvenage, 'The Politics of Memory and Forgetting after Auschwitz and Apartheid,' RAU Seminar Paper, 2002/8. Reprinted at URL: <http://general.rau.ac.za/sociology/duvenage.pdf>. For extended treatments of the concept see Max Pensky, *Melancholy Dialectics: Walter Benjamin and the Play of Mourning* (Amherst: University of Massachusetts Press, 1993); Jurgen Habermas, 'Israel or Athens? Where does Anamnestic Solidarity Belong?', in *Religion and Rationality: Essays on Reason, God and Modernity* (Cambridge: MIT Press, 2002), 129–39; Helmut Peukert, *Science, Action and Fundamental Theology: Toward a Theology of Communicative Action*, trans. James Bohman (Cambridge: MIT Press, 1984).

57   Walter Benjamin, 'Theses on a Philosophy of History', in *Reflections: Essays, Aphorisms, and Autobiographical Writings* (New York: Harcourt Brace, 1978); Peter Osborne, 'Small-Scale Victories, Large-Scale Defeats: Walter Benjamin's Politics of Time', in

Destruction and Experience: Walter Benjamin's Philosophy, eds. Andrew Benjamin and Peter Osborne (Manchester, UK: Clinamen Press, 1978), 80-90. The most famous criticism of Benjamin's position was issued by Horkheimer who argued in a letter to his friend that history is closed and Benjamin's position represented an ill-conceived turn to theology. In South Africa, a practical example of the issue is whether and how harm passes across generations with respect to the need and duration of affirmative action policy. Along a similar track, the problem can be approached through the question of how the past can come to voice, particularly when those who survive testify in a manner that can only (but perhaps must) represent those who did not. The symbolic power of such testimony is thus not without a materialist dimension, particularly to the degree that it immanently details the unfolding force of history with respect to the documents of present culture that express and hold atrocity. For important treatments of this problem see Agamben, *Remnants*; Fiona C. Ross, *Bearing Witness: Women and the Truth and Reconciliation Commission in South Africa* (London: Pluto Press, 2003).

58 One curious manifestation of this neglect was that those named as victims, people characterised as powerless and in desperate need of reparation, were made to hold the banner of a revolt that would occur if such benefits did not appear.

59 Benjamin, *Theses*, 262-3.

60 Treated extensively by Aristotle in his metaphysics, the concept of 'potential' (*dunamis*) has been the subject of substantial contemporary attention. See, for instance, Agamben, *Homo Sacer*, 39-48. There is a key distinction to be drawn between potential and possibility. The former contains the capacity not to become; within themselves, potentials contain the terms of their own negation. This means that a potential is not a hypothetical or an endless projection or deferral towards the future. This risk is underestimated somewhat by Alex Boraine. See Alex Boraine, 'The Language of Potential', in *After the TRC: Reflections on Truth and Reconciliation in South Africa*, eds. Wilmot James and Linda van de Vijver (Cape Town: David Philip, 2000), 81.

61 He adds, 'Equality of freedom to pursue our ends cannot be generated by equality in the distribution of primary goods. We have to examine interpersonal variations in the transformation of primary goods (and resources more generally) into respective capabilities to pursue our ends and objectives.' See Amartya Sen, *Inequality Reexamined* (Cambridge: Harvard University Press, 1992), 87.

62 Sen, *Inequality*, 85.

63 For a consideration of this issue in the South African context, see Steven Friedman, 'Too Little Knowledge is a Dangerous Thing: South Africa's Bargained Transition, Democratic Prospects, and John Rawls' Veil of Ignorance', *Politikon* 25 (1998): 57-80. In debt to Georg Lukacs' claim that the relations of production are shaped by forces of political enlightenment, Jurgen Habermas has argued that historical materialism remains critical only insofar as it concedes that the relationship between base and superstructure is subject to intense political mediation. Blind to the 'sociotechnical' manipulations that sustain modern institutions, 'people's capitalism' forgets that the ability to author history, work that promises both justice and equality, entails a process of collective will-formation in which norms of exchange and resource distribution emerge from (public) deliberations that do not reduce the human condition to an interest in production. See Jurgen Habermas, *Theory and Practice*, trans. John Viertel (Boston: Beacon Press, 1973), 196.

64 Of particular interest is the dynamic that follows when alleged beneficiaries use the standards of law to rebut complicity but then also appeal for the necessity of amnesty in the name of reconciliation. The tension apparent in this movement inside and outside of law may be a basis for the sorts of recognition-oriented questions discussed below.

65 In the early transition, Wilmot James described this problem as a need to undertake a 'campaign of publicity'. The phrase is apt with respect to the problem of how state and quasi-juridical institutions can promote reconciliation initiatives.

66 At base, the problem that appears in contemporary literature on recognition is a presumption for a strong sense of given or authentic identity. As it thus remains tied to the founding presumptions of the liberal, such an identity politics may not only confound the proposed struggle but also run somewhat counter to the historical situation in South Africa. For a discussion of the general dilemma, see Drucilla Cornell and Sara Murphy, 'Anti-Racism, Multiculturalism and the Ethics of Identification', *Philosophy and Social Criticism* 28 (4) 419-449. However, in an important essay, Andre du Toit has examined how the TRC relied on recognition as a kind of root metaphor. See Andre du Toit, 'The Moral Foundations of the South African TRC: Truth as Acknowledgement and Justice as Recognition', in *Truth v. Justice: The Morality of Truth Commissions*, eds. Robert Rotberg and Dennis Thompson (Princeton: Princeton University Press, 2000), 122-40. In drawing from the work done by Axel Honneth (Axel Honneth, *The Struggle for Recognition: The Moral Grammar of Social Conflicts*, trans. Joel Anderson (Boston: MIT Press, 1997)), Du Toit's work makes a careful case for how certain interpretations of recognition figure the South African transition.

67 This double problem can be seen very clearly in the ongoing debate between President Thabo Mbeki and Tony Leon over the politics of race and opposition. The larger issue is how to plot and understand the development of 'constitutive power'. For an important treatment of the issue that is relevant to the South African situation, see Agamben, *Homo Sacer*, 39-48.

68 Hans-George Gadamer, *Truth and Method*, 2d ed. (New York: Continuum, 1994), 374.

9

Out of the Crooked Timber of Humanity:

Humanising Rights in South Africa

Mieke Holkeboer

The compromise that emerged out of South Africa's political settlement – grounded in the 1993 Interim Constitution's Epilogue[1] and interpreted by the subsequent Promotion of National Unity and Reconciliation Act – has been far more complex and agonising (if no less miraculous) than would have been suggested by the parade of praise delivered by international media during coverage of the Truth and Reconciliation Commission (TRC) hearings. Ten years after the adoption of the Interim Constitution and its controversial 'sunset clause' and just five years after the TRC's submission of its *Final Report*, the moral, political and economic complexity of this compromise continues; the truth and reconciliation *process* continues.[2]

Others in this volume have focused more concretely on the meaning of reparation and responsibility as inscribed within the truth and reconciliation process and what sort of moral map this provides for South Africa in the months and years ahead.[3] This chapter has a different set of questions in mind; looking outward to the international community, it considers the ongoing truth and reconciliation process in South Africa within the context of the modern human rights regime. For this truth and reconciliation process – from the negotiated settlement to the present debate about reparation policy – constitutes a controversial interpretation of human rights that has been under-explored. Who, for example, took note when human rights giant Amnesty International (AI) quietly and without fanfare *opposed* the TRC process? What was at stake in what has been described as the gradual marginalisation of human rights groups from the TRC process? And how can we understand present tensions between victims rights groups and their opponents in the reparation debates?

The point of raising these tensions is not to pit 'reconciliation' against 'human rights' but to explore South Africa's truth and reconciliation process as a human rights interpretation in its own right – one that might shed light on some of the tensions and paradoxes inherent in human rights itself and, therein, offer insights that the modern human rights regime would do well to consider for its evolving understanding. With these goals in mind, this chapter appears in three parts. First, I will lay out in greater detail some of the tensions that have arisen between human rights groups and the truth and reconciliation process as a kind of *via negativa* framing of the uniqueness of South Africa's own human rights interpretation. From a close reading of these tensions two very different human rights methodologies emerge: 1) a dismantling method focused on non-negotiable principles of justice and 2) a more constructive, culture-building method with a more process-oriented, dialogue-centred view of justice. Seeking to understand the ongoing tensions between these two methodologies leads to the second part of this chapter. Here I focus on the truth and reconciliation process as a human rights interpretation in its own right, one that I call 'humanising' for its emphasis upon both human interdependence and the paradoxes of the human condition. Finally, I consider what lessons and insights might be gleaned from this humanising interpretation of human rights for the modern human rights regime.

Human Rights Groups and the Truth and Reconciliation Process

As I have noted, in the midst of early international praise for the TRC, Amnesty International took an official position against the Commission's work, and specifically its amnesty component. As Tom Gill, South African country specialist for Amnesty International USA, explains:

> *In official terms, Amnesty [International]'s ... position has been to ... oppose the Truth and Reconciliation Commission and ... the process which was worked out in South Africa, because, according to AI, it allowed too much impunity for past human rights abusers, and [because] AI's position has generally been to ... oppose on principle any process which does not allow for full prosecution of human rights violators.[4]*

To apply a point made above, the clash represented in Amnesty's official opposition to the TRC is not between universal human rights principles and the exigencies of reconciliation. Instead, it signals a conflict between two contesting interpretations of human rights.

In Amnesty's critical stance towards the TRC's amnesty component, at least three characteristics of its approach to human rights stand out: 1) its above-the-fray focus on non-negotiable, universal principles of justice, 2) the emphasis Amnesty International's violations-based approach places on the destructive, dismantling moment in human rights, and 3) its emphasis upon the individual (both in prosecution of individual perpetrators and legal advocacy on behalf of individual victims of human rights abuses). What is especially interesting about Amnesty International's position here is that this methodological approach which precluded a stronger contribution to South Africa's truth and reconciliation process is the very same approach that has made Amnesty International highly effective in combating human rights abuses in so many other contexts over its more than 40-year history. Thus, while Amnesty International's assertion of universal principles provided a critical, morally authoritative voice of impartiality within the international order (particularly during the Cold War), when these same universal principles are intricated within the kind of ethical, political and economic negotiations that have been required in South Africa, the human rights picture gets considerably more complex.

Likewise, Amnesty International's trademark methodologies of monitoring human rights abuses and holding responsible parties accountable have made for watershed work in dismantling dictatorial regimes (indeed, Amnesty International performs this monitoring work in democracies like present-day South Africa as well, shining a needed light on police brutality and other human rights concerns). And yet this work of monitoring and exposing has little to offer the complexities and paradoxes of the truth and reconciliation process. Finally, Amnesty International's consistent focus on the individual – the very focus that has made Amnesty International a friend and advocate for so many prisoners of conscience – played a role in its reservations to the TRC framework. For this framework included formidable tensions between addressing the rights of individual victims and the responsibility of individual perpetrators on the one hand, and efforts to heal and reconstruct a national community based upon human rights on the other. In sum, in South Africa, human rights' destructive moment (where human rights abuses are *exposed)* has been inextricably, agonisingly tethered to the constructive, culture-building moment within human rights (where a societal fostering of human rights must be *imagined*); Amnesty International's violations-based approach – potent as it continues to be in other contexts – has had little to bring to this challenging, ongoing task.

Amnesty International is not the only human rights group to have clashed with South Africa's truth and reconciliation process; human rights non-governmental organisations within South Africa have also been challenged by the amnesty compromise that emerged from the political settlement. Leading up to the passage of the TRC Act, South African human rights groups offered vital resources, researching for and helping to draft the Act, as well as eventually providing the TRC itself with an expansive database of human rights evidence and cases courageously and painstakingly recorded during the apartheid era. These groups were able to make this contribution to the TRC because of their critical work in the years prior to the negotiated settlement. Indeed, during the apartheid years these groups not only monitored human rights abuses and provided critical support to victims, they also provided international funders with a morally authoritative channel for supporting regime change.

And yet as Graeme Simpson, the director of the Johannesburg-based Centre for the Study of Violence and Reconciliation, has suggested, despite these powerful contributions during the apartheid era and even into the beginning of the TRC's work, '... dynamics within the TRC [eventually] did more to isolate human rights NGOs from the process than to draw upon them ...'.[5] Reflecting on the eventual breakdown in relations, he explains further: 'The unfortunate irony is that these [human rights] NGOs were probably marginalized [within the TRC] *precisely because of their past track records of commitment to human rights.*' In other words, precisely because of human rights groups' intimate knowledge of and principled opposition to the human rights violations of the former government, '... elements within the TRC [were able] to easily construe these NGOs as being politically biased [against the former government operatives]'.[6] Indeed, from the perspective of most human rights actors, to fail to have such a 'bias' in the face of the disproportionate number of gross human rights abuses committed by the apartheid regime (in comparison with the opposition movement) would be egregious and forgetful of the victims of these same abuses.

As with Amnesty International, the very methodologies and approaches that made the South African human rights groups so effective during the apartheid era have made for tensions within the context of their work with the TRC and beyond it. Indeed, former TRC commissioner Mary Burton has suggested that not only the 'sunset clause' compromise, but the transition to democratic rule more generally created a kind of identity crisis for the human rights movement within South Africa.[7] The moral clarity and international funding that attended its work in dismantling apartheid were replaced, by the mid-1990s, with a new challenge, namely, to relate this destructive, anti-apartheid work to the newly (if provisionally) constructive, apartheid-subverting vision articulated in the 1993 Interim Constitution. Related to this, the new challenge called for a shift in its methods and thinking from an antagonistic encounter with an apartheid state to a critically constructive encounter with a 'human rights state'.

Jose Zalaquett, former commissioner for Chile's TRC and a former member of Amnesty International's governing board, articulates the challenges of political transition for human rights actors:

Dealing with past injustices and human rights violations is an ethical and a political task. This is true not only for politicians but for human rights activists as well ... [I]n transitions they must face the type of dilemmas politicians face. How does one choose the best course of action rather than simply point out that a norm is being violated? How does one maximize specific resources in order to achieve an end when one does not have the power to achieve it completely? It is one thing for human rights organizations to be above the fray of politics in the face of a dictatorial government, but to do so in a political transition is a different matter.[8]

So far I have spoken about human rights groups that have clashed with the amnesty provision of the truth and reconciliation process. More recently, however, victims' rights groups have become increasingly vocal about the 'other side' of the amnesty compromise, namely, the reparation that was promised to victims of gross human rights abuses in exchange for the amnesty provision's effective denial of their right to redress. Like Amnesty and the other human rights groups, these victims' rights groups have focused on strategies of dismantlement and non-negotiable norms of justice. Zalaquett's questions are worth posing to these groups as well. Do their violation-based, individualist strategies make the best use of limited resources? How seriously are we to take the destabilising impact their lawsuits are capable of having on the South African economy? (On the day of a class action lawsuit against multinationals the Johannesburg stock exchange fell more than 3%.)[9]

If human rights and victims' rights groups are to play a meaningful role in this evolving human rights culture in South Africa, they will have to struggle with the same tough questions that the truth and reconciliation process continues to face: how to navigate ongoing tensions between honouring the suffering individual in the present and growing resources for communities and generations in the future; between supporting an emerging state and being constructively critical when necessary of its decisions and priorities. The work of human rights organisations has hardly become obsolete in this post-settlement context. Rather, I am suggesting that this process, as well as the worldwide profusion of truth and reconciliation commissions over the last 25 years or so, poses fresh questions to human rights methods and thinking.[10] How human rights actors respond to these increasingly vexed 'post-conflict' circumstances and the creative processes that are worked out to address them will be an important measure of their relevance in the 21st century. With this in mind, I will present South Africa's truth and reconciliation process as a human rights interpretation, which for many reasons is worthy of reflection.

The Truth and Reconciliation Process as a Human Rights Interpretation

The history of South African interpretations of human rights is rich with dissonances.[11] Speaking of the 1996 Constitution, legal scholar Makau wa Mutua observes: 'Never has the recreation of a state been so singularly the product of such focused and relentless advocacy of human rights norms.' Indeed, Mutua takes this assertion further, calling post-settlement South Africa '... the first deliberate and calculated effort in history to craft a human rights state – a polity that is primarily animated by human rights norms'.[12] At the same time, within South Africa the language of human rights was rejected until well into the late 1970s, not only by proponents of apartheid, but also by those involved in the anti-apartheid struggle.[13] Thus a rich tradition of social justice and resistance (including, for some of that time, resistance to human rights talk) had already been developing for probably three-quarters of a century before human rights language (and the international funding that attended it) came on the scene in South Africa. As miraculous and unpredicted as the truth and reconciliation process has been, therefore, it did not simply arise *ex nihilo;* the groundwork for its particular interpretation of human rights was laid both in the constitutional embrace of human rights norms and, significantly, in the long struggle that preceded it.

So far I have suggested that South Africa's truth and reconciliation process embodies a unique and controversial human rights interpretation that has found itself in conflict with the aims and interpretations of a number of human rights groups. What then is the nature of this peculiar interpretation? Above all, I believe it is distinctive for its *humanising* of human rights. In 1993 South Africa signalled this unique interpretation of human rights when, at the end of an Interim Constitution based heavily on the norms and language of international human rights law, it spoke of the way forward for the country not in terms of rights, but in terms of *understanding, reparation* and *ubuntu.* A history of 'divisions', 'strife' and 'violent conflicts' could now be addressed, it explained, '... on the basis that there is a need for *understanding,* but not for vengeance, a need for *reparation,* but not for retaliation, a need for *ubuntu* but not for victimisation'. Far from some salutary flourish, these words – and the amnesty provision that followed them – served as the preamble to the TRC Act and largely set the terms for the truth and reconciliation process's interpretation of human rights.

The last term, the African traditional notion of ubuntu, means roughly 'a person is a person through other persons'.[14] Thus ubuntu serves as a kind of social ethic commending respect for fellow people and a recognition of every individual's dependence upon others. Raising this notion within the context of the truth and reconciliation process, two touchstone questions emerge: 'What does it mean to be human?' and 'How can we human beings learn to live together?' Describing the notion in her own words, Afrikaner poet and journalist Antjie Krog reveals the relationship between these two questions with a kind of common-sense complexity:

> *You can only be human in a humane society ... A person is human precisely in being enveloped in the community of other human beings, in being caught up in the bundle of life. To be ... is to participate.*[15]

And yet ubuntu is not solely a positive notion. Placed in the context of South Africa's political transition, the ambivalence of the ubuntu concept

emerges. For as apartheid made clear, this maxim of human interdependence is not always good news. A person's humanity can be
diminished by the inhumanity of other persons and by policies that
prescribe alienation and violence among persons. Thus, to modify the
second touchstone question for the truth and reconciliation process, the
challenge becomes: 'How can South Africans learn to live together not
only in diversity, *but with apartheid's legacy of deep divisions, isolations, violations
and inhumanities?*' How, for example, can South Africans learn to live
together when (as revealed in a 2001 survey) 51% of whites and 35.5%
of black South Africans (34.9% of coloureds; 42% of people of Asian
origin) agree with the statement that 'despite abuses, apartheid ideas
were good ones'? And how can South Africans learn to live together
when, according to the same survey, just 1.5% of black South Africans
and 6.6% of whites (17.7% of coloureds; 19.2% of Asian origin) report
having interracial friendships?[16]

How might the reality of such alienation inform human rights work in
South Africa? In the context of political transition, to inform one's human
rights interpretation with the values of ubuntu requires not only the
incorporation of human rights protections, but equally, a thoughtfulness
about how these human rights ought to be framed. Here, as much as
ubuntu can be read as a kind of Africanised 'do unto others', on a deeper
level it articulates equally the penetrating inhumanity of apartheid and the
intense human price of restoring or *humanising* individuals and communities after official apartheid's end. Cynthia Ngewu (mother of Christopher
Piet, one of the Guguletu Seven killed by security police in 1986) elo-
quently articulated this price and project in her testimony before the TRC:

> *This thing called reconciliation ... if I am understanding it correctly ... if it
> means this perpetrator, this man who killed Christopher Piet, if it means he
> becomes human again, this man, so that I, so that all of us, get our human-
> ity back ... then I agree, then I support it all.*[17]

Thus an ubuntu-framed human rights interpretation requires the transformation of apartheid cartographies, structures and infrastructure. It takes
apartheid's legacy of alienations and isolations seriously in its quest to
understand what is involved in 'learning to live together' and in building a
human rights culture in South Africa. 'It is not enough ... to have minimal decency as one's objective,' Indian political scientist Rajeev Bhargava

incisively notes. 'One must be equally sensitive to the kind of barbarism from which one is extricating oneself.'[18]

Likewise, in addressing the question of what it means to be human, the truth and reconciliation process has had to face the paradox at the heart of human rights, namely, that we humans are not only worthy of dignity but equally capable of barbarous inhumanity. For South Africans have had to confront their inhumanity to one another in its darkest forensic detail and, at the same time, to build and strengthen humanity among South Africans through shared stories. 'A human rights culture,' as South African government minister Kader Asmal once said, 'is based on a special goal. That goal is a shared understanding, a shared history, not the simple imposition of a victor's vision of a united South Africa.'[19] The unbearable dissonance between these two tasks – confronting the history of divisions and barbarism while reaching forward towards a shared history – is at the heart of the truth and reconciliation process's human rights interpretation because it is at the Janus-faced heart of the human condition. In concrete terms, it is manifest in the painful tethering of amnesty for perpetrators with reparation for victims.[20]

In concluding this brief discussion of the truth and reconciliation process's humanising interpretation of human rights, I want to focus on this tethering of amnesty and reparation that in many ways lies at this interpretation's core. Of course this pairing was opposed from the beginning by not only Amnesty International, but also by victims and victims' rights groups within South Africa. And contestation has only intensified since the October 1998 submission of the TRC's *Final Report* as the amnesty committee has continued its work and as government policy made disbursement of reparations contingent upon the completion of this work.[21] The complexities of this debate – and the role of international lawyers within it – have multiplied considerably since the amnesty provision first appeared in the 1993 Interim Constitution and the TRC Act. Yet homing in on the heart of the debate, much that was articulated early on remains relevant to understanding both the truth and reconciliation process and the human rights culture that it is reaching toward.

In 1996, *Azapo v. The President of South Africa and Others* took up the tensions between amnesty for perpetrators and justice for victims within a rights framework. The families of Steve Biko, Griffiths Mxenge, Churchill Ribeiro and other victims of gross human rights violations committed by the apartheid state came before South Africa's highest court to argue that the amnesty provision contained within the 1995 TRC Act (section

20(7)) and the 1993 Interim Constitution Epilogue was unconstitutional. This amnesty should not stand, they averred, because it precluded their constitutional and human right to seek redress for crimes committed against their loved ones, as provided for in the Universal Declaration of Human Rights, Art. 8. Reparation was an unacceptable substitute for the rights to redress and the justice of prosecutions.

The decision of the late Chief Justice Ismael Mahomed, then deputy president of the Constitutional Court, was striking for the way it both upheld the amnesty provision and acknowledged the rights violation that the provision contained. 'The effect of an amnesty,' he explained, 'undoubtedly impacts upon very fundamental rights.'

> *All persons are entitled to the protection of the law against unlawful invasions of their right to life, their right to respect for and protection of dignity and their right not to be subject to torture of any kind. When those rights are invaded those aggrieved by such invasion have the right to obtain redress ... An amnesty to the wrongdoer effectively obliterates such rights.*[22]

And yet, Mahomed continued, '... but for a mechanism providing for amnesty, the "historic bridge" [of the Interim Constitution] itself might never have been erected'.[23] In short, had it not been for the 'unconstitutional' amnesty provision embedded *within* the Interim Constitution, the Constitution itself would never have been politically possible. Mahomed spoke poignantly about this paradox of establishing a human rights culture and the rule of law for all by deferring – indeed effectively denying – the fundamental rights of some. 'The result, at all levels,' he explained, 'is a difficult, sensitive, perhaps even agonising balancing act between the need for justice to victims of past abuse and the need for reconciliation and rapid transition to a new future ... between the correction in the old and the creation of the new.'[24]

To recall a point made early in this chapter, the conflict is not between reconciliation or even 'rapid transition' and human rights. Rather, Mahomed's 'agonising balancing act' occurs *among human rights*. How, for example, can the human right to redress claimed by victims of gross human rights abuses and their families be reconciled with the human rights of generations – born and yet to be born – to a reconstructed society with resources for securing education, housing and health care?[25] How can the rights of the former ever be traded away – for reparation or anything else? What is powerful about Mahomed's Azapo judgment and the truth and reconciliation process of which it is a part is the way this judgment and process retains the tensions and paradoxes at the heart of human rights – between humanity and inhumanity; the past and the future; the destructive and the constructive aspects of human rights work. Indeed, not only does this human rights interpretation make space for the paradoxes at the heart of human rights; in so doing it makes room within human rights for moral regret. Mahomed expresses this regret with eloquence. The ongoing balancing act among rights, he explains:

> ... *is an exercise of immense difficulty interacting in a vast network of political, emotional, ethical and logistical considerations* ... **The results may well often be imperfect and the pursuit of the act might inherently support the message of Kant that 'out of the crooked timber of humanity no straight thing was ever made'.**[26]

In sum, just as apartheid was more than a series of human rights violations, the truth and reconciliation process has recognised that building a human rights culture paradoxically requires (and will continue to require) more than human rights.[27] Rather, this culture-building process has entailed the restoration where possible of human relationships, the venting of identity-based angers and sustained inquiries into the motivations and understandings of perpetrators of gross human rights abuses. It has involved the work of transforming structures and infrastructure originally established to keep apartheid in place.[28] And, finally, it has required efforts, often painfully inadequate and unacceptably delayed, to meet the material and spiritual needs of victims of human rights abuses. In short, the truth and reconciliation process's humanising interpretation of human rights has involved both reconciliation and an honest encounter with deep-seated conflicts and anger at reconciliation's heart. It has been framed by both a recognition that humanity contains inhumanity and an appreciation of the ambivalence, fragility and abiding importance of human interdependence.

Lessons and Insights for the International Human Rights Regime

At the beginning of this chapter I suggested that the truth and reconciliation process offered a human rights interpretation that contained lessons and insights for the modern human rights regime. I argued that its human-ising of human rights has brought forth salient tensions and paradoxes that could inform human rights methods and thinking well beyond South Africa. In one sense, the insights are nothing new. Indeed, this ubuntu-informed human rights interpretation and the political moment in which it was articulated recall the moment out of which the modern human rights regime was born. For the 1948 Universal Declaration of Human Rights (UDHR) was drafted and adopted amidst a human crisis not dis-similar from the one in which South Africans found themselves during the negotiations and constitution-drafting of the early 1990s.

Chastened by the horrors of World War II and the Holocaust and reaching for a more humane future, the Declaration drafters affirmed in the preamble the reality of ubuntu or human interdependence, recognising '... the inherent dignity ... of all members of the human family'. At the same time, they grounded their human rights declaration in an under-standing of the ambivalence of this human interdependence, acknowledging that members of this human family had committed '... barbarous acts which have outraged the conscience of mankind'. Like South African negotiations of the early 1990s, the UDHR drafting was also marked by intense political wrangling. On a deeper level, however, the UDHR drafting also has this in common with the period leading up to South Africa's Interim Constitution: in both processes people came together to articulate a humane moral vision in the face of the worst inhumanity. Under these conditions, ubuntu's questions of human being and human interdependence were articulated as the unavoidable framework for human rights.

More recently, however, any such humanising framework for human rights has fallen out of favour for being too prescriptive and for getting too close to the controversial waters of human nature and metaphysics. In response to challenges to human rights universalism, many human rights defenders have argued instead the philosophical and moral thinness of human rights. As Harvard Carr Center director Michael Ignatieff puts it: '[t]he universalist commitments implied by human rights can be compatible with a wide variety of ways of living only if the universalism implied is self-consciously minimalist'.[29] By this logic, the *thinner,* more abstracted and less culturally prescriptive human rights can be, the more universal, the *thicker* they are (i.e. with values and ideas about human beings and human community), in turn, the more particular and limited will be their scope.

To be clear, these 'thin universal-ists' do not deny that the language and principles of human rights need to be contextualised or translated for every particular context in which human rights are to find a home. However, the assumption is that this is 'one-way traffic'. That is, the journey from the universal to the particular, in this view, goes in one direction only: particular political actors and processes are held to universal human rights principles and standards. Jose Zalaquett describes this kind of one-way-traffic universalism in action:

At times human rights organizations take the high ground during political transitions by stating: 'This is what the articles of the Universal Declaration of Human Rights and other instruments say. You do it. I don't care how'[30]

Human rights principles are normative and universal, according to this 'thin universalist' approach, only insofar as they ultimately transcend – i.e. remain uninformed by – the vagaries of particular contexts. Arguably, at least a few human rights might be said to be universal in this way – e.g. the human right not to be tortured (insofar as *every* person in *every* context has the human right not to be tortured). However, as I have tried to argue in this chapter, human rights considered more expansively and constructively cannot remain thin in this sense because, among other reasons, they are always navigating, never finally transcending, the thick paradoxes of the human condition.

To commit to a framework that accounts for these thick paradoxes is not to give up on human rights universality, but to doggedly affirm and pursue it. It is not a concession to moral relativism, but what turns out to be its opposite: an acknowledgement of moral complexity. This, I suggest, is the critical lesson and possibility that the truth and reconciliation process offers to the modern human rights regime. In this sense, ubuntu is not merely the framework for a particular South African contextualisation of universal human rights, but a universal truth and human rights interpretation in its own right. Human rights universality *lives* not only in the rarefied air of immutable rights and standards (significant as these universal principles remain), but equally insofar as it has the capacity to become informed by particular contexts and to take seriously the insights into human interdependence and the human condition they may provide. To uphold both universal, non-negotiable human rights principles and the wisdom of a process that negotiates agonising balancing acts among them is to accept the human condition and the paradoxes it engenders at the heart of human rights. To recognise, as Judge Mahomed joined Kant in doing, that 'out of the crooked timber of humanity, no straight thing was ever made' is to expect more of human rights, not less.

Notes

1   In 11th-hour negotiations, the amnesty clause was combined with the 'sunset clause' which granted civil servants of the former state job security for five years. See Johnny de Lange, 'The Historical Context, Legal Origins, and Philosophical Foundation of the South African Truth and Reconciliation Commission', in *Looking Back, Reaching Forward: Reflections on the Truth and Reconciliation Commission of South Africa*, eds. C. Villa-Vicencio and W. Verwoerd (Cape Town: University of Cape Town Press, 2000), 22.

2   In this chapter the 'truth and reconciliation process' will refer to the process that began with the 1993 Interim Constitution's controversial epilogue and includes the debating and passage of the 1995 TRC Act, the work of the TRC through to its five-volume report, the 1996 *Azapo v. The President of South Africa and Others* case, the work of the TRC amnesty committee that carried on into 2002 and the ongoing debates around the reparation policy. While healing from apartheid's legacy has no end date, the 'end' of the truth and reconciliation process as I am defining it will coincide with full disbursements of reparation whenever this takes place.

3   '... [I]n the context of the South African Truth and Reconciliation Commission, reparation is essential to counterbalance amnesty. The granting of amnesty denies the victims the right to institute civil claims against perpetrators. The government should thus accept responsibility for reparation.' (TRC, *Final Report*, Vol. 5 (Pretoria: RSA, 1998), 170.

4   E-mail correspondence from Tom Gill, 4 August 2002.

5   Graeme Simpson, *A Brief Evaluation of South Africa's Truth and Reconciliation Commission: Some Lessons for Societies in Transition* (Johannesburg: CSVR, 1998) 24-25.

6   Simpson, *A Brief Evaluation*, 26. My emphasis.

7   Conversation with Mary Burton, former TRC commissioner, former president of Black Sash, and co-founder of the Home to All Campaign, June 2002.

8   A. Boraine, et al., *Dealing with the Past: Truth and Reconciliation in South Africa* (Cape Town: Idasa, 1997), 8-9.

9   In April 2003 South African lawyer John Ngcebetsha and US lawyer Ed Fagan together filed a class action lawsuit in a US court seeking $6.1 billion in damages for workers who were mistreated and whose employment was wrongfully terminated by two of South Africa's mining giants, Anglo American and its diamond subsidiary De Beers (and other multinationals). Anglo American is the single largest company trading on the Johannesburg stock exchange and accounts for more than 16% of its overall value. 'South African Firm Sued.' *Africa Online*, 8 April 2003. See www.africaonline.com

10   For more on this proliferation of truth and reconciliation commissions see Priscilla Hayner, *Unspeakable Truths: Facing the Challenge of Truth Commissions* (New York: Routledge, 2002).

11 It is interesting, if coincidental, that the Universal Declaration of Human Rights was adopted by the UN General Assembly in 1948, the same year the National Party rose to power in South Africa. In adumbration of things to come, South Africa's representative within the UDHR drafting debate, C. T. Te Water, objected to the word 'dignity' as it had been proposed for the Declaration's Article One, complaining that 'dignity' had no universal standard and that it was not a 'right'. Charles Malik, Lebanese delegate and a principal drafter of the UDHR, reminded Te Water that it was South African Field Marshal Jan Smuts who was instrumental in getting the word 'dignity' into the UN Charter. See Mary Ann Glendon, *A World Made New: Eleanor Roosevelt and the Universal Declaration of Human Rights* (New York: Random House, 2001), 144.

12 Makau wa Mutua, 'Hope and Despair for a New South Africa: The Limits of Rights Discourse', *Harvard Human Rights Journal* 10 (1997): 63–64, 65. It is probably worth mentioning that Mutua is in fact critical of what he sees as the dominance of the rights approach in post-settlement South Africa. 'Under the [present] circumstances,' he explains, '... the rights approach gives no more than formal and abstract rights to blacks and other nonwhites. For white beneficiaries of apartheid, by contrast, the rights-based state ... is a golden opportunity to protect most of their privileges ...' 'Hope and Despair', 83.

13 The South African Native National Congress (precursor to the African National Congress) did adopt an African Bill of Rights in 1923 which, in addition to its appeals to constitutional rights and the rights of British subjects, referred in its first article to the rights of the 'Bantu inhabitants ... as human beings ... to a place of abode in this land of their fathers'. Again in 1943 – two years prior to the UN's adoption of the UN Charter and five years prior to the UN's adoption of the 1948 Universal Declaration of Human Rights – the ANC emphasised the importance of rights in a response to the 1941 Atlantic Charter entitled 'Africans' Claims in South Africa'. In 1955 the Freedom Charter became the movement's third major bill of rights document. However, fully explicit appeals to human rights as articulated in international law would await the late 1970s. Ideologically speaking, this rejection of rights talk had to do with the Marxist framework that dominated the struggle and the critique of human rights individualism and abstractness that it contained. Conversation with University of Cape Town political scientist André du Toit, June 2002.

14 As Desmond Tutu explains, ubuntu is '... a central feature of the African *Weltanschauung* ...'. It is from the Nguni group of languages and is the equivalent of *botho* in the Sotho languages. *No Future Without Forgiveness* (New York: Doubleday, 1999), 31. In Zulu its meaning is embedded in the maxim *'umuntu·ngumuntu ngabantu'* (a person is a person through other persons). See Dirk Louw, 'Ubuntu: An African Assessment of the Religious Other' (www.bu.edu/wcp/Papers/Afri/AfriLouw.htm). See Augustine Shutte, *Philosophy for Africa* (Cape Town: University of Cape Town Press, 1993), 46–59. See also P. Coetzee and A. Roux, *The African Philosophy Reader* (New York: Routledge, 1998).

15 Antjie Krog, paraphrasing Desmond Tutu, *Country of My Skull: Guilt, Sorrow, and the Limits of Forgiveness in the New South Africa* (New York: Three Rivers Press, 2000), 143.

16 The survey, entitled 'Truth Yes Reconciliation Maybe: South Africans Judge the Truth

and Reconciliation Process', involved face-to-face interviews with 3 727 South Africans, all over 18 years and drawn from urban and rural populations. The majority of interviews were conducted by interviewers with the racial identity of the interviewee and all of the interviews were conducted in the language of the interviewee's preference. The survey is a link on the Institute for Justice and Reconciliation website (www.ijr.org.za). It was conducted by James L. Gibson and Helen MacDonald in collaboration with Amanda Gouws of Stellenbosch University's Department of Political Science.

17 Quoted in Krog, *Country of My Skull*, 142.

18 Rajeev Bhargava, 'The Moral Justification of Truth Commissions', in *Looking Back, Reaching Forward*, 64.

19 Kader Asmal, 'Victims, Survivors, and Citizens: Human Rights, Reparations, and Reconciliation', Inaugural lecture delivered at the University of the Western Cape, 25 May 1992, Publications of the University of the Western Cape, Series A, No. 64, 28.

20 Within the truth and reconciliation process, amnesty has been granted to qualifying perpetrators before full measures of reparation have been distributed to victims of gross human rights abuses and their families. Now that the TRC's amnesty committee has submitted its final two codicil report volumes, parliamentary debate and final decisions on reparations policy occurred in April 2003. See Chapter 3 by Mary Burton in this volume.

21 That perpetrators have been granted amnesty before victims have received the bulk of measures of reparation has only exacerbated original tensions over the amnesty provision. The amnesty committee's final two codicils, which were held up in fall 2002 due to objections registered by the Inkatha Freedom Party, were finally handed to President Thabo Mbeki on 21 March 2003, Human Rights Day in South Africa. The government will now be expected to begin swiftly the disbursement of final measures of reparation.

22 *Azapo v. The President of RSA CCT 17/96*, 9. My emphasis. See www.concourt.gov.za/judgments/1996/azapo.html

23 *Azapo v. President of RSA*, 19.

24 *Azapo v. President of RSA*, 21.

25 This question of balancing rights to redress with rights to education and health care becomes apparent when one considers the costs of honouring victims' rights to redress. As South African lawyer Paul van Zyl notes, the trial of former minister of defence Magnus Malan and other high-ranking defence force members cost the new state over R9 million (at the time, around 1.5 million US dollars); the trial of former police colonel Eugene de Kock cost taxpayers more than R5 million rand (.8 million US dollars). Van Zyl notes that these figures do not include hidden costs to the state like large teams of state attorneys and the cost of extremely expensive witness protection programmes. Thus Van Zyl estimates that prosecuting officials from the apartheid state could have cost the new government billions of rand, money that might otherwise go towards social programmes and the development of infrastructure. Paul van Zyl, 'Dilemmas of Transitional Justice: The Case of South Africa's Truth and Reconciliation Commission', *Journal of International Affairs* 52 (Spring 1999): 652-653.

26 *Azapo v. President of RSA*, 21.

27 Though let this not be misread: societal restoration cannot be *less than* the prevention of gross human rights abuses and the securing of rights guarantees.

28 Much work of course remains to be done. In 1994, at the beginning of these efforts to reform and transform, over 90% of all regional magistrates (who handle over 95% of all civil and criminal matters) were white and only 4% were women. By 1995, members of the apartheid era South African Defence Force still comprised 65% of the renamed South African National Defence Force. See Mutua, 'Limits of Rights Discourse', 105, 110.

29 Michael Ignatieff, *Human Rights as Politics and Idolatry* (Princeton: Princeton University Press, 2001), 56.

30 Jose Zalaquett, 'Why Deal with the Past?', in *Dealing with the Past*, A. Boraine, et al., p. 9.

10

Doing Justice in South Africa:

Restorative Justice and Reparation

Jennifer J. Llewellyn

The South African Truth and Reconciliation Commission (TRC) has been described and defended as a restorative justice process. In its *Final Report* the Commission identified restorative justice as one of its orienting principles.[1] Precisely, it claimed:

> *[T]he tendency to equate justice with retribution must be challenged and the concept of restorative justice considered as an alternative. This means that amnesty in return for public and full disclosure (as understood within the broader context of the Commission) suggests a restorative understanding of justice, focusing on the healing of victims and perpetrators and on communal restoration.*[2]

Thus, in response to those critics who charged that the TRC sacrificed justice, the Commission maintained it was serving the interests of justice understood restoratively.[3] In previous work I have argued that the South African TRC represents a significant development of the existing truth commission model.[4] Through the inclusion of amnesty within the framework of the Commission, the TRC brought accountability to amnesty and the perpetrators into the process of the Truth Commission. By bringing together the victims, perpetrators and the community into one process, with a view to transcending 'the past of a deeply divided society characterised by strife, conflict, untold suffering and injustice, and [commencing] the journey towards a future founded on the recognition of human rights, democracy and peaceful co-existence' the TRC serves as a promising model of a restorative justice process for societies faced with the challenge of dealing with the past.[5]

Far from sacrificing justice by foregoing prosecution, punishment and civil liability, the Commission sought justice through the restoration of relationships. The TRC has thus, rightfully, in my view, been held up as an example of the possibility and promise of truth commissions to serve as institutions of restorative justice. The significant developments brought about by the South African Commission offer much hope for those seeking to avoid the peace versus justice dilemma in transitional situations.[6] In these kinds of circumstance, South Africa's Commission stands as a model of justice.

There currently exists, however, a significant threat to the ultimate success of the TRC as a restorative justice process, namely, the failure of the South African government to respond in a serious and sufficient way to the Commission's recommendations on reparation.[7] Such a failure risks vindicating those critics who decried the Commission as devoid of justice. The South African government's inaction on the provision of reparation stands as a significant obstacle to the aims of restorative justice and the success of the TRC model. Furthermore, the restorative nature of the TRC serves as a powerful reason to respect and realise its reparation recommendations.

Several arguments have been made as to why the government ought to move on the reparation recommendations of the TRC, including that it is constitutionally and morally compelled to do so.[8] The discussion in this chapter seeks to complement, not supplant, these other arguments for reparation. In order to understand the argument advanced here for reparation in the South African context, it is first necessary to appreciate the role of reparation in restorative justice. Once clear, the fundamental role reparation plays in restorative justice will also serve to strengthen the case for restorative justice processes in transitions from pasts marred by repression or violence to a democratic and peaceful process. This chapter argues that the relationship between restorative justice and reparation is a reciprocal one. Reparation plays a fundamental role in restorative justice theory and practice, and, likewise, restorative justice plays a crucial role in the project of reparation. The chapter considers the implications for the South African context of this relationship between restorative justice and reparation and recommends a way to move towards meeting the TRC's restorative vision.

Reparation in Restorative Justice

Restorative justice is often mistakenly thought of as simply special or alternative practice. Used in this sense, it is no more than a label for those practices that do not conform to those in the mainstream justice system. Restorative justice is, however, more. It is a theory of justice. On a restorative account, justice is relational in nature. It is concerned with responding to the harm caused by wrongdoing. In order to understand the harm with which restorative justice is concerned it is important to first recognise that this idea of justice starts from the premise that the human self is relational – constituted in and through relationships. It views the world relationally, recognising that we live in interconnected webs of relationships. Thus, the harm that results from wrongdoing is, on this account, not limited to that directly experienced by the victim(s) but extends through the web of relationships to their family, friends and communities. Further, restorative justice recognises that the harm resulting from wrongdoing is primary to the relationships between and among the parties involved, including the victim, wrongdoer and community. The harm to the individual parties is not rendered irrelevant by this focus, rather, the restoration of the relationships demands particular attention to the harms experienced by all those involved in order to ascertain what would be required to restore relationships.

The concern of justice understood restoratively is to address this harm to relationships and to restore the relationships at issue to ones of social equality – that is, ones in which all parties enjoy equal respect, concern and dignity. The aim of restorative justice is, thus, not a return to the *status quo ante,* to the way things were before the wrong occurred. Instead, restorative justice is future oriented, aimed at realising the ideal of restored relationships. The term 'restore' often obscures this future orientation of restorative justice, leading some to suppose it is only appropriate in contexts where some prior state of equality can be identified. However, once one grasps that the founding assumption is the relational nature of the human self, the sense in which the term 'restore' is intended becomes clear. Restore in this context speaks to the *ideal* of relationship inherent in the very nature of the human self. Restorative justice thus seeks to restore relationships to this ideal state in which human beings can flourish – that is, in relationships in which they enjoy equal respect, concern and dignity.

This ideal of restoration is, further, aimed at the restoration of *social* relationships and does not necessarily entail the restoration of personal or intimate relationships (although this is not precluded by the theory). The focus on relationships has led some to mistakenly identify the ambition of restorative justice as getting the parties to 'hug and make up'. As is clear from the ideal of relationship to which restoration aims, the rebuilding or creation of personal and intimate relationships is not necessarily its concern. Indeed, there are many situations in which social equality (ensuring equal respect, concern and dignity) will require personal space and the end to an intimate relationship, not its restoration.

Another significant misunderstanding is the identification of restorative justice *itself* with the encounter portion of the restorative process. One of the principled commitments of restorative justice is the need for encounter among the parties affected by, or concerned with, the wrongdoing at issue. On a restorative account, the process of addressing the harm to relationships resulting from wrongdoing needs to be an inclusive one, whereby all those with a stake in the outcome of a situation are brought together to make a plan for the future. Indeed, this is perhaps the most often cited description of restorative justice, based on the early description offered by Tony Marshall:

> *Restorative justice is a process whereby all the parties with a stake in a particular offence come together to resolve collectively how to deal with the aftermath of the offence and its implications for the future.*[9]

The description itself is not problematic. It is the use of it in place of a definition of restorative justice that has led to misconceptions.[10] It has led in the first instance to the view of restorative justice as special practice, as mentioned above. It has also resulted in a related yet more complex problem, that is, the view that restorative justice is nothing more than this process, that is, in the identification of restorative justice with the encounter process. It has caused some to evaluate whether restorative justice was achieved by what happens in the encounter, and, more specifically, by whether an agreement was reached at the end.

This is a complex and difficult problem to grasp. Yet it is essential to our project of comprehending the role of reparation in restorative justice. This point about restorative justice is perhaps so difficult because it reveals the extent to which restorative justice requires a new way of thinking about justice. On a restorative conception, justice is more akin to a process than to an end state. This is not to say that there is no ideal 'just' state envisioned by restorative justice which, when existing, would allow one to identify that justice has been done. Restorative justice has such an end state in that it aspires to relationships of social equality. However, the restoration of relationships is often a lengthy process. Furthermore, given that we live in networks of ever-changing, evolving and sometimes dissolving relationships, the work of restoring relationships is likely to be ongoing. In this way, restorative justice is significantly different from the more familiar retributive notion of justice at work in the criminal justice system.

On a retributive account, justice is done when punishment is meted out to the guilty. Thus, the process of prosecution and punishment can 'achieve' justice. In many ways this is one of the things that makes retributive justice attractive. It can offer, at a general level at least, an easy and standardised answer to the question: what does justice require? Justice requires punishment in proportion to the crime.[11] Once the punishment is done then justice is done. Restorative justice, on the other hand, cannot offer so simple a response to the question of what justice requires. It can only say: 'it depends'. It depends on what is needed to restore the particular relationships at issue.[12] Restorative justice is not, then, as we are used to thinking about justice, something achieved or done, rather it is something we do. There is not the same moment in restorative justice as there is in retributive justice when one can say justice has been done, although this moment may be substituted for by the sense of satisfaction and empowerment people feel as they play a role in doing justice. Perhaps, the feeling justice is *being* done will satisfy our urge to see it done. But so ingrained is the traditional way of approaching the work of justice that even our justice vocabulary makes it difficult to talk about justice differently. People call for justice to be done, to be seen to be done, to meet the demands of justice, etc. Restorative justice, in contrast, involves a commitment to strive continually for just relationships.

Our current mode of thinking about justice as something that is done or achieved is then responsible for the common misconception that restorative justice encounter processes are the sum total of restorative justice. In fact, the actual encounter process is only one part of restorative justice. There is much that needs to happen before and perhaps even more after the encounter. Such encounter processes are necessary but not sufficient for restorative justice. The encounter is often an important step towards the restoration of relationships, but one should not expect, as some of the critics of restorative justice seem prone to do, that this process will alone achieve the restoration of relationships. A restorative encounter process is aimed at understanding the nature of the harm experienced as a result of wrongdoing and to make a plan for how this harm might be repaired and the relationships restored in the future. The encounter process is not intended to do all the work of restoration. Thus, restorative justice encounter processes should not be judged against the restoration achieved by the end of the encounter, but rather by the resulting plan for the future and perhaps, in retrospect, by their contribution to restoration. The confusion between restorative justice and encounter processes seems in fact to be at the root of some of the critiques of the TRC. Many have condemned the TRC because it did not achieve reconciliation. If understood properly as a restorative justice encounter process, the TRC should not have been expected to produce reconciliation or restored relationships. While the Commission did not respond to this critique from the perspective of restorative justice, its response was consistent with this approach. The Commission pointed to its slogan: 'truth the road to reconciliation' as instructive. Its work, the Commission claimed, was only one part of the journey towards reconciliation.[13]

A restorative justice process is not then limited to the encounter stage. Indeed, there is much work that needs to happen in preparation for the encounter and, most significantly for our present discussion, much of the work of restorative justice remains after the encounter. This understanding of the full scope of restorative processes clarifies the role of reparation. In the broadest sense, some measure of reparation might be required to enable an encounter process to go forward. This is particularly so, for example, if the victim needs to be assured that the wrongdoer has admitted responsibility for the event. In such a case a letter from the wrongdoer stating his acceptance of responsibility might be requested. Or, similarly, if the victim has some cause to worry for her safety she might require assurance that the wrongdoer has obtained some assistance in dealing with anger issues before proceeding. The encounter process itself can also involve some reparation in the form of admissions, acknowledgement of harm or apologies. However, generally reparation plays the most significant role in restorative justice as part of the process following the encounter. Reparation forms a significant part of the plan for the future arising from restorative encounters. It is a significant means through which restoration is sought and achieved.

In order to restore relationships, attention must extend beyond the discrete wrong in question to consider the context and causes of the wrong. The plan for the future must address all the harm resulting from the wrongdoing, including that to the victim, the community and even to the offender, and the relationships among them. The recognition that wrong-doing can result in harm to the wrongdoer as well as the victim and the community does not mean that these harms are equal in moral status or require a similar response. The distinction between the status of these harms is reflected in the language that is often used to describe the response to them. The term 'reparation' is generally reserved for responses to the harms suffered by victims while 'rehabilitation' describes the response to the harms experienced by the wrongdoer. A plan resulting from a restorative justice encounter process will generally include both reparation and rehabilitation. Since our current concern is with repara-tion, I leave for another time a fuller discussion of the precise nature of the distinction between rehabilitation and reparation and the role of rehabilitation in restorative justice.

Reparation serves as the most significant vehicle through which the work of restoration is carried out. It forms a significant part of the agree-ments that come out of the encounter process. It is the means through which the parties agree to respond to the harm resulting from the wrong-doing and work towards the restoration of the relationships at stake. As mentioned, reparation is not generally aimed at the offender. However, nor is it limited exclusively to direct victims. Reparation responds to the harm suffered by parties (other than the wrongdoer) resulting from the wrongdoing. This means that reparation might appropriately be made to either the victims (immediate and secondary) or the community to the extent that they suffered harm. Reparation is generally the means through which the wrongdoer acknowledges and responds to the harm he or she caused. However, the wrongdoer is not the only party that might be responsible for reparation. One of the foundational commitments of restorative justice is an understanding that community is an integral part of the creation and solution of social conflict.[14] Thus, insofar as the com-munity bears some responsibility for the creation of the harm, it might rightfully be expected to make reparation to the victim. The community also has a need (in order to ensure its strength) and a responsibility in restorative justice theory to reintegrate both the victim and the wrong-doer. Reparation plays a significant part in that reintegrative task of the community with respect to the victim.[15]

Reparation works to respond to the harm and contribute to the restoration of relationships in two different ways. First, it can address the material needs or harms of the party at issue in an effort to remove any obvious obstacle to the restoration of relationships. This might include, for example, repairing damaged property needed for the party or parties to move on with life after the wrongdoing. The other way in which reparation works is on a symbolic level. Reparation signifies the commitment to, and desire for, restored relationships. It acknowledges the harm suffered and demonstrates a commitment to accord the party with equal respect, dignity and concern in the future. Sometimes it goes beyond demonstrating a commitment to restoring relationships and, through the process of reparation, begins to build these relationships.

Reparation plays a fundamental role in the plan for the future developed out of an encounter process, and thus, in the restoration of relationships, however reparation does not provide that moment of 'justice done' that many seek. That is to say that reparation does not act as punishment does in the retributive system, as the litmus test for justice achieved. Reparation is a step, albeit a significant one, on the road towards justice. But, as noted above, other steps are required, most notably rehabilitation aimed at the wrongdoer. Also, often the steps set out in the restorative agreement create the conditions for, and remove obstacles to, restoration, but restored relationships require further and ongoing work. This is what was meant by the claim that justice understood restoratively is something one does and not something done. This aspect of restorative justice is reflected in the fact that restorative agreements often provide that the wrongdoer must acquire life skills or undergo programmes to address problematic behaviour. These provisions recognise that restored relationships require lasting and ongoing changes to the wrongdoer's mode of being in relationships.

Ultimately, then, the true test of restorative justice will be the extent to which the lessons and commitments of these processes continue to be lived out by the parties in their relationships. This is not to suggest, however, that there is no means of measuring the success of a restorative process beyond some notion of a theoretical future judgement day. The fulfilment of the plan for the future and the perspectives of the parties after completion provide some real sense of the extent to which the harm to relationships resulting from the wrongdoing has been addressed. Nor does the recognition that restored relationships will demand constant attention mean that the work of reparation will be endless. The aim of restorative plans is to take steps towards restored relationships and thus a just future. The dynamic nature of a relationship means that all that can be expected of this plan is to begin the process of restoration, to create the conditions and remove the obstacles to such a just future. The discrete task of reparation, then, and the one that will dictate the extent and type of reparations required in a given case, is to respond to harms resulting from wrongdoing in a forward looking way with a view to the restoration of relationship.

Given the key role that reparation plays as the workhorse of restorative justice, the failure to follow through on reparation is likely to have serious negative consequences for the success of a restorative process. It would certainly impede the project of restoring relationships, but the effects might be even more harmful to the aim of restorative justice than simply stalling progress towards its aim. The failure to provide reparation can constitute a further harm to relationships and thus move the parties further away from justice. This is perhaps particularly true in cases where some measure of restoration was begun at the encounter process. In some real sense the failure to carry through the common agreement that arose out of an encounter process casts doubt on the sincerity and commitment of that party to the process itself. It might thus be interpreted as a further violation of the relationships between and among the parties to the process and thereby undermine what limited level of trust was operating at the encounter session and upon which the agreement was based. Thus, what is lost by the failure to carry out reparation is not simply an unfulfilled promise or the failure of a part of the restorative process – it is the very possibility of restorative justice. Failure to fulfil an obligation to make reparation does not merely leave the work of restorative justice unfinished, it might undermine it entirely.

This does not mean that reparation must be perfectly executed in all cases lest the entire process be deemed a failure. The degree to which an agreement must be completed will depend on the parties' expectations and the surrounding circumstances. For example, in some cases a reasonable and good faith effort to fulfil a condition in an agreement and the attempt to provide reparation may be sufficient to serve the purpose of addressing the harm. This is particularly so if the reparation was largely symbolic in significance. However, what is clear is that the complete failure to provide reparations or a significant failure will doubtless have serious implications for the possibility of restorative justice.

Restorative Justice and Reparation

The above discussion of the role of reparation in restorative justice sheds some light on the nature of reparation itself. Indeed, restorative justice offers a conceptual framework through which to understand reparation. This restorative justice framework makes sense of reparation and the function it serves in response to wrongdoing. This understanding of reparation also makes clear the important role restorative justice processes can have in the project of reparation. Restorative justice processes stand able to play a crucial role in ensuring the legitimacy and success of reparations. This section will explore the role of restorative justice in reparation both as a framework through which to understand the nature and purpose of reparation and as a means of determining appropriate reparation. In the end, the role of restorative justice in reparation serves to strengthen the case for the importance of such processes in transitional contexts.

Restorative justice serves an important function with respect to the project of reparation by providing a conceptual framework within which one can understand the idea of reparation. Further, it serves as the basis for a conception of reparation that is appropriate to transitional contexts. Restorative justice serves to make sense of our instincts about reparation. It offers an explanation of how it is that reparation works to address the harm caused by wrongdoing and why reparation can include monetary and non-monetary components.[16] Restorative justice also serves as a basis for distinguishing between reparation and restitution/compensation, and explaining why reparation is to be preferred as a means of responding to wrongdoing. Finally, restorative justice also offers some principled basis from which to set limits on what reparation might include.

The conception of reparation that emerges from an appreciation of its role in restorative justice is forward-looking and animated by the goal of restoring relationships. Reparation contributes to the process of restoration first by offering redress for harm in an effort to remove obstacles to restoration, and, secondly, by demonstrating a commitment to relationships in which the parties enjoy equal respect, concern and dignity. At times, the process of reparation itself models these relationships, for example, when the process of reparation engages a wrongdoer in a relationship with the victim – whether it be visiting an elderly victim who requires company or working for a victim's business harmed by the wrongdoer's actions. Thus it is clear why reparation often includes both monetary and non-monetary elements. Given that the concern of reparation is the restoration of relationships, the means and methods of reparation have to demonstrate a commitment to, and capacity for, restored relationships. This often requires more than a material transfer from wrongdoer to victim. It requires a creative and context-specific reparation plan that might include monetary payments and/or the performance of particular acts or undertakings.

The lens of restorative justice also makes clear that reparation is future-oriented and not intended simply as payment for some past act. This is notably what distinguishes reparation from restitution and compensation, both of which aim, although in slightly different ways, at a return of the *status quo ante*. Restitution as a common law concept roughly denotes the idea that a gain or benefit wrongly taken or enjoyed should be returned. At its base restitution takes the view that through his or her actions the wrongdoer has been enriched at the expense of the victim. By disgorging him- or herself of the benefit of the offending actions and returning that which was taken from the sufferer, the wrongdoer 'rights' the wrong he or she created. The restitutionary aim is thus that things be returned to the way they were before the wrong occurred. The wrong-doer must return that *thing* which he or she has taken from the victim. Compensation is similar in focus to restitution, although it entails a recognition that it is often not possible to return the *thing* that was taken, and, in that case, what will be required is the return of something commensurate with the loss. That something very often involves a material transfer from wrongdoer to victim. The term reparation as understood within the framework of restorative justice denotes a commitment to addressing the harms resulting from the wrong consistent with restitution and compensation, but reparation combines this with a commitment to understanding and addressing the implications of that wrong for the future. Reparation, then, is animated by a forward-looking cause – the restoration of relationships to the ideal of social equality – in contrast to the backward focus of restitution and compensation. This forward-looking orientation is what makes reparation more appropriate to contexts facing the challenge of dealing with their past with a view to making the transition to a new and democratic future.

Finally, a restorative justice framework provides a principled basis upon which to determine what can properly be included in a plan for reparation. That is to say, restorative justice can generate appropriate limits for reparation. Reparation, aimed as it is at the restoration of relationships, could not involve or cause harm. For example, it cannot be designed with a view to punishing or causing pain or humiliation to the wrongdoer. Quite simply this would defeat the purpose of reparation as it would take the parties further away from relationships of social equality. The nature of restored relationships is such that they cannot be achieved by diminishing or harming the wrongdoer. Restorative justice does not aim at an equality of harm but rather at respect, concern and dignity.

This last point is closely connected to the other function restorative justice serves with respect to reparation. Restorative justice furnishes legitimacy for reparation; it provides a process through which reparation can be determined so as to ensure their legitimacy and increase the likelihood of their success. Reparation that grows out of a restorative process has legitimacy because it is designed by the parties who have a stake in the outcome of the situation – those who will perform or receive this reparation. Their participation and input into the determination and design of reparation means they are more likely to be committed to, and satisfied by, the reparation. Legitimacy also derives from the fact that this reparation is designed by those most aware of what is needed to address the harm and restore their relationships. Thus reparation resulting from a restorative justice process is more likely to be successful in that it will be meaningful for the parties at which it is aimed. It will be successful in responding to the needs and wants of the victims and/or community because it is born out of a process that took full account of them. This role of restorative justice with respect to reparation is yet another factor commending the use of restorative processes in transitional contexts. Further, it might give some pause for thought as to the chance for success of those reparation plans designed without such a process.

South Africa and the Issue of Reparation

The proposed relationship between restorative justice and reparation has significant implications for South Africa and in particular for the current debate over their government's position on reparation. Specifically, the relationship between restorative justice and reparation ought to give cause to the South African government to rethink its delay and inaction with respect to the TRC's recommendations on reparation. While there has been some provision of urgent interim reparation, the majority of victims still await the fulfilment of the reparation promise. The government indicated that the delay on reparation resulted in part from their desire to review the addendum to the *Final Report* of the TRC which addresses the work of the Amnesty Committee and provides further information on those accorded victim status. Given that this further report of the TRC will not alter its original recommendations on reparation, the strength of this argument for delay is questionable. Regardless, at the time of writing the government was in receipt of the *Report* from the TRC and thus there ought to be no further reason to delay the implementation of the reparation recommended by the Commission. There have, however, been indications that even with the work of the Commission completed the government does not intend to implement the TRC's reparation recommendations. Doubt has been cast on the government's commitment to individual reparation in general and specifically with respect to the TRC's reparation plan.

The discussion of the relationship between restorative justice and reparation suggests strongly that the South African government needs to make good on the promise of reparation and in particular why they ought to implement reparation according to the recommendations of the TRC. In the event, however, that the government chooses to revisit the TRC recommendations and develop its own plan for reparation, the importance of restorative justice to the project of reparation has significant implications for the way in which such a plan ought to be developed.

The fundamental role reparation plays in the work of restorative justice grounds two arguments for reparation in the South African context. First, the failure to make reparation seriously threatens the possibility of restorative justice. Justice understood restoratively cannot be achieved through words and intention alone. It must be realised through a demonstrated commitment to restored relationships and the stage set through attention to addressing the harms resulting from wrongdoing. Thus, restorative justice requires much more than its critics suggest – hugs and apologies are not nearly enough. Reparation does much of the work of restoration, and, in their absence, the prospect of restorative justice is seriously diminished if not entirely removed. This serves as a compelling reason to take reparation seriously in the South African context. The restoration of relationships to ones of social equality is a fundamental element of the transition to a future marked by respect for human rights. Inaction on reparation thus threatens the restoration of relationships and, by extension, the ultimate success of the transition to a rights-respecting future. The failure to provide reparation not only threatens the prospects of restorative justice in South Africa, but in the process stands to undermine the work and the ultimate success of the TRC.

This provides another reason for the government to make good on the promise of reparation. The success of the TRC as a restorative process will depend upon the fulfilment of the promise of reparation. It was this promise that prompted many victims to come forward to participate in the process and tell their story. Further, this reparation is the mechanism through which the plan for the restoration of relationships is carried out. In its absence the groundwork laid for such restoration by the Commission process will be left unfulfilled. Worst still, from the perspective of the victims, in the name of restoration the Commission has already provided amnesty to the perpetrators. Yet since restoration also requires reparation to be realised, failure in this respect leaves the perpetrators free, while removing the primary mechanisms through which the work of restoration is to be accomplished. Inaction on reparation, then, runs the risk of undermining the work done by the TRC as it casts doubt on the commitments at the very heart of the Commission and leaves its plan for the future unrealised.

These arguments make the case for reparation but not necessarily for the implementation of the TRC's recommendations. The provision of reparation is indeed important to the goal of restorative justice; however not just any reparation will do. The nature of the reparation matters as to whether it will fulfil its role in restorative justice. As indicated in the discussion above, in order to play this role, reparation must contribute to and not detract from the restoration of relationships. Reparation developed through a restorative process (one that is inclusive of the parties with a stake in the outcome of the situation and one committed to the restoration of relationships) is more likely to be successful in its work towards restorative justice. This ought to serve as a persuasive reason for the South African government to respect the recommendations of the TRC on reparation. The TRC as a restorative justice process was in the best position to determine appropriate reparation.

It is important to acknowledge, in making this case for the implementation of the TRC's recommendations, that the argument is not intended to suggest, nor need it prove, that the TRC was a perfect model of a restorative justice process. Indeed, there are many ways in which the TRC process might have been improved from the perspective of restorative justice. The use of restorative justice as a framework through which to understand the work of the TRC means that this standard also ought to be used to evaluate the TRC. An evaluation of the weaknesses and strengths of the TRC as a restorative process might offer significant and important insights for how this model might be developed and applied in other contexts. However, the acknowledgement that the TRC may not have been perfect as a restorative process does not mean it was not restorative in its orientation. Further, it does not affect the claim that its recommendations on reparation ought to be respected. The TRC process, while not perfect, was restorative in its orientation and approach, and its reparation recommendations were born out of this process and thus reflect a commitment to restorative justice. The TRC's recommendations then ought to be taken very seriously by the South African government as they are more likely to serve the function required of reparation in restorative justice in that they were designed out of a process consciously aimed at the restoration of relationships.

The South African government then ought to implement the recommendations of the TRC because they are more likely to be successful for several reasons. First, because they were designed with the aim of restoration in mind. Second, because they were designed through an inclusive process through which the input of the interested parties was taken as the foundation for the reparation recommended. By dealing with victims and perpetrators within the same process, the Commission was able to draw upon their views and perspectives to provide significant insight and information to the Reparation & Rehabilitation Committee. The Committee was also intentional about soliciting and incorporating the views of the community.[17] The recommendations of the Committee were thus drawn from a process that brought together the parties with a stake in the outcome of the situation – a restorative process. Third, the participation of the relevant parties ensures that the reparation will not only respond to their needs and be satisfying, but also increases the likelihood that the parties will be committed to their fulfilment because of their role in the process through which they were developed.

That the TRC embodied, in significant measure, restorative principles, in particular with respect to its reparation recommendations, offers a compelling reason for the South African government to make good on the Commission's recommendations. There is, however, some significant reason to worry that this might be unlikely. The government has not only delayed implementation of the recommendations, but has given some signals that if reparation is provided it will be the result of the government's own plan. Further, the discourse surrounding the recommendations for reparation from the TRC (particularly the opinions and views of the government) might leave little choice but to rebuild the foundation for reparation since it may undermine the effectiveness of reparation in the restoration of relationships even if they were to be implemented now. For example, comments made by President Mbeki may significantly diminish the restorative value of reparation even were it to be implemented by the government.

> *Honourable members, we must again ask ourselves — what do we understand by reparation? Did our people engage in a gigantic struggle, with some deciding to lay down their lives, with the prospect of financial reward in their minds? I have said, and I will say again, that any such suggestion is an insult to them and to all of us who now enjoy the freedom that they fought for.[18]*

If the government does face the task of revisiting or rewriting the TRC reparation plans, what insights does the discussion of the relationship between reparation and restorative justice have to offer the government as to how it ought to proceed? First it suggests that the South African government must make some serious and substantial effort to provide reparation soon. It also suggests that if the government intends to table its own plan (either distinct from the TRC's recommendations or in order to implement them) it needs to take seriously the importance of restorative justice processes to the legitimacy and success of reparation. Thus they ought to arrive at their plan through a process consistent with restorative principles — most importantly, then, it must be an inclusive process that brings together the stakeholders with a view to designing reparation that would work towards the restoration of relationships.

This is not a call for a new truth commission, or to revisit the recommendations of the TRC. Indeed it is my view that the TRC recommendations, coming as they do out of a restorative justice-based process, ought to be implemented, or at least serve as an important basis for any further discussion about reparation. Rather, I am suggesting that the government, insofar as it intends to make its own plan with respect to reparation and its implementation, ought to come to its decision through an inclusive process.

This suggestion must be tempered by one significant fact — time is of the essence. Victims have waited a long time and the delay has likely already harmed the cause of restoration, so it is important that such a process not be used as a further stalling or avoidance tactic. Whatever is to be done must happen in a timely manner and be attentive and sensitive to the concerns of the victims whose patience must already be at an end. On the other hand, however, a rush to reparation without sufficient attention to ensure that it is legitimate, meaningful and appropriate for victims and the community is not an acceptable solution. In terms of timelines, the easiest path would of course be to recognise that the reparations recommended by the TRC have the virtue of being the result of a restorative justice-oriented process and should be implemented. Should the government decide to do otherwise, to alter the recommendations, or develop a plan for implementation, such a plan ought to be developed through a restorative justice process and must take the work and insights of the TRC as a starting point. Such a process must include consultation with victims, perpetrators and the community, and use the insights from the TRC experience, and the information arising from it, as a fundamental starting point.

Notes

1 Truth and Reconciliation Commission of South Africa, Final Report, Vol. 1 (Pretoria: RSA, 1998), 117–131.
2 TRC, *Final Report,* 117.
3 TRC, *Final Report,* 119–120.
4 See Jennifer J. Llewellyn, 'Justice for South Africa: Restorative Justice and the Truth and Reconciliation Commission', in *Moral Issues in Global Perspective,* ed., Christine Koggel (Peterborough, Ontario: Broadview Press, 1999) 96–111; Jennifer Llewellyn and Robert Howse, 'Institutions for Restorative Justice: The South African Truth and Reconciliation Commission', in *University of Toronto Law Journal* (1999) 49: 355–388.
5 Speech by the justice minister when introducing the Promotion of National Unity and Reconciliation legislation (the TRC Act) to Parliament. As quoted in TRC, *Final Report,* 106.
6 Or the truth versus justice dilemma posited by the editors of a recent collection on the morality of truth commissions. See Robert I. Rotberg and Dennis Thompson (eds.), *Truth v. Justice: The Morality of Truth Commissions* (New Jersey: Princeton University Press, 2000).
7 For a general description of the government's failure in this respect see Paul van Zyl, 'Unfinished Business: The Truth and Reconciliation Commission's Contribution to Justice in Post-Apartheid South Africa', in *Post-Conflict Justice,* ed. M. Cherif Bassiouni (New York: Transnational, 2002) 745–759.
8 See generally Michael Lapsley and Karin Chubb, 'Common Guilt or Common Responsibility? Moral Arguments for Reparations in South Africa', in *From Rhetoric to*

Responsibility: Making Reparations to the Survivors of Past Political Violence in South Africa (Centre for the Study of Violence and Reconciliation). Reprinted at: http://www.csvr.org.za/papers/papr2r3.htm (accessed 6 March 2003); Shadrack Gutto, 'Constitutional, International and Comparative Law Perspectives on Reparation', in *From Rhetoric to Responsibility.*

9   Tony Marshall, *Restorative Justice: An Overview* (London: Home Office Research Development and Statistics Directorate, 1999), 5.

10 For a full discussion of the need for a definition of restorative justice see generally Jennifer J. Llewellyn and Robert Howse, *Restorative Justice – A Conceptual Framework* (Ottawa: Law Commission of Canada, 1998).

11 The answer is of course not quite as simple as it appears as it requires an answer to the question: what is proportional punishment? Much ink has been spilt by criminal justice theories and policy-makers seeking an answer to this question. They have offered a partial answer by identifying those punishments that are never appropriate, namely those that are cruel and unusual. Despite the intractability of the debate over proportionality, retributive justice can at least satisfy with a general answer as to what is required for justice – punishment – even if the details of how much or what kind of punishment remain to be worked out.

12 It is perhaps not entirely correct to say 'it depends' for there are some responses that cannot be accepted if justice means the restoration of relationships. Specifically, justice cannot be served on a restorative account by any response that isolates and removes a party from the relationship altogether. For a relationship to be restored both parties must remain in the relationship. Most obviously this would preclude the death penalty as a possible requirement of justice. Notice that this is a point often missed by those who maintain restorative justice as victim-centred rather than as it is properly conceived of as 'relationship-centred'. In a victim-centred account, the aim of restorative justice is understood as restoring the victim. This conception of restorative justice would place the victim in a privileged position since he or she would know better than others what would restore harm and make him or her whole. A victim could, for example, assert that only the death of the perpetrator would suffice.

13 TRC, *Final Report,* 48–49.

14 For a full discussion of the principles of restorative justice see Llewellyn and Howse, *Conceptual Framework.*

15 Again for an elaboration of this point see generally Llewellyn and Howse, *Conceptual Framework.*

16 Regarding the oft-used distinction between monetary and symbolic reparation, by its very nature reparation understood from the perspective of restorative justice serves some symbolic function, monetary or not.

17 For an overview of the work of the Reparation and Rehabilitation Committee see TRC, Final Report, Vol. 1, Chapter 10.

18 As quoted in Yasmin Sooka, 'The Unfinished Business of the TRC', in *From Rhetoric to Responsibility.*

11

Across the Divides of Perception:

The Strategic and Moral Demands of Reparation at the End of the TRC

Karin Lombard

On the eve of a decade of democracy, South Africa has a great deal to celebrate. However, the recently released 2001 census figures reveal that South Africa's young democracy still faces many of the economic concerns it faced prior to its first democratic elections. Moreover, South Africa's socio-economic divisions largely continue to reinforce racial cleavages in terms of the demographic profile of the poorest of the poor still being almost exclusively black.[1] Although research clearly demonstrates that the racial composition of the middle class is changing, the proportion of the entire population that this middle class represents renders the impact of this change on the transformation of the larger society minimal.[2] This research indicates that most whites and some blacks now enjoy a relatively high level of socio-economic affluence, but that racial divisions are still apparent in the unacceptably high proportions of black South Africans whose daily experience is that of grinding poverty.

Public opinion data reveals that South Africans' attitudes on reparations and reconstruction run along racial lines.[3] Concerned with the precise terms of these perceptions, this chapter contends that the obvious disjuncture between black and white opinion raises a number of difficult questions about South Africa's capacity to sustain a process of transformation that might redress gross socio-economic inequality. The data considered here suggests reasons why white South Africans are apparently unwilling to take significant responsibility for reparation and the larger reconstruction process. More precisely, the evidence indicates that those who possess the country's human and economic capital are unlikely to become involved in the reduction of inequality if such programmes are premised on a need or duty to 'take responsibility for past injustice'. As the memory of apartheid brutality fades from immediate view, the risk of this failure is compounded by time. Although certainly not a perfect solution, it may be to the nation's advantage to adopt a strategy premised on the notion that it is in the interests of present capital holders, and not their moral obligation, to become active participants in economic transformation.

Under the mandate of the Promotion of National Unity and Reconciliation Act, the Truth and Reconciliation Commission (TRC) made recommendations for institutional reforms, legal and administrative measures, symbolic reparations in the form of memorials and monuments, community rehabilitation programmes and monetary payments. The recommendation for financial compensation, however, elicited the most vigorous and heated debate – a debate that was certainly not restricted to victims and perpetrators.

The complex knot of emotional, material and psychological needs of the victims of gross human rights violations identified by the TRC renders it very difficult to assess the degree to which monetary payment is important to them.[4] The liveliness of the debate about reparation payments to the victims of gross human rights violations appears to suggest, however, that monetary compensation is very important to South Africans. A national survey conducted in 2000 provided a reliable source for investigating this assumption.[5] The national data set in question does not allow for any evaluation of the salience of this issue to victims on an individual level, focusing instead on the significance of victim reparations on a macro-level to a national sample of South Africans.

The data revealed that approximately six out of every ten respondents thought national reconciliation requires material compensation, suggesting that monetary payments are broadly important to the majority of South Africans. However, the data also revealed that fewer respondents identified material compensation than any of the other potential preconditions provided as being critical for the national reconciliation process. More respondents claimed that the need for greater forgiveness, understanding and the healing of memories was indispensable, and even the provision of amnesty as a prerequisite for reconciliation was supported by more South Africans than was financial payment. This implies that while material compensation is generally important, it certainly does not take precedence over other prerequisites of reconciliation, with those addressing the subjective mending of relationships between previously

Table 1: South African support for different preconditions for national reconciliation

	Percentage in agreement					
	All SA (%)	Black (%)	White (%)	Coloured (%)	Indian (%)	
National reconciliation requires that South Africans understand one another better	74.4	76.9	63.1	80	60	χ^2=191.060, p<.000.
National reconciliation requires[6] material compensation for victims of apartheid	58.9	69.6	20.6	54.1	26	χ^2=471.158, p<.000.
National reconciliation requires that people forgive one another	77.9	80.7	63.8	84.5	64	χ^2=195.023, p<.000.
National reconciliation requires forgetting the past	65.9	66 6	3.5	74.1	56	χ^2=124.407, p<.000.
National reconciliation requires the healing of memories	70.8	73.5	56	78.6	59	χ^2=190.733, p<.000.
National reconciliation requires amnesty as provided by the TRC	60.7	69.1	30.6	59.1	28	χ^2=354.96, p p<.000.
	N = 2 200	N = 1 560	N = 320	N = 220	N = 100	

divided parties being more frequently identified as mandatory preconditions.

Consequent experimental survey research, undertaken in 2001, to evaluate the importance of material compensation in influencing judgements of fairness of the TRC outcomes to victims, yielded similar findings.[7] The payment of material compensation to victims had the greatest positive effect on people's assessment of the fairness, but the effect was not very large and the effect of giving people an opportunity to talk about their experiences in public and/or receive an apology was also substantial.[8] Whether South Africans evaluate the salience of the issue of material compensation for national reconciliation or for the fairness of the TRC outcome for victims, the results appeared similar. Material compensation is important, but giving people a voice or an apology (in the case of evaluations of fairness to victims) or understanding and forgiveness (at a national reconciliation basis) are equally, if not more, important.

Intuition suggests, however, that the salience of material compensation will largely depend on whether the respondent is a potential benefactor or beneficiary of such policy decisions. This intuition appears substantiated by the empirical data, as out of all the issues addressed in the 2000 study, the issues of material compensation, and to a lesser degree amnesty, revealed the biggest divide in opinion between black and white South Africans. Seventy per cent of black South Africans claimed material compensation was necessary for the process of national reconciliation, while only 21% of white South Africans believed this to be the case. There is a palpable reluctance by white South Africans to agree that these aspects are essential parts of national reconciliation.

While this is probably to be expected in the case of material compensation, the results of the amnesty statement are unanticipated, as one might have expected whites to be more positive about this aspect, with more members of the white community potentially benefiting from this provision. Less than a third of white respondents agreed that national reconciliation requires amnesty as provided by the TRC. This is potentially the result of the disapproval of the TRC as a whole displayed by many white South Africans.[9]

These findings were substantiated in a later national survey conducted in early 2001, which revealed that almost three-quarters of blacks (72%) approved of amnesty, despite the fact that amnesty was sometimes given to those committing abuses in defence of the apartheid state, while among white South Africans the portion approving was substantially less at 39%. Coloured and Indian South Africans, as for most of the questions, fall between black and white opinion. The other components did not demonstrate any major racial differences.

The divergence between black and white South Africans on the relative importance of material payment appears replicated with regard to the question of who bears responsibility for reparation. Despite considerable opposition, the new democratic government took the responsibility of reparation for victims of human rights violations in the past upon itself.[10] Former TRC commissioner Yasmin Sooka articulates the obvious injustice in this arrangement:

> *What is tragic is that the new government, who inherited a bankrupt structure, has to bankroll reparations for the sins committed by the past government.*

Those who benefited from the spoils of apartheid are still benefiting. There has been no special tax imposed, no need for any act of personal contrition, no need for an act of restitution to the victims directly, no loss of jobs or land.[11]

To investigate the level of support for non-state actors, and in particular 'beneficiaries' of the apartheid regime, bearing the responsibility for financial reparations, respondents to the 2001 national survey were asked whether they would support or oppose nine different institutions or groups of people footing the reparation bill. These included big businesses in South Africa, the Afrikaans churches, white South Africans, individual companies that profited from apartheid, South African farmers, the perpetrators themselves, black beneficiaries of affirmative action, all South Africans – via new taxes – and wealthy South Africans – via a special wealth tax. Both the previous government and the present government were intentionally left out of the list.

Not surprisingly, the data in Table 2 revealed that the perpetrators themselves (79%) were most frequently selected as those who should be responsible for compensation. White farmers were also frequently selected (66%) as benefactors of victim compensation, although the support is substantially less than for perpetrators. This wide-ranging support for holding white farmers accountable and responsible is not unexpected in light of the finding that settlers of European descent misappropriated 90% of all land, while enjoying the benefits of cheap black labour and generous government subsidies.[12]

Sixty-five per cent of respondents were in support of compensation being the responsibility of all white South Africans. This, no doubt, speaks in part to the extent to which a large portion of the South African population recognise the degree to which whites aided and abetted apartheid by not presenting overt opposition to the system, as well as the extent to which they profited from apartheid.

The strong precedent set by Archbishop Desmond Tutu in his capacity as chairperson of the TRC, when he proclaimed business as being 'central to the economy that sustained the South African state during the apartheid years,'[13] appears to have manifested itself in the minds of South Africans, as the data also demonstrated substantial support for business to bear responsibility for the compensation of victims of apartheid. While more respondents felt that only those companies which had directly and clearly benefited from apartheid – as opposed to big business in general – should

Table 2: South African support for potential benefactors of reparations for victims of apartheid

	Percentage in agreement					
	All SA (%)	Black (%)	White (%)	Coloured (%)	Indian (%)	
Large business	69.3	82.1	24.2	44.8	53.1	χ^2=1320.961, p<.000.
Afrikaans churches	64.3	78.1	15.6	32.3	58.0	χ^2=1383.515, p<.000.
White South Africans	64.8	78.9	10.0	37.5	60.4	χ^2=1624.722, p<.000.
Individual companies that profited	71.5	81.9	34.0	54.2	63.7	χ^2=1064.277, p<.000.
South African farmers	65.9	80.4	9.5	40.0	52.2	χ^2=1628.743, p<.000.
The perpetrators themselves	79.3	84.8	63.4	65.2	87.8	χ^2=707.089, p<.000.
Black beneficiaries of affirmative action	43.9	47.8	33.7	28.0	59.2	χ^2=316.929, p<.000.
All South Africans – via new taxes	26	30.9	12.3	12.9	12.2	χ^2=348.759, p<.000.
Wealthy South Africans – via special tax	52.1	62.6	14.7	35.1	42.4	χ^2=819.615, p<.000.
	N = 3 727	N = 2 002	N = 987	N = 480	N = 245	

be responsible, the difference is insignificant at less than 2%. This could suggest that, in the minds of the majority of South Africans, the lines between companies which obviously benefited from apartheid and those which did not are by no means clear. What appears to be clear is that the majority of South Africans feel that the compensation of victims is the responsibility of the business sector.

These findings raise some interesting questions about the extent of popular support for the recent class actions instituted on behalf of victims of apartheid.[14] Despite the fact that even former president Nelson Mandela has now criticised apartheid lawsuits against South African companies in foreign courts there is unequivocal support for business to pay. But whether South Africans believe corporate involvement should occur on a voluntary basis, as advocated by the South African government, or be dictated by law, as is the case with the apartheid lawsuits, is open to debate.

There is also the question of whether South Africans would perceive actions taken outside of the national criminal justice system as legitimate.[15] This issue ties in with the larger question of how to involve more proactively those who hold the country's human, intellectual and economic capital in the process of capacity-building and socio-economic transformation. While the government certainly has an important role to play, it is corporate South Africa, both black and white-owned and managed, that has the real capacity and resources to bring about wide-ranging change.

The disaggregated data reported in Table 2, however, reveals that despite the presence of policies such as affirmative action and black economic empowerment leading to a greater share of corporate power held by black South Africans, blacks as a whole are still far more willing to single out big businesses as benefactors of reparation. On the other hand, the table reveals far more congruence between the race groups on the issue of black beneficiaries of present-day affirmative action policies footing the bill. Interestingly enough, more black than white South Africans were in favour of these recently enriched black South Africans bearing the responsibility of reparation. Equally interesting is the empirical fact that three times more whites selected black beneficiaries of affirmative action as opposed to white South Africans as benefactors of reparation.

South Africans of differing racial backgrounds appear intractably divided on the questions of South African farmers, white South Africans and the Afrikaans churches being responsible for reparation. The less than 10% of all whites holding farmers accountable is sharply juxtaposed to the 80% of blacks who do so. In a similar vein 79% of blacks hold whites accountable, yet only 10% of whites agree.

The government's recent decision to fulfil, at least in part, the recommendation by the TRC for individual monetary grants to victims of gross human rights violations, renders the apparently inflexible racial cleavages in opinion on this issue less consequential. Unfortunately, this gross disjuncture between beliefs is also evident when South Africans are questioned about their views on affirmatively redressing the grievances of those groups and communities that have suffered previous discrimination. The consequences of black and white South Africans not being able to see eye to eye on this issue may, however, prove more significant.

The SA Reconciliation Barometer national survey conducted in 2002[16] included a number of questions designed to evaluate respondents' support of compensatory or redistributive measures. Respondents were questioned whether they would support or oppose the government implementing the following policy decisions: 'people in formerly disadvantaged racial categories must be given special consideration in education, hiring and promotion decisions, even when their credentials on paper are not as good as their competitors'; 'introducing a compulsory community service year for graduating teachers, to address the quality differences between previously disadvantaged and other schools' and 'introducing a basic yearly financial payment for all previously disadvantaged people'.

All three questions yielded majority support, although immediate financial payment for all previously disadvantaged persons yielded the lowest level of support, at only 54.8%.[17]

Table 3 reports that South Africans reveal a remarkable degree of willingness to make compromises in the present for future benefit, with almost three-quarters of the population registering their support. But disaggregation of the data once again reveals distinct differences across race groups, with far larger percentages of blacks and coloureds than whites willing to make the previously mentioned compromises. While past privileges enjoyed by white South Africans are likely to leave them on the losing end

Table 3: South Africans' support for present socio-economic compromise[18]

	All SA (%)	Black (%)	White (%)	Coloured (%)	Indian (%)
Supporting compromise	72.5	25.4	82.9	71.0	38.8
Uncertain	19.6	33.5	15.9	22.8	19.6
Opposing compromise	7.9	41.1	1.3	6.2	7.9
	N = 3 375	N = 935	N = 1 998	N = 388	N = 170
χ^2=1122.728, p<.000.					

of these kinds of sacrifices, the data belies both a lack of any thoroughgoing realisation that present sacrifices may result in future political, social and – most importantly – economic arrangements that are beneficial to all South Africans, as well as a lack of any substantial recognition that future arrangements need to be infused with *a strong consciousness of the past.*[19]

Consequent research corroborates this absence of significant acknowledgment of past or continued economic benefits ascribed to whites as a result of the colour of their skin. The 2002 survey revealed that only 22.4% of whites agreed with the following statement: 'In the past, whites profited greatly from Apartheid, and most continue to profit today from the legacy of Apartheid.' The percentage of black South Africans who agreed was 73.7%. This denial of beneficiation appears to hinder, as former MP Carl Niehaus explains, 'the beginning of a more mature process of taking joint responsibility for the future of our country',[20] the beginning of a process of whites and other 'haves' becoming actively involved in capital sharing, capacity-building, development and reconstruction drives that extend beyond those projects emphasised by the government.[21] It is an absence of this kind of commitment that prevents greater socio-economic justice and consequent thoroughgoing reconciliation. The extent of denial that whites have and continue to have has prompted some to toy with the idea of a truth commission to inform South Africans of the extent to which white people benefited and enriched themselves at the cost of South Africans of colour.[22]

With the dust of a heady transition beginning to settle, the outlines of a stalemate appear increasingly visible. Corporate South Africa, already at the business sector hearings of the TRC, resolutely refused to recognise any responsibility for upholding apartheid and, despite some exemplary efforts by some businesses, as a whole continue to make inadequate contributions to transformation.[23] The SA Reconciliation Barometer survey found that only 22% of ordinary white South Africans acknowledge that they benefited, economically and otherwise, from apartheid. As a result, very few play an active role in the transformation and reconciliation process. Meanwhile a mass of disenfranchised, marginalised and critically poor black South Africans continue to live under the oppressive regime of historically induced poverty.

It would seem that somewhere between the flood of relief of the 1994 elections and the TRC's final broadcasting of the horrors of apartheid, a sense of complacency emerged. The result of this apathy has been inadequate economic transformation and socio-economic development. The latest *Employment Equity Report* announced that while blacks constitute

77% of all employees, they constitute only 25% of top management positions.[24] According to *Statistics SA*, the average annual household income for urban blacks was R28 816, while white households earned an average R134 489. The differences are far greater in rural areas where the average for a black South African household was R15 269 and in the case of white households R168 919.[25]

In the early 1990s, the risk of economic crisis counselled vigilance over the course of the transition, the need for an ongoing struggle to ensure sustained and equal development. However, this concern for socio-economic rights has proven difficult to sustain, especially as the urgency of pursuing reconciliation has faded from view. In the new South Africa, many of those who found themselves still comfortably off, along with those who found themselves newly comfortable, have found few reasons to promote change. Meanwhile, those still bearing the burden of under-development appear increasingly powerless and voiceless. This dynamic has led some analysts to suggest that the primary weakness of the negotiated settlement was the absence of any agreement on a coherent economic strategy to address the gross poverty and inequality in the country.[26]

Post-TRC South Africa faces the very real possibility of lapsing into stagnation, within which *complacency of the powerful and increasing frustration of the weak becomes the norm.*[27] The outcome of this complacency can be any of a host of new conflicts. The potential for such conflict in South Africa is boldly present. It is nascent in illegal land grabs. The media has reported on ex-liberation fighters involved in cash heists, executed with military precision. The rumble of mass discontent among the hungry and destitute is growing louder.

Most political analysts forecast that there is little chance of a left-wing revolutionary upsurge in the near future. But, as Neville Alexander, commenting in his recent book *An Ordinary Country*, explains there is 'a powerful, potentially explosive, movement of the poor, led substantively, if not formally, by public-service workers ... evolving under the eyes of the new ruling elites of a very old South Africa'.[28] While this upsurge will probably be geared towards a government that has not fulfilled the promise of a 'better life for all', taking joint responsibility for the attainment of socio-economic justice in South Africa's transition is surely in the moral and strategic interests of the privileged.

Frederik van Zyl Slabbert reminds us of the countless 'historical examples that show that if there is no development accompanying the freedom that democracy promises, freedom will be destroyed. First it will be destroyed by crime, corruption and social disintegration, and then by political despotism'.[29]

It is surely in the interest of every single South African that the country is not subject to this kind of degeneration. But other than the obvious role ascribed to government, the South African middle class, into which most whites fall, has the capacity to prevent further decline and eventually even a reverse of this trend. The data has revealed that whites are unlikely to respond to any requests based on moral grounds – there is a general sentiment of having paid enough 'guilt money'. Yet crime, corruption, political instability, precarious worker-employee relations and decreased investment, all intricately linked to the present socio-economic status quo, are some of the biggest threats facing the middle class. It may thus be in the country's best interests and to the primary benefit of the millions of unemployed and virtually unemployable people to put all energies behind a strategy that emphasises that it is in the strategic interests of present capital holders, and not their moral obligation, to become active participants in economic transformation. The time for institutional change and political compromise has come and gone with largely positive results. The time for expansive development, historic redress, reconstruction and economic compromise is upon us.

Notes

1   It should be noted that in making reference to South African racial subgroups – black, white, Indian and coloured – no approval of the apartheid-era classification system or its underlying theory of race is intended. The nature of present-day South African society still bears the scars of an apartheid past, and as such substantial differences between the conditions and orientations of the four main racial groups often persist and need to be rigorously analysed.

2   See N. Nattrass, and J. Seekings, 'Race and Economic Inequality in South Africa', in *Daedalus*. Winter 2001, 45-72; J. Seekings, 'Inequality, Mobility and Politics in South Africa', paper presented at the 19th Annual International Political Science Association Congress, Durban: South Africa, 30 June 2003.

3   Although these terms are often used interchangeably and can take on different connotations in various contexts, in this chapter reparation refers to the redressing of past injustices through some form of recognition, be it symbolic or financial, while reconstruction refers to the larger process of reducing the country's present socio-economic inequality through wide-ranging development and poverty-alleviation strategies. The lines of distinction between the two are, however, very fine and the interconnectedness of these two processes should not be ignored.

4   Some have remarked that reparation is 'a double-edged sword'. While financial compensation and some form of public acknowledgement go some distance towards ameliorating past hurts, 'they can never wholly meet all the psychological needs of the survivors as these are disparate, inchoate and contradictory'. Reported in B. Hamber and R. Wilson, 'Symbolic Closure Through Memory, Reparation and Revenge in Postconflict Societies', paper presented at the Traumatic Stress in South Africa Conference hosted by the Centre for the Study of Violence and Reconciliation in association with the African Society for Traumatic Stress Studies, Johannesburg, South Africa, 27-29 January 1999.

5   The survey included face-to-face interviews with 2 200 South Africans across the country. The questions were translated into eight official languages and the sample was drawn in a scientific manner to replicate the broader South African population. The survey was carried out during July 2000.

6   As this statement does not refer explicitly to the TRC recommended reparations, respondents may have understood this statement to refer either to those victims of gross human rights violations identified by the TRC or, alternatively, all South Africans who were victimised by apartheid in some way.

7   Face-to-face interviews were conducted with a sample of 3 727 South Africans in late 2000/early 2001. The sample is representative of people 18 years and older, throughout the entire country (urban and rural). The interviews were conducted in English, Afrikaans, Zulu, Xhosa, North Sotho, South Sotho, Tswana, Tsonga and Venda, according to the preference of the respondent.

8   J. L. Gibson, 'Truth, Justice and Reconciliation: Judging Amnesty in South Africa', paper delivered at the 59th Annual Meeting of the Midwest Political Science Association, Chicago: Illinois, 19-21 April 2001.

9   76% of blacks approved of the TRC, yet only 37% of whites did. Reported in J. L. Gibson and H. Macdonald, 'Truth – Yes, Reconciliation – Maybe: South Africans Judge the Truth and Reconciliation Process', research report, Institute for Justice and Reconciliation, Rondebosch: South Africa 2001.

10 The TRC Report states, 'the present government has accepted that it is morally obliged to carry the debts of its predecessors and is thus equally responsible for reparation'. TRC, Final Report, Vol. 5, Pretoria: South Africa, 1998, 174.

11 Yasmin Sooka, speaking at Reparations and Memorialisation: The Unfinished Business of the TRC conference, hosted by the Institute for Justice and Reconciliation, 4 October 2000.

12 In this volume, see the chapter by Ntsebeza.

13 TRC, Final Report, Vol. 5, Pretoria: South Africa, 1998, 252.

14 None of the surveys contained questions that referred explicitly to the court cases against various multi-national corporations that have been filed in US courts.

15 Justice Minister Penuell Maduna submitted a nine-page affidavit to a US court, accusing the victims' representatives of seeking to establish a 'surrogate government' and thereby attempting to undermine South Africa's sovereignty.

16 This survey of South Africans, 16 years and older, was conducted between 18 October and 25 November 2002. Face-to-face interviews were conducted with 3 491 South Africans. The survey instrument was first prepared in English and then translated into

Afrikaans, Xhosa, Zulu, North Sotho, South Sotho and Setswana. Respondents were interviewed in the language of their choice.

17 The responses to the three questions were statistically analysed and one underlying construct or index that summarised respondents' support or opposition to actions designed to redress past benefits for greater future equality was distilled. Altogether 63.1% of South Africans supported people in formerly disadvantaged racial categories being afforded special consideration in education, hiring and promotion decisions, even when their credentials on paper are not as good as their competitors, while 61.4% were in favour of introducing a compulsory community service year for graduating teachers to address the quality differences between previously disadvantaged and other schools.

18 The factor loadings on the three items in the order of the table were .829, .806 and .833 respectively. The reliability score was .76.

19 H. Taylor, 'The Future of Remembrance in South Africa's Deeply Divided Society', paper presented at The Future of Remembrance conference, Germany, 6-9 September 2000.

20 In a newsletter to members of the Home For All Campaign, quoted in *Time*, 8 January 2001.

21 Such as the mandatory 1% of payroll training levy that is now required from corporations.

22 Suggested by philosophy professor Hennie Lotter in an article in *The Star*, 30 April 2003.

23 A *Financial Mail* report on 4 April 2003 reported that an annual Trialogue survey of the top 100 companies on the JSE puts South Africa's annual corporate donations at R2,2 billion or 1,2% of pre-tax profits. It also reported that research by the SA Foundation reveals only 1% of after-tax profits. At that stage the Business Trust had received donations to the extent of R800 million.

24 Department of Labour: Commission for Employment Equity Report 1999-2001. http://www.labour.gov.za/docs/reports/CEE%20Annual%20Report.pdf

25 Statistics SA, *Income and Expenditure of Households, 2000,* published in November 2002.

26 A. Habib and V. Padayachee, 'Economic Policy and Power Relations in South Africa's Transition to Democracy', *World Development,* Vol. 28, 2, 2000, 245–263.

27 C. Villa-Vicencio, 'The Courage to Live Together: Material and Subjective Reconciliation', paper delivered at Conference on Truth, Justice and Reconciliation, Stockholm: Sweden, 23-24 April 2002.

28 N. Alexander, *An Ordinary Country* (Pietermaritzburg: University of Natal Press, 2003). These include issue-based movements or organisations rallying against the privatisation of municipal services, the termination of access to water and electricity, evictions for faulting on bond or rent payments, the government's refusal to roll out anti-retroviral drugs and the withholding of burial rights on white-owned farms.

29 *Financial Mail,* September 8, 2003.

12

Reconciliation, Reparation and Reconstruction in Post-1994 South Africa:
What Role for Land?

Lungisile Ntsebeza

In keeping with the provisions of the 1993 Interim Constitution of South Africa, the Truth and Reconciliation Commission (TRC), which was established in terms of the Promotion of National Unity and Reconciliation Act of 1995, embarked on a process whose aim was to reconcile South Africans and transform South African society. The TRC was established against the backdrop of a society characterised by deep racial and class divisions, suffering and injustice. An area where these divisions and injustices of the past manifested themselves and which forms the basis of this chapter is land.

Unlike Zambia where white settlers seized only about 3% of the land surface of the entire country or Malawi where they took 5% or Namibia where they grabbed 43% or Zimbabwe where they acquired about 50%, in South Africa white settlers appropriated more than 90% of the land, thus dispossessing the vast majority of the indigenous population and confining them to reserves in the remaining marginal portions of land.[1] The skewed distribution of land in the country is one of the pillars underlying the success of white commercial agriculture in South Africa. There is another crucial pillar that needs to be highlighted: captured cheap black labour.

This chapter raises the issue of the relevance of land in the reconciliation and reparation debate in post-1994 South Africa. It does so against the background of the establishment of the South African land reform programme soon after the advent of democracy in South Africa in 1994. The chapter raises serious questions about the adequacy of the land reform programme in addressing the fundamental land reform, which must shift substantial ownership of land from whites to previously dispossessed blacks. It contends that there is a fundamental contradiction in the Constitution's objectives of safeguarding the existing land rights of property owners while at the same time aiming to redistribute land to blacks. The legacy of colonialism and apartheid in South Africa has indeed led to vast racial economic inequalities. Consequently, the chapter argues, a much more comprehensive land reform policy is required if the need 'truly to transform South Africa into the truly non-racial, non-sexist, prosperous and human society visualized in our Constitution' is to be met.[2] The chapter concludes with some thoughts on how a comprehensive land reform policy could heal the wounds of the past in keeping with the spirit of the Promotion of National Unity and Reconciliation Act.

The Colonial and Apartheid Legacy: the Question of Land Dispossession

One of the abiding legacies of colonialism and apartheid is that despite the advent of democracy in 1994, the vast majority of land continues to be under white control and ownership. Colonialism and apartheid systematically dispossessed Africans of their land, confined them to small reserves in the remaining land while at the same time constraining African access to land outside these reserves.[3] In the process, colonialism created two agricultures: commercial agriculture for white settlers and subsistence agriculture for African rural people. Central to the success of white commercial agriculture was the availability of a captured cheap black labour. These Africans were bound to white farms in various tenant relationships, mainly as farm workers and labour tenants. Often, some were available as seasonal migrant workers, driven by poverty in the rural areas of what was then the Bantustans, the so-called communal areas under the jurisdiction of chiefs.

The immediate origins of the current land inequalities can be dated back to the introduction of the 1913 Natives Land Act.[4] It is this Act that restricted Africans to reserves after the establishment of the Union of South Africa in 1910. As is well known by now, the 'scheduled areas' that became the reserves amounted to only 7% of the land. The bulk of the land, the so-called prescribed areas, was put aside for white ownership. Provision was made after the 1913 Land Act to release more land to Africans, a process that led to the introduction of the 1936 Natives Trust

Act which extended the reserve areas to 13% of the South African land surface. This was the situation until 1994.

White commercial farmers, who constitute a mere 55 000 of the 42 million South African population, own the bulk of land in South Africa. The total area of land in South Africa is 122.5m hectares. Of this, around 85.2m hectares is used for commercial agriculture. This means that just over 70% of the land, at the advent of democracy in 1994, was owned by fewer than 1% of the population – an average of 1 500 ha per white farmer.[5] By contrast, about 1.4 million Africans engaged in cultivation eked out a lingering existence in less than 13% of the land. The following breakdown in 1994 tells the story: about 50% cultivated an area of less than one hectare, 22% an area between one and two hectares and only 1% had more than ten hectares under cultivation.[6]

Apart from owning vast tracts of land, white farmers established themselves through their naked and thorough exploitation of a captured cheap black labour.[7] Sampie Terreblanche argues: 'The agricultural sector benefited from paying extraordinary wages to farm workers whose mobility and bargaining power were seriously constrained by the strict application of the pass laws.'[8] African farm workers in particular were the worst paid category of worker in South Africa, earning an average of R535 per month in 1996. This is despite the fact that surveys suggest that African wages increased steadily between 1994 and 1996. The average income of African farm workers contrasts sharply with their white counterparts who earn on average R4 613 a month.[9]

It is worth noting that the TRC found that 'the white agricultural industry benefited from its privileged access to land and that it failed to provide adequate facilities and services for employees and their dependants'.[10] However, Terreblanche is of the opinion that the TRC was mild in its findings:

> The Commission is in fact mistaken to think that the agricultural sector benefited mainly from its privileged access to land. Although access to land was important, its really privileged position was based on its access to very cheap and bounded black labour.[11]

Until recently, most farm workers lived on the farms where they were employed. The majority did not have any other home. These farm workers lived with their families, some of whom were not even employed.

However, since the late 1980s, farm workers have been losing their jobs. Out of about 1 323 694 farm workers in 1985, about 180 000 regular employees and about 210 000 casual and seasonal employees lost their jobs between 1985 and 1996.[12] The loss of jobs has further aggravated the plight of farm workers not only in terms of not having income, however small, but also in terms of security of tenure.

The South African Land Reform Programme: Post-1994 South Africa's Response

Since 1994, the Department of Land Affairs has embarked on a land reform programme. This programme is anchored in three components, land restitution, redistribution and tenure reform. Of the three elements, this chapter will focus on land redistribution for the simple reason that it is this component that has the potential of redressing the fundamental issue of land inequality in South Africa. The restitution leg of the programme has severe limitations, for example, the 1913 cut-off date means that claims based on land dispossession before June 1913 cannot be lodged; the fact that some claims could be settled through cash payments; and, finally, that an unknown, though potentially significant, number of claimants missed the 31 December 1998 closing date for the submission of claims, largely due to lack of information and guidance.

In the almost ten-year period since the advent of democracy in South Africa, the Department of Land Affairs has made various pledges and promises in addressing the land question. The first was based on the pledge contained in the election manifesto of the ANC, the Reconstruction and Development Programme (RDP). Based on the recommendations of the World Bank, the RDP promised to redistribute 30% of white-owned agricultural land over a five-year period from 1994. However, by the end of the five years, in 1999, less than 1% of white-owned agricultural land had been redistributed. Some months after her appointment as the Minister of Agriculture and Land Affairs, Thoko Didiza announced in her Strategic Direction in Land Issues address in February 2000 a new target: transfer of 15% of agricultural land to black ownership over a five-year period. This changed again in August 2001 when the Department of Land Affairs launched its Land Redistribution and Agricultural Development Programme. In terms of this programme, 30% of land will be transferred to emerging black commercial farmers over 15 years.[13] It is not clear in the formulation whether the 30% will be white-owned agricultural land or whether state land, including communal land in the former Bantustans, will be part of this percentage.

To date, very little has been achieved. At the end of 2002, a total of 2.3% (around 2m hectares) of the land had been transferred. The breakdown is as follows: 1.7% (about 1.5m hectares) through land redistribution and tenure reform and .6% (about .5m hectares) through restitution.[14] It is worth noting that to achieve even the conservative target of 30% over 15 years, the South African state would have to deliver about 2m hectares per annum. The current average rate over the eight-year period to the end of 2002 was about .25m hectares.

Will the Existing Land Reform Programme Resolve the Land Question?

There is clearly a huge disjuncture between the political freedoms enshrined in the Bill of Rights and the economic realities of post-1994 South Africa. The land question is an important indicator in this regard. The land reform programme in its current form is clearly unable to meet even the modest and conservative targets that the Department of Land Affairs has set for itself. It merely tinkers with the legacy of massive land inequalities. The bulk of the land in this country is still firmly in the hands of a few whites. The question that forces itself on us is why the political emancipation project of post-1994 South Africa is not translating into economic liberation.

Part of the answer can be traced to the fundamental contradiction that exists in the South African Constitution between the objectives of protecting existing property rights on the one hand and a commitment to redistributing land to the dispossessed majority.[15] The two objectives cannot be achieved at the same time simply because the bulk of land outside the former Bantustans is under private ownership and consequently safeguarded by the Constitution. In this regard, a declaration that land will be made available to blacks is rendered void for the simple reason that most land is privately owned by whites. As Mafeje puts it, the declaration eschews the land question and in so doing confirms the status ante.[16]

The mechanism adopted by the South African state to try to resolve the above contradiction, namely the market-led mechanism of purchasing land from white farmers, is linked to this. There is growing evidence of white commercial farmers who are withholding their land in the hope that they can fetch the highest possible price for the land. Thus, the market-led mechanism is not only restricted by the willing-seller-willing-buyer condition, but has also got huge budgetary implications.

Indeed, the low budget allocated for land reform since the inception of the programme will not meet even the conservative target of 30% of land over 15 years. For example, the budget allocations to the Department of Land Affairs over the last three years have been less than 1% of the total budget. The current 2003/4 budget, the highest so far, amounts to about R1.6 billion, a mere .49% of the total budget. This budget falls far below the required amount to meet the current government target.

Although it is not possible to give a precise figure of what the budget should be, the reason being that land prices differ from area to area, the Western Cape gives us a clue of the inadequacy of the current budget. This province has estimated that to meet the 30% departmental target, it would require a budget of about R1.5 billion per annum, that is, over 90% of the entire current budget. Using the Western Cape as an example, it would appear that the state would have to budget around 4-5% of the total budget for land redistribution to meet its current target.

Given the colonial context and the extent of dispossession in South Africa, the targets set by the Department of Land Affairs are indeed very modest, even if sufficient funds were budgeted. It would mean that after 15 years, a maximum of 43% of the land would be under black control. Additionally, the market-led mechanism based on willing-seller-willing-buyer does not seem to take into account the success behind commercial agriculture in South Africa, in particular the super exploitation of black labour and state subsidies. Expropriation, which appears to be a route that the Constitution opens, is itself limited and rendered ineffectual as a result of the property clause in the Constitution and the fact that land will still be purchased. Tinkering is not going to address the vast racial inequalities in land in South Africa. A comprehensive and fundamental land reform programme is needed. In the true spirit of reconciliation and reconstruction, a comprehensive land reform programme is necessary and possible.

Truth and Reconciliation in South Africa as a Healing Process

To ensure a smooth transition from the atrocities of apartheid to democracy, the TRC was established in South Africa in 1995. In terms of the law that set it up, 'the Constitution of the Republic of South Africa, 1993, provides a historic bridge between the past of a deeply divided society characterized by strife, conflict, untold suffering and injustice, and a future founded on the recognition of human rights, democracy and peaceful coexistence for all South Africans, irrespective of colour, race, class and sex'. The Act goes further: 'the Constitution states that the pursuit of national unity, the well-being of all South African citizens and peace, require reconciliation between the people of South Africa and the reconstruction of society ... There is need to understand but not for vengeance, a need for reparation but not for retaliation, a need for ubuntu but not for victimization.'

In his address to Parliament on the occasion of accepting the TRC's Final Report on 15 April 2003, President Thabo Mbeki captured the essence of the above Act when he laid stress on the ideal of 'peace, reconciliation among the people of South Africa and the reconstruction of society'.[17]

With regard to the circumstances and process through which the envisaged reconciliation and reconstruction of society would be achieved, the TRC head of the Investigative Unit, Dumisa Ntsebeza, has recounted:

> *In dealing with reconciliation between victim and perpetrator at the truth commission, perpetrators were compelled to come forward in exchange for absolution from prosecution and civil liability. They had to give a full account of their gross violations of human rights. Victims had the opportunity to have their civil and human dignity restored by telling the stories of their suffering.[18]*

A critical question is how victims and perpetrators were defined by the TRC. It would appear that the Commission took a narrow definition of these groups to mean those who directly suffered or inflicted injury. This definition would exclude those who gave the instructions or created an environment for gross human rights violations. It is in this group that business, including commercial farmers, would fall. According to Ntsebeza:

> *Business is central to the mission of reconciliation and reconstruction, but it has never been called to account. There has never been any legislative framework for business to come before the TRC to give a full disclosure of what they did ... there was no threat to business, whether they came or not. They were under no obligation to make a full disclosure ... Business went to the*

TRC out of courtesy rather than out of conviction that it was the right thing to do. For the most part, they were in denial. They still are.

Yet, as has already been pointed out, business, including commercial farmers, benefited from the apartheid regime. According to Mafeje, the success of capitalist agriculture, not only in South Africa, but in the southern African settler societies was premised on the following:

- Dispossession of the majority of rural dwellers;
- Unlimited captive black labour; and
- An unchanging subsistence sector in the form of Native Reserves.[19]

What Mafeje omitted to add was that the taxpayer, through state subsidies, contributed to the development and enrichment of the agricultural sector in the region. Under these circumstances, it would not be remiss to expect the business sector to come to the party and deliver its side of the bargain in the project of national reconciliation and the reconstruction and transformation of South African society. As Ntsebeza puts it:

For as long as they [business] have not [made a disclosure] in an open and transparent way there will be victims who will seek other solutions to complete the unfinished business of the truth commission. Holding beneficiaries to account is in the interest of promoting national reconciliation. After all, perpetrators ... were compelled to go through a harrowing process of full disclosure before we could, as a society, grant them amnesty and, where possible, forgive them. Why should we not compel our corporate citizens in a similar way?

In an earlier newspaper article, another former TRC commissioner, Yasmin Sooka, was equally forthright about business: 'At the heart of the debate is whether business is prepared to acknowledge the fact that decades of profits were based on the systematic violations of human rights of the vast majority of South Africans.'[20]

Those in the business sector, including commercial farmers, should go beyond merely making full disclosures and disgorge the profits they made under apartheid. I will attempt to show in the following section how this could be achieved in the area of agricultural land.

The Role of Land in the Healing Process in South Africa

The greatest challenge to reconciliation and reconstruction in South Africa is how to end vast racial inequality, of which land is a visible example. Within the context of colonialism and apartheid in South Africa, land is, first and foremost, a political issue. No political stability, democracy or peace are imaginable as long as the bulk of the land is in the hands of whites. Not only was land in the settler societies forcibly taken away from the indigenous majority, white commercial farmers made profits through the thorough exploitation of cheap black labour and state subsidies.

Under these circumstances, a market-based land reform programme, including the willing-seller-willing-buyer approach that the post-1994 South African state has adopted, hardly seems appropriate. If the process of reconciliation and reconstruction in South Africa is to gain the credibility it deserves, land that has been acquired and made profitable in the manner described above cannot be morally and politically justified. The one critical role that white commercial farmers can play if they are serious about reconciliation and reconstruction in South Africa is to donate land and make it available to blacks whose livelihood is dependent on land-based activities. This would apply particularly to the poor, including former and existing farm dwellers, those living in the overcrowded rural areas in the former Bantustans and the urban poor.[21] Moyo has reminded us that the demand for land redistribution in terms of both redressing historically and racially grounded inequalities and of the growing need by both the black poor (rural and urban) and black elite has been a consistent feature of southern Africa politics and policy-making. Examples are the war veterans, landless peasants and the urban poor in Zimbabwe, and the landless in urban and peri-urban South Africa.[22]

A question that forces itself on us is how to achieve this objective without, in the words of the economist Michael de Klerk, 'at the same time seriously impairing the productive capacity of agriculture'.[23] This chapter takes into account this caution while simultaneously not losing sight of the urgent need for enduring reconciliation and restructuring in this country.

A logical starting point, it seems, would be for the state to expropriate land that is unused or under-utilised. This category could also include farms that are in debt. In the case of Zimbabwe, unused and under-utilised land included abandoned farmland.[24] These farms were abandoned during the anti-colonial and independence war of the 1970s. However, the extent of unused and under-utilised land in South Africa is not clear. More research seems desperately needed in this regard. De Klerk is of the view that very little land was abandoned in South Africa for military reasons. Work done by Craig McKenzie, Dan Weiner and Nick Vink in the late 1980s, after the completion of a similar study in Zimbabwe by Dan Weiner and Sam Moyo, came to the conclusion that, unlike in Zimbabwe, there was not substantial unused land in South Africa.[25] In addition, it is quite possible that unused and under-utilised land will be marginal, rather than high potential land.[26]

In the circumstances, the question of putting a ceiling on the farm size becomes critical. The question of farm size would definitely have to take into account the quality of the land. Again, Sam Moyo and Archie Mafeje have revisited the question of farm size in their thinking about land redistribution in southern Africa. Both scholars are extremely critical of the colonial large-scale commercial farm model. The rationale for this model includes the following assumption:

- The freehold landholding system and private land markets are efficient and superior to customary (so-called communal) tenure, thus justifying their preservation;
- That smallholder farmers are less efficient and misuse their land ecologically while large-scale farmers are more efficient in utilising their land; and
- White farmers are technically superior and efficient producers, while blacks are subsistence farmers who contribute little to the broader economy.[27]

Moyo has noted that most post-colonial states have uncritically adopted this model.[28] According to him, the 'rural elites' are calling for access to larger plots on the commercial farms. He points out that in Zimbabwe, for example, the black elites hold 11% of Zimbabwe commercial farmlands.[29] The Land Redistribution and Agricultural Development (LRAD) programme of the Department of Land Affairs in South Africa, with its emphasis on promoting emerging black commercial farmers, appears to be mimicking the large-scale commercial farm model. Moyo contests this kind of thinking. His position is that post-colonial states should reject the large-scale commercial farm model in favour of smallholders. According to him, and here he might be referring specifically to Zimbabwe, the output performance of smallholders, including resettled black farmers, and including those who have invested in peri-urban areas, demonstrates that with adequate access to land blacks can contribute substantially to domestic and export markets.[30]

It is not the intention of this chapter to debate and discuss the technical details about the merits and demerits of large-scale commercial farms. Neither does the chapter wish to weigh the merits of large-scale commercial versus small-scale farms. The main concern of this chapter is the need to redress historical racial land inequalities and ensure social justice in the context of reconciliation and societal transformation in South Africa. As Mafeje has argued, white capitalist agriculture was not liberating. It flourished at the expense of the vast majority of the rural population, catering for a small minority, and through monopolisation of the land and agricultural inputs directly contributed to the underdevelopment of the native reserves or the so-called communal areas, some of which are nothing more than rural slums. Mafeje concludes:

> *The first step in instituting any agrarian reform in the sub-region would be the total abolition of the system of land reservation. The so-called communal areas must be rent asunder so as to allow the surplus population to flow out to any surplus land that has been artificially kept out of their reach. For those who are cynically concerned about 'loss of productivity' in the case of transfer of land from 'more productive' commercial/white farmers to 'less productive' African peasant producers, this need not entail appropriation of land that is under production by whosoever is concerned.*[31]

A group that Mafeje does not address himself to, though, and that has been a victim in the growth and development of capitalist commercial farms in the southern African region is farm dwellers.

Conclusion

This chapter has raised issues around land and its significance within the context of the unfolding reconciliation and reconstruction processes in post-1994 South Africa. It has been argued in this chapter that one of the legacies of colonialism and apartheid in South Africa is the vast racial inequalities in landholding. The chapter has gone on to show the severe limits of the post-1994 South African land reform programme conducted under the auspices of the Department of Land Affairs in addressing the need for a fundamental shift of substantial ownership of land from whites to previously dispossessed blacks. A number of factors have been highlighted as contributing to the rather poor performance of the Department of Land Affairs. These include the fundamental contradiction in the Constitution's objectives of safeguarding the existing land rights of property holders while at the same time aiming to redistribute land to blacks; the market-led approach based on the principle of willing-seller-willing-buyer; and a palpably inadequate budget for land reform.

As a way forward, this chapter has argued that the ideal of reconciliation and reconstruction that is enshrined in the South African Constitution potentially provides the necessary conditions for a comprehensive land reform programme. However, the chapter has shown that the TRC, the vehicle that was supposed to meet the obligations of the Constitution, failed to pin down a critical actor in the process of reconciliation and reconstruction: business, including commercial farmers. Business, it has been argued, benefited from colonialism and apartheid and cannot conceivably be left out of the healing process. In this regard, the chapter proposes that the market-led approach, including the willing-seller-willing-buyer principle, should be dropped. Commercial farmers should make their contribution to the healing process in the form of donating a portion of their land. This could be land that is underutilised or not used at all. If this land is not enough, their contribution could be to donate land that goes beyond an agreed maximum size of land to be held by an individual. The land would be made available especially to poor blacks who need and want land for residential and food security purposes.

Notes

1   F. Hendricks and L. Ntsebeza, 'The Paradox of South Africa's Land Reform Policy: Failed Decolonisation?', paper presented to the annual colloquium of the Southern African Regional Institute for Policy Studies (SARIPS), Harare, Zimbabwe, 24-27 September 2000, 1.

2   Statement by President Thabo Mbeki at the handing over of the Final Report of the TRC, Pretoria, 21 March 2003. See http://www.anc.org.za/ancdocs/history/mbeki/2003/tm0321.html

3   The reserves were later renamed Bantustans and homelands. Between 1976 and 1981, some Bantustans were granted independence by the apartheid regime, but were never recognised by the rest of the world.

4   Scholars argue that this Act drew extensively from the Cape tradition, in particular Cecil John Rhodes' Glen Grey Act of 1884, and the South African Native Affairs Commission of 1905. See F. T. Hendricks, *The Pillars of Apartheid: Land Tenure, Rural Planning and the Chieftaincy* (Uppsala: Acta University, Studia Sociologica Upsaliensa, 1990); M. Lacey, *Working for Boroka: Origins of the Coercive Labour System in South Africa* (Johannesburg: Ravan Press, 1981).

5   Figures from the Monitoring and Evaluation Directorate of the Department of Land Affairs, requested by the Programme for Land and Agrarian Studies (PLAAS), University of the Western Cape.

6   F. M. Orkin and B. Nlobe, *Employment Trends in Agriculture in South Africa* (Pretoria: Statistics South Africa and National Department of Agriculture, 2000), 23.

7   The term 'black' is used here in the Black Consciousness sense of including Africans, so-called coloureds and Indians. All these groups were, to varying degrees, victims of white domination and exploitation.

8   S. Terreblanche, 'Dealing with Systematic Economic Injustice', in *Looking Back, Reaching Forward: Reflections on the Truth and Reconciliation Commission of South Africa*, eds. C. Villa-Vicencio and W. Verwoerd (Cape Town: University of Cape Town Press and London: Zed Books, 2000), 266.

9   Orkin and Njobe, *Employment Trends*: x.

10 TRC, Final Report, Vol. 4, 54, as quoted in Terreblanche, 'Dealing with Systematic', 266.

11 Terreblanche, 'Dealing with Systematic', 266.

12 *Government Gazette* No. 22648, Vol. 435, 13 September, 50.

13 See the following: http://land.pwv.gov.za/redistribution/PROPOSAL.DG.html, http://www.gov.za.search97cgi/s97_cgi, http://land.pwv.gov.za/redistribution/lrad.htm

14 Monitoring and Evaluation Directorate, Department of Land Affairs, 31 December 2002.

15 The property clause is contained in Section 25 of the Constitution and reads thus: (1) No one may be deprived of property except in terms of law of general application, and no law may permit arbitrary deprivation of property. (2) Property may be expropriated only in terms of a law of general application – a) for public purposes or in the public interest; and b) subject to compensation, the amount, timing and manner of which must be agreed, or decided or approved by a court and this compensation should be just and equitable.

16 A. Mafeje, 'The Land and the Agrarian Question in Southern Africa.' Seminar paper presented to the Sociology and Industrial Sociology Department, Rhodes University, Grahamstown, 8 October 2002, 12.

17 http://www.anc.org.za/ancdocs/history/mbeki/2003/tm0415.html

18 'Let us Wipe the Slate Clean', *Sunday Times*, 20 April 2003.

19 Mafeje, 'The Land and the Agrarian Question', 11-12.

20 'Victims of Repression Deserve Reparations', *Sowetan*, Friday, 11 April 2003.

21 The term farm dweller is used to refer to a range of people who reside(d) on white-owned commercial farms either as farm workers, ex-farm workers still residing on the farms, family members of farm workers not necessarily working on the farms and labour tenants.

22 S. Moyo, 'Land Reform and Land Redistribution in Southern Africa', paper presented

at a conference hosted by the Central Policy Unit, KwaZulu Natal, South Africa, at the Blue Waters Hotel, Durban, 14-15 March 2003, 13. Detailed research is needed to determine the extent of land demand and need, particularly in South Africa. Pertinent questions in this regard include: who wants land and for what?

23 M. de Klerk, *A Harvest of Discontent: the Land Question in South Africa* (Cape Town: Idasa, 1991), 259.

24 Ibid., 269.

25 E-mail communication with Nick Vink, 14 July 2003.

26 See de Klerk, *A Harvest of Discontent*, 269-270. I am also indebted to Fani Ncapayi, Senior Programmes Officer of the Cala University Students Association (CALUSA), for drawing my attention to this possibility.

27 See Moyo, 'Land Reform and Land Redistribution', 5-6.

28 Moyo reminds us that the 'rural elites' are also calling for access to larger plots on the commercial farms. In Zimbabwe, for example, the black elites hold 11% of Zimbabwe commercial farmlands. Moyo, 'Land Reform and Land Redistribution', 9-14.

29 Ibid., 9-14.

30 Mafeje is another protagonist of the small producer model. According to him, 'small producers in Africa sell a certain amount of their produce to earn cash to buy consumer goods'. Mafeje defends the African supposition that land is there to be used to guarantee livelihood for all members of the community and not simply to be owned as property. Mafeje, 'The Land and the Agrarian Question', 11-14.

31 Ibid., 16.

13

For the Next Generations:
Remaking South Africa's Juvenile Justice System

Ann Skelton

The standard response to crime and punishment in the Western world is failing. The increasingly heavy court caseload and over-crowding in prisons bears testimony to the fact that it is not working. The irony is that although Western nations increasingly put more offenders behind bars, the public does not seem to be feeling any safer. The calls for ever more punitive approaches continue.[1]

Concern and public anger about crime is highest in relation to children committing crimes. This is not because children commit the most crimes nor the most serious crimes. The facts reveal quite the contrary. In the United States in 1997, attorney general Janet Reno announced that there had been a 30% reduction in serious crimes committed by children. This positive news, however, was totally overshadowed by the announcement in the same week of two murders committed by juveniles in the United States. Advocates for juvenile justice policy reform complain that there is an enormous disparity between research and data about juvenile crime and public policy in this area. A major reason for this is that media coverage of crime, particularly crime committed by children, obscures people's understanding of what is happening and what the solutions are.

Coverage of juvenile crime is badly skewed toward hyper-violent, idiosyncratic acts, presented out of context with social forces that foster delinquency. This non-contextual, exaggerated coverage negatively affects both public opinion and policy making in the field of juvenile justice.[2]

Bernadine Dohrn observes that there has been a tidal wave of fear associated with children during the last decade, and a major consequence of this is that adults have responded through legislative and policy decisions to criminalise vast sectors of youth behaviour.[3] The American zero tolerance and 'get tough' approaches have begun to permeate other juvenile justice systems in the world. South Africa, too, has shown signs of opting for this approach with minimum sentencing, tougher bail laws and hard-hitting anti-gang legislation passed by Parliament in the late 1990s.[4]

A voice of dissent

Among the clamour for tougher measures, zero tolerance and labelling children as 'predators', a small voice of dissent has begun to make itself heard. A different meaning of 'justice' is being discussed and debated and, unlike most of the putative answers to the problem of crime in the modern era, its genesis is not in the Western world. In searching for a different approach to crime, some criminal justice reformers have called for a re-examination of the basic principles and concepts underpinning the standard criminal justice response to crime. The last decade of the 20th century saw a rapid growth in a new movement based on restorative justice. Restorative justice researchers and practitioners begin from the observation that the standard criminal justice focus is on questions such as 'who has committed this crime and what punishment should follow from it?' In contrast, they suggest a turn to the questions 'who has been hurt by this crime and how can the person who caused the harm put things right again within the context of the community?'

Definitions of restorative justice abound. But most attempts to define the concept include the idea of holding offenders accountable through getting them to face up to what they have done wrong, often through facilitated processes that bring them face to face with victims. Restorative justice requires the offender to listen to the needs of the victim and other people affected by the crime, and make reasonable attempts to meet those needs as a way of repairing the harm. The restorative justice lexicon emphasises words such as reconciliation, restitution, healing and harmony.

Scholars of restorative justice have underscored the fact that this approach accords well with indigenous conflict resolution. The focus in a small, cohesive community is on rebuilding relationships that have been damaged by the wrongful actions of a member or members of that community. The search for harmony and healing is common to many indigenous justice systems, including those that existed in South Africa prior to colonisation. Some customary courts, known as *izinkundla*, *izigcawu* or *makgotla,* are still used in South Africa today, mostly in rural areas. With the emphasis on 'problems' rather than offences, these structures hear the stories of the parties involved and then make decisions regarding outcomes. These outcomes aim to heal relationships, and they ensure restitution or compensation to victims.[5] Symbolic gestures, such as sacrifice of animals and sharing of meals, indicate that the crime has been expiated and the offender can be reintegrated.[6]

Until the last decades of the 20th century it seemed as though the importance of these traditional practices was waning. However, in the search to provide fresh answers to dealing with crime, scholars all over the world are turning to indigenous models of justice to harness the wisdom that existed before the colonisers' way of dealing with crime became official practice.[7] This does not necessarily mean a wholesale return to the way things used to be done. Jean-Marie Makang explains the role that African traditional approaches can bring to modern discourse:

> *Tradition as an ideology of society or as a utopia aims at enlightening African people in their striving for adaptation to new material conditions of the present works, with their self-determination and a better quality of their humanity as their common purpose. By appealing to the praxis and wisdom of our African foreparents, we do not mean to repeat them but we mean to make use of this praxis and wisdom as interpretive tools to enlighten present generations of Africans.[8]*

Can Africa Provide New Insights into Dealing with Crime?

In an essay on the ethics and values needed for peace in the 21st century, Horace Campbell asserts that the world has been organised according to the views of Western male leaders who have relied on concepts such as the importance of the individual as espoused by John Locke, the free market as propounded by Adam Smith and the survival of the fittest as described by Charles Darwin. Campbell suggests that it may be possible to provide alternatives to this approach of maximising self-interest by focusing on other values such as peace, reconstruction and reconciliation.[9]

The starting point of this alternative ideation is the moral ethic of social collectivism. While Western ideation is premised on individualisation, African ideation is based on a theory of collective living, which finds voice in a number of key African concepts. The philosophy of *ujamaa,* used by Julius Nyerere to describe the kind of life he believed Tanzanians should live, is an example. It involved individuals living a simple life in harmony with their close families. Wealth belonged to the family as a whole, and no one could use wealth to dominate others. 'We want the whole nation to live as a family', was how Nyerere explained the idea. He recognised that this approach was akin to socialism, but used the term *ujamaa* because he wanted to root the concept of socialism in the African philosophy of collectivism, and because he wanted to be sure that no one would act as 'master over servant'.[10] The importance of people living together at the same level, recognising differences but not allowing domination or discrimination, was further illustrated by Nyerere in his promotion of the concept of *ndugu,* meaning brotherhood or sisterhood.[11]

What the Truth and Reconciliation Commission (TRC) Tells Us about an African Response to Wrongdoing

In South Africa it may be argued that the ethic of social collectivism is captured in the concept of ubuntu. Scholars note that this concept is not easily translated into English, except by drawing together strands of concepts such as 'a person is a person through other people' and 'the very essence of being human'.[12] The spirit of ubuntu has been described as being at the heart of the decision to go the TRC route in South Africa. The Interim Constitution drafted by the negotiating parties in 1993 set out the rationale for the TRC. It includes in its postscript the assertion that the Constitution provides a foundation for South Africans to transcend the divisions of the past, which had generated violations of human rights and led to a legacy of hatred, fear, guilt and revenge. The postscript goes on to say:

> *These can now be addressed on the basis that there is a need for under-standing but not for vengeance, a need for reparation but not for retaliation, a need for* **ubuntu** *but not for victimisation.*[13]

Charles Villa-Vicencio, director of research of the TRC at the time, observes that South Africans needed to learn to live together again, a process described by Chileans as *reconvivencia.* For this to happen, it was necessary to find out what had happened during the years of apartheid, why it had happened and who was responsible. He observes that while the goals of truth-telling and reconciliation were generally supported by the South African public, there was a concern with what was perceived by some as 'a lack of justice'. Villa-Vicencio asserts that the TRC was a process that embodied a different kind of justice, a 'political restorative justice' which addressed the legitimate concerns of victims and survivors while seeking to reintegrate perpetrators into the community.[14]

South Africa's TRC has subsequently been explicitly characterised as a restorative justice process by a number of authors.[15] (It should be noted it has also been described as an incomplete attempt to apply restorative justice principles.[16]) The chairperson of the TRC, Archbishop Desmond Tutu, has stated quite clearly that in his view the TRC's work was based on the concept of restorative justice, which, he asserts, is a concept compatible with an African view of justice. In an interview about the TRC he is reported to have said:

> *Retributive justice is largely Western. The African understanding is far more restorative – not so much to punish as to redress or restore a balance that has been knocked askew. The justice we hope for is restorative of the dignity of the people.*[17]

Applying a More African Approach to Juvenile Justice Law Reform

The TRC proved that South Africans accept that the 'convict and punish' approach is not the only road to justice. This having been demonstrated at the macro-level, the next inquiry is the extent to which this 'other kind of justice' has permeated the criminal justice system at the ground level. On a practical level, there is little evidence that South African courts are working in a restorative way. The court system is part of the country's colonial inheritance; the values on which it is based are Eurocentric and generally punitive. The South African Constitution provides protection to individuals who are accused of crimes, and there is a general feeling that victims of crime are left out of the equation. It is true that the South African criminal justice system, while not soft on offenders, is offender-focused.

However, the transition to a constitutional democracy opened the door to the possibility of far-reaching changes to the law. One of the most radical pieces of draft legislation to emerge from the South African Law Reform Commission in recent years is the Child Justice Bill.

The law-making process began when the minister of justice at the time, Dullah Omar, requested the South African Law Commission (now the South African Law Reform Commission) to include an investigation into juvenile justice in its programme. He appointed to the Juvenile Justice Project Committee individuals from civil society who he knew to be advocates for restorative justice and who had been part of the non-government lobby group calling for substantial reform to the juvenile justice system. The Juvenile Justice Project Committee of the South African Law Commission commenced its work in 1997 and a discussion paper with a draft Bill was published for comment in 1998. The Commission's final report was completed and handed to the minister of justice in August 2000.[18] The Department of Justice introduced the Bill into Parliament in August 2002 and public hearings on the Bill began in February 2003.

The stated objective of the Child Justice Bill is to promote ubuntu in the child justice system through:

* fostering children's sense of dignity and worth;
* reinforcing children's respect for human rights and the fundamental freedoms of others by holding children accountable for their actions and safe-guarding the interests of victims and by means of a restorative justice response;
* supporting reconciliation by means of a restorative justice response;
* involving parents, families, victims and communities in child justice processes to encourage the reintegration of children who are subject to the provisions of the Act.[19]

Restorative justice is defined in the Bill as the promotion of reconciliation, restitution and responsibility through the involvement of a child, a child's parent(s), family members, victims and communities. The proposed system includes alternatives to arrest, the compulsory assessment of each child by a probation officer and an appearance at a preliminary inquiry within 48 hours of the arrest. The main purpose of the preliminary inquiry is to promote diversion.

Diversion is a way of getting children to take responsibility for what they have done without taking them through the courts and prisons. If a child acknowledges responsibility for the wrongdoing, he or she can be set specific tasks, or required to attend a programme, or in some way made to put right what he or she has done wrong. In this way the child avoids the stigmatising and even brutalising effects of the criminal justice system. Diversion gives children a chance to avoid a criminal record. At the same time, the aim is to teach them to take responsibility for their actions and to avoid situations that lead to trouble.

Diversion is practised informally in South Africa. Although the current law does not specifically provide for diversion, since 1992 the National Institute for Crime Prevention and Reintegration (Nicro), a non-governmental organisation partially subsidised by the government, has experimented with diversion of young offenders with the co-operation of prosecutors and probation officers. Diversion tends to be carried out on an *ad hoc* basis, relying largely on positive working relationships between prosecutors, probation officers and service-delivery organisations. In the proposed system diversion will be a core component, and the range of options set out in the legislation will formalise and encourage its use.

The provisions on sentencing also reflect a restorative justice approach. The Bill sets out the sentencing options under four rubrics; community-based sentences, restorative justice sentences, sentences involving correctional supervision and sentences with a compulsory residential requirement. The postponement or suspension of sentences is linked to a number of conditions, and the list of conditions includes requirements such as 'restitution, compensation or symbolic restitution' and 'an apology'. Children may be required to make symbolic restitution or a payment of compensation to a specified person or group.

The Bill includes the possibility of a child being referred to a family group conference. The family group conference is empowered to regulate its own procedures and make a plan as it deems fit, provided that these are appropriate for the child and family and consistent with the principles contained in the Bill. The plan must specify the objectives for the child and the family, the period in which they are to be achieved, details of the services and assistance to be provided for the child and family and other matters relating to the education, employment, recreation and welfare of the child, as are relevant. According to the Bill, family group conferences can be diversion options prior to trial. A court can also stop its proceedings in the middle of a trial and refer the matter to a family group conference. The court can also, after conviction, send the matter to a family group conference to determine a suitable plan which the court can then make into a court order for the purposes of sentencing. Similar provisions for victim offender mediation are included in the Bill.

Although changes may still be made to the Bill in the legislature, at the time of writing indications are that the diversion and restorative justice orientation of the Bill will be retained. Once the Bill is passed there will be a legal framework for practitioners to undertake restorative justice work with child offenders in South Africa. This will be a positive step, but work on developing effective restorative justice practice in South Africa will still need to be done.

Restorative Justice Within the South African Context Today

If less serious crimes committed by children are to be dealt with through family and community structures, these units needs to be coherent and strong. It must be acknowledged that South Africa has in recent decades experienced a breakdown of families and communities. The constant drift of people off the land into cities began with the migrant labour policy of the apartheid government, but continues as people search for employment. The departure from the carefully structured traditional family life has led to many children being raised in female-headed households, rarely seeing their fathers. The impact of diseases such as HIV/Aids and tuberculosis has pushed children closer to the edge of overstretched families. Democratisation has led to the growth of more affluent African families. They live in cities, develop nuclear family patterns and tend to have little connection to their communities. These family structures may make it difficult to bring the vital concept of ubuntu to the centre of the future child justice system. On the other hand, it has been observed that the process of conferencing itself may provide a catalyst to rebuild families and communities and provide a springboard for a recommitment to ubuntu.[20]

Recognising Children's Individual Rights Within a Collective Approach

The issue of children's rights has been high on the agenda of those working to reform the law relating to children who commit crimes, and it has been observed by Julia Sloth-Nielsen that international human rights law profoundly influenced the juvenile justice reform process.[21] However, the African approach embodied in the proposed new law does stand in some tension with the rights of the individual child as they are espoused in the UN Convention on the Rights of the Child (CRC). In short, the CRC's interpretation does not always match African concepts of childhood. The balancing of children's rights and responsibilities within the context of the extended family is better reflected in the African Charter on the Rights and Welfare of the Child. Although the Charter contains many concepts and ideas that are included in the CRC, positive African traditions are given special attention, while customs that are harmful to children are discouraged to the extent that they are inconsistent with the Charter.

One way in which the African Children's Charter differs markedly from the CRC is that it expressly places responsibilities on children. These responsibilities arise from the view of the child as part of a community. Children have a duty to work for the cohesion of the family, to respect their parents, superiors and elders at all times, and to assist them in case of need. Parents are also given responsibilities by the African Children's Charter – in fact they are seen as being primarily responsible for the 'upbringing and development' of children. In this process, the best interests of the child must remain their basic concern.

Frans Viljoen has observed that if one compares the UN CRC with the African Children's Charter some of the views regarding children and childhood conflict.[22] From one perspective children are seen as being vulnerable and in need of protection. On the other hand, the child is seen as a self-asserting bearer of rights. There is a tension between individualism and the community. Children have rights as individuals. If they are at risk from their families the state is required to intervene to prevent abuse or neglect. At the same time, children are seen as deriving their personhood and therefore their rights through their role as members of families and communities. Kwame Gyeke, drawing on a number of other African writers, recognises that a communitarian ethos underpins African social structures. But Gyeke goes further, attempting to balance the idea of 'personhood' with 'communitarianism'. He poses the following question:

The metaphysical question is whether a person, even though he/she lives in a human society, is a self-sufficient atomic individual who does not depend on his/her relationships with others for the realisation of his/her ends, or whether the person is by nature a communal (or communitarian) being, having natural and essential relationships with others.

Gyeke concludes that a purist approach to communitarian ethical and political theory should be moderated in a manner that allows for communal values as well as values of individuality. He believes that although the general thrust gives prominence to duties towards the community, it does not do so to the detriment of individual rights, the existence and value of which should be recognised by the community.[23] This way of thinking is also echoed by Ruel Khoza: '*Ubuntu* would seem to be broadening respect for the individual – respect for the dignity and the rights of each person in the social unit – and purging collectivism of its negative elements.'[24]

Here the negative elements of collectivism relate to the Western-style collectivism, which Khoza views as authoritarian. He refers to formulations such as Rousseau's idea of submission to the 'general will' and Marx's idea of the determination of people's consciousness by their social being. Khoza says that ubuntu allows for individual efforts, which are rewarded as long as they are altruistic.

Certainly individual children's rights must be protected in South African society. In addition to having ratified the UN CRC and the African Charter on the Rights and Welfare of the Child, the South African Constitution provides clearly and directly for the protection of children's rights. Concerns have been raised about children's rights and restorative justice for juveniles.[25] There is a view that restorative justice practice may erode due process rights such as the right to remain silent and the right to be considered innocent until proven guilty. These fundamental elements may be placed at risk by a tendency to coerce children to admit guilt in order to be considered for diversion to restorative justice options. All diversion entails some risk, as we remove offenders from a system that has built up many procedural protections over the centuries. The protection of rights is surely important, but in restorative justice we are striving for more than formalistic protection – we are aiming higher, hoping for behaviour change, hoping to prevent re-offending, hoping to balance the needs of the offender with the needs of the victim.[26]

Conclusion

The TRC proves that African responses to wrongdoing can transcend the simple knee-jerk response of retribution and lead instead to reconciliation and harmony. The Child Justice Bill holds the promise of transferring this knowledge to the criminal justice system for children. The Bill embraces the principle of ubuntu and sets the stage for the practice of restorative justice that will see the majority of children being diverted away from the criminal justice system of courts and prison towards programmes that will hold them accountable and give them a chance to make up for what they did and change their behaviour. This legislative step is a bold move, especially at a time when many countries in the West, especially the United States, are cranking up the penalties levied against children who commit crimes and increasingly releasing youths into the adult justice system. An essential difference in these approaches is identified as the Western focus on the individual on the one hand, and the more communitarian approach of traditional African society on the other. This article has attempted to show that these concepts are not mutually exclusive; a child may enjoy rights as an individual within the framework of the family and community.

Bringing about a restorative justice system for children in South Africa will not be an easy task, despite the positive background factors. To remake the law is one thing. To rebuild communities into a powerful force for communal value transmission and child protection is quite another. The concept of ubuntu and all that it teaches about communitarian living has been overlaid by education based on Western values. Where wealth is in the hands of a few as is the case in South Africa, the Western approach based on maximising self-interest in a struggle for scarce resources is bound to contribute to crime. While acknowledging the challenges to the practical achievement of a more restorative justice system for children, it is nevertheless possible to conclude that new child justice legislation provides scope for the reactivation of an African response to the problem of crime within the broader context of communal values.

Notes

1   Gerry Johnstone, *Restorative Justice: Ideas, Values, Debates* (Cullompton, Devon: Willan Publishing, 2002), 10.

2   Vincent Schiraldi and Jason Ziedenberg, 'How Distorted Coverage of Juvenile Crime affects Public Policy', in *Zero Tolerance: Resisting the Drive for Punishment in our Schools*, eds. W. Ayers, B. Dohrn and B. Ayers (New York: The New Press, 2001), 114-125, at 114.

3   Bernadine Dohrn, 'Look Out Kid/It's Something You Did', in *Zero Tolerance*, eds. W. Ayers, Dohrn and B. Ayers, 89-107.

4   Ann Skelton, 'Juvenile Justice Reform: Children's Rights and Responsibilities versus Crime Control', in *Children's Rights in a Transitional Society*, ed. C. J. Davel (Pretoria: Protea Book House, 1999), 88-106.

5   Karen van Eden, 'What Can Indigenous African Customs Teach Contemporary Juvenile Justice?', unpublished paper, Institute of Criminology, University of Cape Town, 1995.

6   David Kgosimore, 'Restorative Justice as an Alternative Way of Dealing with Crime', conference paper presented at the Conference on Restorative Justice and Community Facilitation, Johannesburg, November 2001.

7   Jim Consedine, *Restorative Justice – Healing the Effects of Crime* (Christchurch: Ploughshares, 1999); C. Taylor Griffiths and R. Hamilton, 'Sanctioning and Healing: Restorative Justice in Canadian Aboriginal Communities', in *Restorative Justice: International Perspectives*, eds. B. Galaway and J. Hudson (Monsey, New York: Criminal Justice Press, 1996).

8   Jean-Marie Makang, 'Of the Good Use of Tradition: Keeping the Critical Perspective in African Philosophy', in *Postcolonial African Philosophy*, ed. E. C. Eze (Oxford: Blackwell Publishers Ltd, 1997), 324-338, at page 338.

9   Horace Campbell, 'The Ethics, Qualities and Values Necessary for Leadership and Peace in the Twenty First Century', in *Emerging African Leadership: Opportunities and Challenges for Peace and Development,* ed. G. Wildschut (Cape Town: Desmond Tutu Leadership Academy, 2002), 91-160.

10 Julius Nyerere, 'Leaders Must Not Be Masters', in *African Philosophy: An Anthology,* ed. E. C. Eze (Oxford: Blackwell Publishers Ltd, 1998), 77-80.

11 Campbell, 'Ethics, Qualities and Values', 142.

12 Tutu, *No Future without Forgiveness* (London: Rider, 1999), 34.

13 Constitution of the Republic of South Africa Act, 1993.

14 Charles Villa-Vicencio, 'A Different Kind of Justice: The South African Truth and Reconciliation Commission', in *Contemporary Law Review,* Vol. 1, Issue 4 (1999): 403-428.

15 Alex Boraine, *A Country Unmasked: The Story of South Africa's Truth and Reconciliation Commission* (South Africa: Oxford University Press, 2000), 426-428; Medard Rwelamira, 'South Africa's Truth and Reconciliation Commission', unpublished paper presented at the ancilliary sessions on restorative justice at the 10th UN Crime Congress, Vienna, 2000; Villa-Vicencio, 'Different Kind', 407.

16 Howard Zehr, 'When Justice and Healing Go Together', *Track Two*, 6/3 (1997): 20.

17 Cited in Martha Minow, *Between Vengeance and Forgiveness* (Boston: Beacon Press, 1998), 81.

18 South African Law Commission, Report on Juvenile Justice, Project 106, 2000.

19 Child Justice Bill no. 49 of 2002.

20 Ann Skelton and Cheryl Frank, 'Conferencing in South Africa: Returning to our Future', in *Restorative Justice for Juveniles,* eds. A. Morris and G. Maxwell (Oxford: Hart Publishing, 2001).

21 Julia Sloth-Nielsen, 'The Role of International Law in Juvenile Justice Reform in South Africa', LLD thesis, University of the Western Cape, Cape Town, 2001.

22 Frans Viljoen, 'The African Charter on the Rights and Welfare of the Child', in *Introduction to Child Law in South Africa,* ed. C. J. Davel (Lansdowne: Juta and Co., 2000), 214-231.

23 Kwame Gyeke, 'Person and Community in African Thought', in *The African*

Philosophy Reader, eds. P. H. Coetzee and A. P. J. Roux (London: Routledge, 1998), 317-335.

24 Ruel Khoza, 'Ubuntu as African Humanism', unpublished conference paper read at Ekhaya Promotions, 1994, quoted in Erasmus D. Prinsloo, 'Ubuntu Culture and Participatory Management', in *African Philosophy Reader,* eds. Coetzee and Roux, 41-51.

25 Els Dumortier, 'Neglecting Due Process for Minors: A Possible Dark Side of Restorative Justice', paper presented at the ancilliary sessions on restorative justice at the 10th UN Crime Congress, Vienna, 2000. Available at: http://www.restorativejustice.org/rj3 (accessed 15 January 2003).

26 Ann Skelton, 'Restorative Justice as a Framework for Juvenile Justice Reform: A South African Perspective', *British Journal of Criminology* 42 (2002): 496-513.

14

Amnesty, Reparation and the Object of Reconciliation in the Context of South Africa's Truth and Reconciliation Commission

Ilan Lax

This brief chapter will examine the relationship between the 'right to reparation' for victims on the one hand and the amnesty process on the other, both within the context of the South African Truth and Reconciliation Commission (TRC) and on the imperative of reconciliation, one of the inarticulate premises that permeated the activities and objects of the Commission.[1] The chapter will briefly look at the ethos of the TRC and examine the amnesty process, making some observations and comments thereon. It will thereafter examine the aspect of reparation, the role of victims in the amnesty process, the rather elusive notion of reconciliation and then conclude with an analysis of how the TRC process tried to balance these difficult and at times irreconcilable imperatives.

The Ethos of the TRC

The preamble of the Promotion of National Unity and Reconciliation Act No. 34 of 1995 (the Act) makes it clear, quoting the 1993 Interim Constitution, that the purpose of the TRC is to achieve a set of objectives within the context of a constitutional state where the constitution provides a 'bridge between the past of a deeply divided society characterised by strife, conflict, untold suffering and injustice, and a future founded on the recognition of human rights, democracy and peaceful co-existence for all South Africans irrespective of colour, race, class, belief or sex'.[2]

To this end, the preamble to the Act postulates that 'the pursuit of national unity, the wellbeing of all SA citizens and peace *require* reconciliation between the people of SA and the reconstruction of society' and that 'there is a need for understanding, but not for vengeance, a need for reparation but not for retaliation, a need for ubuntu and not for victimization'. It concludes that 'in order to advance such reconciliation and reconstruction amnesty *shall* be granted ...'.[3]

Through this frame, it is possible to see the kinds of issues that determined some of the TRC's ethos. It is interesting to note that, apart from the foregoing, the Act contains very few references to the term reconciliation. It is, as far as I can ascertain, only mentioned in the principles for dealing with victims.[4] It is for this reason that reconciliation stands as an inarticulate premise of the TRC, although it is obviously apparent from the name of the Commission. As a consequence, many of its members understood that they needed to take steps to ensure that the TRC's processes were implemented in a manner that fostered reconciliation.

It is also interesting to note that national unity was set out in the Act as something that required both reconciliation and the reconstruction of society. With respect to amnesty, the mandate that it '*shall* be granted' had important implications for the adjudication of amnesty applications. Specifically, the applications were approached on the basis that if the applicants complied with all the formal requirements and satisfied the criteria set out in the Act, the Amnesty Committee was obliged to grant amnesty.

How the Amnesty Process Worked

Any person could voluntarily apply for amnesty provided he or she completed the prescribed form. Where people applied on the wrong documentation, the Amnesty Committee sent them the correct forms to complete.[5] This had to be done before the cut-off date, 30 September 1997. The received application was registered, scrutinised for completeness and formal compliance and thereafter captured on the central database. The application would then be passed onto the TRC's investigative unit. Thereafter, if necessary, further particulars were requested, and once these were clarified and the investigations completed, the committee members would then evaluate the applications and confirm whether a decision could be made 'in chambers', i.e. behind closed doors, or if the application would be heard in public.[6] The workings of the Amnesty Committee thus comprised two parallel processes.

Requirements for the Granting of Amnesty

To briefly paraphrase section 20 of the Act, in order to be granted amnesty an applicant had to, *inter alia*:

- Be in formal compliance with the statute;
- Show that the act, omission or offence applied for was an act associated with a political objective committed in the course of the conflicts of the past but during the window period,[7] and
- Provide full disclosure of all relevant facts.

An act associated with a political objective was defined to include the following criteria:

- The conduct must have been committed as a member or supporter of a publicly known political organisation or liberation movement or state structure;
- The conduct must have been bona fide in furtherance or support of or on reasonable grounds believing s/he was authorised to do so; and
- There could not have been personal gain, malice, ill will or spite.

Applicants also had to satisfy the Committee that their conduct was in line with a range of other criteria related to the motive, context, legal or factual nature of the act, the relationship between the act and the objective, and whether the person applying for amnesty acted under orders.[8]

Processing the Chamber Matters

These applications dealt with offences or delicts that did not involve gross violations of human rights.[9] Committee members were required to evaluate the file by verifying:
- The completeness of the amnesty application form;
- The particularity of the acts applied for; and
- That sufficient investigation or corroboration had been conducted.

Processing the Hearable Matters

In addition to some of the above issues, this process involved incidents alleged to involve gross violations of human rights. Here, the focus included ensuring the proper representation of parties, issuing notice to implicated persons, victims and other interested parties, and checking the preparation of the bundles of documentation ('bundles') for the hearing.[10]

Members of the Committee generally sat in panels[11] of three with a High Court Judge (also a committee member) as chairperson. All members contributed to factual and legal rulings during the course of the proceedings. The hearings proceeded on the basis that applicants would lead the evidence on which they intended to rely. They could be cross-examined by the victims or their legal representatives, by other applicants or their legal representatives where there were material differences in their respective versions and by the committee's leader of evidence, and then re-examined.[12] The panel could ask questions, and when it did, the parties were offered an opportunity to deal with any new issues. The victims and thereafter the Commission, through its leader-of-evidence, would then lead their evidence, if any was relevant, on the same basis as outlined above. After this, the parties presented their legal arguments, either orally or in writing.

Often in situations where victims were unable to add to the factual nature of the evidence in issue, they would make a statement rather than testify *per se*. Such statements related to how they felt about what had happened or provided some background to the events or persons affected by the actions of the applicants. Although such statements had little probative value, they contributed to a sense of catharsis and closure for the victims. Occasionally we witnessed spontaneous heart-warming reconciliatory encounters between the parties. The parties sometimes called for a private session at which to explore such matters further.

Legal Representation

Legal representation of parties before the TRC had the potential to throw up difficult issues.[13] While some people wanted this right restricted to only the most deserving cases, others felt it was an essential safeguard in view of the possible legal consequences faced by the parties. It is my personal view that while lawyers are required to protect their clients' rights and interests, they did not always facilitate the hearings process, the finding of the truth or attempts at reconciliation. This was due to a number of factors. Lawyers tend to adopt an adversarial approach. In South Africa this has been our primary training and experience, although we have seen mediation and other alternative dispute resolution processes being more widely used in various areas of legal practice in more recent times.

The amnesty process was more inquisitorial in nature. Once clients had committed themselves to a version, some lawyers appeared to defend this version rather than facilitate the clients changing their version in line with what was more probably 'the truth'.[14] This approach appeared to flow from a failure to understand the open nature of the inquisitorial process or a lack of trust in the process. In many cases parties testifying gave a new version of events, despite having given contradictory testimony in other forums. However, they were required to explain such contradictions. Some legal representatives (and their clients), particularly those used to practising in criminal courts, seemed to struggle with this idea of clients 'coming clean', and some applicants suffered as a result, despite efforts by the panels to encourage a more frank and transparent approach.

Some of the reasons why this situation arose were: Many applicants and implicated parties had reservations about the process and/or were apprehensive about telling the full truth. Thus some of them stated only the bare minimum in their application forms and adopted a 'wait and see' approach. In addition, because some applicants were 'flushed out' by the TRC's investigative unit as a result of being notorious perpetrators or having been mentioned in the Human Rights Violations Committee statements or other amnesty applications, their applications reflected a defensive approach with obvious subsequent implications.

The Nature of the Evidence Presented

In the Amnesty Committee process, the primary focus was on whether or not the applicants were *entitled* to amnesty and whether there were people who might be victims. The person driving the application was the applicant. In many cases there was very little evidence presented other than that given by the applicants. In part, this was because the victims were in many cases unaware of the actual facts concerning the incidents applied for. Although at times the Committee was left with the distinct feeling that an orchestrated version of what had transpired was being offered, in the absence of actual evidence to the contrary (and, for a variety of reasons, contrary evidence was rarely available), they had to decide on the evidence before them. Indeed, even where there were inconsistencies and contradictions in the versions presented by applicants and witnesses on the same matter, these were seldom significant enough to provide a sufficient basis for rejecting the applicants' versions.

Cross-examination

Section 34(2) of the Act provided for 'reasonable limitations' in respect of the cross-examination. The Human Rights Violations Committee relied on this provision to limit cross-examination by legal representatives quite substantially. The Amnesty Committee, on the other hand, allowed much more leeway and seldom restricted questions except where relevance was an issue. Of course there were notable exceptions, but these were limited to a few hearings. Unfortunately, when lawyers did tend to get carried away during cross-examination, some committee members were loathe to interfere or restrict them because they did not want to create a negative perception with the party concerned and thereby risk compromising impartiality.

Writing, Discussion and Confirmation of Decisions

Decisions were largely made by consensus. Members tried to write decisions as soon after the hearings as possible. In very complex matters one needed to wait for the written transcript of the hearing to be prepared so as to ensure a thorough deliberation of all the facts and arguments presented at the hearing. Decisions written by co-panellists were read and amendments suggested. Occasionally dissenting decisions were written.

Reconciliation

The title of the TRC's governing act is the *Promotion of National Unity and Reconciliation Act*.[15] As something to be promoted, it is self-evident that reconciliation is not an event. It is a process, a long and difficult journey that can sometimes end quite suddenly for some or last centuries for others. It often means different things to different people and is bound up in culture, tradition and faith.

The TRC's chairperson, Archbishop Tutu, speaking of reconciliation said this: 'The trouble is there are erroneous notions of what reconciliation is all about. Reconciliation is not about being cosy; it is not about pretending that things were other than they were. Reconciliation based on falsehood, on not facing up to reality, is not true reconciliation and will not last.' He went on to say, 'it is only on the basis of truth that true reconciliation can take place'.[16] In my view, seeking out this 'basis of truth' has been the gist of our work in the TRC.

According to Jurgen Habermas, the notion of truth comprises three essential elements:[17]

- It should correspond to the facts. In other words, it must involve an accurate description of the instance, including the context and background;
- It should comply with a normative system in the sense that both those who make a statement (of 'facts') and those who receive it are able to make a judgement. Thus, it must appear to be a 'fair' conclusion, in language that is accessible and it must conform to 'normal' practices;
- The statement should be sincere in the sense that it must have integrity. In other words, it should be the result of a process which is credible and which involves credible and committed adjudicators.

If the process and the resultant 'truth' conform to these qualities or criteria, they are more likely to contribute to reconciliation. In the context of the TRC, reconciliation can be understood at different levels of complexity.[18] These include:

- Coming to terms with the painful truth. In this sense, we are talking about the *individual's* ability to be reconciled with the fact that, for example, a loved one who 'disappeared' is actually dead. This in turn facilitates the potential for closure. Sometimes this can lead to denial and the need for revenge. We saw very little of this during our process. Most people appear to have been satisfied with finding out the truth of what happened.[19] Another aspect of this is the difficulty some perpetrators had in coming to terms with their guilt or accepting moral responsibility for their actions. In our amnesty process remorse was not a requirement for being granted amnesty.[20]
- Reconciliation between *victims and perpetrators*. Although the actual number of instances of this kind of scenario was limited because of the relatively few cases which received a public hearing, a fairly large number of instances of reconciliation took place.[21] The primary issue here is that victims generally expressed a sentiment that 'I am ready to forgive, but I need to know who to forgive and for what'. This is common to the attitude of victims in many other jurisdictions. Victims need to believe they are hearing the full truth. If they remain unconvinced, they will be reluctant to reconcile with perpetrators.
- Reconciliation at a *community* level. The nature of the conflict led to huge divisions within communities. These occurred at various levels, between young and old, men and women, neighbours and within families, as well as between ethnic and racial groups. To some extent, the

Commission was able to facilitate reconciliation meetings where such elements found common ground. Often the truth-telling led people to see each other in a different light, as they were able to understand or relate to the motives and context described by the applicants as a basis for their actions. Another important cultural factor that is of relevance in this context is the concept of ubuntu. This is a traditional African concept that includes, among other things, the notion that the individual finds expression and identity through his/her community. This traditional worldview has helped to facilitate reconciliation in some divided communities because the community is able to find healing through the acknowledgement by its members of their differences and their commitment to this shared sense of community.

• Promoting *national* unity and reconciliation. The work of the Commission highlighted the different understandings people have of this notion. It also focused attention on the differences between individual responses, often based in personal and religious notions of reconciliation, and those that have a political or ideological application to a society in transition or transformation. In this sense, some of us believed that the difficulties of a truth-finding process with its robust legalistic processes was not ideally suited to facilitating reconciliation. Nevertheless, we sought to conduct ourselves in a manner that would facilitate a perception of even-handedness on the part of all the parties and generally allowed the parties a measure of latitude with regard to their statements and approach if we thought this would promote reconciliation.

One process that proved useful was the public hearings into various sectors of society, for example, the legal system, business sector, health sector, etc. Here leaders and other prominent people sometimes made public apologies, which had the potential for reconciliation. These gestures, coupled with the restoration of dignity that the public acknowledgement of victims represents, were fundamental to ensuring that people begin to own the new culture of democracy and human rights and restoring credibility to state structures.

Further features that may have served to underpin these aspects were the public and inclusive nature of the Commission's work and the fact that many previously unknown facts were made public. These small beginnings coupled with the other transformations taking place in our country represent a substantial shift away from the depravations of the past. Thus, the work of the Commission should contribute to a strengthening of the rule of law. In this regard, the recommendations aimed at preventing future abuses of human rights are also important. To quote the old adage: 'those who fail to learn the lessons of history are doomed to repeat them.'

The challenge facing us as a nation is how to ensure that the vast majority of our people who were victims of apartheid become beneficiaries of the new order. In this regard, we struggle with gross disparities and structural inequalities. The Commission resolved that its terms of reference restricted its focus primarily to looking at gross violations of human rights and thus it was unable to look more widely at the whole gamut of the effects of apartheid. This decision gave rise to some heated criticism from commentators who argued that the TRC missed an opportunity to address the past in a more systemic manner. Nevertheless, the various measures recommended to the president, including those dealing with reparation and the ongoing transformation taking place in South Africa, could go a long way to helping promote reconciliation in this sense. One area of caution is that problems could arise if reparation is dispensed in a way that emphasises or results in differentiation between those found to be 'victims' and the rest of their communities.

Although reconciliation was part of the Commission's brief, many of the critics of the Commission have complained that it failed to bring this about. I do not share this complaint because reconciliation is a process, a journey that requires a variety of fellow travellers and a host of integrated factors. Furthermore, I do not believe that it was intended that the TRC should be the sole agent for reconciliation in South Africa. As indicated above, our role, along with others, has been to help facilitate a beginning to the process. It is the task and responsibility of society at large to ensure the process continues in a meaningful way.

Reparation

I do not intend to canvass and describe the reparation provisions in the Act or comment on the debate about the nature of the recommendations made by the TRC. This will no doubt be done by other contributors better equipped to expound on the issues. Nevertheless, there can be no doubt, in my view, that the issue of reparation and the long delays and uncertainty experienced by many victims has the potential to impact directly and negatively on reconciliation.

Flowing from the amnesty process people became eligible to apply for reparation on two bases. Firstly, as a result of the granting of amnesty, and where the Amnesty Committee 'is of the opinion that a person is a victim', the names of the victims (or their relatives and dependants) were forwarded to the Reparation & Rehabilitation Committee to be considered in terms of section 26 of the Act.[22] Similarly, where amnesty was refused, but the Amnesty Committee was of the opinion that a gross violation of human rights had occurred and the person was a victim, the matter was also referred to the Reparation & Rehabilitation Committee on the same basis.[23] As mentioned above, amnesty was granted for matters that were not necessarily gross violations of human rights but, as amnesty meant the loss of rights to prosecute or sue, eligibility for reparation was a necessary corollary.

Section 26 of the Act provides that: 'Any person referred to the Committee in terms of section 25(1)(a)(i) **may** apply for reparation.'[24] Reparation is thus a voluntary process and only people who apply will be considered. In this context, it is worth noting that there is also an interesting tension that arises when amnesty is refused. The refusal of amnesty means the right to sue or prosecute remains intact. However, there is a conundrum as to how to deal with the evidence contained in or led during the amnesty application. This difficulty relates to the issue of the problem of the inadmissibility of derivative evidence (i.e. independent of the amnesty application) because the application and anything testified to by the applicant is inadmissible against him. This creates problems where the only evidence against a person is the content of their application for amnesty and the related evidence. The use of this would violate the rule against self-incrimination.

A further tension relates to the fact that if the victim wants or urgently needs reparation their best chance to achieve this would in fact be for the amnesty application to be granted, thereby making them eligible for reparation. This in turn would mean that they would be more inclined not to oppose an application for amnesty as to do so would lessen the likelihood of receiving reparation. I am not aware of many instances where victims may have been less inclined to oppose an application on this basis.

Although the Commission made its recommendations almost five years ago, the response by the government has been slow. While it is true that the president has recently announced plans for implementation of the reparation process, the full impact, extent and process are still to be deter-mined.[25] This issue is fundamental to the validation of the whole TRC process. As was said by Justice Didcott in the Azapo case, reparation offers 'some *quid pro quo* for the loss of ... legal claims'.[26] The state's failure to put in place a credible and viable reparation mechanism could have the effect of undermining many of the gains achieved by the Commission to date. It is noted that it must be extremely galling for many victims to see applicants being granted amnesty while they have had to wait for the state to implement reparation, their quid pro quo, in lieu of justice.

Analysis

Many critics of the amnesty process believed that those who applied for amnesty did not suffer at all. From a traditional criminal justice perspect-ive, this may be true in the sense that they did not have to go to or remain in prison if granted amnesty.[27] However, this fails to take account of the intense and at times punishing process many perpetrators experienced through public exposure of their deeds. Indeed, in many cases people who knew the perpetrators from other contexts like churches and community structures were not aware of their participation in gross violations of human rights and thus many found themselves newly shunned and ostracised. Spouses, children, relatives, friends and associates of perpetrators also came to see them in a different light, and many perpetrators have undergone divorces and continue to suffer from psychological problems as a consequence of their deeds and the revelations and the internal con-tradictions that go with the realisation of what their deeds entailed. These may not seem like severe consequences, but for many perpetrators their revelations to the TRC have clearly had a profound effect on their lives and in some cases their attitudes.

The TRC process has also been criticised for denying justice to the victims of human rights violations. Some say that the moral compromise, in which justice was traded for truth, has irrevocably undermined the position of victims. While there may be some truth in this, we must not lose sight of the fact that the country was able to avoid an escalation of the armed struggle and secure relative peace through this compromise, a com-promise brokered between the main parties engaged in a low intensity civil war that was by and large conducted by people many of whom were themselves victims of gross violations of human rights.

These activities were conducted in a covert manner in two senses. Many of the activities of the apartheid state's own agents were 'denied' by the state itself, either through cover-ups at various levels or by making it appear as if the perpetrators were members of the other side. This made it difficult to ascertain who the actual perpetrators were and provided a basis for denial by the state, false accusations against opposition elements, and even the ensuring of retribution by their own constituencies against people falsely implicated as perpetrators.

A further aspect is that the state and sometimes other parties' denials of the activities of their agents and the avoidance of accountability left many victims feeling that their suffering was 'unreal' and unacknowledged. Thus their reality or life experiences were undermined or denied in the sense that their human dignity was impaired, and consequently healing and closure seemed extremely unlikely and difficult to achieve. The TRC thus offered many victims an opportunity for acknowledgement and closure. While it is thus true that some people still feel aggrieved at the lack of justice in the formal sense of criminal prosecutions, many others have found the process uplifting and helpful.

The notion of justice in the strict sense of crime and punishment fails to take account of the difficulty of achieving successful prosecution. This is particularly so when there is very little evidence available to prove matters beyond a reasonable doubt, the standard criminal liability test. There are numerous examples where failed prosecutions have in fact contributed to perpetuating impunity rather than preventing it because the perpetrators could say in the face of continued accusations: 'see a court has found me not guilty!!' What the amnesty process and TRCs generally achieve is to make 'the known and suspected (as well as the previously unknown)' acknowledged as 'official truth' in the sense that an official body makes a finding that the allegations in fact occurred. This prevents what Michael Ignatief called the 'permissible lie' from being perpetuated and thus in fact undermines impunity.[28]

One of the tasks of the Commission was 'the restoration of the human and civil dignity of victims of gross violations of human rights through testimony'.[29] Put differently, this meant the acknowledging of victims by having their testimony put before the TRC. Only a small percentage of people who made statements to the TRC actually got an opportunity to testify. This was due to time, logistical and resource constraints. However, many of those who elected to tell their stories publicly were explicitly chosen because their stories were representative in nature, demographics and situation. Thus many victims were able to relate to and share in the narratives and the experiences of others, thus validating their own experiences. We believe that as a result large numbers of people achieved vicarious acknowledgement and possibly even catharsis through hearing such testimonies being publicly acknowledged before the Commission.

Much of the TRC process revolved around the acknowledgement of those who had previously been denied a voice. However, within the context of the amnesty process, a quasi-judicial forum and procedure, we were faced with a number of constraints. The more formal evidentiary procedures outlined above meant that victims often had very little to contribute as a result of the fact that many crimes for which amnesty was applied were committed covertly and much misinformation was spread to facilitate cover-ups. Thus in such hearings the victims' legal representatives could do little more than cross-examine the applicants in the hope that vigorous and/or clever cross-examination might result in material contradictions surfacing, thus leading to a collapse of the version. Where victims did choose to testify themselves and managed to find witnesses who could give evidence to counter what the applicants were alleging, they sometimes had to face difficult and at times gruelling and robust cross-examination by the applicants' legal representatives. This seldom contributed to the parties' eventual reconciliation but more often than not resulted in a further hardening of attitudes.

In addition, despite our efforts to make the proceedings less formal and more accessible, the mere fact that lawyers were involved and conducted themselves like lawyers, i.e. using legal jargon, taking technical points, conducting cross-examination, coupled with the issues of representation referred to above, meant that victims often found the process difficult to understand and alienating. It was a difficult balancing act because too much informality and a lack of clear and formal procedures can sometimes result in people perceiving the process as lacking credibility.

As mentioned above, one way in which we were able to ensure that victims were heard was to allow them the opportunity to make statements, either under oath or not, about a range of issues that they wanted to bring to the Commission's attention. This might include their feelings or intuition about the facts, how the events being related had affected them and their families, what their and their families' current needs were, requests for explanations of what had happened and sometimes statements of forgiveness.

A further issue of relevance here is that although much of the TRC process was inquisitorial in character, the amnesty process involved more adversarial elements. This meant that the panels conducted the hearings more in the nature of trials, using the balance of probability test to analyse and decide the evidence presented during the hearing. This invariably resulted in the applicant having a 'duty' to present evidence in support or furtherance of the application. It was then left primarily up to parties to challenge the version presented by the applicant/s in order to contest the application. The panellists rarely intervened except to prevent obvious miscarriages of justice.

A question often asked of us is: 'Did the process unearth the truth?' I believe that the process was largely successful in revealing much more of 'the truth'. However, as noted earlier, in many cases the Amnesty Committee had no choice but to rely upon or accept the evidence presented to it. In other words, where an applicant was the only party to testify in respect of a gross violation of human rights (as was often the case), the panel was faced with *only one version of the event*. This was true except where an applicant or other party broke ranks, or where the victim or other affected parties were able to get witnesses to testify to a different version or provide facts that formed the basis for challenging the applicants' version. In some cases, the applicants' cases failed due to internal inconsistencies or improbabilities. This formed the basis for a finding that full disclosure of all relevant facts had not been made. However, as alluded to above, there were cases where panels were left with the uneasy feeling that we had not been told the full truth. In spite of such misgivings, in the absence of evidence to the contrary, we were compelled to grant amnesty to applicants who fitted all the other criteria, even when it appeared as if the parties may have conspired and presented a fabricated version.

On the whole we were satisfied that many applicants did make full disclosure of facts that had previously been unknown. Several instances of disappearances were resolved, permitting some level of closure for the relatives. Also, many of the cases where members of communities had been suspected of involvement in acts against their own people were exposed as acts of terror by the state. In addition, some individuals who had been wrongly or unfairly accused were vindicated or exonerated posthumously. This all had a positive effect on the individuals and their families, many of whom had been ostracised by the communities in which they lived.

In short, much of what was 'known' to have happened in the past, despite not necessarily being 'recognised as fact' by all sides, was now 'acknowledged' as fact by an official body. In this regard, many of the findings of the Commission were accurate and have been accepted as such by society at large. This is true in respect of perpetrators and victims on both sides.

Conclusion

My own experience of being part of the South African TRC has been enriching and humbling. I have watched the literal 'unearthing' of the truth at exhumations and extra-judicial burial site visits. I have seen and experienced first-hand the dynamic potential such processes have for personal and vicarious acknowledgement and catharsis. I have watched in wonder as intense anger and deep sadness are transformed as people set off on the journey towards reconciliation and a measure of closure. However, I have also witnessed and experienced the intense frustrations that are generated when people have tried and sometimes succeeded in abusing such processes for their own narrow personal or political agendas. In conclusion I'd like to quote a passage written by Ignatief which rang true for me in relation to the process:

All that a truth commission can achieve is to reduce the number of lies that can be circulated unchallenged in public discourse. In Argentina, its work has made it impossible to claim, for example, that the military did not throw half-dead victims into the sea from helicopters. In Chile, it is no longer permissible to assert in public that the Pinochet regime did not dispatch thousands of entirely innocent people. Truth commissions can and do change the frame of public discussion and public memory. A truth commission cannot overcome a society's divisions. It can only winnow out the solid core of facts upon which society's arguments with itself should be conducted. But it cannot bring those arguments to a conclusion. Critics of truth commissions argue as if the past were a sacred text, which has been stolen and vandalized by evil men and which can be recovered and returned to a well-lit glass case in some grand public rotunda. The past is an argument and the function of truth commissions, like the function of honest historians, is simply to purify the argument, to narrow the range of permissible lies.[30]

Where this passage is so apposite in relation to the amnesty process, reparation and issues of reconciliation is the following: The South African TRC's amnesty process can be distinguished from other amnesties granted in other jurisdictions in the world. The amnesties granted in other jurisdictions were generally wide and non-specific. They entailed no voluntary application process, no admission of culpability or accountability, no duty of full disclosure nor the evaluation of the versions being proffered by the applicants against a range of other legislated criteria. Furthermore, no provision was made for the participation of victims or their families in the process.

In this sense the South African process amounted to a 'due-process' amnesty and this, in my view, makes it more palatable in the context of the prevailing international human rights and humanitarian law regimes. It also makes the process more likely to measure up to the *indiciae* paraphrased from Habermas above and, therefore, more likely to contribute to a lasting and meaningful reconciliation. Added to these factors is the necessary and important component of reparation. While the reparation is relatively small in comparative terms and thus primarily symbolic, it does represent together with acknowledgement a small part of the *'quid pro quo'* the Azapo decision refers to. While this can never bring back the dead or assuage the loss and hurt suffered by so many, it can go some way towards restoring their human and civil dignity.

However, since reconciliation must go hand-in-hand with reconstruction, reconciliation without transformation is a meaningless notion while many victims and the majority of South Africans continue to live in dire circumstances, in many cases not much better than those of the past. This is not to say that there has not been progress in reconstruction; however, the pace and extent needs to be extended at a much greater rate in order to ensure more effective improvements for the mass of South Africans.

Thus, for there to be meaningful reconciliation in South Africa there must necessarily be meaningful reconstruction and transformation in every sphere of our society. This is the challenge we must face if the seeds sown during the TRC process are to bear fruit in the future.

Notes

1 In writing this paper, I have been very aware that hindsight is more or less a perfect science. I am conscious that when the TRC process in South Africa started there were

very few precedents to follow and much of what we decided to do had to be made up and thought through as the process unfolded. Our statute did not always provide as much guidance as its drafts may have intended. Where I make criticisms of the processes, I do so with the hope that the lessons to be learnt will be beneficial. As a member of the Commission I accept that whatever criticisms I make of the process and people involved are equally applicable to me.

2   See the preamble to the Act.

3   Emphasis added.

4   See §11 (g) of the Act.

5   The vast majority of applications were completed by lay people without the assistance of lawyers. In addition, most applicants were in prison.

6   See §19 (3) (a) and (b) of the Act, which provides for certain applications being decided without a public hearing. These were called chamber matters. In contrast, with respect to so-called hearable matters, see §19 (4) of the Act.

7   1 March 1960 to 10 May 1994 (see §20 (2) of the Act).

8   See §20 (2), (3) & (4) of the Act for a more detailed exposition.

9   These are defined as 'killing, abduction, torture or severe ill-treatment of any person; or any attempt, conspiracy, incitement, instigation, command, or procurement to commit' one of these. See §1 (1) of the Act.

10   See §19 (4) of the Act.

11   Such panels were not fixed. Members worked in different permutations. The minimum quorum was three committee members and the maximum number in a panel was as far as I can recall five. This avoided the perception that certain panels may have a particular approach or bias.

12   Note §34 (2) of the Act which provides for placing 'reasonable limitations with regard to time allowed' for cross-examination 'in order to expedite proceedings'.

13   §34 (1) of the Act provided for parties '... questioned by an investigation unit and ... subpoenaed or called upon to appear before the Commission ... [being] entitled to "legal representation"'.

14   Most lawyers said that their clients stuck to the original instruction despite their efforts to explain the nature of the process.

15   The writer's emphasis added. See the discussion above dealing with the ethos of the TRC.

16   See TRC, Final Report: Vol. 1 (Pretoria: RSA, 1998), Chapter 1, 17, 18.

17   Jurgen Habermas, 'Theory of Communicative Action' quoted in Daan Bronkhorst, *Truth and Reconciliation – Obstacles and Opportunities for Human Rights* (Amsterdam: Amnesty International, 1995), 145-146.

18   See TRC, Final Report: Vol. 1, Chapter 5, 106–110 and Vol. 5, Chapter 9, 350 to 435. I have drawn on some of the frameworks but also added other aspects.

19   Of course, where victims feel that the truth has not been revealed they are usually reluctant to be reconciled with the perpetrators but this is different to the issues of closure or accepting the painful truth.

20   Perpetrators who applied for amnesty were required to accept categorically responsibility for their actions in the sense of admitting guilt in unambiguous terms. However, the issue of moral responsibility and acknowledging that their actions were morally

reprehensible was a difficult issue. With regard to the aspect of remorse, one reason for not including it as a criterion is that it is very difficult to gauge the sincerity of an expression of remorse.

21 Without making too fine a point of it, such interactions were often superficial and took place in the heat of the moment. However, because reconciliation is a process that is quite individual to each person it is not easy to gauge the genuineness or otherwise of such interactions. Although I do not profess to be an expert in this field, I found some of the instances I witnessed extremely moving and uplifting.

22 See §22 (1) of the Act.

23 See §22 (1) & (2) of the Act.

24 The writer's emphasis added. See §26 (1) of the Act. §25 (1) (a) (i) of the Act provides for the consideration of referrals from the TRC, the Human Rights Violations Committee and the Amnesty Committee.

25 More detail has in the interim become available, including the extent of the reparation to be paid out to victims.

26 *Azapo and Others* v. *The President of the RSA and others*, 1996 (8) BCLR 1015. More detail has in the interim become available including the extent of the reparation to be paid out to victims.

27 Some applicants were granted amnesty but nevertheless continued to serve sentences for other crimes that they either did not include in their amnesty applications or for which they were refused amnesty for various reasons.

28 See the fuller discussion and reference below.

29 See TRC, Final Report: Vol. 1, paragraph 32c, 57.

30 In 'Articles of Faith', *Index on Censorship* – Vol. 25 No. 5 (1996): 111–113.

15

The Promise and Pitfalls of Apology

Trudy Govier and Wilhelm Verwoerd[1]

The South African Truth and Reconciliation Commission (TRC) was a moral and political experiment on a vast scale.[2] It offers many examples of individuals and institutions struggling to make a moral response to the enormous evils that constituted apartheid. The TRC transcripts provide examples of sincere and profoundly important apologies, illustrating the promise of apology as an important step towards rectifying relationships disrupted by wrongdoing.[3] They also provide illustrations of apologies severely flawed by hypocrisy, grandstanding and denial.

Our central thesis is that it is through *acknowledgement* that the importance of apologies to victims, and their power as a step towards reconciliation, can be explained. We discuss the relationship between apology and the means that perpetrator individuals or groups may employ to make amends to victims harmed by wrongdoing. We also seek to clarify the relationship between individual and institutional apologies. Throughout we draw on material from the proceedings of the TRC to highlight some of the pitfalls of public apologies.

Dictionary entries for 'apology' reveal three basic senses: the apology as a defence (as in Socrates' *Apology*), the apology as excuse or account (sorry I was late, but I was interrupted just as I was leaving) and the moral apology, which is an expression of sorrow for moral wrongdoing (I am profoundly sorry I injured you). The last implies a request for forgiveness and is an initiative towards reconciliation. Here we are concerned with *moral apologies*. We are not concerned with apologies for small matters such as arriving late or spilling fruit juice on a freshly washed floor. In particular, we are interested in *public moral apologies for serious wrongdoing*. A moral apology involves an admission of wrongdoing and will be weakened if it includes attempted justifications or excuses. A public apology is one that is expressed in the public domain on the assumption that it is relevant to the public at large and not solely to the victims of the wrongdoing. Public apologies may be issued by individuals purely as individuals, or by individuals acting as spokespersons for groups or institutions.

The Promise of Apology

The power and importance of apology lie in its potential to offer victims a *moral recognition* or *acknowledgement* of their human worth and dignity. In the case of serious wrongs, a wrongdoer has implied that the victim has little or no moral worth, which is a moral insult. In apologising, the party responsible for the insult accompanying the wrongdoing is implying that the wronged human beings should not have been injured, thus withdrawing the moral insult.[4]

In her recent book, *Between Vengeance and Forgiveness*, Martha Minow includes a brief and useful discussion of apology, noting that there is a sense in which an apology grants power to victims – the power to accept, refuse or ignore the apology. No apology can undo wrongs of the past, but apologies can offer moral acknowledgement to victims and correct a public record, assigning responsibility appropriately to parties who committed the wrongs.[5] If there is no apology, no cancellation of the message, the message of moral insult persists to wound again: 'You were treated as worthless, people have said you were worthless, and no one is going to do anything about it or take that message back.' At this point, the implication is: 'You really are worthless.'

The Japanese military treated Korean Comfort Women as instruments of sexual pleasure; the English treated the Irish like worthless peasants; under apartheid in South Africa, 'non-whites' were systematically dehumanised. Insofar as moral apologies express acknowledgement of the *human dignity and moral worth of victims* as well as *respect for victims' feelings of resentment*, they can provide reason for an emotional shift on the part of victims. A complete and heartfelt apology unstates, or cancels, such messages of degradation and worthlessness. No one can remake the past and some harms are irreparable – but that does not mean that sincere and well-implemented apologies are useless. To those who have been humiliated and treated as morally negligible, a genuine apology is profoundly significant and may soothe their wounds.

A corollary of the idea of soothing by acknowledgement is that there is further insult to, and harm of, victims/survivors when acknowledgement is lacking. If a society pays no heed to brutalities and offences suffered by its citizens, it further damages these vulnerable people because *moral contempt can be as devastating as the original wrong itself.* In literature on the treatment of trauma, this lack of acknowledgement has been termed a second injury to victims, and its effects are referred to as the second wound of silence.[6]

One should not deny the legitimacy of resentment against a moral wrong. This point has been emphasised by Jeffrie Murphy, who claims that resentment of wrongdoing against oneself is an assertion of self-respect.[7] An especially strong person with a keen sense of his or her own moral dignity might maintain dignity in the face of repeated affronts. But resentment in the wake of wrongdoing is an extremely natural response, and one expressive of our sense that we deserve better. If a perpetrator, through an apology or other action, expresses respect for a victim's right to feel angry and resentful, that gives the victim a reason to forgive and overcome resentment. An apology acknowledging that victims legitimately have bitter feelings may help to bring such feelings to the surface. That is essential, if victims are to reflect on them and eventually overcome them.

The importance of this acknowledgement of resentment is implicit in the following statement by Professor Trevor Jenkins of the Medical Faculty of the University of the Witwatersrand at the TRC's health sector hearing:

> *A great deal of hard work though, and creative thinking, will undoubtedly be needed if members of the faculty are to be reconciled with one another. The privileged members of the faculty, who were not the victims of apartheid in the teaching hospital settings, must listen to the accounts of their black colleagues and former students. They must be reminded of the many ways in which they wittingly or unwittingly collaborated with the system. They must be prepared to experience and share some of the pain and hurts which their colleagues of colour experienced because of an accident of birth.[8]*

Moral Amends and Practical Amends

Although wrongs cannot be undone and the past cannot be 'fixed', it is often possible to mitigate the effects of wrongdoing. In granting moral acknowledgement, apologies have the potential to make *moral amends* to victims of wrongdoing.[9] In addition, apologies incorporate an implicit or explicit recognition of the importance of making *practical amends* (some form of restitution or compensation) in the light of that acknowledgement. Serious wrongdoing has resulted in real damage to the victim. A complete apology for serious wrongdoing must include some commitment to practical amends – concrete practical measures to address the damage brought by these wrongs. An oft-cited illustration of the importance of concrete amends is provided by Reverend Mxolisi Mpambani's haunting parable of the bicycle:

> *There were two boys living opposite each other. John stole a bicycle from Tom and then after a year John came to Tom and said: 'Tom, I stole your bicycle and what I need now is reconciliation.' Then Tom looked at John and said: 'Where is my bicycle?' He said: 'No, I am not talking about your bicycle now, I am talking about reconciliation.'*[10]

Another illustration of the close connection between moral amends and material amends may be found in this statement by Cynthia Ngewu, the mother of an activist shot dead by the police:

> *In my opinion, I think the best way to demonstrate a truthful commitment to peace and a truthful commitment to repentance is that perpetrators of acts of violence would make a contribution, a financial contribution, to the families of victims and, in that way, they would then cleanse themselves of their own guilt, and they will then demonstrate with extreme confidence that in fact they are sorry about what they did.*[11]

As the TRC debate about reparation after apartheid highlights dramatically and painfully, victims and victim communities are likely to question the sincerity of an apology if the speakers are *in no way* willing to commit themselves to concrete measures to repair damage that has been done to the victim.

At a TRC hearing Laurie Nathan, former director of the Centre for Conflict Resolution in Cape Town, said that the white community should accept collective responsibility for its acquiescence in maintaining a 'wretched' racist system.

> *To invoke theological terminology, we should confess and engage in meaningful acts of contrition. These acts of contrition could take many forms: establishing or funding memorials like those which commemorate the*

*Holocaust in Nazi Germany, funding bursaries for black students or basic
facilities for pupils, providing medical supplies to amputee hospitals in
Mozambique and Angola ... training in respect for human rights and
multi-cultural diversity for teachers and pupils ... it's critical that they are
undertaken, not as charity, but in partnership with black communities.[12]*

A further illustration of the importance of concrete measures of reparation
is to be found in this statement on behalf of the Natal Law Students. (This
was an organisation representing previously disadvantaged law students.)

*As students, we can say that we do not want the money of these practi-
tioners, we do not want them to go on their hands and knees and beg for
forgiveness, we do not want any more platitudes and token gestures. The
apology of the Pretoria Bar, amongst others, is noted. However, we need to
go beyond this and ask ourselves, what are we going to do in concrete terms
to redress the imbalances, to demonstrate that we really are sorry?[13]*

An apology in which there is no willingness to undertake any practical
measures of reparation is likely to seem insincere or hollow and may even
be worse than no apology at all. An insincere and hollow apology may add
insult to injury and amount, in effect, to a third wound of insincerity. This
negative dynamic was illustrated by an exchange between a representative
of the (former ruling) National Party and Commissioner Mapule
Ramashala at the TRC hearing into an event where a number of unarmed
and peaceful black demonstrators were shot and killed by members of a
homeland security force. Concerning the perpetrators, Ramashala said:

*None of them has said: 'This is my contribution. I would like to do the fol-
lowing.' It stops with, 'I am sorry.' None of them has said: 'As a demonstration, perhaps of how sorry I am, this is what I would like to do.' None
of them have done that. So as you prepare that submission, could you please
address that, because that is the more tangible thing that people are asking,
and people say **that is a re-victimisation, that is a de-humanisation**
and that has caused more pain than you realise. [Emphasis added.][14]*

Because practical gestures may include efforts to improve attitudes and
relationship, and need not always have a material focus, we prefer to speak
of *practical amends* instead of *material amends*. For potential reconciliation

between the parties, and for good evidence of sincerity on the part of perpetrators, a fully fledged moral apology should include a commitment to practical amends.

Individual and Institutional Apologies

When an institution, through its practices, policies and acts, has been instrumental in wronging an individual or a large number of individuals or a group, the issue of institutional apology arises. Institutions or groups may be involved in wrongdoing in various ways. They may have policies that positively require or sanction a kind of wrongdoing, or they may turn a blind eye to wrongs that are officially prohibited. If an organisation comes to see its policies and actions as having been wrong and harmful to others, then the question of an institutional apology, indicating regret for the commission of these harms, arises. In an institutional or individual apology, a speaker expresses sorrow or moral regret for a wrong committed, either by himself or herself as an individual or by individuals acting under the auspices of a group or institution he or she represents.

The expression of sorrow in institutional apologies, however, needs to be clarified further. If people in an institution have come to regard past actions as *wrong* and *the actions of their institution, the one with which they are currently identified*, there is a sense in which we can say that the institution as a collectivity morally regrets those actions and is sorry for them. However, the expression of emotion, which is strikingly important in many contexts of individual apology, tends to be diminished in the institutional case. One relevant factor here is that the spokesperson who issues the apology may not personally have been involved directly in any wrongdoing. Tony Blair apologised for the potato famine in 19th century Ireland, but when he did so he was removed by a century and a half from that event and any role the British government had in worsening it. Given that distance, it is unlikely that Blair felt any remorse about what happened; the apology can better be regarded as an acknowledgement of fault on the part of the British government than as an expression of feelings of sorrow on the part of the individual who issued it.

Another relevant consideration with regard to institutional apologies is that they tend to be made in public contexts and for the public record. Typically, in Western cultures at least, norms of public behaviour require low emotionality in public space. Our emphasis on *acknowledgement* as the basis of moral apologies is consistent with these considerations.

Offering an institutional apology is a public event, one that may carry implications of legal liability or a duty to compensate victims. Third parties are present, offering opportunities for grandstanding and hypocrisy. The shift from the private to the public realm alters the grounds for the interaction and imposes constraints on flexibility. A public apology is mainly fashioned for the record, and may exist primarily to appear on a record. Prestige, honour and reputation may be at stake, and sorrow is likely to be present only in a diminished form.

An understanding of institutional apologies is enhanced if we focus our attention on moral acknowledgement of victims as contrasted with expression of emotion by perpetrators, because such acknowledgement can be a feature of institutional apology even when little or no emotion is indicated. It is not crucial that acknowledgement is expressed through the *emotion* of an institutional representative, much less that it be expressed (somehow) by the whole institution. What is crucial for the significance of the apology in beginning to address the wrongs of the past is that it constitute an acknowledgement of wrongdoing, thereby implying an acknowledgement of the human dignity and legitimate feelings of those people who were wronged. Whether or not a collective or institution can in any sense *feel sorrow or regret*, it is clear that it can, through spokespersons, acknowledge wrongdoing. Institutions, and especially the state, are often in especially powerful positions to acknowledge wrongdoing because they have the power to issue official statements and documents and to establish memorials and compensation programmes.

We now move to a number of further considerations regarding institutional apologies. One obvious and central difference between an individual and an institutional or collective case is that the person who issues the apology is characteristically not identical with the *agent(s)* of wrongdoing. A speaker who issues an apology on behalf of an institution or collective is speaking for that institution or collective, not for himself or herself.

A further difference is that institutions are typically involved in *plural or ramified actions*, which occur over a considerable period of time and involve many people. A prominent case at the TRC was that of the Medical Association of South Africa (MASA).[15] This group has about 14 000 members. At issue were policies and the behaviour of doctors who, over many years under apartheid, helped create a climate within which violations of human rights took place. In some cases district surgeons assisted in the torture of detainees and failed to testify accurately in court about damage resulting from torture.

Because institutions and collectives such as the Medical Association of South Africa are typically more extensive and more powerful than individuals, there is often a financial and physical capacity for many further actions. Thus reparation and commitment not to re-offend are of special importance. To be willing to extend some kind of forgiveness and work for reconciliation with an institution that has been oppressive or cruel in the past, victims need the assurance that that institution is not going to lapse into its bad old ways. An institution that has encouraged, authorised or negligently permitted wrongdoing by its personnel and officers will have much to do to reform itself.[16] The need for sustained institutional effort is recognised in this statement from the Medical Association of South Africa:

The transformation of MASA of which I speak is an ongoing process. A significant event along the way was the unconditional apology for the past wrongs of the Association that was made in June 1995. We stand by every word that was spoken in that apology ... The apology was a necessary step along the road we are travelling, but it was only a step. Our wholehearted participation in the work of this Commission is yet another step on this road, but again only a step ... [T]here is much that remains to be done. We intend to participate fully in the work of the proposed over-arching Health and Human Rights Organisation. We propose to enlarge and to strengthen the office and the activities of our ombudsman, our public protector. Our peer review system has already been sharpened and structured much more effectively than it ever was before. We are currently engaged in a programme designed to promote structured ethics education in all the medical schools in this country, and we are planning formal structured training for prisons' health service personnel.[17]

The implementation of reforms in such cases is no short and easy matter. In a collective or institutional apology the spokesperson must have an appropriate mandate. That mandate should emerge from processes within the institution, before the apology is issued, so that when a representative speaks, he or she is genuinely speaking for the many others within the institution and is not at risk of having his or her words undercut by subsequent denials from others within it. The importance of having a mandate becomes immediately clear if we imagine a spokesperson issuing an important and profound public apology on behalf of an institution, only to have his or her apology followed shortly thereafter by denials on the part of other individuals in the institution. The mandate is necessary for the apologising person to be genuinely a spokesperson; it is required for rhetorical effectiveness and to ensure plausibility and viability of the commitments to abide by pertinent moral rules in the future and to make amends.

An individual who speaks for an institution and apologises may have had little or nothing to do with the wrongful acts in question. This can lead to confusion. The individual will, of course, appear to be himself or herself and speak with a name and personal history. However, as the issuer of an institutional policy, he or she must also appear to be the spokesperson for a collective. The individual may seem most conspicuously to be himself or herself – but what is most important, in the context of an institutional apology, is that person's status as spokesperson for the institution. The individual is not speaking for himself or herself, but rather for a collectivity that he or she serves, in this context, as an authorised representative. Thus there is a crucial distinction to be drawn between the *role* of spokesperson for an institution which is acknowledging institutional wrongdoing and the *role* of the individual wrongdoer. A collectivity can act, and be responsible for acts, without every individual in it being personally implicated.[18] In institutional contexts, response may be given by the leadership of the group. In cases where the people affected by the original wrong do not have an official authorised leadership, there are likely to be indications of acceptance or rejection from outstanding persons with less formal and structured positions of leadership.

A public institutional apology is addressed to victims of the wrongs: primary victims (those directly harmed), secondary victims (the family and close friends of primary victims) and tertiary victims (affected members of their community or group). Any victim receiving a public apology for an act that has affected him or her has a choice to make about how to respond. A victim can accept or reject the apology. It is also possible to withhold judgement, waiting to see whether future actions show commitment to reform and practical amends. Such withholding is significant, because it often represents a powerful conviction that in the wake of serious wrongdoing words are not enough.

A Poignant Application

In the light of these distinctions, we wish to comment in some detail on an apology by former state president, F. W. de Klerk, before the TRC.[19] In a highly significant appearance, De Klerk said:

Let me place once and for all a renewed apology on record. Apartheid was wrong. I apologise in my capacity as leader of the National Party to the millions of South Africans who suffered the wrenching disruption of forced removals in respect of their homes, businesses, and land. Who over the years suffered the shame of being arrested for pass law offences. Who over the decades and indeed centuries suffered the indignities and humiliation of racial discrimination. Who for a long time were prevented from exercising their full democratic rights in the land of their birth. Who were unable to achieve their full potential because of job reservation. And who in any other way suffered as a result of discriminatory legislation and policies. This renewed apology is offered in a spirit of true repentance, in full knowledge of the tremendous harm that apartheid has done to millions of South Africans.[20]

On the face of it, this striking statement by a former state president sounds like a sincere and credible apology. However, grave problems emerged during the subsequent questioning of De Klerk by the TRC staff and commissioners. By the end of the day of hearings, Archbishop Tutu, literally in tears, expressed his deep disappointment with De Klerk's performance. The ANC issued an angry press statement in which it rejected De Klerk's apology 'with contempt'. What went wrong?

Several features of our account help to explain the failure of De Klerk's apology. First, the acknowledgement of responsibility for wrongdoing was partial and compromised. Second, there was no clear commitment to practical amends. And third, De Klerk's role as a spokesperson for the National Party in its previous governing role was unclear.

De Klerk's responses to TRC questioning reveal a contradiction between his initial acknowledgement of responsibility for the moral and material injuries of apartheid and his later highly selective acknowledgement of responsibility for gross human rights violations. The glaring gap between his 'full knowledge of the tremendous harm that apartheid has done to millions of South Africans' and his persistent denial of any knowledge of or responsibility for widespread, systematic torture and severe ill-treatment by state agents made a mockery of what was supposed to be a 'spirit of true repentance'. De Klerk accepted responsibility for 'all our policies, decisions and actions' and acknowledged that the security legislation and the state of emergency created circumstances conducive to abuses of human rights. However, even after detailed and persistent questioning by TRC staff, who had reviewed extensive verbal and written testimonies of consistent, widespread human rights violations by police and defence personnel, he maintained that such 'crimes' were never government policy. '(I)t has never been the policy of the government, the National Party, that people should be murdered, should be assassinated,' De Klerk maintained. Tortures, murders, rapes and abductions were deplorable and detestable acts – but none were done under official instruction; there was no government or cabinet responsibility for them. As presiding chairperson, Archbishop Tutu noted that some highly placed police and army employees had admitted wrongdoing and applied to the TRC for amnesty. De Klerk stonewalled, moving back and forth between denial (we never did it, accepted it or recommended it) and excuses (torture in jails happens all over the world; the ANC too had been guilty of abuses; it was a period of violent struggle). He insisted that it had never been government policy to murder, torture, rape or abduct anti-apartheid activists. He said that he *regretted* what went wrong in the perpetration of these horrors, but he *did not apologise* for them because he – and by implication his National Party government – *accepted no responsibility for them*.

Vagueness about any practical or material amends made De Klerk appear even more insincere. The lack of an explicit commitment by his political party to a process of practical amends stood in stark contrast to some other institutional apologies such as those by MASA, described earlier.

De Klerk's appearance was a highly public one, in a public context with extensive media publicity. He was concerned to protect his personal self-image and that of the National Party. 'We abolished apartheid and we are proud of it,' he said. He wanted to take a position of pride, insisting that his government had succeeded in ending apartheid, rather than a position of shame in which he would have to admit that his government was responsible for gross violations of human rights.

De Klerk had an inadequate and unclear mandate to speak for the National Party. Members of the older (pre-transition) party, such as former state president P. W. Botha, were not present and had not authorised De Klerk to speak for them. Botha publicly criticised some of De Klerk's statements, immediately revealing that De Klerk's mandate as a spokesperson was questionable. Confounding matters was a confusion between the older pro-apartheid National Party and the new National Party, which constituted the Parliamentary opposition in 1997. Although he was accompanied by members of the reformed National Party, De Klerk insisted on being the only one to answer questions.

Tragically, this was a case of an apology gone wrong. The subsequent denials compromised acknowledgement; there was no commitment to practical amends; the public format pushed De Klerk in the direction of cover-up rather than commitment and his mandate as a collective representative was unclear. The millions of South Africans hurt by apartheid were hurt again by this promising but partial, and ultimately ineffectual, effort. Instead of 'pouring balm on the wounds of many', this compromised apology only served to rub salt in those wounds.

Conclusion

As noted, the practice of issuing apologies for serious moral wrongs has recently been prominent in the proceedings of the TRC and, indeed, around the globe. We have offered a stringent account of what it is to offer a credible moral apology in such cases because we believe that apologies for such past wrongs are serious business. As we have argued here, and as is illustrated in the case of F. W. de Klerk, there are many pitfalls one can encounter in the process of apologising. There are also profound moral reasons for avoiding these pitfalls. The most important of these is that by issuing a facile or insincere apology, one will injure the victims again. One will briefly raise their hopes only to disappoint in the end – when one's acknowledgement is partial, setting in question the commitment to moral reform; when one is unwilling to commit to moral and practical amends; or when one cannot properly represent a group or institution on whose behalf one purports to speak. If one is going to apologise, it is important to do it right to avoid a bitter third wound in which the insincere apology adds moral insult to the original moral injury.

We have also alluded to the promise of apology. The promise is that a whole-hearted apology, followed up with proper commitment to reform and practical amends, can provide a major initial step towards restoring injured relationships. As such, a whole-hearted apology offers benefits of moral reform and self-acknowledgement to the perpetrator; benefits of moral recognition and reparation to the victim; an improved relationship to both; and positive ripple effects to the broader community. Credible moral apologies take past wrongs seriously and deal deeply with them. For that reason, they can constitute an important stage in the arduous process of morally addressing wrongs of the past.

Notes

1   In this paper we draw on Trudy Govier and Wilhelm Verwoerd, 'The Promise and Pitfalls of Apologies', in *Journal of Social Philosophy*, 33 (2002): 67-82, and to a lesser extent on our 'Taking Wrongs Seriously: A Qualified Defence of Public Apologies', in *Saskatchewan Law Review*, 65 (2002): 153-176. Thanks to Anton Colijn, David Crocker, Susan Dwyer, Larry May, Janet Sisson and Bob Ware for comments on earlier versions of this paper.

2   The Promotion of National Unity and Reconciliation Act, No. 34 of 1995, mandated the TRC to (a) get as 'complete a picture as possible' of the 'nature, causes and extent' of politically motivated gross human rights violations (i.e. acts of torture, killing, abduction and severe ill-treatment) which occurred during the period of 1 March 1960 to 10 May 1994; (b) help restore the human and civil dignity of victims by granting them an opportunity to relate their own accounts of the violations of which they are victims; (c) grant amnesty to those individuals giving 'full disclosure' of politically motivated crimes during this period of resistance to and defence of the apartheid system; and (d) make recommendations to the president and Parliament on reparation and rehabilitation measures to be taken, including measures to prevent the future commission of human rights violations. Under the chairpersonship of Archbishop Desmond Tutu, these tasks included making findings on tens of thousands of alleged gross violations of human rights contained in 20 300 statements taken from victims or survivors of these violations. A comprehensive report was handed to the president on 28 October 1998, with the last volume finally handed over in April 2003. See Truth and Reconciliation Commission of South Africa, Final Report (Pretoria: RSA, 1998).

3   TRC, Final Report, Vol. 5, 382-392.

4   Jean Hampton, 'The Retributive Idea', in *Forgiveness and Mercy*, Jeffrie Murphy and Jean Hampton (Cambridge: Cambridge University Press, 1988), 111-161.

5   Martha Minow, *Between Vengeance and Forgiveness: Facing History after Genocide and Mass Violence* (Boston: Beacon Press, 1998), 112-116.

6   M. Symonds, 'The "Second Injury" to Victims', in *Evaluation and Change* (1980): 36-38; Yael Danieli, 'Confronting the Unimaginable: Psychotherapists' Reactions to Victims of the Nazi Holocaust', in *Human Adaptation to Extreme Stress*, eds. J. P. Wilson et al. (New York: Plenum Publishing Corporation, 1988).

7   Jeffrie Murphy, 'The Retributive Emotions', in *Forgiveness and Mercy*, Murphy and Hampton, 16.

8   Transcript of TRC health sector hearing, Cape Town, 18 June 1997. See also TRC, Final Report, Vol. 4, 109-157.

9   See Marcel Golding, 'Forgiveness and Regret', in *Philosophical Forum*, 16 (1986): 121-137.

10 Transcript of TRC public meeting, University of Cape Town, 24 January 1997.

11 Transcript of public forum on Reconciliation, Reconstruction and Economic Justice in Cape Town, 19 March 1997.

12 Transcript of TRC special hearing on compulsory military service/conscription, Cape Town, 23 July 1997. See TRC, Final Report, Vol. 4, 220-245.

13 Transcript of TRC hearing on the legal system, Johannesburg, 27-29 October 1997. See TRC, Final Report, Vol. 4, 93-108.

14 Transcript of TRC hearing on the Bisho massacre, Bisho, 11 September 1996. See TRC, Final Report, Vol. 3, 136-145.

15 Currently renamed as the South African Medical Association (SAMA).

16 This commitment to reform is, of course, complicated by the fact that within institutions questions of *causality* and *responsibility* (who did what) are more complicated than they are in the case of individuals. If a man acting as an individual rapes a woman, we know who did what. Issues of responsibility and wrongdoing are relatively straightforward in such a case. If, however, a government sets up a homeland system including petty black dictators who have a defence force, and a general within that defence force authorises a foot soldier to shoot during what was supposed to be a peaceful demonstration, it is less clear who is the wrongdoer. This example is a simplified version of issues arising in the TRC hearings concerning the Bisho massacre.

17 Transcript of TRC health sector hearing, Cape Town, 18 June 1997. See TRC, Final Report, Vol. 5, 387-388.

18 At this point it is useful to keep one's mind resolutely fixed on a logical fallacy known as the Fallacy of Division. It is a logical mistake to make inferences straightforwardly from wholes to parts.

19 F. W. de Klerk was leader of the National Party and state president of South Africa between 1989 and 1994 and a cabinet minister under the presidency of P. W. Botha during the 1980s. Jointly with Nelson Mandela, he received the Nobel Peace Prize in 1993 for his role in the negotiated settlement in South Africa. For further reflections on De Klerk see Timothy Garton Ash, 'True Confessions', *New York Review of Books*, 44, 12 (1997): 33-38.

20 Transcript of political party submissions, Cape Town, 14 May 1997. The appearance of De Klerk on behalf of the (reformed or new) National Party was the first in a series of follow-up hearings in which the TRC questioned representatives of various political parties on submissions presented to the TRC in August 1996.

16

The Rupture of Necklace Murders:
A Need for Psychological and Broader Strategies of Reparation

Pumla Gobodo-Madikizela

There was hardly any space to move in the tiny room. Mrs Zamela's home in the black township of Mlungisi in the Eastern Cape town of Queenstown consisted of two rooms. This was her bedroom. In 1985, she had to flee Mlungisi township after young anti-apartheid activists, suspecting that her daughter Nosipho was an informant for the police, put a car tyre around Nosipho's neck, doused it with petrol, and forced her to set it aflame, burning her to death. As the rubber melted, the crowd sang and danced around her until there were no signs of movement left in her body and they were sure she was dead.

Between 1984 and 1989, some 450 people, almost all blacks, were killed by this grisly method. Death by tyre – a burning tyre – came to be known simply as 'the necklace'. The necklace was the kiss of death. It was almost as if the seething anger that many young blacks felt towards the agents of apartheid, with nowhere for it to go, found an outlet by turning against any fellow black who was thought, for real or imaginary reasons, to be in cahoots with the architects of oppression. In Mlungisi, as elsewhere, the violence of blacks against other blacks, even in the form of the necklace, was in many cases an expression of rage towards the system of apartheid. The significance of the event transcends what is literally taking place before one's eyes. The violence becomes a symbol of something larger. It is not just about the person who is the target of the crowd. The person stands as a cipher for a larger story, a larger crime, for it is not about hatred of a fellow black but rather accumulated long-term frustration that suddenly gets focused by one event and onto one person.

Mrs Zamela had somehow found the courage to return to live in Mlungisi. This morning she was sitting on her queen-size bed, which had seen better days and now yielded quite readily to the heft of her substantial body as she bent forward over a large aluminium bath filled with dirty water. There was another large tin tub sitting on the bedroom floor, in which she had deposited the clothes already washed. In the darkened corner of the room stood a sturdy chest of drawers that supported a tall, oblong yellowing mirror suspended between two wooden panels. Various objects decorated the top of the chest: Vaseline, sewing basket, bottles of medicine, a Bible, stacks of envelopes, a clock. In the other corner, a bench with clothes piled up on it doubled as a makeshift wardrobe. Next to the second tub, a chair with red upholstery.

As I walked in she stopped, sudsy water dripping from the brassiere she was washing, and looked up, half-surprised to see a stranger in her home. Her grandson had led me through the front room where five or six men were sitting drinking beer and simply let me into her room unannounced. She greeted me pleasantly, dropping the laundry back into the water and extending her arm, offering me her wrist instead of her soapy hand. I shook her wrist. Her hands were of course covered in suds up to her wrists, but the courteous thing to do was to accept the offer. After exchanging greetings, I was warmly directed to the red chair.

I had made inquiries at the East London office of the Truth and Reconciliation Commission (TRC), which was where Mrs Zamela would have made a statement, and found out that she had not made a submission about her daughter's killing. I desperately wanted to encourage her to agree to tell the story of what had happened to her daughter. This was the reason for my visit. The Commission had conducted quite an extensive outreach programme in Mlungisi township. I wondered why Mrs Zamela hadn't approached the TRC to tell what had happened to her daughter. Perhaps the pain was still too fresh, too unmanageable, to bring it all to the surface again. 'Necklace' cases always seemed to evoke strong ambivalence among people attending TRC hearings, and even among TRC members. In almost every case, I sensed some uncertainty in the family members of victims of necklace murders, as if the shame they bore prevented them from sharing the same platform as families of victims whose lives were snuffed out by the very enemy with whom their loved ones had been accused of collaboration.

Perhaps Mrs Zamela had been reluctant to submit her statement because she knew that many who would come forward to give statements at the Commission's hearings had been bystanders to her daughter's killing. They had stood by and watched, perhaps even sang and clapped, and she wanted to avoid encountering them, and the powerful emotions this might unleash in her, in the context of a hearing.

Yet I knew that Mrs Zamela deserved to be heard. Like so many in the township of Mlungisi, she had suffered immensely, and deserved the relief, albeit small, that would come from the reparation the government had promised to victims of gross human rights abuses. For that alone, her daughter's death needed to be part of the Commission's record.

To understand why Nosipho was killed – although there is, in the end, no explanation that can fully make sense – you have to understand something about the emergence of the young leaders who led the countrywide wave of grisly necklace murders that swept South Africa at the height of President P. W. Botha's rule of 'Total Strategy'.

In 1983, Botha established a tripartite Parliament that allowed for power sharing among whites, coloureds and Indians, but excluded blacks from participation in matters of government. For blacks, the government created a separate system of black 'counsellors' who were given formal authority, but little real power or support, to manage the affairs of their urban areas. Among blacks, the counsellors had essentially no mandate as leaders. Beginning in 1983, therefore, a consensus began to form in the black community that unless the resistance to the regime of terror shifted to a new and higher gear, the cause might never be won. In response to having been shut out of the three-way power-sharing arrangement in Parliament and rendered voiceless, the anti-apartheid struggle launched the United Democratic Front (UDF), a system of locally based organisations charged with a national campaign for redress of local grievances. In the concerted effort that ensued to dismantle the separatist tripartite arrangement, a consumer boycott of white-owned businesses was launched. Yet, almost immediately, leaders of the UDF were detained and imprisoned, leaving a leadership vacuum. Left to manage the movement's policies were young, inexperienced marshals like the ones who killed Nosipho. It was out of this inexperience that intolerance of black dissent, even perceived dissent, emerged. The 'necklace' method of dispensing with those perceived to be 'enemies of the people' was one result of this development.

Mrs Zamela's daughter, Nosipho, was accused of having an affair with a policeman and so she was fingered as a police informant. On 8 December 1985, she was burnt in broad daylight in the centre of Mlungisi township by a small crowd of youths who sang hateful songs and danced as they watched her burning body.

'How can I help you, my daughter?' Mrs Zamela began as I sat opposite her in her tiny room. There is something comforting about visiting
the home of a fellow black South African, I find myself thinking even
before I answer. In a black home, the linguistic exchanges themselves have
inflections embedded in them that immediately float you on a bed of
comfortable hospitality. The warmth of a people who have little to offer
one another materially but the warmth of ordinary kinship – *ubuntu*.

I tell her my name, that my home is in the nearby town of Cala. I
explain that I work for the Truth Commission, that I was one of the people
from the Commission who came to launch the outreach in Mlungisi two
years ago. I tell her that I know about Nosipho and that I can imagine
how painful, how terrible, it all must still be. Has she considered sharing
what happened to Nosipho with the Commission, I ask?

A cloud descends over her face as I mention her daughter's name. Her
eyes become a well of grief, her face a picture of anguish. There is a pause,
a painful pause. She starts to speak, but no words come out. She looks
away. As her eyes well up with tears, she reaches back for a piece of cloth
lying on her bed. She holds it in her hands, but instead of wiping her eyes
she looks down at the cloth, stretching and turning it as if within its folds
she might somehow discover an answer to my question, that it might
somehow slip from its folds and save her from having to speak words that
are still unspeakable.

She begins to wipe her hands – her fingers, one by one, first the fingers
on one hand, then the other. She is lost in thought; where she is gone, I
dare not follow. Tears roll down her hands. She puts the cloth away. Then
she looks up and stares out in space somewhere above me. I know there is
nothing there to see but darkness in the corner of her bedroom, and a ticking clock. I imagine she has been staring into this darkness for many years.
She is remembering, thinking, and not seeing. She is one who, like many
in our country, has become familiar with not seeing. Her head now bent,
her eyes look down but her gaze seems fixed at something on the floor,
beyond the floor, beneath the floor, something far away. Her stare is the
stare of one who has lost something so precious, so profound, that the
mind can no longer put it into words that others can understand.

In the distance, I can make out the sounds of life in the neighbourhood
– small children shouting, a passing van, a dog barking. Here, all I can hear
is the ticking of the clock on the wall as we sit together in this crowded darkness, sharing a moment of humanity that neither of us can describe. Have

you considered sharing what happened to Nosipho with the Commission, I ask again, not knowing what else to do or say.

'I didn't think they wanted to hear from me,' she finally replies. Her voice is so sad, so filled with loneliness, like a child abandoned by her parents, by the world. Her voice sags with weariness. I don't know what to say. 'These people who injured my child, aren't they the ones who are being invited to take their grievances to this commission?'

'*Injured* my child …' It is as if she can't bring herself to mention her daughter's death, as if using the word 'killed' would be disrespectful to her daughter's name by violating some sacred commitment she has privately made to Nosipho's memory, as if pronouncing the word would finally make it real – or worse, enact it all over again.

'These people …' *They* are the ones who can lay legitimate claim to victim status. *She* has no right to claim that status. As for her daughter, what was she but a spy, an outcast, an informant who had been caught sleeping with the enemy, a witch burnt at the stake of the anti-apartheid struggle. This is what the whole community said. She must live with it, she says, and has lived with it ever since her daughter was taken away from her that Saturday morning. What does the TRC want with the mothers of such people? I feel her shame, guilt and sadness as she speaks; I can see it in the slump of her shoulders, a woman who has borne the burden not only of having been unable to protect her daughter but also of being branded the mother of a 'collaborator'. The doors of the Truth Commission, she imagined, must surely be closed to the mother of a collaborator.

I explain to her that the TRC has been inviting and receiving statements from any South African whose child, parent, spouse, partner or relative was killed, tortured, abducted or suffered any kind of abuse in the past. She shakes her head and says slowly: 'All I can tell you is that nobody was there, except for a very small group of family members …' Her voice breaks as she chokes with tears, looking blankly at the dirty laundry in the tub in front of her. 'We had to leave for the cemetery before dawn,' she continues, 'in the early hours. There was nobody. Nobody. Nobody came there. Nobody came afterwards. That's all I can tell you.' Her voice breaks again, and this time she lets go of her tears.

Trauma and the Need for Psychological Reparation

Necklace murders left gaping, aching wounds on many levels; the psychological damage of individuals whose loved ones were murdered by people who, in many cases, were neighbours and/or peers, as well as the damage inflicted on those who were witnesses to this tragedy. Financial compensation of victims of gross human rights abuses is often seen as the best approach to reparation that can bring about closure. Where there has been a major rupture within communities, however, because of a breakdown of a sense of trust, confusions and divisions as a result of the horrific practice of necklace killings, the question is not how much is given in material terms to individual victims, but whether the reparation strategy responds to the need to rebuild trust and community bonds. How well a reparation strategy addresses the aftermath of trauma will be measured by the extent to which it bestows psychological healing on victims.

The central part of healing in any aftermath of trauma is helping victims and survivors of trauma to gain a certain level of control. The violation of a necklace murder extends far beyond the individual victim and her/his loved ones. It is about a system of power in which both the victim and the community of bystanders have absolutely none. Often many of the bystanders of a necklace murder, by virtue of their silence – they have no power to speak – become an extension of the perpetrators. They are the accomplices in this bitter crime. In this atmosphere of active perpetrators and silent bystanders, victims are voiceless. Victims continue to be silenced long after the event because bystanders of these hideous crimes of crowd murders are afraid to listen, lest memory forces them to turn their faces towards the past, and perceive the destruction of which they are guilty by association, to see the ruins that lie waste in the wake of their silence. Much more needs to be repaired in the communities that were shattered by the necklace epidemic.

Trauma is an affliction of the powerless, Judith Herman informs us.[1] When the trauma is human-induced, one loses a sense of power over those things that are usually under one's control, including one's sense of identity. Human-induced trauma strips victims of all that defines who they are. Susan Brison refers to this as the 'un-making' of the self.[2] To repair this damage to the self requires not only a focus on the individual, but also on one's community to restore broken bonds and rebuild the trust that was crushed by the traumatic experience.

For many survivors and family members of victims, coming before the TRC was a time of solidarity and shared pain. For those whose loved ones were murdered by the necklace, however, the moment of testimony was a moment of remembering their family's shame and the tragic rejection by the same community that must now listen to victims' stories of pain that they in their silence and inaction helped to bring about. Mrs Zamela's wound is deep, like so many mothers whose children were burnt to death. Their narratives of trauma show evidence of the shame and guilt of having failed to protect their children and the humiliation of being outcasts in their communities. While other victims are assured of the support and affirmation of their communities, and even the entire society, these victims' trauma lives indelibly on their bodies, and remains unresolved, unresolved that is, until the trust and the solidarity with their communities can be re-established.

Stories of necklace murders always carry an overwhelming sense of loss and pain precisely because very few people – or none at all – reach out. 'Nobody came,' said Mrs Zamela. Not during the burial of her daughter, not after. Nobody mourned with her. For her loss, there was no *sense* of community to speak of. Yet the most crucial ingredient for healing of traumatic wounds, many trauma specialists say, is community support. For family members and victims of necklace murders then, the best form of psychological reparation lies in gaining solidarity with their community, to be at peace with them, to live in harmony with them, to be able to reclaim their dignity and respect, and, finally, to have freedom from guilt and shame.

Reparation for More than Victims: the Route of Cleansing Rituals

Incidents of necklace violence offer evidence of how ordinary people in one's community are capable of the worst kind of evil we could have imagined. But so are we capable of the greatest virtue we might have thought. People can and do heal. Broken bonds within communities can be rebuilt, repaired, and trust and hope in the human spirit restored. The challenge is how communities can break the chains of denial and fear, rise above guilt and seek instead engagement with the tragic drama of necklace murders in which communities were silent witnesses, engagement, that is, with the shameful past. In order to heal, survivors and family members of necklace killings need to be released from shame. Yet, the burden of shame is also on the shoulders of those who perpetrated the murders, who, ironically, were heroes at the time they committed the gruesome murders. They, too, are in need of reparative intervention.

With Nosipho Zamela's death, for instance, the cycle of madness in the township of Mlungisi finally ended. But a sense of tragedy continues to pervade the lives of many in this township community. Nosipho's mother and others whose loved ones died through the bitter 'justice' of a necklace execution still live with unanswered questions. But perpetrators wear their own albatross around their necks. For unlike their leaders in the anti-apartheid struggle, and unlike apartheid's henchmen who have kept their jobs and their freedom, and many of the privileges of being white in a country long dominated by whites, *they* have no jobs, no privileges. The necklace murderers are the black sheep of the liberation movement. Once they had felt like heroes when they were managing the consumer boycott. Now, like veterans of a war that nobody wants to remember, they are neither remembered nor treated as heroes, a shaming anonymity. Those who once pushed hard against the envelope of apartheid under difficult and ill-defined circumstances, making up the rules of the struggle as they went, now move from one bottle of beer to the next, steeped in a perpetual haze – in pursuit of perpetual forgetfulness.

The hope for inner reparation, the resolution of the inner turmoil in these men, the ghosts that refuse to be silenced, could be in cleansing rituals. African traditional cleansing rituals can be a symbol of personal reparation, a reconnection with one's community and a symbolic act of reconciliation with victims.

The image of human blood is an image that is normally not seen. Blood carries a lot of symbolism for people in general, but has particular significance for many African people. When blood is made visible by unnatural means through murder or an accident, there are certain associations that are made, which in turn define the way people relate to these events. A person responsible for exposing blood unnaturally by murdering is referred to as having *isinyama* (blackness) in Zulu and *isithunzi* (shadow) in Xhosa. For those affected, the 'blackness' or 'shadow' of the victim hovers over them, or follows them like a burden, and they have to be 'washed' of its presence in their lives in order that they can live normally. For others, for example, members of a community, casting their eyes on those who are affected may colour their lives with the same 'blackness' or 'shadow' of the perpetrator. The cleansing process, then, has a reparative element, and includes both the perpetrator as the one who is affected, and the community of people who inhabit the world of the perpetrator. The effect of the cleansing goes far beyond 'removing' the stains of guilt. It is a way of finding, through ritual expression, something that is unspeakable, finding comfort in symbolic language that brings pain, responsibility, shame and guilt into the common pot of shared empathy. Thus, the ritual becomes an instrument of psychological rehabilitation, and its effect is the validation and affirmation of victims' suffering.

Notes

1   Judith Herman, *Trauma and Recovery: From Domestic Abuse to Political Terror* (New York: Basic, 1992).
2   Susan Brison, 'Trauma Narratives and the Remaking of the Self', in eds. M. Bal, J. Crew & L. Spitzer, *Acts of Memory: Cultural Recall in the Present* (Hanover, NH: Dartmouth, 1999), 39–54.

17
Building Sites of Repair:
Freedom Park and its Objectives

Revel Fox

Freedom Park is part of the cabinet-approved Legacy Project which 'has undertaken to approve and facilitate the setting up of new monuments, museums and museum programmes, plaques, outdoor art works and other symbolic representations that will create visible reminders of the many aspects of our formerly neglected heritage, widely distributed throughout the country'.[1]

Freedom Park is intended to fulfil a wide spectrum of complex and highly sensitive functions, which will find expression in the components comprising the project: a memorial, a museum and a garden of remembrance.

The museum's role is described as 'the acknowledgement, preservation, presentation and narration of South Africa's history, arts, culture and heritage for present and future generations ... The Freedom Park development will provide a unique opportunity to design and implement a narrative centre which makes a significant contribution to the processes of reparation, reconciliation and nation building'.[2]

The Freedom Park memorial is described as: 'A national memorial seeking to facilitate a communal process of commemorating the pain, and celebrating the victories of the past, by preserving the memories of victims, conflict and human rights abuses caused by slavery, colonialism and racism, and honouring the victims, heroes and heroines of the struggle against apartheid.' The description continues as follows: 'The memorial is the spiritual sanctum of the entire Freedom Park precinct, expressing a national human experience of heroism sacrifice, human suffering and loss.'

The memorial is further described as taking cognisance of all the categories of the victims of conflict as stated in the National Heritage Resources Act, and special reference is made to 'apartheid victims, including, but not limited to, those named by the Truth and Reconciliation Commission [TRC]'.

It is the garden of remembrance that is identified as a place where sculptures commemorating national heroes and heroines or historic events would be located. Within the garden, provision is being made for a gathering space, which must accommodate 5 000 people on significant national days. It will also become a venue for cultural and other appropriate performances.

A board of trustees, of which Mongane Wally Serote is Executive Chairman, was established to oversee the project and a number of officials were appointed to an administration responsible for its implementation.

In a preface to the brief and conditions of the architectural competition organised by the Freedom Park Trust, President Thabo Mbeki referred to Freedom Park as 'the most ambitious heritage project to be undertaken by the new democratic government'.

While the central theme of Freedom Park could be described as a memorial to the struggle for freedom and dignity in South Africa, the scope of the heritage extends from the genesis of the earliest life forms to the present day and reaches into an exploration of a great future for our nation.

The capital city, Pretoria, was selected as the location for the site which, in terms of the National Heritage Resources Act No. 25 of 1999, Section 7,1 (a), should be classified as a 'Grade 1 project, because it is a heritage resource with qualities so exceptional that they are of special national significance'.

Salvokop, the site chosen, is one of several hills that surround the city. It is clearly visible from the major approaches to Pretoria and from the city itself. It is believed that the area was used for grazing and initiation ceremonies by Sotho-Tswana people whose descendants were later removed to the outlying areas of Mamelodi and Atteridgeville. The decision to make use of high ground, particularly for the places of spiritual significance, is consistent with customs and choices in many different cultures and religions.

An extract from the Freedom Park Trust programme reads: 'The Project will be established at a 52-hectare site, identified as Salvokop in Pretoria. The Project aims to be inclusive of all South Africans, and will place the country's entire history in a context whose integrity will be respected nationally and internationally.'

The implementation of Freedom Park will comprise three phases, spread over several years. These phases will include the construction of the state-of-the-art museum which will be South Africa's narrative space; the memorial, which will be the country's spiritual space; and the garden of remembrance.

An international architectural competition began in January 2003. The

first stage was adjudicated in April 2003, and the second stage, comprising
a short list of selected entries, was assessed in July 2003.

The scope of the competition includes the museum, the memorial and
the garden of remembrance. In the brief for competitors, this garden
includes an amphitheatre or gathering space of 4 500 square metres and a
garden of 20 000 square metres. The remainder of the open space on
Salvokop does not form part of the architectural competition, and is the
subject of an ongoing and independent research programme involving a
broad spectrum of interests, which will guide and inform policy at
Freedom Park.

As a guide to those entering the architectural competition, certain basic
principles have been outlined, and the concept for Freedom Park is set
out as follows:

> *Salvokop Hill has been divided into three distinct zones: the base of the hill,
> which is a public area engaging with the inter city; the crest which is for the
> more special, symbolic and sacrosanct aspects of Freedom Park such as the
> museum, memorial and garden of remembrance; and the slope between the
> base and the crest which is a transitional space where the journey takes place
> from the public to the sacrosanct, from the real world to the spiritual world ...
> The narrative path from the base of the hill to the crest occurs in a number of
> ways. Access to the crest can be a short steep walk following the general routes
> of the 'vistas'. An alternative route would be a spiral route commencing at the
> axial view from the hill to Church Square adjacent to the Salvokop Village
> and winding up the hill to the sacrosanct space on top. This walk is longer but
> less steep and will allow paraplegic access to the top in special electric vehicles or
> wheelchairs ... Access to the crest for service vehicles and ceremonial vehicles
> will be allowed along an improved road in the west ... Narrative points are
> placed along the spiral path at the intersection of the axes. The axes are re-
> inforced by the conscious establishment of vistas of the various historic land-
> marks. Due to the ecological, geological and environmentally sensitive nature
> of the site, development has been kept to the northern side of the hill. Parking
> areas are located in poor environment access generally in bluegum areas, and
> all parking areas have been sensitively located. The location of the museum,
> memorial and garden of remembrance has taken account of the geology and the
> highly sensitive aspects of the environment and landscape.*

The wish has also been expressed that a head of state guesthouse be located on or near the top of the hill. This will be used by important visitors, and will ensure their privacy and security.

The Environmental Impact Assessment that has been carried out has recommended minimal clearing, keeping the environment as natural as possible. It also recommended that endangered species be transplanted and reared while invader species be controlled. It further recommended that all areas disturbed through the development be rehabilitated, and as little construction as possible take place in areas where indigenous species occur. The assessment also identified particularly sensitive areas on the site where all development should be avoided.

A Freedom Trust Administration building is included, located close to a place of arrival at the base of the Salvokop Hill, which will provide current and future office accommodation, with the possibility of conference facilities in future.

On the remainder of the site, not included in the scope of the competition, provision is made for services and infrastructure, including the spiral pedestrian route leading to the apex of the hill, with contemplative spaces along the route.

These elements constitute the first phase of the Freedom Park project, intended for delivery by 2004.

At a special meeting of the Board of Trustees of Freedom Park, held in April 2003 for approving the commencement of construction of the garden of remembrance, Executive Chairman Serote made the following remarks:

> *Our country and people know the deepest pain, the deepest agony and suffering. We have, as South Africans, experienced the highest forms of cruelty and evil meted by human beings against other human beings ... But we have also as South Africans been inspired by the noblest ideals of the human race; we have been motivated by the freedom of all people, by justice for all and have spared nothing to defend, protect and enshrine these values in our consciousness, and fought that all we do is motivated by this understanding and commitment.*

As a consequence of an extensive research and consultation process, including workshops with key stakeholders, a policy document was prepared to define a framework within which symbolic reparation, cleansing and healing would be undertaken, and to guide many of the decisions taken in the development of Freedom Park.

The document discusses the processes of nation-building and

reconciliation, and refers to both monetary and symbolic reparation. It notes the importance of symbolic reparation, which can be expressed in terms of buildings, monuments and the names of streets and places, and Freedom Park is confidently expected to ensure that symbolic reparation for the whole South African nation is realised.

Reference is made to the TRC Report on the context of Freedom Park, and attention is given to the need for symbolic reparation to assist in the process of healing by focusing reflection on past memories in an attempt to deal with the trauma and the pain. In identifying the recommendations of the TRC, the policy document singles out symbolic reparation as one of the principal objectives for Freedom Park. It highlights the importance of memorials at both national and provincial levels as reminders of things past and as safeguards against future abuses. The document reminds us that reparation is not solely the concern of government, but touches all aspects of civil society and requires a concerted and integrated approach by all concerned South Africans.

An important function of Freedom Park will be its role as a final resting place for all who died in what are described as the seven events of conflict – genocide, slavery, wars of resistance, the Anglo-Boer War, the First World War and its impact on South Africa, the Second World War and its impact on South Africa, and the struggle for liberation. Symbolic reparation and cleansing and healing ceremonies are intended to be directly associated with these seven events of conflict. These are described in great detail in the document, beginning with the skirmishes between the Portuguese and the Khoi in 1492, and tracing all recorded accounts of oppression and genocide, all wars of resistance, the participation of all South Africans in international wars against oppression and fascism, the beginnings of African unity, the strategies of the ANC's Defiance Campaign of the 1950s and the armed struggle, leading ultimately to the Government of National Unity.

The detailed account of the seven events of conflict concludes with this undertaking: 'Therefore Freedom Park commits itself to the three pillars of government as a means towards reconciliation, rehabilitation and symbolic reparation to contribute towards nation building, common patriotism and unity for all South Africans.'[3]

The policy document further gives special attention to the cleansing and healing ceremonies that are considered to be an inseparable part of reparation. Cleansing ceremonies have occurred in several places around the country, and will no doubt continue. They have taken many forms, but all emphasise the need for overcoming hatred and bitterness before the traditional or more orthodox religious healing processes through prayer and forgiveness can begin.

It is emphasised that Freedom Park, in carrying out its mandate, should present a balanced view based on close communication with all stakeholders. With this in mind, it is intended that a steering committee be formed consisting of, *inter alia*, the South African Council of Churches, the National Forum of Traditional Healers, the National Forum of Traditional Leaders, the National Khoi-San Consultative Conference, the National Khoisan Council, the National Division of Museums, the Moral Regeneration Movement, Members of the Executive Councils, the TRC, the Afrikaanse Taal en Kultuurvereniging and the Phoenix Settlement Trust. Several other representatives of civil society, including youth, labour unions, artists, women and the media, are also included.

Participation in the establishment of Freedom Park is planned at local, provincial, national and international levels. To this end, there will be provincial and embassy involvement in proposals for the Garden of Remembrance. As Freedom Park is intended to be the central point for collecting and storing written and oral history, as well as a place of national reconciliation, provinces and embassies are invited to give inscribed boulders, lists of names, soil and in certain instances plants. It is planned that these elements will be incorporated in the layout of the garden of remembrance, which includes special places for reflection and contemplation or prayer.

A heavy burden of responsibility rests with the Freedom Park Trust to oversee the establishment of this important addition to our national heritage sites. It is required to ensure the satisfactory completion of a complicated set of physical structures in a sensitive ecological location, and has the much more difficult task of ensuring, in the words of President Mbeki, that Freedom Park 'must not be a lifeless decorative monument, but a hallowed place that inspires all to continue the infinite journey of freedom from ignorance and superstition, fear, poverty, oppression and violence, moved to help develop the country that is the cradle of humanity into the home of human freedom'.[4]

Notes

1 Freedom Park Conceptual Framework.
2 Freedom Park Architectural Competition Brief and Guidelines.
3 Freedom Park Symbolic Reparations, Cleansing and Healing Policy Document.
4 Freedom Park Architectural Competition Brief and Conditions.

18

Pursuing Private Actors for Reparations for Human Rights Abuses Committed in Africa in the Courts of the United States of America[*]

Jeremy Sarkin

Questions relating to accountability for human rights abuses have never been more in the news or more favourably viewed than at present.[1] Both criminal and civil processes have seen major developments over the last few years.[2] Criminal accountability has been established at both the international and domestic levels.[3] The creation of the International Criminal Tribunal for Yugoslavia, the International Criminal Tribunal for Rwanda and the International Criminal Court has resulted in criminal accountability for gross human rights violations becoming far more of a reality. Domestically, the way states deal with past human rights abuses is often dependent on the way in which political change has occurred and the way the state deals with the tensions between justice,[4] truth and reconciliation.[5]

The issues of apology and reparation for violations committed during colonialism,[6] slavery and apartheid have also never been so high on the agenda. This is seen to be a critical issue, as during the years of colonialism and apartheid untold numbers of human rights abuses occurred in the race to possess and exploit the resources of the colonised countries. The crimes committed in the process of carving out the spoils for the colonisers

---

[*]   This article was previously published in Eva Brems and Pieter van der Heede (eds.) *Bedrijven en Mensenrechten,* Maklu Publishers, Belgium, 2003, 174–204. Publication herein with the permission of the editors.

include crimes against humanity,[7] war crimes,[8] genocide (even before the word was coined),[9] extermination, disappearances, torture, forced removals, slavery, racial discrimination, cruel, inhuman or degrading treatment and more. In fact, a key issue, and a defence that has been raised by the countries or corporations that perpetrated these deeds, is that the crimes committed at that time were not then defined as crimes. It is contended that only later were they defined as such.[10]

Many countries where colonialism occurred are still underdeveloped[11] and the legacy of the colonial years is still a major feature of the landscape in these places.[12] In some countries, certain communities assert that the way in which they were exploited in the past is the reason they now suffer economic and other hardships.

In this vein, the issue of compensation for victims of human rights abuses has become a critical concern for these countries and the individuals who live in them. Until recently, it was believed that remedies were not available and that the only mechanism to achieve some type of redress was some measure of foreign aid from the former colonial masters who could be made to feel guilty about the past and, consequently, provide such assistance.

The issue of reparation has become more important not only for the money that is being sought but also because reparation is seen to fulfil at least three functions. First, it directly assists victims who are coping with financial loss they have suffered; second, it provides official acknowledgement of what happened in the past; and third, it may act as a deterrent to the perpetration of human rights abuses in the future.[13]

One reason why reparation for these abuses has become an issue of considerable significance is that there has been a growing awareness and acceptance internationally of the need for and right to reparations for victims of human rights violations. Many international human rights instruments recognise that a victim is entitled to a remedy, which includes the means for full rehabilitation.[14] In fact, receiving some reparation for harm suffered is a well-established principle of international law.[15] Such a right is now also found in regional human rights instruments and in the jurisprudence of regional human rights courts.[16] What is also developing in international human rights law is the notion that, in principle, this law governs the conduct of state actors as well as private parties, including juridical bodies such as corporations. There is also a growing acceptance of the principles of universal jurisdiction.[17]

These developments have been bolstered by claims and payments made recently in a number of cases related to the Holocaust.[18] These claims and their significance will be discussed later. In addition, a growing number of civil cases are being filed in relation to these types of violations. The majority of these are in the United States under the Alien Torts Claims Act (ATCA).[19]

There are also at least three major cases against multinationals pending in the courts of the United States for violations committed during the colonial and apartheid periods.[20] One suit has been filed by the Herero people of Namibia for violations committed in that country in the early 20th century and two claims have been filed by South African victims for violations committed during the apartheid era.

The issue of reparation is also now so topical because the matter of reparation for slavery and colonialism was a major and highly contested agenda item at the World Conference against Racism, Racial Discrimination, Xenophobia and Related Intolerance (WCAR), held in Durban, South Africa from 31 August until 8 September 2001.[21] A considerable part of the World Conference was devoted to these themes. A formal apology, coupled with an undertaking to effect reparation in some way, has been requested from those who were the beneficiaries of slavery and colonialism.[22] The WCAR declaration[23] has many sections relevant to the issues under discussion.[24]

This chapter examines the issue of reparation for colonialism and apartheid. It does so on the understanding that, while world opinion or moral authority might be that there are very valid reasons for countries that were colonisers to pay reparation, it is unlikely that these states will acknowledge and apologise for past human rights abuses or be willing to pay reparation for these. If reparation is forthcoming in the future this will be the result of changes in the political climate and agreement being reached.[25] For this reason, it is more likely that multinational corporations or other companies who conducted business and benefited where violations were committed, or are seen to have benefited during those years, will be sued. As has been noted by Joel Paul

Why has international law turned its gaze to multinational corporations at this time and in this way? After all, many of the claims against multinational companies arise out of the Holocaust and the Second World War. After more than a half century, why are litigants seeking redress from these

corporate giants? One simple answer to the question is that the companies may be the only tortfeasors still available to provide any compensation. The individual bad actors are often dead, missing, beyond the jurisdictional reach of domestic courts, or unable to satisfy large damage claims. The immortality of the multinational corporate entity, its size, wealth and omnipresence in a variety of jurisdictions make it uniquely attractive as a defendant.[26]

These institutions are also pursued, as it is unlikely that international courts will permit such cases before them. For a variety of reasons, these courts are not really available for victims who seek redress. This is unlikely to change. In any case, victims have difficulty in gaining access to these courts as, in the main, they do not permit non-state actors to litigate before them and private corporate entities bear almost no obligations under public international law. The long and the short of it is that the legal status of multinational corporations under international law has not advanced significantly in a quarter of a century.[27]

At the level of state liability, reparation is at present a political rather than a legal issue.[28] As a consequence of the difficulties in pursuing state actors,[29] victims often view corporations rather than governments as easier targets for such claims.[30] Part of the reason for this is that multinational corporations often have assets in jurisdictions that have easier procedural rules for litigation. While claims by victims of human rights abuses have until now been relatively limited, there has been a major growth in such claims over the last five years. The precedent cases relating to World War II claims have resulted in victims, who did not see such possibilities previously, taking legal steps to seek redress. As Ellinikos has noted, 'eventually as business leaders are now finding out, somebody has to take responsibility'.[31] Thus, the case that is being made, especially in litigation, is against corporations for the role they played, and the manner in which they benefited from acts committed in particular countries in the past.

While the United States system allowing foreigners to sue in its courts, mostly under the ATCA, is evaluated in this chapter, it is not an extensive evaluation of those laws but rather an overview of the types of cases that have been filed and what possibilities exist for claims relating to colonialism and apartheid. The focus is, thus, rather on what we can learn, for possible cases in these areas in the future, from the cases already brought. Why the United States is the major site of such litigation is also explored to some degree, to determine whether the courts in other countries have similarities that may be applicable to these types of cases. Additionally, the lessons and possibilities raised by the US cases may be relevant for bringing lawsuits in either the US or other countries.

The Role of Multinational Corporations in Committing Human Rights Abuses

The role of multinational corporations in their conduct of business in the third world is very controversial. Their role in the colonial era is even more contentious than their role in many parts of the world today. As Jonathan Charney has noted, the involvement of transnational corporations, particularly with third world governments, has often resulted in substantial transnational corporation influence on host governments, and that influence has not always served those governments' best interests.[32]

In many instances where plaintiffs allege that corporations have been implicated in human rights abuses, the claim is not that the violations were committed by the company itself or its agents.[33] However, this is not always true of human rights abuses that occurred during colonialism or of the activities of companies that made use of slaves. While it is generally the case that the abuses were committed by local state actors and that the company's participation was in regard to its complicity in the human rights violations, there are cases of direct involvement.[34]

A corporation's awareness of ongoing human rights violations, combined with its acceptance of direct economic benefit arising from the violations, and continued partnership with a host government, could give rise to accomplice liability. Thus, it could be that such an entity may be liable directly for human rights violations as an accomplice or as a joint actor with a state actor (e.g. security forces) in a venture that violates international law.[35]

Anita Ramasastry considers the precedents on the issue of corporate complicity by reviewing the United States Military Tribunal at the Nuremberg prosecution of two bankers.[36] There the Tribunal found: 'Loans or sale of commodities to be used in an unlawful enterprise may well be condemned from a moral standpoint ... but the transaction can hardly be said to be a crime ... we are not prepared to state that such loans constitute a violation of [international] law.' The Tribunal, therefore, emphasised a key distinction between providing capital and active participation in Nazi crimes.

A critical question is whether corporations have an obligation to respect human rights. The debate on the duty of corporations is now very advanced, and few argue that corporations have no role.[37] The current question is what the duty is of corporations vis-à-vis their role and the manner in which they benefited during colonialism and apartheid. The answer could be a clear position from 1948, when the Universal Declaration of Human Rights was adopted. This instrument demands that 'every individual and every organ of society ... promote respect for these rights and freedoms and by progressive measures, national and international, to secure their universal and effective recognition and observance.'[38]

In this regard, Clapham and Jerbi claim that although 'companies may not be in the habit of referring to themselves as 'organs of society', they are a fundamental part of society. As such, they have a moral and social obligation to respect the universal rights enshrined in the Declaration'.[39]

Professor Louis Henkin has seized upon the same language in the Declaration, emphasising that: 'Every individual includes juridical persons. Every individual and every organ of society excludes no one, no company, no market, no cyberspace. The Universal Declaration applies to them all.'[40] The International Court of Justice in the Barcelona Traction, Light and Power Co. case found that the legal personality of a transnational corporation is equal to that of a regular citizen.[41] Professor Steven Ratner has asked: '[C]an decisionmakers transpose the primary rules of international human rights law and the secondary rules of state and individual responsibility onto corporations? If corporations are such significant actors in international relations and law, then can they not assume the obligations currently placed on states or individuals, based on those sets of responsibility?'[42]

Ratner argues that 'the unique role for states in securing some rights ... does not preclude duties for corporations with respect to other, related rights'.[43] Thus, duties on states are not simply transferable to corporations, but the same human rights that create duties for states may impose the same or different duties upon corporate actors.[44]

Ratner also explores, among other things, how corporations could or should be held responsible for acts of governments, subsidiaries or other actors in the stream of commerce.[45] In a related inquiry, Anita Ramasastry questions how broadly the accomplices net should be cast. What about the fear of deterring investment, especially in developing countries? And, practically, how can corporations make decisions about moving forward with international investments, when they fear that their very presence in a country that may have a questionable government may rise to the level of complicity?[46]

As Ratner has observed: '[S]imply extending the state's duties with respect to human rights to the business enterprise ignores the differences between the nature and functions of states and corporations. Just as the human rights regime governing states reflects a balance between individual liberty and the interests of the state (based on its nature and function), so any regime governing corporations must reflect a balance of individual liberties and business interests.'[47]

A key question, often asked in regard to colonialism and apartheid, is what duties were owed then. Other significant issues are procedural problems, such as statutes of limitations on how far back claimants are entitled to bring a claim.

The Development of the Notion and Acceptance of Reparation

Historically, claiming reparation for damages that have been suffered is not an issue of recent vintage. In fact, at the conclusion of warfare, agreements were often reached in terms of which a payment or a forfeit of land was a consequence. What is a recent phenomenon, however, is for reparation or damages to be paid to individuals. It is in the post-World War II era that such reparation began, at first negotiated and later because of the enactment of a statute or because of the decisions of courts of law. At the level of statute, various countries have made provision for reparation to be paid in the wake of human rights abuses. Such countries include Argentina, Chile and South Africa.

For a number of years, there has also been a solid movement internationally towards recognising a legal basis for victims of human rights and humanitarian abuses to claim reparation. There has, for example, been an ongoing effort to establish international principles on reparation. In 1989, the UN Sub-Commission on Prevention of Discrimination and Protection of Minorities selected Professor Theo van Boven to determine whether a set of basic principles and guidelines on remedies for gross human rights violations could be drafted. A draft version of the basic principles and guidelines on the right to reparation followed.[48] As a result of the UN Commission on Human Rights' 1998 session, Professor Cherif Bassiouni was appointed to prepare a draft for the next session so that the principles could be clarified and sent to the UN General Assembly for approval. This task is still in the process of being completed, but the Basic Principles and Guidelines on the Right to a Remedy and Reparation for Victims of Violations of International Human Rights and Humanitarian Law[49] is at an advanced stage.[50]

In various regions of the world there have also been initiatives towards obtaining reparation. In 1992, Chief Moshood Abiola of Nigeria activated the establishment of the Organisation of African Unity (OAU) Group of Eminent Persons for Reparation. The OAU mandated them to press forward with ensuring that reparations for the African slave trade were made. In 1993, the group assembled the First Pan-African Conference on Reparations in Abuja, Nigeria. The Abuja Declaration further committed the OAU to attempt to obtain reparation for slavery.

The two international tribunals in the 1990s set up to adjudicate on gross human rights violations in Yugoslavia and Rwanda have come to accept reparation as a right. The governing statutes of the two tribunals, in fact, established such rights for victims.[51] Indeed, the Rome Statute, which governs the International Criminal Court, provides greater rights to victims for compensation than ever before.

As far as individual claims are concerned, it is the post-World War II era that defines the movement towards the granting of reparations for violations of human rights. It was at the end of the 1940s that the German government discussed the issue of reparations with the Israeli government, and the Conference on Jewish Material Claims against Germany resulted in the Luxembourg Treaty with Israel in 1952 and the 1953 enactment of the Final Federal Compensation Law. In terms of this agreement, Germany agreed to pay $714 million to Israel to support the assimilation of displaced and impoverished refugees from Germany or areas formerly under German control.[52] The treaty required individual compensation as well as payment of $110 million to the Conference of Jewish Material Claims against Germany for victims. The process ran from 1952 until 1965. Another limited reparations scheme was agreed to in 1993 to assist some of those left out of earlier agreements.

Two other important examples of reparation occurred in the United States. The first concerns reparation paid by the US government as a result of the internment of Japanese-Americans during World War II.[53] The second concerns compensation paid to the Aleut Indians, thousands of whom were relocated from South-East Alaska during the same period as the internment of the Japanese-Americans. Both of these communities negotiated for nearly 50 years to secure compensation reparation. In the 1980s the Americans passed a law – the Civil Rights Act – which permitted reparation to be given to Japanese-Americans.

Especially relevant for claims relating to events that occurred many years ago is that the Aleut Indians obtained damages for the children of survivors as well as for the villages that were affected by the relocations, even though it took almost 50 years for this to happen. It was recognised that the problems that had been caused by the relocation not only affected the communities at the time but were still having effects four or five decades later. It was determined that those consequences would continue for the foreseeable future.

The movement towards obtaining reparation by individuals was assisted by two court cases in the 1980s. In the first case, *Filartiga* v. *Pena-Irala*,[54] the US courts recognised that aliens could sue for reparation for human rights abuses committed against them by individuals who were not citizens of the US. The court noted that the 'international community has come to recognise the common danger posed by the flagrant disregard of basic human rights and particularly the right to be free of torture'.[55] This case has had enormous consequences and it and its progeny will be examined in detail below.

The other major case was the Inter-American Court of Human Rights decision of Velásquez-Rodriguez, in which the court decided that individuals who had had human rights violations perpetrated against them would be able to pursue damages claims against perpetrators, because 'under international law a State is responsible for the acts of its agents undertaken in their official capacity and for their omissions even when those agents act outside the sphere of their authority or violate internal law'.[56]

However, there have been failures in other courts to claim damages for events that happened 50 or more years ago. It is largely the US courts that have been sympathetic to some extent to this type of litigation. Many ex-Comfort Women from Korea and other countries have filed suit against the Japanese government in the courts in Japan.[57] Of those cases only one was successful, but it, too, was overturned later by the high court.

Major developments in the move to obtain reparation occurred when the Holocaust cases were filed in the US. The first of these claims occurred in October 1996, when a class action lawsuit was filed in the federal district court of Brooklyn, New York against the Swiss banks, Credit Suisse, Union Bank of Switzerland and Swiss Bank Corporation. All the filed cases were brought together in 1997 as *In re Holocaust Victim Assets Litigation*. The consolidated claim alleged that the banks did not return assets deposited with them, the banks traded in looted assets and the banks benefited by trading in goods made by slave labour. The case was settled in 1998 with a payment by the banks of $1.5 billion. Not only Jews benefited in terms of the settlement but also homosexuals, physically or mentally disabled or handicapped persons, the Romani (Gypsy) peoples and Jehovah's Witnesses.[58]

The Holocaust cases against the Swiss banks were followed up with suits filed against German and Austrian banks in June 1998. These cases were launched by Holocaust survivors, American citizens, who filed a class action lawsuit against Deutsche Bank and Dresdner Bank alleging profiteering from the looting of gold and other property belonging to Jews. All the cases were merged in March 1999 as *In re Austrian and German Bank Holocaust Litigation*.[59] French banks or banks that had branches in France during the war, such as the British bank, Barclays, were also sued. A settlement agreement was reached with them in 2001. Also sued by Holocaust survivors were more than a dozen European insurers.[60] Nor were German corporations spared. Former slave labourers also launched cases against a host of German companies. However, a number of these were dismissed on the basis that they were excluded by statutes of limitations or because of treaties signed by Germany and the Allied powers at the conclusion of the war. A settlement was reached, however, relating to slave labour for about $5 billion on the condition that all other slave labour cases would be dropped. The US government also agreed to intercede in any future lawsuits filed against Germany in relation to claims arising from World War II.[61]

The suits filed against German companies have also resulted in cases being filed by soldiers captured by the Japanese during the war as well as by civilians against Japanese companies. During the war, thousands of American, British, Canadian, Australian and New Zealander prisoners of war were used as slave labour by Japanese companies, including Mitsubishi, Mitsui, Nippon Steel and Kawasaki Heavy Industries. Also used as slave labour were Chinese, Korean, Vietnamese and Filipino civilians.[62]

To get around the length of time between injury and claim, the state of California enacted a law in July 1999 that permitted any action by a 'prisoner-of-war of the Nazi regime, its allies or sympathizers' to 'recover compensation for labor performed as a Second World War slave victim ... from any entity or successor in interest thereof, for whom that labor was performed'.[63] The statute was enacted when it seemed that the case against the German companies was not proceeding. It permitted such lawsuits to be filed until 2010.[64] The courts there were thus able to deal with these claims.[65] The claims by all former Allied soldiers were dismissed in 2001, however, after the US government intervened in the case, on the basis that in terms of the 1951 Peace Treaty with Japan, the US and other Allied powers had relinquished all of their claims against Japan, including those against Japanese companies.

Regarding the civilian claims, the court ruled later that as far as the Filipinos were concerned, they were also excluded as the Philippines had also ratified the treaty. The court also dismissed the other claims and declared the California statute unconstitutional as it was held to be an encroachment on the powers of the federal government to perform foreign policy.[66]

A number of other cases were also filed before the US courts. One case saw foreign civilians sue Japanese companies for having used them as slave labour and another saw former Comfort Women sue. Both were dismissed in 2001 and are being appealed.

In a case that goes further back in time, a number of descendants of Armenians (mostly US citizens) who died in the Armenian genocide that occurred around World War I, and who had purchased insurance policies from European and American insurance companies, sued the New York Life Insurance Company.[67]

In *Marootian v. New York Life Insurance Company* it was argued that time barred the proceedings and that the policies had clauses stating that the French or English courts had jurisdiction in the event of litigation. Once again, California enacted a statute permitting suits relating to Armenian genocide-era policies and extended the time limit to 2010. This case was then settled. The lessons from the case are, nevertheless, important as the time limit for claims was shifted to almost 100 years ago. In addition, the beneficiaries were not those who had taken out the policies.[68]

Recently tens of thousands of Russians who were forced into Nazi slave labour camps during World War II were able to share a E427m payout. Almost 500 000 people applied to the foundation, while the relevant authorities had planned for just 57 000 claims.[69]

Thus, it does seem as though there are possibilities for litigation for claims going back to the beginning of the 20th century or possibly earlier.[70] This is a key issue as it is a potential obstacle for possible claims that relate to events during colonialism. The year 1885 is an important point marking the carving up of Africa by the various European powers. Although colonial occupation occurred before this time, it was the Berlin Conference of 1884-85 that clarified which European country would occupy which part of Africa.[71] The General Act of the Berlin Conference on Africa in Chapter I noted: 'All the powers exercising sovereign rights or influence in the aforesaid territories bind themselves to watch over the preservation of the native tribes, and to care for the improvement of the conditions of their moral and material well-being and to help in suppressing slavery, and especially the Slave Trade.'

The issue of reparation or damages for slavery is much more difficult.[72] Such an action would be for events that occurred much earlier, and also for individuals where there may not even be direct descendants. These problems were seen to be critical when a 1995 case filed by African American plaintiffs was dismissed.[73] The Ninth Circuit, affirming this, noted that the United States had sovereign immunity, the claims were too long ago and the plaintiffs themselves could not claim as they themselves were never slaves. The court stated: 'Discrimination and bigotry of any type is intolerable, and the enslavement of Africans by this country is inexcusable. This Court, however, is unable to identify legally any cognizable basis upon which plaintiff's claims may proceed against the United States. While plaintiffs may be justified in seeking redress for past and present injustices, it is not within the jurisdiction of this Court to grant the requested relief. The legislature, rather than the judiciary, is the appropriate forum for plaintiff's grievances.'[74]

It is therefore clear that it cannot be the courts only where such claims ought to be brought for resolution. Clearly, many of these issues are political rather than legal. The courts are not the only avenue where these claims can, and should, be pursued. It is at the political level, in the legislatures and in other fora (including the fora of national and international public opinion) that efforts can be made.

In this regard, there have been attempts, each year since 1989, to introduce legislation in the US Congress to deal with the legacy of slavery. The bill, H.R. 40 The Commission to Study Reparations Proposals for African Americans Act, seeks the establishment of 'a commission to examine the institution of slavery, subsequent de jure and de facto racial and economic discrimination against African Americans, and the impact of these forces on living African Americans, to make recommendations to the Congress on appropriate remedies ...'.[75] Other efforts have also been made in various individual US states, and there has been an attempt in the US Congress to make an apology for slavery.

Using Courts as a Means to Obtain Reparation or Damages

Using the courts as a means to obtain damages or reparation for these types of claims is a relatively recent phenomenon. It mostly emerges out of the US *Filartiga* decision in 1980.[76] In fact, almost all of the relevant litigation has occurred in common law, rather than civil law, jurisdictions.[77] As one commentator has explained:

> *With the exception of one action brought in Quebec against a Canadian corporation registered in Montreal, all of the claims so far have been brought in common law jurisdictions. The established legal cultural links between Anglo-Saxon lawyers and procedural rules, such as those that determine what defendants have to disclose in litigation, may be contributory factors. But for the longer term it is not unlikely, as legal practitioners' understanding of the relevant principles of law evolves, that cases will emerge in the civil law systems of European Union (EU) member states such as the Netherlands or France.[78]*

However, by far and away the majority of these types of cases are being brought in the United States under the ATCA.[79] As Beth Stephens explains: 'Civil human rights litigation in the United States is the natural product of a legal culture that relies on private lawsuits both as a means to obtain compensation for injuries and also as a tool to address societal problems.'[80] Pointing out that the *Filartiga* decision[81] 'has been called the *Brown v. Board of Education* of transnational law litigation, invoking the legacy of the great civil rights cases that dismantled legal segregation across the United States',[82] Stephens notes an 'absence of core *Filartiga* cases' elsewhere.[83] 'Indeed,' Stephens writes, 'despite a great deal of interest in the *Filartiga* doctrine in England, a British international law study group recently concluded that the likelihood of such litigation in Britain was slim.'[84] In an attempt to explain this phenomenon, Stephens offers a list of five factors that render US courts the most attractive arena for international human rights litigation. These include:

- no penalty for losing;
- contingency fees;
- punitive damages;
- default judgments; and
- broad discovery rules.[85]

Stephens has also noted that the 'the use of civil litigation as a means of impacting human rights policies is a natural development in the U.S. legal system'.[86] The fact that the system of jury trials is advantageous to litigants in these types of cases should also be noted. The nature of the US legal system is thus a critical determinant as to why so many of these cases have been brought before the courts in that country. As Lord Denning observed: 'As a moth is drawn to light, so is a litigant drawn to the United States. If he can only get his case into their courts, he stands to win a fortune.'[87]

Using the United States Courts to Pursue Perpetrators

While the United States has various laws that permit victims of human rights abuses committed outside the US to be sued, it is the ATCA that has been used the most.[88]

This law was enacted in 1789 as part of the Judiciary Act and has since generated a considerable number of suits alleging violations of human rights committed in countries outside America by state and non-state agents. The key provision that has elicited increasing international attention stipulates: 'The district courts shall have original jurisdiction of any civil action by an alien for a tort only, committed in violation of the law of nations or a treaty of the United States.'

While there have been many successes since the 1980 case of *Filartiga* v. *Pena-Irala*[89] for claims in terms of the Alien Torts Claims Act, Ramsey provides a useful overview of some of the issues and critiques related to the application of the Act.[90] Ramsey argues that 'the sheer number of controverted points upon which corporate ATCA litigation rests may suggest that expansive application of ATCA liability is a project requiring much judicial sympathy for its success'.[91] While Ramsey does not suggest that this is a reason to reject Alien Torts Claims Act litigation, he does advise caution in the area of expansive Alien Torts Claims Act litigation, as there is a whole host of doctrines[92] that permit judges to dismiss Alien Torts Claims Act claims even if subject-matter and personal jurisdiction have been established.[93] These include the international comity doctrine, which is premised on respecting the legislative, executive or judicial acts of another nation,[94] as well as the doctrines relating to political questions, *forum non conveniens*[95] and acts of state, which prohibit US courts from reviewing the validity of the public acts of a recognised foreign sovereign that are carried out in the foreign territory.

However, the courts are not applying these doctrines strictly, as can be seen in *Kadic v. Karadzic*.[96] Here the court stated that while the act of state doctrine might be applicable to some cases brought under the Alien Torts Claims Act, it doubted 'that the acts of even a state official, taken in violation of a nation's fundamental law and wholly unratified by that nation's government, could properly be characterized as an act of state'.[97]

This case also has relevance for the question of whether private actors could fall under the Alien Torts Claims Act provisions. *Kadic v. Karadzic* expanded the scope of the Act by holding that acts committed by non-state actors also fell squarely within its ambit. The Court of Appeals observed that: '[T]he law of nations as understood in the modern era does not confine its reach to state action. Instead, certain forms of conduct violate the law of nations whether undertaken by those acting under the auspices of a state or only as private individuals.'[98] The court found that certain violations of the law of nations provided for by the Act, such as piracy, slave trade, slavery and forced labour, genocide, war crimes and other offences of 'universal concern' did not require state involvement. Thus, private actors could be held liable for such activities as well as other gross human rights violations.

In *Doe v. Unocal*,[99] a case involving farmers from Myanmar/Burma suing the oil companies Unocal and Total SA operating in Myanmar/Burma, it was argued that these companies were engaged in a joint venture of gas exploitation with the military government of the country. To clear the way for a pipeline, the government had forcibly relocated villages, displaced local inhabitants from their homelands, and tortured and forced people to work on the project.[100] It was argued, therefore, that the corporations were liable for these violations since they funded the repressive regime and the project with full knowledge of the abuses, and derived benefit from them.[101] It was alleged that 'in the course of its actions on behalf of a joint venture ... the regime carried out a program of violence and intimidation against area villagers'. It was further alleged that 'women and girls in the ... region have been targets of rape and other sexual abuse by regime officials, both when left behind after male family members have been taken away to perform forced labor and when they themselves have been subjected to forced labor'.[102] In its decision in September 2002, the court declared that 'forced labor is a modern variant of slavery to which the law of nations attributes individual liability such that state action is not required'.[103] Making a finding on a question of material fact regarding Unocal's liability under the Alien Torts Claims Act for aiding and abetting the Myanmar/Burma military regime in subjecting plaintiffs to forced labour,[104] the 2002 Unocal decision reversed the earlier summary judgment previously won by Unocal, holding that 'the standard for aiding and abetting under the ATCA is ... knowing practical assistance or encouragement that has a substantial effect on the perpetration of the crime'.[105]

The court in *Iwanova* v. *Ford Motor Co.* examined circumstances where the company acted in close co-operation with Nazi officials in compelling civilians to perform forced labour. The court found that the fact that the company pursued its own economic interests did not preclude a determination that Ford Motor Co. acted as an agent of, or in concert with, the German government, and that no logical reason existed for not allowing private individuals and corporations to be sued for universally condemned violations of international law even if they were not acting 'under color of law'.[106]

In *Wiwa* v. *Royal Dutch Petroleum Co.* the plaintiffs alleged that Royal Dutch Shell was complicit in acts of torture, arbitrary arrest, detention and killing in the Ogoni region of Nigeria.[107] The plaintiffs claimed that they and their next of kin 'were imprisoned, tortured and killed by the Nigerian government in violation of the law of nations at the instigation of [defendant Shell companies], in reprisal for their political opposition to the defendant's oil exploration activities'. It was further claimed that Royal Dutch Shell 'provided money, weapons, and logistical support to the Nigerian military, including the vehicles and ammunition used in the raids on villages, procured at least some of these attacks, participated in the fabrication of murder charges ... bribed witnesses to give false testimony against them'.[108] The Second Circuit's ruling in this case has had a major effect on the *forum non conveniens* principle, making it easier to bring an action based on a foreign human rights violation despite the availability of an alternative forum.[109] The court's reasoning stresses the concern of the United States in supporting human rights abroad, and that this principle imposes a different standard of inconvenience on wealthy parties than on poorer ones.[110]

In *Beanal* v. *Freeport-McMoran, Inc.*[111] it was alleged that Freeport-McMoran committed human rights violations, environmental torts, genocide and cultural genocide while conducting mining activities in Indonesia. Plaintiffs alleged that Freeport companies 'systematically engaged in a corporate policy both directly and indirectly through third parties that has resulted in human rights violations against the Amungme Tribe and other Indigenous tribal people. Said actions include extrajudicial killing, torture, surveillance and threats of death, severe physical pain and suffering by and through its security personnel employed in connection with its operation at the Grasberg mine'. The case was dismissed, however, as the court found that there were insufficient facts concerning abuses to make out a cause of action.

Also relevant to possible claims in the US for events that occurred during colonialism and apartheid are issues in the Foreign Sovereign Immunities Act (FSIA). This Act contains the rules governing whether and how states can be sued. It is relevant as far as the present discussion is concerned in that there is one exception to immunity given to a state or its officials: this is the commercial activity exception. The Foreign Sovereign Immunities Act provides that sovereign immunity shall not be granted when 'the action is based upon an act outside the territory of the United States in connection with a commercial activity of the foreign state elsewhere and that act causes a direct effect in the United States'.

According to the United States Supreme Court in *Saudi Arabia* v. *Nelson,*[112] a state conducts commercial activity within the definition of the Foreign Sovereign Immunities Act when it acts as though it is a private citizen in the marketplace; in this regard, it is important to look at the activity performed rather than its purpose.

The court in *Adler* v. *Federal Republic of Nigeria,*[113] however, considered the meaning of 'in connection with a commercial activity', in contrast to the finding in *Saudi Arabia* v. *Nelson*, which looked at the issues by examining the phrase 'commercial activity'. Thus, states in Africa, for example, could sue where there is a connection to commercial activity. However, it must have had a direct effect on the US. In some cases, for example slavery, this is clear; in others, it would be more difficult to establish.

From the above discussion of the various cases brought under the Alien Torts Claims Act, it does seem that the US courts could be sympathetic to the types of claims that arise out of colonialism and apartheid.[114]

Time Limits

A major issue for cases concerning human rights abuses committed during colonialism, as well as those committed during apartheid, is the time-line factor. This issue of the length of time between injury and claim is crucial, as often such procedural questions prevent a claim from getting past even the first hurdle.[115]

The Alien Torts Claims Act has no inherent statute of limitations,[116] but the Torture Victim Protection Act (TVPA) does. The report of the US Senate that accompanied the Torture Victim Protection Act stated: 'A ten-year statute of limitations insures that the Federal Courts will not have to hear stale claims. In some instances, such as where a defendant fraudulently conceals his or her identification or whereabouts from the claimant, equitable tolling remedies may apply to preserve a claimant's rights.[117] ... The ten-year statute is subject to equitable tolling, including for periods in which the defendant is absent from the jurisdiction or immune from lawsuits and for periods in which the plaintiff is imprisoned or incapacitated.'[118]

Under federal law, a cause of action, in terms of the time limit to bring such an action, starts running from the time the damage occurs.[119] In *Bussineau v. President & Dirs. of Georgetown College* the court found that a 'cause of action is said to accrue at the time injury occurs'.[120] The court in *Xuncax v. Gramajo* applied the Torture Victim Protection Act period to an Alien Torts Claims Act claim.[121]

However, for years the courts have been willing to extend the time limit. In 1947 in *Osbourne v. United States* the plaintiff had been interned by Japan during World War II and claimed that the statute of limitations did not apply because of 'extraordinary circumstance that throughout the period when he ought to have brought suit the courts were unavailable to him as a prisoner in the hands of the enemy'.[122] The court tolled the limitation period for an injury that occurred immediately prior to his internment because these circumstances were sufficiently extraordinary. In this regard, the court held: 'All statutes of limitations are based on the assumption that one with a good cause of action will not delay in bringing it for an unreasonable period of time; but, when a plaintiff has been denied access to the courts, the basis of the assumption has been destroyed.'[123]

In 1987, the doctrine was extended in *Forti v. Suarez-Mason*. There the court held: 'Federal courts have also applied a theory of equitable tolling similar to an "impossibility" doctrine. Where extraordinary events which are beyond [a] plaintiff's control prevent a plaintiff from bringing his claim, the limitations period is tolled until the barrier caused by these events is removed.'[124]

The court held that even though the Argentine courts were available, 'as a practical matter' the military regime controlled those courts, making it impossible for those wanting to sue to get a fair trial. The court held that: 'Equitable tolling occurs under federal law in two types of situations: (1) where defendant's wrongful conduct prevented [a] plaintiff from timely asserting his claim; or (2) where extraordinary circumstances outside [a] plaintiff's control make it impossible for [a] plaintiff to timely assert his claim.'[125]

In *National Coalition Government of Union of Burma v. Unocal, Inc.*[126] the court noted that, in applying the Forti test for equitable tolling, the court in *Hilao* concluded that fear of intimidation and reprisal were extraordinary circumstances outside the plaintiff's control.[127] As such, claims against Marcos for injury from torture, disappearance or summary execution were tolled until he left office. This is a crucial ruling for apartheid and colonialism cases. The Court in *Unocal* applied the *Hilao* ruling to the facts of the case and held: 'Under federal law, equitable tolling is available where (1) defendant's wrongful conduct prevented [a] plaintiff from asserting the claim; or (2) extraordinary circumstances outside the plaintiff's control made it impossible to timely assert the claim.' The court further noted that: 'In fact, based on the Ninth Circuit's decision in *Hilao* John Doe I's claims may well be tolled as long as [the State Law and Order Restoration Council] SLORC remains in power if he can show that he is unable to obtain access to judicial review in Burma.'[128] This may have major significance for future cases.

In *Iwanowa v. Ford Motor Co*[129] the claims related to World War II forced labour. The plaintiff sued Ford in Germany and its American parent company, seeking compensation for forced labour in Ford's German manufacturing plant. As far as the period to sue was concerned with regard to the German claim, the court held that the limitation period was tolled until 1997 when the moratorium on claims (imposed in various post-war treaties) was finally lifted. This was not alleged with respect to the United States corporation. Thus, it was the treaties that prevented the bringing of claims rather than the fault of the defendant. The court held: '[E]quitable tolling may be appropriate, *inter alia*, where the defendant has actively misled the plaintiff. To avoid dismissal, a complainant asserting equitable tolling must contain particularized allegations that the defendant "actively misled" the plaintiff.'[130] Although the plaintiff made claims of misrepresentation and concealment in brief and in oral argument,[131] because these were not contained in the complaint the court denied the relief.[132] A similar result occurred in *Fishel* v. *BASF Group*.[133]

In *Sampson* v. *Federal Republic of Germany*[134] a suit lodged for damages for unlawful detention in a Nazi concentration camp was disqualified because of the length of time between the injury and bringing the suit. In *Kalmich* v. *Bruno*[135] a claim for the return of property confiscated by the Nazis was time barred.

In *Jane Doe I* v. *Karadic* the court found that 'the TVPA's limitations period is subject to equitable tolling, including for periods in which the defendant is absent from the jurisdiction or immune from lawsuits and for periods in which the plaintiff is imprisoned or incapacitated'.[136] In *Estate of Cabello* v. *Fernandez-Larios* the court held: 'Equitable tolling of the TVPA is appropriate in this case because Chilean military authorities deliberately concealed the decedent's burial location from Plaintiffs, who were unable to view the decedent's body until 1990.'[137]

In *Cabello* v. *Fernandez Larios* the court held, 'the pre-1990 Chilean government's concealment of the decedent's burial location and the accurate cause of death prevented Plaintiffs from bringing this action until 1990. Accordingly, the ten-year limitation period did not begin to accrue until 1990. Since Plaintiffs brought this action within ten years, and Defendant has not presented the Court with any compelling reason to alter its previous ruling that the limitation period commenced in 1990, the Court finds that the claims alleged in the Second Amended Complaint are not time barred'.[138]

Thus, it seems that the time limit may not always be a definite bar to such claims. Plaintiffs will need to show specific circumstances that fit in with the above rulings to ensure that statutes of limitations do not act as obstacles to such cases.

Other Jurisdictions

While the majority of cases of this nature have been brought in the US, there has been international human rights litigation in courts elsewhere.

This has primarily been in England. Such cases have included:

- *Cape plc*: arising from asbestos-related injuries suffered by South African victims during the 1960s and 1970s;[139]
- *RTZ*: arising from a Scottish worker's case of laryngeal cancer contracted from working at the defendant's uranium mine in Namibia;[140]
- *Thor Chemical Holdings Ltd*:[141] in response to government health and safety criticisms in England, Thor relocated its facility to Natal, South Africa, where it continued to operate with the same deficiencies that necessitated its departure from England, and did little to reduce the danger to workers. Thor became subject to the court's jurisdiction by serving a defence, which precluded a *forum non conveniens* dismissal, and ended up settling for 1.3 million British pounds.[142]

The issues in these cases appear to revolve entirely around personal jurisdiction, choice of law and *forum non conveniens*, with the merits not being reached; hence, Stephens' comment that non-US jurisdictions lack a 'core *Filartiga*' case. The litigation that has occurred in Australia surrounding Broken Hill Proprietary indicates the same problem.[143]

The Hereros of Namibia's Claim for Reparation

One of the first cases to be fought on issues relating back to colonial days is the case filed in 2001 in Washington DC by the Herero People's Reparations Corporation and the Herero tribe, through its Paramount Chief Riruako and other members of the Herero tribe. They[144] are suing Deutsche Bank, Terex Corporation[145] a.k.a. Orenstein-Koppel and Woermann Line, now known supposedly as Deutsche Afrika-Linien Gmblt & Co.[146] While most see South Africa[147] as being responsible for many of the atrocities that have occurred in southern Africa, Namibia's colonial legacy under Germany includes one of the worst atrocities committed – the genocide of nearly 100 000 people at the beginning of the 20th century. In June 2001 the Herero People's Reparation Corporation filed suit against the corporations for two billion dollars.[148] They accuse these companies, including Woermann Lines, of forming an alliance to exterminate more than 65 000 Hereros between 1904 and 1907.

The case revolves around a genocide committed at the beginning of the 20th century in Namibia when more than 65 000 Hereros were killed in pursuit of a shoot on sight policy in that country.[149] This policy was announced on 2 October 1904 when General Lothar von Trotha decreed: 'The Herero people will have to leave the country. Otherwise I shall force them to do so by means of guns. Within the German boundaries, every Herero, whether found armed or unarmed, with or without cattle, will be shot. I shall not accept any more women or children. I shall drive them back to their people – otherwise I shall order them to be shot. Signed: the Great General of the Mighty Kaiser, von Trotha.'

Besides the 65 000 people who were killed, water wells were sealed and poisoned to prevent Herero access to water. Thousands were condemned to slavery[150] on German farms, and surviving Herero women were forced into becoming Comfort Women for the settlers. German geneticists came to the country to perform racial studies of supposed Herero inferiority. Von Trotha also established five concentration camps, in which the mortality rate was more than 45%.

Von Trotha almost succeeded with the genocide. The Herero population was diminished by about 80% to approximately 16 000 people, the majority in concentration camps. The court papers state: 'Foreshadowing with chilling precision the irredeemable horror of the European Holocaust only decades later, the defendants and imperial Germany formed a German commercial enterprise which cold bloodedly employed explicitly sanctioned extermination, the destruction of tribal culture and social organisation, concentration camps, forced labour, medical experimentation and the exploitation of women and children in order to advance their common financial interests.'

Thus, the Hereros are suing Deutsche Bank as it is alleged that it was the principal financial and banking entity in German South West Africa. It is alleged that Disconto-Gesellschaft, which was acquired by Deutsche Bank in 1929, combined with Deutsche Bank, controlled virtually all financial and banking operations in German South West Africa from 1890 to 1915. The case asserts that these entities were major and controlling investors, shareholders in and directors of the largest mining and railway operations in German South West Africa during that time. It is further claimed that Deutsche Bank, itself and through Disconto-Gesellschaft, was a critical participant in German colonial enterprises and that Deutsche Bank is directly responsible for, and committed, crimes against humanity perpetrated against the Hereros. The Hereros are suing Deutsche Bank as they allege that the bank specifically financed the then government and companies linked with Germany's colonial rule.[151]

Terex was also sued, as it is alleged that it is the successor in interest to or merger partner of Orenstein-Koppel Co., the principal railway construction entity in German South West Africa from 1890 to 1915. The court papers state that Arthur Koppel, the principal of Orenstein-Koppel, was a powerful German executive; his business specialised in earthmoving technology and had contracts all over the world at the beginning of the 20th century. It is alleged that Terex and its predecessors prospered over the 125 years of its existence through organising, participating in and taking advantage of a slave labour system. It is further alleged that they profited enormously from the system and were directly responsible for, and committed, crimes against humanity perpetrated against the Hereros.

The claimants later temporarily withdrew their legal claim for reparation against Terex as the corporation claimed that it had been under different management at the time the atrocities were committed.[152] However, the claimants did then file against the German government.[153] In this regard, Chief Kuaima Riruako stated: 'I am suing legitimate governments and companies who happened to function in the colonial days ... We're equal to the Jews who were destroyed. The Germans paid for spilled Jewish blood. Compensate us, too. It's time to heal the wound.'[154]

Also being sued is Woermann Line who allegedly controlled virtually all of the shipping into and out of German South West Africa from 1890 to 1915. It is asserted in the plaintiff's claim that Woermann employed slave labour, ran its own concentration camp, was a critical participant in the German colonial enterprise and that 'individually and as a member of that enterprise, Woermann is directly responsible for and committed crimes against humanity perpetrated against the Hereros'.[155]

It is alleged that the Otavi Mines and Railway Company (OMEG) was founded on 6 April 1900 with the legal status of a German colonial company whose purpose was the exploitation of copper deposits and the construction of a railway system. Deutsche Bank, it is alleged, was a member of the OMEG governing board from 1900 to 1938. The applicants aver that Disconto-Gesellschaft, one of Germany's largest banks by 1903, was a principal investor in OMEG and that the Woermann Shipping Line had, by 1900, established complete control of the shipping and harbour enterprises in South West Africa. All materials for the OMEG railway were shipped by, and through, Woermann who used the slave and forced labour of over 1 000 people to load and unload ships at Swakopmund.

The case has enormous relevance for a number of reasons. Firstly, it indicates how the German Holocaust was predated by an earlier genocide. Secondly, the case indicates how the courts can be used to pursue human rights violators even in another country. In this regard the Herero Chief has argued: 'We are taking our case to America because it's easier and fairer and we can get support from the public there. Jews could not take their case to Germany, what chance then do we have of succeeding [in Germany]?'[156]

Thirdly, the case could be a precursor to a number of other cases where former colonial governments and commercial concerns, which benefited from the period of conquest and domination, are sued by the inhabitants of the territories then under their control. This is because the Hereros were not the only group to be the victims of colonial atrocities. For example, the Belgians under King Leopold II massacred thousands of Congolese. The French are also guilty of such crimes, as are the British. As Sydney Harring has argued:

> [I]t factually represents one of the best cases possible for opening the question of reparation for colonial oppression against the various imperial powers. The direct founding of this claim in the specific context of Germany's responsibility for reparation for Jewish victims of World War Two era genocide directly raises the question: how is colonial era genocide different from modern European genocide? In an impoverished Africa, it cannot be surprising that the indigenous people there cannot accept the legitimacy of two regimes of international law, one for Europeans, another for Africans. Because the Herero claim is narrow based on a particular – and well-documented – act of twentieth century genocide, in a particular colonial war, against a nation with a record of recidivism at genocide, it is an appropriate case for a reparations claim against Germany.[157]

On a visit to Namibia at the beginning of March 1998, German President Roman Herzog said that too much time had passed for Germany to give any formal apology for slaughtering Hereros during colonial rule. Herzog said that German soldiers had acted 'incorrectly' between 1904 and 1907 when about 65 000 members of the Herero group were killed for opposing colonialism. Herzog rejected the payment of compensation, stating that this was not possible as international rules for the protection of the civilian population were not in existence at the time of the conflict and no laws protected minority groups during the colonial period.[158] He also said that Germany had significantly assisted Namibia for many years and he pledged that Germany would live up to its special historical responsibility towards Namibia.[159] Germany has also stated that the issue of reparation would not be considered as Namibia was already receiving preferential financial support from Germany.[160]

The Namibian government has not supported the Hereros' claim. Prime Minister Hage Geingob has said that the approach by Herero leaders to seek compensation only for Herero-speaking Namibians is wrong.[161] 'We are being condemned by the Chief for not taking action. But we cannot just say we want money for the Hereros. Not only the Hereros suffered the consequences of war. All Namibians suffered and the best would be to help all Namibians by providing roads and schools.'[162]

The Namibian prime minister said it was unfortunate that the issue of reparations had been politicised, and questioned why the issue of Herero reparation had not been brought before the Namibian Parliament. However, this has not happened because the Herero accuse the governing party of diverting $500 million in German aid to Ovambo voters.[163] They, therefore, want Germany to establish a fund to allow Hereros to purchase land and cattle. Gottlob Mbaukaua, an opposition party Herero leader in Okahandja, has argued: 'What we are saying is that the Germans, because they only killed the Herero and no one else, must uplift us.'[164]

Eckhart Mueller, chairman of the German-Namibian Cultural Organisation, argues: 'Genocide is a relative term if you are involved in a war and you lose. I think they're taking a long shot to get some money. If not genocide, it will be something else. We must bury the past and look to the future.'[165]

Victims of Apartheid Claims

Human rights abuses abounded against South Africa's majority during apartheid. Many people were dispossessed of their land, had their language and culture marginalised, and suffered gross human rights violations.[166] The majority of South Africans were denied access to an enormous variety of amenities, institutions and opportunities, including many places and types of employment, particularly in state institutions. The South African state systematically violated the rights of black people and subjected them to socioeconomic deprivation.[167] Black South Africans were disenfranchised and many were forcibly removed from where they lived and deprived of their citizenship.[168] State employees, and others acting with state sanction and assistance, routinely carried out torture, assault and killings.[169] Many detentions[170] and deaths in custody occurred.[171] Freedom of expression and association were severely limited. As a consequence, in 1973 the UN declared apartheid a crime against humanity. While state action was a major cause of human rights abuses, other actors also contributed to these violations, including multinational corporations who either aided or abetted or benefited from their relationship with the regime. It has been alleged that more than \$3 billion in profits were transferred out of apartheid South Africa by foreign banks and businesses each year between 1985 and 1993.[172] In 1987, an investigation by the UN Commission on Human Rights into the responsibility of multinational corporations for the continued existence of apartheid concluded that, 'by their complicity, those transnational corporations must be considered accomplices in the crime of apartheid and must be prosecuted for their responsibility in the continuation of that crime'.[173]

South Africa's process to deal with the past internally has been its Truth and Reconciliation Commission (TRC), wherein victims could testify about abuses committed against them and those who perpetrated human rights abuses could apply for amnesty from criminal prosecution as well as civil liability.[174] In addition, the TRC held hearings into various sectors including the judiciary, the health sector and political parties. Hearings were also held on the role of business. However, until the two cases brought in the US, which will be discussed below, multinationals or other corporations who benefited from the system during those years were not pursued. Reparation to victims has been discussed as an obligation of the state. While recognising that it is required to provide some compensation, the state has, however, not been quick to respond to the TRC's recommendations about when and how much to pay the 21 000 people deemed to be victims by the TRC.

As far as business is concerned, all that has happened in South Africa is that the TRC reported on the role of business and labour during apartheid. It found that a 'vast body of evidence points to a central role for business interests in the elaboration, adoption, implementation and modification of apartheid policies throughout its dismal history'.[175] In reaching this conclusion, the TRC did not lump together, in either its reportage or analysis, all business involvement, but instead attempted to provide a more nuanced and structured – and perhaps, therefore, more credible – indictment[176] of business's role during apartheid.[177] Accordingly, the TRC divided the culpability of business into three categories:

- *first order involvement*: 'direct involvement with the state in the formulation of oppressive policies or practices that resulted in low labour costs (or otherwise boosted profits)';[178]
- *second order involvement*: 'knowing that their products or services would be used for morally unacceptable purposes';[179]
- *third order involvement*: 'ordinary business activities that benefited indirectly by virtue of operating within the racially structured context of an apartheid society', but '[t]aken to its logical conclusion, this argument would need to extend also to those businesses that bankrolled opposition parties and funded resistance movements against apartheid. Clearly not all businesses can be tarred with the same brush'.[180]

One commentator wrote of this categorisation: 'The TRC found the first two levels reprehensible per se … Yet its nuanced conclusions regarding other businesses reflected an appreciation of the extent to which apartheid clearly benefited them and of the complexity of business interactions with the government. In the end, while concluding that government and business "co-operated in the building of an economy that benefited whites", it rejected both a condemnation of all business people as collaborators as well as an exculpation of them for taming and helping end the system.'[181]

The Role of Banks

The TRC Report appears to place banks (both foreign and domestic) in the second and third culpability categories.[182] In discussing second order involvement, the Report notes the example of banks that provided police with covert credit cards, finding that: 'A bank that provides a covert credit card to the police to help them with, say, investigations into white-collar fraud, is in a different position to one which knowingly provides covert credit cards to death squads to help them lure their victims.'[183]

Nevertheless, the TRC Report found that 'there was no obvious attempt on the part of the banking industry to investigate or stop the use being made of their facilities in an environment that was rife with gross human rights violations'.[184] Moreover, the Council of South African Banks (COSAB) 'acknowledged that being a bank "inevitably" meant doing business with a variety of bodies that were an integral part of the apartheid system'.[185] However, the TRC Report did not draw its own conclusions (it quotes but does not clearly adopt the submissions of others) regarding the consequences of a bank's 'doing business' with the apartheid regime.

Similar to the first apartheid case, discussed later, and most likely due to the same lack of information, the TRC Report did not attempt the extra step of analysing any particular transaction or relationship between a bank and an apartheid institution to ascertain: (1) to what extent lending activities aided and abetted oppression, and (2) to what extent banks should have foreseen or known that lending activities would aid and abet oppression. For example, the Report quoted COSAB's submission to the TRC:

> *By the very nature of their business, banks were involved in every aspect of commerce during the apartheid years. Without them, government and the economy would have come to a standstill. But it would have been an 'all or nothing' decision. There could have been no halfway position. Either you are in the business of banking, or you are not. It does not lie in the mouth of a bank to say that it will accept the instruction of its client to pay one person but not another.[186]*

Therefore, although the TRC Report acknowledged that while 'banks were "knowingly or unknowingly" involved in providing banking services and lending to the apartheid government and its agencies', it also noted that banks 'were similarly involved in the movement of funds from overseas donors to organizations resisting apartheid'.[187] This manner of allowing the murkiness of the picture to emerge, but without addressing it fully, is equally evident in the TRC's approach to the role of 'business' generally.

The Role of Business

Although finding that the general involvement of business during apartheid spanned all three categories of culpability, the TRC Report paid close attention to the dual role of business in (often simultaneously) helping and hindering apartheid. For example, the Report noted: '[m]any business organisations were uncertain how to react to the economic crisis and political unrest. As SACOB put it: The business community was caught between a recognition of the inevitability and desirability of significant political reform, and a range of developments which resulted in a great deal of instability and which were, quite simply, bad for business stakeholders.'

Their response to this acute dilemma was, on the one hand, to try to speed up the reform process and facilitate contact between the different political interests – both within and outside of South Africa – and, on the other, to fight a rearguard action against the sanctions and disinvestment campaign and the rising levels of violence, which threatened the economy and job creation.[188]

While the Report chronicled efforts by business to accelerate reform – such as 'visits by leading business representatives to the ANC in exile'[189] – it also emphasised 'rearguard actions' such as business's involvement with Joint Management Committees (JMCs), which formed part of the National Security Management System.[190] While making clear that the goal of the JMCs was 'essentially to prolong white domination',[191] the Report also observed: 'Where [businesses] participation resulted in the channelling of resources to townships, the moral issues are more opaque. While JMC-facilitated development in townships was certainly motivated by counter-revolutionary aims, there is an important difference between counter-revolutionary strategies based on providing infrastructure to people, and strategies based on torture and repression. Again, not all businesses played the same role in the process.'[192]

On the subject of sanctions, the Report noted that businesses opposition to sanctions, in addition to arising from profit-driven self-interest, 'also stemmed from a belief by some businesses that economic growth rather than the intensification of poverty promotes democracy'.[193] Remarkably, the Report made little attempt to evaluate either this belief itself, how widespread and representative it truly was, or the reasons why a self-interested actor might choose to embrace (or claim to embrace) it.

In the TRC's defence, however, there were few corporations – particularly multinational corporations – that offered to make submissions to the TRC.[194] In addition, the fact that the TRC was not 'in a position to impose – or eliminate – legal, let alone criminal, liability upon corporations'[195] may have influenced both its own hesitation to issue condemnations and, in the air of relative impunity, multinational corporations to see fit to ignore the proceedings. As a result of these processes, two cases have been filed in the United States claiming damages for events during apartheid.

The First Apartheid Case

In June 2002 thousands of South African claimants filed a class action suit against several multinational corporations[196] in the Southern District of New York under the Alien Torts Claims Act.[197] By August, a lawsuit targeted the following 12 companies as co-conspirators with the apartheid regime: Citigroup, Credit Suisse, UBS, Deutsche Bank, Dresdner Bank, CommerzBank, IBM, Amdahl Corporation, ICL Ltd, Burroughs, Sperry and Unisys (the parent company of Sperry and Burroughs).[198] According to their lawyers, the mining companies Anglo American and De Beers may be added to this list of defendants. In addition, the lawyers have written to over 27 banks and corporations proposing settlement talks.[199] Aside from potential defendants Anglo American and De Beers, the lawsuit does not target domestic businesses.[200]

The complaint, originally lodged solely against Swiss and United States banks, contends that '[f]or justice to be done, the financial institutions and companies that fuelled and made possible the apartheid regime's reign of terror must account for their sins, crimes and profiteering, just as did the companies that fuelled and made possible the Nazi reign of terror'.[201] The complaint seeks $50 billion in damages,[202] asserting that but for the banks' loans, the apartheid regime would not have survived as long as it did[203] and that the computer companies 'knew full well that their equipment, technology and systems were used within the apartheid system in a manner that facilitated and encouraged the violation of human rights and the commissioning of atrocities against the majority of South Africa's population'.[204] The mining concerns are being targeted to include racist and exploitative labour practices during the apartheid era.

Ed Fagan, the US lawyer leading the case, sent out a press advisory highlighting a portion of the complaint that traces the German banks' behaviour to their Third Reich history.[205] Fagan 'has been variously described as an opportunistic showboater'.[206] Responses to Fagan and the lawsuit have, not surprisingly, been mixed, with government unreservedly chilly, and news media somewhat less so, but probably not as supportive as Fagan had hoped.[207]

The Second Apartheid Case

On 12 November 2002 the second case, *Khulumani et al.* v. *Barclays et al.*,[208] was filed in the New York Eastern District Court against eight banks and twelve oil, transport, communications technology and armaments companies from Germany, Switzerland, Britain, the United States, Netherlands and France.[209]

It was filed on behalf of the Khulumani Support Group and 108 individual 'victims of state-sanctioned torture, murder, rape, arbitrary detention, and inhumane treatment'. Jubilee South Africa stated: 'The corporations aided and abetted a crime against humanity whose persistent social damage requires urgent repair … They made massive profits while the suffering of the victims of apartheid intensified. The banks and businesses have consistently ignored our attempts to engage in discussion about their role in supporting broad social programmes for the reconstruction and development of affected communities and in compensating specific individuals for the damage that the corporations made possible.'[210]

In their press statement, the plaintiffs averred that they had for four years been attempting, unsuccessfully, to 'get multinational banks and businesses that propped up the apartheid state to account for their odious profiteering'. The Khulumani Support Group noted that this case 'is the only route left open to us to ensure that the truth is known about the extent of corporate complicity in apartheid abuses and that justice is delivered to those who suffered. The victims cannot be left to pay for their own suffering. Multinational corporations must be put on notice that complicity in crimes against humanity does not pay.'[211]

In its press release, the Apartheid Debt & Reparations Campaign said: 'In this claim, we express our commitment to the future of apartheid's victims, to the protection of human rights, and to the rule of law … This suit has been filed after extensive international consideration of its legal and factual basis, and after thorough consultation amongst key organisations. Further complaints of similar weight in regard to other aspects of apartheid crimes will be filed in coming months.'[212] The US law firm representing the plaintiffs noted in their press release[213] that the complaint:

[s]eeks to hold businesses responsible for aiding and abetting the apartheid regime in South Africa in furtherance of the commission of the crimes of apartheid, forced labor, genocide, extrajudicial killing, torture, sexual assault, and unlawful detention. The world community recognized apartheid itself as a crime against humanity and a violation of international law. Apartheid could not have been maintained in the same manner without

> the participation of the defendants ... The suit is based on common law principles of liability and on the Alien Tort Claims Act, 28 U.S.C. 1350, which grants U.S. courts jurisdiction over certain violations of international law, regardless of where they occur ... Recent historical evidence demonstrates that the involvement of companies in the key industries of mining, transportation, armaments, technology, oil, and financing were not only instrumental to the implementation of the furtherance of the abuses, but were so integrally connected to the abuses themselves that apartheid would probably not have occurred in the same way without their participation.

In South Africa, these two cases have been viewed somewhat contentiously. Former president F. W. de Klerk has come out against the cases, stating that he will advise the companies to fight the lawsuits. He has also said these cases would raise false hopes of enrichment among poor South Africans.[214]

As far as the South African government is concerned, it has stated that it will not support the claims against multinationals cited for having propped up apartheid. Minister of Justice and Constitutional Development, Penuell Maduna, has been quoted as saying that the cabinet had taken a decision of 'indifference', neither supporting nor rejecting the lawsuits. He stated: 'We are not supporting the claims for individual reparations. We are talking to those very same companies named in the lawsuit about investing in post-apartheid SA. The focus is on getting those companies to keep investing in SA to benefit the entire population.'[215]

The South African minister of finance, Trevor Manuel, has stated that the lawsuits cannot solve the problems apartheid caused: the 'enormity of the crime is apartheid itself. And for that there can't be compensation individually ... This kind of adventurism, when you look for victims ... does not see apartheid itself as a serious violation of human rights, but looks for physical assault, and battery and torture and killings.'[216]

Conclusion

The role of multinational corporations in the perpetration of human rights abuses during the colonial and apartheid eras was considerable. Their role is under greater scrutiny now than at any other time in history. Part of the reason for this is that more and more norms and standards are being developed on the conduct of companies in respect of human rights. As this happens, so the role played by corporations in the past is being examined in much finer detail. Another reason for the increased scrutiny and calling to account is the fact that there has been a growth of accountability mechanisms at both international and domestic levels. As this scrutiny intensifies, still more attention is being focused on these questions and, as more information emerges, the possibilities for redress expand.

Recently, the reparation movement has been growing in leaps and bounds. On a number of fronts over the last few years, the likelihood of reparation for human rights abuses has become more of a reality. It is, therefore, possible that a solution to the thorny issues of reparations for violations committed a relatively long time ago might be achieved in the future. Developments relating to universal jurisdiction might also assist in this regard. At the domestic level, it is largely the United States legal system that permits, or is useful for, foreign claimants seeking redress. However, it is possible that claimants may seek to use the courts in other countries to pursue violators. The time–limit question will be one of the major issues that may hinder these claims. The lessons of other cases, particularly those relating to the Holocaust, show that these types of claims are often successful not because a court makes a finding but because of the pressure placed on defendants who then wish to settle because of the adverse publicity attracted. This has not yet occurred with the claims relating to colonialism or apartheid, but these cases are still in their early stages. The extent to which they are successful, either in the courtroom or because the defendants settle, will determine whether and how many other cases are filed.

However, these cases are not the panacea to the problems that the affected countries and individuals who live there face, as 'virtually no judgments ... have been collected, and many defendants have chosen to flee the United States during the course of the litigation'.[217] Additionally, the courts are not yet sufficiently disposed towards such cases, and very few have been successfully concluded in the courts. Although it seems that the climate is improving, it will take time for the courts in the United States, or elsewhere, to become more sympathetic towards this type of litigation. It must also be borne in mind that:

Corporations, unlike the other defendants in ATCA lawsuits, have the motivation, money and experience to litigate fully all jurisdictional limits and advantages of corporate structure available to them to avoid a litigation on the merits. In order to circumvent or overcome such corporate defenses, plaintiffs suing MNCs are pushed in two different directions. On the one hand, plaintiffs have to target the behavior of the MNC as it directly led to the alleged human rights violations in the host State (requiring a focus on the MNC operations in and with the host State) because ATCA cases demand a higher than normal factual basis at the initial stages; on the other hand, plaintiffs must concentrate on the MNCs' activity at its corporate headquarters in order to facilitate the court's assertion of personal jurisdiction over the MNC defendant and to avoid impermissible intrusions upon the government of the host State and its relationship with the U.S. The synthesis of these opposing trends may make life difficult for some human rights litigators, but in the long run will serve to ensure that only meritorious cases, properly heard in the U.S., will proceed.[218]

Because of these factors, which will stymie or limit such cases for some time to come, the political route for redress will become more important in the future. This will occur as the issues receive more international acceptance and more pressure is brought to bear by those who endured the brunt of colonial and apartheid human rights abuses.

Notes

1   See generally T. de Pelsmaeker, P. van der Auweraert, J. Sarkin and J. van de Lanotte (eds.), *Social, Economic, and Cultural Rights – An Appraisal of Current International and European Developments* (Antwerpen: Maklu, 2002).

2   See generally J. Sarkin and W. Binchy (eds.), *Human Rights, the Citizen and the State* (Dublin: Round Hall, Sweet and Maxwell, 2001).

3   See further J. Sarkin, J. van de Lanotte and Y. Haeck (eds.), *Resolving the Tensions Between Crime and Human Rights: European and South African Perspectives* (Antwerpen: Maklu, 2001).

4   An example of pursuing a human rights abuser is the prosecution of the former leader of Chad, Hissene Habre. See R. Brody, 'Universal Jurisdiction: Myths, Realities, and Prospects: The Prosecution of Hissene Habre. An African Pinochet', in *New England Law Review*, (Winter) 2001, 35, 321. See also B. Crossette, 'Dictators Face the Pinochet Syndrome', in *The New York Times*, 22 August 1999, section 4, 3.

5   See further J. Sarkin, 'The Trials and Tribulations of South Africa's Truth and Reconciliation Commission', in *South African Journal on Human Rights*, 1996, 12, 617; J. Sarkin, 'The Truth and Reconciliation Commission in South Africa', in *Commonwealth Law Bulletin*, 1997, 528; J. Sarkin, 'The Development of a Human Rights Culture in South Africa', in *Human Rights Quarterly*, 1998, 20 (3), 628; J. Sarkin,

'The Necessity and Challenges of Establishing a Truth and Reconciliation Commission in Rwanda', in *Human Rights Quarterly*, 1999, 21 (3), 767; J. Sarkin, 'Preconditions and Processes for establishing a Truth and Reconciliation Commission in Rwanda: The Possible Interim Role of Gacaca Community Courts', in *Law, Democracy and Development*, 1999, 223; J. Sarkin, 'Transitional Justice and the Prosecution Model: The Experience of Ethiopia', in *Law, Democracy and Development*, 1999, 253; J. Sarkin, 'Promoting Justice, Truth and Reconciliation in Transitional Societies: Evaluating Rwanda's Approach in the New Millennium of using Community-Based Gacaca Tribunals to Deal with the Past', in *International Law Forum*, 2000, 112, 2 (2); J. Sarkin, 'Dealing with Past Human Rights Abuses and Promoting Reconciliation in a Future Democratic Burma', in *Legal Issues on Burma*, 2000, 2, 2 (2), 1; J. Sarkin, 'The Tension Between Justice and Reconciliation in Rwanda: Politics, Human Rights, Due Process and the role of the Gacaca Courts in dealing with the Genocide', in *Journal of African Law*, 2001, 45, 2, 143; and J. Sarkin, 'To Prosecute or Not to Prosecute? That is the Question. An Examination of the Constitutional and Legal Issues Concerning Criminal Trials for Human Rights Violations Committed in the Apartheid Era and the Giving of Amnesty to Those who did not Apply or Were Refused Amnesty in Post Truth and Reconciliation Commission South Africa', in C. Villa-Vicencio and E. Doxtader (eds.), *Amnesty in South Africa*, (forthcoming) 2003.

6   Most countries in Africa, for example, went through a colonial period under the domination of countries such as France, Germany, Great Britain, Italy, Belgium and Portugal.

7   The concept of crimes against humanity is found in the Martens Clause of the 1899 Hague Convention II and the 1907 Hague Convention IV. The earlier version of the Martens Clause (Preamble, 1899 Hague Convention II) refers to 'laws of humanity'; the later version (Additional Protocol I) refers to 'principles of humanity'. E. Kwakwa, *The International Law of Armed Conflict: Personal and Material Fields of Application* (Dordrecht: Kluwer Academic, 1992), 36. The 1907 Convention states that: 'Until a more complete code of the laws of war has been issued, the high contracting Parties deem it expedient to declare that, in cases not included in the Regulations adopted by them, the inhabitants and belligerents remain under the protection and the rule of the principles of the law of nations, as they result from the usages established among civilised peoples, from the laws of humanity, and the dictates of the public conscience.' An even earlier use of the term is found in the 1868 Saint Petersburg Declaration of an International Military Commission. This declaration limited during war the use of certain explosive or incendiary projectiles, because they were declared 'contrary to the laws of humanity'.

8   The Convention with Respect to the Laws and Customs of War on Land and its annex, Regulations Concerning the Laws and Customs of War on Land of 1899, are seen as 'the first significant modern treaties on jus in bello'. See S. R. Ratner and J. S. Abrams, *Accountability of Human Rights Atrocities in International Law, Beyond the Nuremberg Legacy* (Oxford: Clarendon Press, 1997), 45. It is relevant only to some degree, because it is binding on the parties that are signatories to them. Where there was war between signatory parties there were provisions that demanded that prisoners of war were treated humanely, and that these prisoners 'shall be treated as regards food,

quarters, and clothing, on the same footing as the troops of the Government which has captured them'. Article 23 (c) prohibited the killing or wounding of enemies that are unable to defend themselves or have surrendered. Also relevant for future claims could be Convention (IV) in respect of the Laws and Customs of War on Land and its annex, Regulations Concerning the Laws and Customs of War on Land of 1907.

9   The term 'genocide' only received formal and legal recognition at the Nuremberg trials, although the Charter of the Tribunal did not expressly use the term. The term was coined in the 1940s by Raphael Lempkin. The Genocide Convention was only adopted by the UN General Assembly in 1948.

10 An example of this, which will be dealt with in much greater detail below, is the case of the genocide committed on the Hereros in Namibia at the beginning of the 20th century. The argument made by President Roman Hertzog of the Federal Republic of Germany, when visiting Namibia in 1998, was that no crime had been committed as no law existed then which proscribed such conduct.

11 The declaration of the World Conference against Racism held in 2001 recognised in article 158 'that these historical injustices have undeniably contributed to the poverty, under-development, marginalization, social exclusion, economic disparities, instability and insecurity that affect many people in different parts of the world, in particular in developing countries. The Conference recognizes the need to develop programmes for the social and economic development of these societies and the Diaspora, within the framework of a new partnership based on the spirit of solidarity and mutual respect ...' United Nations A, General Assembly Distr., General, A/Conf. 189/24 September 2001, Original: English, World Conference Against Racism, Racial Discrimination, Xenophobia and Related Intolerance, Durban, 31 August – 8 September 2001. Adopted on 8 September 2001 in Durban, South Africa (final version released on 31 December 2001).

12 For example, the legacy of the 1884–85 Berlin conference, where the colonial powers of Europe met in Berlin to carve up Africa among themselves as colonies and dependencies, still has a major effect on the extent to which conflict racks the continent. See J. Sarkin, 'Finding a Solution for the Problems Created by the Politics of Identity in the Democratic Republic of the Congo (DRC): Designing a Constitutional Framework for Peaceful Co-Operation', in *The Politics of Identity*, Konrad Adenauer Foundation (ed.), 2002. It is not surprising that, against the backdrop of these inexcusable and arbitrary colonial border placements and policies of rigid ethnic identity in a pervasive environment of underdevelopment, 20 of the 48 genocides and 'politicides' that occurred worldwide between 1945 and 1995 took place in Africa. See H. Solomon, 'Analysing Conflicts', in *Searching for Peace in Africa: An Overview of Conflict Prevention and Management Activities*, Amsterdam, The European Platform for Conflict Prevention and Transformation, 1999, 34. See further P. Brogan, *World Conflicts – Why and Where They are Happening* (London: Bloomsbury Publishing Ltd), 1992.

13 N. Kritz, *The Dilemmas of Transitional Justice* (Washington DC: United States Institute for Peace, 1998) xxvii.

14 See Universal Declaration of Human Rights Article 8; International Covenant on Civil and Political Rights Article 2 (3) (a) and the Convention Against Torture and Other Cruel, Inhuman, or Degrading Treatment or Punishment, Article 14 (1).

15 See the Chozrow Factory case, Publications of the Permanent Court of International Justice, Collection of Judgments, Series A, No. 9, 21; Series A, No. 17, 29 (June 27, 1928). This case was cited with approval in the 14 February 2002 judgment *Democratic Republic of the Congo* v. *Belgium*, where the court held that 'reparation must, as far as possible, wipe out all the consequences of the illegal act and re-establish the situation which would, in all probability, have existed if that act had not been committed'.

16 An example is the finding of the Inter-American Court of Human Rights decisions in the Velásquez–Rodriguez case. See Inter-American Court of Human Rights, Velásquez–Rodriguez v. Honduras, Serie C, nr. 7, Judgment of 21 July 1989 (Compensatory Damages), para. 71. See further C. Tomuschat, 'Reparation for Victims of Grave Human Rights Violations', in *Tulane Journal of International and Comparative Law* (Spring), 2002, 10, 157.

17 See further K. Rendall, 'Universal Jurisdiction Under International Law', in *Texas Law Review*, (March) 1998, 66, 785; B. Brown, 'Universal Jurisdiction: Myths, Realities, and Prospects: The Evolving Concept of Universal Jurisdiction', in *New England Law Review*, (Winter) 2001, 35, 383; R. Brody, 'Universal Jurisdiction: Myths, Realities, and Prospects: The Prosecution of Hissene Habre. An African Pinochet', in *New England Law Review*, (Winter) 2001, 35, 321; N. Roht-Arriaza, 'Universal Jurisdiction: Myths, Realities and Prospects: The Pinochet Precedent and Universal Jurisdiction', in *New England Law Review*, (Winter) 2001, 35, 311; L. Sadat, 'Universal Jurisdiction: Myths, Realities, and Prospects: Redefining Universal Jurisdiction', in *New England Law Review*, (Winter) 2001, 35, 241; and M. Scharf and T. Fischer, 'Universal Jurisdiction: Myths, Realities, and Prospects: Foreword', in *New England Law Review*, (Winter) 2001, 35, 227.

18 See M. J. Bazyler, 'The Holocaust Restitution Movement in Comparative Perspective', in *Berkeley J. Int'l L.*, 2002, 20, 11.

19 Cases have also been filed in terms of the Torture Victims Protection Act of 1991. Act 12, 1992, P.L. 102-256, 106 Stat. 73. However, the court in *Beanal* v. *Freeport-McMoran, Inc.* held that because the TVPA used the term 'individual', Congress did not intend to include corporations as defendants. 969 F. Supp. 362, 382 (E.D. La. 1997).

20 An example of the growth in the number and type of suits filed is one against Royal Dutch Petroleum Company and Shell Transport and Trading Company (Royal Dutch/Shell). In *Wiwa* v. *Royal Dutch Petroleum*, 96 Civ. 8386 (S.D.N.Y. filed 8 November 1996) 226 F.3d 88 (2d Cir. 2000), Shell was charged with complicity in the 10 November 1995 hanging of Ken Saro-Wiwa and John Kpuinen, two of nine leaders of the Movement for the Survival of the Ogoni People (MOSOP), the torture and detention of Owens Wiwa, and the wounding of a woman, peacefully protesting the bulldozing of her crops in preparation for a Shell pipeline, who was shot by Nigerian troops called in by Shell. The case was brought under the Alien Tort Claims Act and the Racketeer Influenced and Corrupt Organisations Act. Another case was brought against President Robert Mugabe of Zimbabwe. This case was, however, objected to by the US government, citing concerns that he might be entitled to diplomatic immunity. See 'Zimbabwe President Accused of Orchestrating Terror in United States Suit', *CNN.com*, 10 September 2000. See further F. L. Kirgis, 'Alien Tort Claims Act

Proceeding against Robert Mugabe', in *American Society of International Law Insights*, (September) 2000, 2.

21 M. Bossuyt and S. van de Ginste, 'The Issue of Reparation for Slavery and Colonialism and the Durban World Conference against Racism', in *Human Rights Law Journal*, 2001, 22, 25.

22 See A. J. Sebok, *Slavery, Reparations, and Potential Legal Liability: The Hidden Legal Issue Behind the U.N. Racism Conference*, http://writ.news.findlaw.com/sebok/20010910.html (last visited on 23 May 2002).

23 United Nations A, General Assembly Distr., General, A/Conf. 189/24 September 2001, Original: English, World Conference Against Racism, Racial Discrimination, Xenophobia and Related Intolerance, Durban, 31 August–8 September 2001. Adopted on 8 September 2001 in Durban, South Africa (final version released 31 December 2001).

24 Just two examples of this are articles 13 and 14. Article 13 reads: 'We acknowledge that slavery and the slave trade, including the transatlantic slave trade, were appalling tragedies in the history of humanity not only because of their abhorrent barbarism but also in terms of their magnitude, organized nature and especially their negation of the essence of the victims, and further acknowledge that slavery and the slave trade are a crime against humanity and should always have been so, especially the transatlantic slave trade, and are among the major sources and manifestations of racism, racial discrimination, xenophobia and related intolerance, and that Africans and people of African descent, Asians and people of Asian descent and indigenous peoples were victims of these acts and continue to be victims of their consequences.' Article 14 reads: 'We recognize that colonialism has led to racism, racial discrimination, xenophobia and related intolerance, and that Africans and people of African descent, and people of Asian descent and indigenous peoples were victims of colonialism and continue to be victims of its consequences. We acknowledge the suffering caused by colonialism and affirm that, wherever and whenever it occurred, it must be condemned and its reoccurrence prevented. We further regret that the effects and persistence of these structures and practices have been among the factors contributing to lasting social and economic inequalities in many parts of the world today.'

25 In the context of the Herero of Namibia's claim, Harring argues that the 'Herero are aware that reparations regimes operant in the world today are political and not legal. But, these political actions have a common history of being moved by extensive legal posturing, creating a powerful moral climate supporting reparations, and shaping public opinion'. S. L. Harring, 'German Reparations to the Herero Nation: An Assertion of Herero Nationhood in the Path of Namibian Development?', in *West Virginia Law Review*, (Winter) 2002, 393, 410.

26 J. R. Paul, 'Holding MultiNational Corporations Responsible Under International Law', in *Hastings International and Comparative Law Review*, (Spring) 2001, 285, 291.

27 S. Zia-Zarifi, 'Suing Multinational Corporations in the U.S. for Violating International Law', in *UCLA Journal of International & Foreign Affairs*, 1999, 4, 81, 85. See further B. Frey, 'The Legal and Ethical Responsibilities of Transnational Corporations in the Protection of Human Rights', in J. Minn, *Global Trade*, 1997, 6, 153.

28 See, for example, L. Fernandez, 'Possibilities and Limitations of Reparations for the

Victims of Human Rights Violations in South Africa', in M. Rwelamira and G. Werle (eds.), *Confronting Past Injustices. Approaches to Amnesty, Reparation and Restitution in South Africa and Germany,* Durban, Community Law Centre, University of the Western Cape, 1996, 65-78.

29 See M. Penrose, 'It's Good to Be the King! Prosecuting Heads of State and Former Heads of State under International Law', in *Columbia Journal of Transnational Law,* 2000, 39, 193; A. Perez, 'The Perils of Pinochet: Problems for Transitional Justice and a Supranational Governance Solution', in *Denver Journal of International Law and Policy,* (Spring) 2000, 28, 175; C. Pierson, 'Pinochet and the End of Immunity', in *Temple International and Comparative Law Journal,* (Fall) 2000, 14, 263, and A. Hasson, 'Extraterritorial Jurisdiction and Sovereign Immunity on Trial: Noriega, Pinochet and Milosevic – Trends in Political Accountability and Transnational Criminal Law', in *Boston College International & Comparative Law Review,* 2002, 25, 125.

30 There are obstacles that plaintiffs would have to surmount for a claim to succeed against a country. In the US, the Foreign Sovereign Immunities Act often operates to insulate state actors from liability. See further L. Saunders, 'Rich and Rare are the Gems They War: Holding De Beers Accountable for Trading Conflict Diamonds', in *Fordham International Law Journal,* 2001, 1402. The *Supreme Court in Argentine Republic v. Almerada Hess Shipping Corporation* held that the act of 1976 established a general immunity of foreign states from suits before American courts. See *Argentine Republic* v. *Amerada Hess Shipping Corp.,* 488 U.S. 428 (1989).

31 M. Ellinikos, 'American MNCs Continue to Profit from the Use of Forced and Slave Labor. Begging the Question: Should America Take a Cue from Germany?', in *Columbia Journal of Law and Social Problems,* (Fall) 2001, 35, 1, 26.

32 J. Charney, 'Transnational Corporations and Developing Public International Law', in *Duke Law Journal,* 1983, 766.

33 C. Forcese, 'ATCA's Achilles Heel: Corporate Complicity, International Law and the Alien Tort Claims Act', in *Yale J. Int'l L.,* 2002, 26, 487.

34 See the case of *Eastman Kodak Co.* v. *Kavlin,* where the plaintiff was involved in a contractual dispute with a Bolivian company and claimed a conspiracy on the part of the firm and the Bolivian authorities to imprison him. The District Court observed that 'it would be a strange tort system that imposed liability on state actors but not on those who conspired with them to perpetrate illegal acts through the coercive use of state power'. 978 F. Supp. 1078 (S.D. Fla. 1997).

35 A. Ramasastry, 'Corporate Complicity: From Nuremberg to Rangoon. An Examination of Forced Labor Cases and Their Impact on the Liability of Multinational Corporations', in *Berkeley J. Int'l L.,* 2002, 20, 91.

36 A. Ramasastry, op cit. 91.

37 The corporation, at times, could be seen to be an accomplice with the regime that actually carries out the abuses. In this regard, the International Criminal Tribunal for Yugoslavia has found that an accomplice is guilty if 'his participation directly and substantially affected the commission of that offence through supporting the actual commission before, during, or after the incident. The court furthermore required that the defendant act with knowledge of the underlying act.' Quoted in S. R. Ratner, 'Corporations and Human Rights: A Theory of Legal Responsibility', in *Yale L. J.,* 2001, 111, 443, 501.

38 A. Clapham and S. Jerbi, 'Categories of Corporate Complicity in Human Rights Abuses', in *Hastings International and Comparative Law Review*, (Spring) 2001, 339, 340 (quoting UNDHR preamble).

39 Ibid The authors also note that although corporations are not bound by the UDHR, a number of them are responding to the societal condemnation that arises from violating it by incorporating 'an explicit commitment in their business principles' to upholding human rights.

40 L. Henkin, 'The Universal Declaration at 50 and the Challenge of Global Markets', in *Brook. J. Int'l L.*, 1999, 25, 17, 25, as quoted in B. Stephens, 'The Amorality of Profit: Transnational Corporations and Human Rights', in *Berkeley J. Int'l L.*, 2002, 20, 45.

41 *Barcelona Traction, Light and Power Co., Belgium* v. *Spain*, INT.GERI 3, para.70 (1970).

42 S. R. Ratner, op. cit., 492.

43 Ibid. at 493.

44 Ibid. at 494.

45 See generally Ibid.

46 A. Ramasastry, 'Banks and Human Rights: Should Swiss Banks be Liable for Lending to South Africa's Apartheid Government?', in *FindLaw*, 3 July 2002, available at http://writ.findlaw.com/ramasastry/20020703.html (hereinafter 'Ramasastry'). See also A. Ramasastry, 'Corporate Complicity: From Nuremberg to Rangoon. An Examination of Forced Labor Cases and Their Impact on the Liability of Multinational Corporations', in *Berkeley J. Int'l L.*, 2002, 20, 91.

47 S.R. Ratner, op. cit., 493.

48 T. van Boven, *Study Concerning the Right to Restitution, Compensation and Rehabilitation for Victims of Gross Violations of Human Rights and Fundamental Freedoms*, U.N. GAOR 4th Comm., 45th Sess., Provisional Agenda Item 4, para. 57, U.N. Doc. E/CN.4/Sub.2/1993/8 (1993).

49 See UN Commission on Human Rights document E/CN.4/2000/62 of 18 January 2000.

50 See further C. Tomuschat, 'Reparation for Victims of Grave Human Rights Violations', in *Tulane Journal of International and Comparative Law*, (Spring) 2002, 10, 157.

51 In the decision *Prosecutor* v. *Tadic* IT-94-1-A (15 July 1999) the tribunal considered international principles for attributing actions of private actors to state actors. The tribunal held that a state can be held responsible because of its request to a private individual to discharge tasks on its behalf. (Judgment of the Appeals Chamber, at para 119.)

52 K. Parker, 'Compensation for Japan's World War II Rape Victims', in *Hastings Int'l & Comp. L. Rev.*, 1994, 497, 502.

53 Another more recent example where the US government agreed to pay $5 000 and issue an apology to 2 200 Latin-American Japanese who were removed from Latin America during World War II and held in internment camps in the US. This resulted from a settlement agreement arising out of the case *Mochizuki* v. *United States* No. 97-924C, 41 Fed. Cl. 54 (1998). See N. T. Saito, 'Justice Held Hostage: U.S. Disregard for International Law in the World War II Internment of Japanese Peruvians – a Case Study', in *Boston College Law Review*, (December) 1998, 275.

54 630 F.2d 876, 880 (2d Cir. 1980).

55 Ibid. at 890.

56 9 Hum. Rts. L.J. 212 (1988).

57 See T. Yu, 'Comment, Recent Development: Reparations for Former Comfort Women of World War II', in *Harvard International Law Journal*, 1995, 36, 528; T. Tree, 'Comment, International Law: A Solution or a Hindrance Towards Resolving the Asian Comfort Women Controversy?', in *UCLA J. Int'l L. & Foreign Aff.*, 2000, 5, 461, 466-68; and K. Park, 'Comment, The Unspeakable Experience of Korean Women Under Japanese Rule', in *Whittier Law Review*, 2000, 21, 567.

58 See M. J. Bazyler, 'The Holocaust Restitution Movement in Comparative Perspective', in *Berkeley J. Int'l L.*, 2002, 20, 11.

59 M. J. Bazyler, op. cit., 11.

60 M. J. Bazyler, op. cit., 11.

61 M. J. Bazyler, op. cit., 11.

62 M. J. Bazyler, op. cit., 11.

63 See further R. Foos, 'Righting Past Wrongs or Interfering in International Relations? World War II-Era Slave Labor Victims Receive State Legal Standing After Fifty Years', in *McGeorge L. Rev.*, 2000, 31, 221, 232.

64 M. J. Bazyler, op. cit., 11.

65 M. J. Bazyler, op. cit., 11.

66 M. J. Bazyler, op. cit., 11.

67 See generally V. N. Dadrian, 'The Historical and Legal Interconnections between the Armenian Genocide and the Jewish Holocaust: from Impunity to Retributive Justice', in *Yale Journal of International Law*, (Summer) 1998, 503.

68 M. J. Bazyler, op. cit., 11.

69 See http://www.theaustralian.news.com.au/common/story_page/0,5744,5134326%255E401,00.html

70 Even at that time questions relating to statutes of limitations were being asked. For example, Oliver Wendell Holmes asked: 'What is the justification for depriving a man of his rights, a pure evil as far as it goes, in consequence of the lapse of time?' O. W. Holmes, Jr, 'The Path of the Law', in *Harv. L. Rev.*, 1897, 10, 457, 476. This issue will be explored later in more detail.

71 Fifteen countries attended the conference: Austria-Hungary, Germany, Belgium, Denmark, France, Germany, Great Britain, Italy, the Netherlands, Portugal, Russia, Spain, Sweden-Norway, Turkey and the USA.

72 It is a highly controversial issue. See R. W. Tracinski, 'America's "Field of the Blackbirds": How the Campaign for Reparations for Slavery Perpetuates Racism', in *Journal of Law in Society*, (Winter) 2002, 3, 145.

73 *Cato v. United States*, 70 F.3d 1103 (9th Cir. 1995).

74 At 1105. Cited in A. A. Aiyetoro, 'The Development of the Movement for Reparations for African Descendants', in *Journal of Law in Society*, (Winter) 2002, 3, 133.

75 See A. A. Aiyetoro, 'The Development of the Movement for Reparations for African Descendants', in *Journal of Law in Society*, (Winter) 2002, 3, 133, 138.

76 *Filartiga v. Pena-Irala*, 630 F.2d 876 (2d Cir. 1980) where the court found that 'deliberate torture perpetrated under color of official authority violates universally accepted norms of the international law of human rights, regardless of the nationality

of the parties. Thus whenever an alleged torturer is found and served with process within United States borders, the ATCA provides jurisdiction'. 630 F.2d 876, 880 (2d Cir. 1980).

77 For an analysis of why non-US jurisdictions in general have seen so few civil international human rights claims see B. Stephens, 'Translating Filartiga: A Comparative and International Law Analysis of Domestic Remedies for International Human Rights Violations', in *Yale J. Int'l L.*, 2002, 27, 1.

78 H. Ward, 'Securing Transnational Corporate Accountability Through National Courts: Implications and Policy Options', in *Hastings Int'l & Comp. L. Rev.*, 2001, 27, 451, 454-55. For discussion of how Dutch courts might handle the jurisdictional remedies and choice of law issues if cases were brought involving harms suffered in foreign countries see generally A. Nollkaemper, 'Public International Law in Transnational Litigation Against Multinational Corporations: Prospects and Problems in the Courts of the Netherlands', and G. Betlem, 'Transnational Litigation Against Multinational Corporations Before Dutch Civil Courts', both in M. T. Kamminga and S. Zia-Zarifi (eds.), *Liability of Multinational Corporations under International Law*, Kluwer Law International, 2000, 265-82 and 283-305.

79 J. Glaberson, 'US Courts Become Arbiters of Global Rights and Wrongs', in *New York Times*, 21 June 2001, 1-4.

80 B. Stephens, 'Translating Filartiga: A Comparative and International Law Analysis of Domestic Remedies for International Human Rights Violations', in *Yale J. Int'l L.*, 2002, 27, 1, 24.

81 *Filartiga v. Pena-Irala*, 630 F.2d 876 (2d Cir. 1980).

82 B. Stephens, op. cit., 13.

83 B. Stephens, op. cit., 18.

84 Ibid. Obviously the Pinochet process in the UK gives some impetus to the idea of pursuing human rights violators. See R. Brody, 'One Year Later, The "Pinochet Precedent" puts Tyrants on Notice', in *The Boston Globe City Edition*, 14 October 1999, A 19. See also www.hrw.org/editorials/1999/reed-oped.htm (last visited 22 March 2002). See also C. Nicholls, 'Reflections on Pinochet', in *Virginia Journal of International Law*, (Fall) 2000, 41, 140.

85 B. Stephens, op. cit., 14-16.

86 B. Stephens, 'Corporate Liability: Enforcing Human Rights Through Domestic Litigation', in *Hastings Int'l & Comp. L. Rev.*, 2001, 24, 401, 413.

87 *Smith Kline & French Labs v. Bloch*, 2 All E.R. 72, 74 (Eng. 1983).

88 These include the Torture Victims Protection Act, the Foreign Sovereign Immunities Act and terrorism laws.

89 630 F.2d 876, 880 (2d Cir. 1980).

90 D. M. Ramsey, 'Multinational Corporate Liability Under the Alien Tort Claims Act: Some Structural Concerns', in *Hastings Int'l & Comp. L. Rev.*, 2001, 24, 361.

91 Ibid. at 364.

92 These include *forum non conveniens*, international comity, act of state and the political question doctrines.

93 See generally E. Gruzen, 'The United States as a Forum for Human Rights Litigation: Is this the Best Solution?', in *Transnat'l Law*, 2001, 14, 207; 'Development in the Law: "Corporate Liability for Violations of International Human Rights Law"'

in *Harv. L. Rev.*, 2001, 114, 2025, and M. D. Ramsey, 'Multinational Corporate Liability Under the Alien Tort Claims Act: Some Structural Concerns', in *Hastings Int'l & Comp. L. Rev.*, 2001, 24, 361.

94   *Iwanowa v. Ford Motor Co.*, 67 F. Supp. 2d 424, 489-90 (D.N.J. 1999).

95   A. X. Fellmeth, 'Note from the Field: Wiwa v. Royal Dutch Petroleum Co.: A New Standard for the Enforcement of International Law in U.S. Courts?', in *Yale H.R. & Dev. L. J.*, 2002, 5, 241, 249.

96   70 F.3d 232 (2d Cir. 1995). Here the plaintiffs were Croat and Muslim citizens of Bosnia-Herzegovina. They sued the leader of the other forces for having committed gross human rights violations such as genocide and war crimes. See also J. Lu, 'Jurisdiction Over Non-State Activity under the Alien Tort Claims Act', in *Colum. J. Transnat'l L.*, 1997, 35, 531.

97   At 350.

98   At 239.

99   *Doe v. Unocal Corp.*, 2002 U.S. App. LEXIS 19263 (9th Cir. 18 September 2002) at 32-33.

100   See further J. Sarkin, 'Examining the Competing Constitutional Processes in Burma/Myanmar from a Comparative and International Democratic and Human Rights Perspective', in *Asia-Pacific Journal on Human Rights and the Law*, 2001, 2 (2), 42-68.

101   See e.g., *Doe v. Unocal*, 110 F. Supp. 2d at 1294, 1306-1307 (C.D. Cal. 2000); *Iwanova v. Ford Motor Co.*, 67 F. Supp. 2d. 424, 443 (D.N.J. 1999).

102   963 F. Supp. 880, 885 (C.D. Cal. 1997).

103   *Doe v. Unocal Corp.*, 2002 U.S. App. LEXIS 19263 (9th Cir. 18 September 2002) at 32-33.

104   See Ibid. at 35-55.

105   Ibid. at 36.

106   *Iwanova v. Ford Motor Co.*, 67 F. Supp. 2d. 424, 445 (D.N.J. 1999).

107   226 F.3d 88, 93 (2d Cir. 2000).

108   See further A. X. Fellmeth, 'Note from the Field: Wiwa v. Royal Dutch Petroleum Co.: A New Standard for the Enforcement of International Law in U.S. Courts?', in *Yale H.R. & Dev. L. J.*, 2002, 5, 241.

109   See further A. X. Fellmeth, op. cit., 241.

110   A. X. Fellmeth, op. cit., 241.

111   197 F.3d 161 (5th Cir. 1999).

112   507 U.S. 349 (1993).

113   107 F.3d 720 (9th Cir. 1997).

114   E. Schrage, 'A Long Way to Find Justice. What Are Burmese Villagers Doing in a California Court?', in *Washington Post*, 14 July 2002.

115   Very relevant to this issue internationally is the fact that the General Assembly, in 1968, adopted the Convention on the Non-Applicability of Statutory Limitations to War Crimes and Crimes against Humanity. See further M. Lippman, 'The Pursuit of Nazi War Criminals in the United States and in other Anglo-American Legal Systems', in *Cal. W. Int'l L. J.*, 1998, 29, 1, 12. The first sentence of Article 1 states that 'no statutory limitation shall apply to the following crimes, irrespective of the

date of their commission' following the definitions of war crimes and crimes against humanity. However, Article 2 reads: 'If any of the crimes mentioned in Article I is committed, the provisions of this Convention shall apply to representatives of the State authority and private individuals …' The key word is 'is'. Does this mean that the convention only applies prospectively?

116   In *Iwanowa* v. *Ford Motor Co.* 67 F. Supp. 2d at 433-34 the court found that the Torture Victim Protection Act of 1991, 28 U.S.C. 1350, which has a 10-year statute of limitations, was the most comparable statute to the ATCA. See Iwanowa at 462.
117   US Senate report S.Rep. No. 249, 102d Cong., 1st Sess., (1991) 5.
118   US Senate report S.Rep. No. 249, 102d Cong., 1st Sess., (1991) 11.
119   In Forti, at 1549 the court held: 'Although the limitations period of a claim under the Alien Tort Statute is governed by state law, because the claim itself is a federal claim, federal equitable tolling doctrines apply.'
120   518 A.2d 423, 425 (D.C. App. 1986).
121   886 F. Supp. 162, 191 (D. Mass. 1995).
122   164 F.2d 767 (2d Cir.1947).
123   At 769. This statement is reproduced in Forti at 1550.
124   At 1550.
125   See *Forti* v. *Suarez-Mason*, 672 F. Supp. 1531, 1549 (N.D. Cal. 1987).
126   176 F.R.D. 329 (C.D. Cal. 1997).
127   Citing the Ninth Circuit's ruling in *Hilao* v. *Estate of Marcos* 103 F.3d 767 at 772.
128   At 360.
129   67F. Supp. 2d 424, 462 (D.N.J. 1999).
130   At 467.
131   See also *Pollack* v. *Siemens AG*, No. 98CV-5499 (E.D.N.Y.) filed 30 August 1998. The Pollack complaint alleged significant concealment on the part of the defendant corporations and that important documents were made public only in the mid-1990s. See J. Roy, 'Strengthening Human Rights Protection: Why the Holocaust Slave Labor Claims Should be Litigated' in *Scholar*, 1999, 1, 153. The issue of concealment is also seen to be important; Bilenker, for example, argues that for the claims against banks for World War II acts 'the court could apply the "fraudulent concealment" doctrine to the banks' situation if it finds evidence that the banks in fact concealed essential information from plaintiffs regarding the status of their accounts and the deposits of looted assets'. See S. A. Bilenker, 'In Re Holocaust Victim's Assets Litigation: Do the US Courts Have Jurisdiction over the Lawsuits Filed by Holocaust Survivors Against the Swiss Banks?', in *Md. J. Int'l L. & Trade*, 1997, 21, 251.
132   See M. J. Bazyler, 'Nuremberg in America: Litigating the Holocaust in the United States Courts', in *U. Rich. L. Rev.*, 2000, 34, 1.
133   Civ. No. 4-96-CV-10449, 1998 U.S. Dist. LEXIS 21230, at 30-31 (S.D. Iowa, 11 March 1998).
134   975 F. Supp. 1108, 1122 (N.D. Ill. 1997) aff'd, 250 F.3d 1145 (7th Cir. 2001).
135   450 F. Supp. 227, 229-30 (N. D. Ill. 1978).
136   No. 93 Civ. 0878 (PKL), 2000 WL 76861, 1 n. 3 (S.D.N.Y. 13 June 2000).
137   157 F.Supp.2d 1345, 1368 (S.D. Fla., 2001).

138   205 F. Supp. 2d 1325; (S.D. FLA 2002) 2002 U.S. Dist. LEXIS 10323; 15 Fla. L. Weekly Fed. D 336.

139   See *Lubbe* v. *Cape plc*, (1999) Int'l Litigation Procedure 113, CA.

140   See *Connelly* v. *RTZ Corp. plc*, (1996) 2 WLR 251; [1997] 3 WLR 373.

141   See *Ngcobo and others* v. *Thor Chemical Holdings Ltd* and another, (1995) TLR 579; *Sithole and others* v. *Thor Chemical Holdings Ltd* and another, (1999) TLR 110.

142   For further discussion see R. Meeran, 'Liability of Multinational Corporations: A Critical Stage in the UK', in M. T. Kamminga and S. Zia-Zarifi (eds.), *Liability of Multinational Corporations under International Law*, Kluwer Law International, 2000, 258-61 and R. Meeran, 'The Unveiling of Transnational Corporations: A Direct Approach', in *Human Rights Standards and the Responsibility of Transnational Corporations*, M. K. Addo (ed.), Kluwer Law International, 1999, 164-69.

143   See *Dagi* v. *Broken Hill Proprietary Co. Ltd*, (No. 2) (1997) 1 VR 428.

144   The Herero People's Reparation Corporation, the Herero tribe by and through its Paramount Chief Kuaima Riruako, 199 individuals and the Chief Hosea Kutako Foundation filed in the Superior Court of the District of Columbia a case captioned *The Herero People's Reparation Corporation*, et al. v. *Deutsche Bank AG*, et al., 01 CA 4447.

145   The Terex claim was later dropped, at least temporarily. See UN Integrated Regional Information Network, 21 September 2001.

146   Various strategies have been attempted to claim reparations for the atrocities committed against the Herero. Speaking at the commemoration of Herero Day at Okahandja in 1999, Chief Riruako stated: 'On the threshold of the new millennium the Hereros, as a nation, have decided to take Germany to the International Court for a decision regarding reparations. We also warn the Namibian Government not to stand in our way as we explore this avenue to justice.' Each year in August, the Hereros come together in memory of their fallen heroes who died during the 1904–1907 Herero-German war. See C. Maletsky, 'International Court Dashes Hereros' Reparation Hopes', in *The Namibian*, 8 September 1999.

147   South Africa has also been called on to provide reparations to the Hereros. Herero Paramount Chief Kuaima Riruako has called on the Namibian government to institute a legal suit, similar to the one of the Hereros against the German government, against their South African counterparts. He has stated: 'I'm not quite happy (with the state of affairs against SA). We suffered a lot (at the hands of SA) and we can't let them off the hook.' The South Africans responded that they will not pay reparations and compensation to the Herero people in Namibia. Foreign affairs spokesman Ronnie Mamoepa stated that the current South African government was composed of former victims of colonisation and apartheid and can you ask for reparation or compensation from the same victims who suffered under those regimes? See C. Maletsky and T. Mokopanele, 'SA Refuses to Consider Reparation for Hereros', *Business Day*, 28 September 2001.

148   On 19 September 2001, plaintiffs filed a similar claim against the Federal Republic of Germany, see *The Herero Peoples' Reparation Corporation*, et al. v. *Federal Republic of Germany*, 1:01CV01987CKK.

149   Chief Riruako has expressed dismay at the Namibian government's lack of interest in the Herero case stating that: 'For the (Namibian) government or any one to say, "I'm

not part of it" … must be nuts.' See C. Maletsky and T. Mokopanele, 'SA Refuses to Consider reparation for Hereros', in *Business Day*, 28 September 2001.

150   It is interesting to note that the Special Rapporteur to the UN Sub-Commission in 1993, Theo van Boven, notes: 'it would be difficult and complex to construe and uphold a legal duty to pay compensation to the descendants of the victims of the slave trade and other early forms of slavery.' (E/CN.4/Sub.2/19993/8.) He refers to a report of the UN Secretary-General on the Right to Development (E/CN.4/1334) who notes, with regard to 'moral duty of reparation to make up for past exploitation by the colonial powers', that 'acceptance of such a moral duty is by no means universal'.

151   F. Bridgland, 'Germany's Genocide Rehearsal' in *The Scotsman*, 26 September 2001.

152   C. Maletsky, 'Hereros Temporarily Drop Claim in $2bn Suit', in *Business Day*, 20 September 2001.

153   On 19 September 2001, plaintiffs filed against the Federal Republic of Germany. See *The Herero Peoples' Reparation Corporation, et al. v. Federal Republic of Germany*, 1:01CV01987CKK. See also C. Maletsky and T. Mokopanele, 'SA Refuses to Consider Reparation for Hereros', in *Business Day*, 28 September 2001.

154   F. Bridgland, 'Germany's Genocide Rehearsal', in *The Scotsman*, 26 September 2001.

155   Herero complaint.

156   *The Independent* – London, 9 September 2001.

157   S. L. Harring, 'German Reparations to the Herero Nation: An Assertion of Herero Nationhood in the Path of Namibian Development?', in *West Virginia Law Review*, (Winter) 2002, 393, 414-5.

158   C. Maletsky, 'Hereros Temporarily Drop Claim in $2bn Suit', in *Business Day*, 20 September 2001.

159   'Reparations not on the Table', in *The Namibian*, 31 August 2000.

160   Comments of the spokesperson for the Southern African Development Community (SADC) in the German Parliament, Hans Buttner, during a meeting with Prime Minister Hage Geingob in Windhoek reported in 'Reparations not on the Table' in *The Namibian*, 31 August 2000.

161   'Reparations not on the Table', in *The Namibian*, 31 August 2000.

162   'Reparations not on the Table', in *The Namibian*, 31 August 2000.

163   T. Bensman, 'Tribe Demands Holocaust Reparations: Germany's Genocidal War Against Namibia's Herero was Rehearsal for World War II Atrocities', in *The Salt Lake Tribune*, 18 March 1999.

164   T. Bensman, 'Tribe Demands Holocaust Reparations; Germany's genocidal war against Namibia's Herero was rehearsal for World War II atrocities', in *The Salt Lake Tribune*, 18 March 1999.

165   T. Bensman, 'Tribe Demands Holocaust Reparations; Germany's genocidal war against Namibia's Herero was rehearsal for World War II atrocities', in *The Salt Lake Tribune*, 18 March 1999.

166   See J. Sarkin, 'The Development of a Human Rights Culture in South Africa', in *Human Rights Quarterly*, 1998, 20 (3), 628, 644.

167   J. Sarkin, 'Can South Africa Afford Justice? The Need and Future of a Public Defender System', in *Stellenbosch Law Review*, 1993, 4 (2), 261.

168 See D. D. Mokgatle, 'The Exclusion of Blacks from the South African Judicial System', in *South African Journal on Human Rights*, 1987, 3, 44.

169 See H. Varney and J. Sarkin, 'Failing to Pierce the Hit Squad Veil: An Analysis of the Malan Trial', in *South African Journal of Criminal Justice*, 1996, 10, 141.

170 See J. Sarkin, 'Preventive Detention in South Africa', in A. Harding and J. Hatchard (eds.), *Preventive Detention and Security Law: A Comparative Survey* (Dordrecht/Boston: Martinus Nijhoff, 1993), 209, 271.

171 M. Coleman (ed.), *A Crime against Humanity: Analysing the Repression of the Apartheid State* (Cape Town: David Philip, 1998).

172 Calling Apartheid's Profiteers to Account – Archbishop Njongonkulu Ndungane, Jubilee South Africa Patron, Anglican Archbishop of Cape Town, Action for Southern Africa (http://Www.Actsa.Org/News/Features/011002_Reparations.htm)

173 Calling Apartheid's Profiteers to Account – Archbishop Njongonkulu Ndungane, Jubilee South Africa Patron, Anglican Archbishop of Cape Town, Action for Southern Africa (http://Www.Actsa.Org/News/Features/011002_Reparations.htm)

174 See further J. Sarkin, 'The Trials and Tribulations of South Africa's Truth and Reconciliation Commission', in *South African Journal on Human Rights*, 1996, 12, 617; J. Sarkin, 'The Truth and Reconciliation Commission in South Africa', in *Commonwealth Law Bulletin*, 1997, 528; J. Sarkin, 'The Development of a Human Rights Culture in South Africa', in *Human Rights Quarterly*, 1998, 20 (3), 628; and J. Sarkin, 'To Prosecute or Not to Prosecute? That is the Question. An Examination of the Constitutional and Legal Issues Concerning Criminal Trials for Human Rights Violations Committed in the Apartheid Era and the Giving of Amnesty to Those Who Did Not Apply or Were Refused Amnesty in Post Truth and Reconciliation Commission South Africa', in C. Villa-Vicencio and E. Doxtader (eds.), *Amnesty in South Africa*, 2003.

175 Final Report of the Truth and Reconciliation Commission, v. 4, ch. 2, Institutional hearing 'Business and Labour' (TRC Report on Business and Labour), ¶ 21.

176 I use the term 'indictment' with full knowledge that this was exactly not what the TRC Report was intended to be. Nevertheless, the term does not seem altogether inappropriate given that (1) Ntsebeza, who was a TRC commissioner who helped draft the Report, is now leading the lawsuit that is in part based on the TRC's findings; and (2) Terry Bell, who provided research for the TRC and subsequently wrote *Unfinished Business: South Africa Apartheid & Truth*, infra, with Ntsebeza, is also involved with the lawsuit.

177 See e.g. ibid. at ¶ 49 ('Business was not a monolithic block and it can be argued that no single relationship existed between business and apartheid').

178 TRC Report on Business and Labour at ¶ 23.

179 Ibid. at ¶ 28.

180 Ibid. at ¶ 32.

181 S. R. Ratner, 'Corporations and Human Rights: A Theory of Legal Responsibility', in *Yale L. J.*, 2001, 111, 443, 503.

182 Although brief mention of banks is made in the Report's discussion of first order involvement, the Report shies away from ascribing principal liability to banks. Instead, the Report records without concurring, in the view of The Apartheid Debt Coordinating Committee, that 'even the seemingly most pristine ... trade loans were

tainted by apartheid. The simple fact of trade with South Africa inescapably meant helping to sustain and reproduce … apartheid. No loan could avoid this institutional contamination.' TRC Report on Business and Labour at ¶ 25.

183 Ibid. at ¶ 28.
184 Ibid. at ¶ 31.
185 Ibid. at ¶ 29.
186 Ibid. at ¶ 35.
187 Ibid. at ¶ 30.
188 Ibid. at ¶ 118.
189 Ibid. at ¶ 119.
190 Ibid. at ¶ 120. It is unclear whether or not multinational corporations participated in such Joint Management Committees with the apartheid regime.
191 Ibid.
192 Ibid. at ¶ 122.
193 Ibid. at ¶ 123.
194 See e.g. ibid. at ¶ 5 (reporting that multinational oil corporations (which were the largest foreign investors in South Africa) did not respond to the invitation to participate); and ¶ 131 ('The failure of multinational corporations to make submissions at the hearing was greatly regretted in view of their prominent role in South Africa's economic development under apartheid. It was left to the AAM Archives Committee to explain the role of foreign firms in South Africa').
195 Ratner at 503.
196 C. Terreblanche, 'Anglo and De Beers Could Be Targeted in Class Action Suit', in *Sunday Independent*, 29 September 2002.
197 A. Ramasastry, 'Banks and Human Rights: Should Swiss Banks be Liable for Lending to South Africa's Apartheid Government?', in *Find Law*, 3 July 2002, available at http://writ.findlaw.com/ramasastry/20020703.html
198 J. Lauria, 'Explosive Start to "Apartheid Victims" Lawsuit', in *Sunday Independent*, 11 August 2002.
199 B. Boyle, 'At Least 27 Entities on Apartheid Lawsuit List', in *Star*, 12 July 2002.
200 See *Weekly Mail and Guardian*, 25 July 2002.
201 N. Deane, 'South Africans take on the Giants', in *Weekly Mail and Guardian*, 27 June 2002. The article appears to be quoting the complaint.
202 'More Join Apartheid Victims' Suit' in *Star*, 24 June 2002. A letter Fagan sent to the chief executive of Barclay's Bank in London employs a strikingly less hyperbolic approach: 'We hope to enter into a dialogue with you and others and through which we can find a meaningful way that can address both objectively and proportionately the nature and extent of your company's involvement in South Africa during apartheid and what your company has done to help redress the wrongs that were committed. Entering into this dialogue would be taken as an expression of your company's desire to work together to find a resolution for the benefit of victims of apartheid.' D. Carew, 'Apartheid "Collaborator" Companies Asked to Respond to Class Action Lawsuit', in *Saturday Weekend Argus*, 13 July 2002.
203 See *Ntzebesa, Mequbela, Molefi, Mpendulo et al. v. Citigroup Inc., UBS A.G., Credit Suisse Group et al.* Affidavit in Support of Motion for Preservation of Evidence at 5–6.

204 C. Terreblanche, 'Apartheid Victims File $35bn Suit in the US' in *Cape Times*, July 2, 2002. See also Affidavit at 5–6. In his book, Terry Bell notes how '(g)reater reliance on computer technology was seen as one of the ways of making more efficient the maintenance of the apartheid system,' and why 'Botha and his generals ... saw more centralised and efficient information processing as the key'. As Bell explains, and as noted earlier, 'close, collaborative ties with international business and the links through South African corporations, were not explored much locally and not at all by the TRC'. Touching on the role of companies such as IBM, Bell writes: 'The whole racial classification system, from "influx control" for blacks to the "books of life" for other categories, had been maintained since the 1950s, by electronic hardware and software provided by companies such as Britain's ICL, IBM of the United States and the Burroughs Corporation. The shortage of military personnel in the 1970s had partially been overcome by the use of computers supplied by "Big Blue", the IBM corporation. By the time of the bloody decade of the Eighties, South Africa had become the biggest spender in terms of percentage of national wealth (GDP) on computers after the US and Britain.' In addition, Bell draws the connection between the information infrastructure provided by foreign corporations, and the functioning of the Civil Co-operation Bureau, 'the military's full-time murder and terror squad'.

205 See 'Press Advisory', 1 July 2002, 2.

206 Sapa-AFP, 'Justice with a Hefty Price Tag', in *Cape Argus*, 27 June 2002.

207 See e.g. 'Govt Wise to Shun Compensation Suit', in *The Herald* (*EP Herald*), 25 June 2002; A. Dasnois, 'Fagan's Campaign is Unlikely to Enrich Citizens', in *Star*, 22 July 2002 ('There is a danger that Fagan's campaign will serve his own ends more than those of justice').

208 The Khulamani Support Group is a coalition partner organisation in Jubilee SA. Khulumani is an organisation of about 32 000 victims of gross apartheid human rights violations.

209 From the United States of America – Citigroup, J. P. Morgan Chase (Chase Manhattan), Caltex Petroleum Corporation, Exxon Mobil Corporation, Fluor Corporation, Ford Motor Corporation, General Motors, International Business Machines (IBM); from the United Kingdom (UK) – Barclays National Bank, British Petroleum P.L.C., Fujitsu ICL (previously International Computers Limited); from the Federal Republic of Germany – Commerzbank, Deutsche Bank, Dresdner Bank, Daimler Chrysler, Rheinmetall; from Switzerland – Credit Suisse Group, UBS; from France – Total-Fina-Elf; from The Netherlands – Royal Dutch Shell.

210 Press release by the Apartheid Debt & Reparations Campaign, Tuesday, 12 November 2002.

211 Press release Khulumani Support Group, 12 November 2002.

212 Press release Apartheid Debt & Reparations Campaign, 12 November 2002.

213 Press statement by Cohen, Milstein, Hausfeld & Toll, 12 November 2002.

214 'Manuel Doubts Value of Apartheid Lawsuits', SABC news 26 November 2002 (http://www.sabcnews.co.za/south_africa/general/0,1009,48214,00.html).

215 'Manuel doubts value of apartheid lawsuits' SABC news 26 November 2002 (http://www.sabcnews.co.za/south_africa/general/0,1009,48214,00.html).

216   'Manuel doubts value of apartheid lawsuits' SABC news 26 November 2002 (http://www.sabcnews.co.za/south_africa/general/0,1009,48214,00.html).
217   S. R. Ratner and J. S. Abrams, *Accountability for Human Rights Atrocities in International Law, Beyond the Nuremberg Legacy* (Oxford: Clarendon Press, 1997), 211.
218   S. Zia-Zarifi, 'Suing Multinational Corporations in the U.S. for Violating International Law', in *UCLA J. Int'l L. & Foreign Aff.*, 1999, 4, 81, 120-1.

19

Reparation Efforts in International Perspective:

What Compensation Contributes to the Achievement of Imperfect Justice

Pablo de Greiff

Despite recent increased attention to the topic of reparation and its long history, it is surprising that the issue has received significantly less attention than other transitional justice mechanisms. There are few in-depth studies of reparation, and even fewer systematic comparative analyses of the different reparation measures established by a fairly large number of countries in the aftermath of conflict or of a democratic transition. The Research Unit at the International Center for Transitional Justice (ICTJ) has embarked on an ambitious research project which attempts to remedy this situation.[1] This chapter summarises some of the results of that research.[2] But rather than limiting itself to brief synopses of some of the cases in the larger project – as useful as this, in itself, might be – this chapter constitutes an effort to systematise some of the crucial challenges faced by those entrusted with the design of massive reparation programmes.

After briefly outlining three reparation efforts, the chapter will sketch a taxonomy of these cases in the expectation that this will shed some light on some of the critical variables in the design of reparation programmes. Finally, the chapter will offer some concluding reflections on the notion of justice that these programmes arguably aim to satisfy. This chapter hence moves from the factual to the normative.[3]

Three reparation efforts

Once the difficulties of information collection are solved, the primary challenge in writing a paper on this topic is choosing from among the ample selection of cases. The three selected cases illustrate the breadth of alternatives open to policy-makers. These cases differ significantly from one another across a variety of factors including their historical location, the type and magnitude of the benefits they distributed, the numbers of beneficiaries they covered, the types of crimes they sought to redress, their programmatic or non-programmatic nature, and their relationship with other legal instruments, in particular with civil suits. The cases are post-World War II Germany, Argentina and Chile. In this section the cases will be ordered chronologically for ease of presentation. In the next section, in sketching a taxonomy, the cases will be ordered along multiple axes.

German Holocaust reparations[4]

There is no point in attempting in a chapter of this nature to trace in any detail the historical roots of reparation programmes that benefit victims of human rights abuses. It is obvious, however, that post-bellum reparation between states are the main source. German reparations for the victims of the Holocaust, however, constitute a watershed; in some ways they responded to the familiar model of inter-state reparation, in others they are the first example of reparation for individuals. They are also the first reparation programmes negotiated with the participation of what would come to be known as non-governmental organisations (NGOs). As of December 2001, the Federal Republic of Germany (FRG) had paid approximately $61.5 billion USD (70 billion DM) in reparation, including $37.5 billion (42.5 billion DM) under federal individual indemnification laws.[5]

The 1952 Luxembourg Agreement negotiated by the FRG, the new state of Israel and Jewish NGOs included a commitment by Germany to draft national legislation to provide for individual reparation. The eventual nation-wide law in the Federal Republic of Germany outlining reparation (*Bündesentschädigungsgesetz* of 1953, 1956 and 1965) was foreshadowed in individual laws promulgated in German provinces, the Allied Restitution Law of 1947 and the law of compensation established in the US occupied zone in 1949. Though the first Chancellor of the FRG, Konrad Adenauer, argued for a West German reparation policy on moral grounds, German popular acquiescence to such a programme – for initially it would be an overstatement to talk about support – was also motivated by political reasons, including an interest in reconciliation and integration with the West and the North Atlantic Treaty Organisation.

Representatives of Israel, for their part, were also divided on whether to demand compensation from West Germany. Part of the compensation agreement involved the transfer of capital and other goods from Germany to Israel, some of which would be resold by Israel. This, in the eyes of reparation opponents, made Israel a partner with their former executioners. Supporters of reparation relied on both political and religious arguments, including the economic needs of the new Israeli state and Talmudic teachings that a criminal should not profit from his/her crime. The key architects of the reparation negotiations maintained a strict separation between, on the one hand, the *legal* grounds for reparation and, on the other, the *moral* unredeemability of the German crimes that provided the grounds for reparation in the first place.

The 1952 Luxembourg Agreement
After close to eight months of negotiations, representatives of Israel, the FRG and the Claims Conference[6] agreed that: 1) the FRG would pay the state of Israel three billion DM or $882 million dollars between 1953 and 1965; 2) in Protocol One, the FRG agreed to implement a series of laws to govern reparation to individual victims; 3) in Protocol Two the FRG agreed to pay 450 million DM or $107 million to the Claims Conference. This amount was actually paid to Israel in goods, which were sold and funds were then transferred to the Claims Conference.[7]

Israel agreed to use the payments to purchase German goods within the following categories: 1) steel, iron and non-ferrous metals; 2) products from steel-processing industries; 3) products from chemical and other industries; 4) agricultural and food products; 5) services and administrative costs. Germany also agreed to provide a third of the total 3.45 billion DM in foreign exchange for the purchase of oil from Great Britain. A 'Mixed Commission' of appointed German and Israeli officials could approve purchases of non-German origin and changes in the schedule of payments or purchases.

The Claims Conference distributed its annual payment to various Jewish assistance organisations, such as the American Joint Distribution Committee (JDC) and the Jewish Relief Survivor Organisation (JRSO). Utilising their own networks, these organisations developed humanitarian programmes (cash relief, medical and psychological treatment or assistance); cultural programmes (exchange programmes with Israeli universities) and non-emergency assistance programmes (for the elderly and childcare). These organisations also assisted Jewish populations in France, Belgium or Holland.

The Individual Indemnification Laws:
1953 Federal Supplementary Law[8]; 1956 Federal Compensation
Law[9]; 1965 Federal Compensation Final Law[10]
The first nationwide law on individual compensation established eligibility
and procedures for those who, due to their political views, race or religion,
were persecuted by the National Socialist Party. Damages incurred for
reasons other than persecution were not eligible for compensation, but
victims could claim damages to their career or property as a result of persecution even if they did not suffer physical or psychological harm.
Compensation was limited to former German citizens, refugees and stateless people (as defined by the Geneva Convention). Eligible claimants had
to prove they were persecuted through 'officially approved measures',
which was a difficult standard to meet given the atmosphere of generalised and diffuse xenophobia of the Third Reich.[11]

Victims had to file individual claims that would be sent to provincial
(*Land*) reparation agencies. If the claimant disagreed with the agency's
decision, she or he could contest the settlement first in provincial courts
(*Landgerichte*), then courts of appeal (*Oberlandsgerichte*) and finally the
Federal Supreme Court (*Bündesgerichthof*). Claimants over 60 years old,
the needy, sick and infirm whose earning capacity had been reduced by at
least 50%, received priority within the decision-making process.[12]
Claimants could simultaneously pursue damages in each of the various
categories: 'harm to life, body, health and freedom; harm to possessions
and assets; and harm to career and economic advancement' for persecution from 30 January 1933 till 8 May 1945.

Compensation for life
Widows, children and dependent relatives could apply for a pension for
wrongful death, based on the amount paid to families of civil servants who
suffered accidental death on duty, an amount that depended on the civil
servant's seniority.[13]The deceased's average income for the last three years
before his death was the basis for determining to which category of civil
service compensation the deceased would be assigned, which would in
turn determine the relevant pension. Claimants were also eligible to
receive a one-time capital payment based on the monthly pension multiplied by the number of months between the persecuted's death and the
beginning of annuity payments.

The 1965 law expanded the eligibility for compensation for loss of life to recognise deaths that occurred within eight months of 8 May 1945. Similarly, this category of loss of life was made available to the surviving relatives of those who died from harm to body or health as a result of persecution even if the death occurred beyond the eight-month grace period.[14] As of December 2001, the German government has paid approximately $3.5 billion (3.9 billion DM) in claims for compensation for life.[15] In 2001, the average pension under this category was approximately $697 per month (792 DM).

Compensation for health

For 'not insignificant'[16] damage to health or spirit, claimants were entitled to medical care. For reparation beyond the provision of medical care, such as a monthly pension, claimants needed to prove that their persecution caused health problems that led to at least a 30% reduction in their earning capacity. Doctors often relied on tables for quantifying the damage; loss of an eye constituted a 30% reduction and loss of an arm constituted a 50% reduction in earning capacity.[17] The reduction in earning capacity was measured using the victim's average income for the three years before persecution against him or her began as a benchmark.[18] The percentage reduction in earning capacity was then correlated with a percentage of civil servants' benefits, for example, for a 30–39% reduction in earning capacity a claimant was entitled to 15–40% of the relevant civil servants' disability pay. For the time between the injury (or reduction in earning capacity) and the annuity, claimants were entitled to a once-off capital payment as calculated for compensation to life capital claims.

In 1956, the minimum 30% reduction in earning capacity necessary to claim monetary damages was lowered to 25%. Funds were made available to assist claimants who needed physical therapy. The 1965 law significantly eased the burden on claimants to prove that damages to their health were linked to their earlier persecution. It established the presumption that if a claimant had been incarcerated for a year in a concentration camp, subsequent health problems could be causally linked to their persecution under the Nazi regime. By December 2001, the German government had paid approximately $21.8 billion (24.7 billion DM) in health-related claims.[19] In 2001, the average pension under this category was approximately $450 per month (510 DM).

Compensation for damages to freedom

To qualify, claimants must have been subjected to conditions listed in the

1953 law, §16, including incarceration in a political or military jail, detention in a concentration camp, detention for interrogation or punishment or forced residence in a ghetto. The law also included forced labour insofar as the persecuted lived under jail-like conditions. Claimants were entitled to 150DM per month of detention (approximately $35 at the time).[20] In 1956, this category was expanded to include claimants forced to wear the Star of David or to live 'underground' in inhuman conditions. By December 2001, the German government had paid approximately $1.27 billion (1.4 billion DM) in claims for damages to freedom.[21]

Compensation for property, assets,[22] discriminatory taxes

Claimants were entitled to compensation (not restitution) for damage to property, assets lost due to boycotts or payment of discriminatory taxes such as the Reich Flight Tax.[23] The loss of property must have occurred because the claimant fled the country or emigrated or was 'robbed of his freedom'. The maximum amount (including all three categories) was 75 000DM, approximately $18 750 at the time.[24] Of this amount, claims for personal belongings could only constitute 5 000DM or one and a half times the 1932 annual salary of the victim.

In 1956, this category was divided into three separate classes, each with separate ceilings on compensation (except for discriminatory taxes, which were no longer subject to a ceiling). For property, claimants could file for the replacement value, not to exceed a maximum award of 75 000DM. The law also recognises other instances in which claims for property are eligible, including being expelled or deported and forced to flee and live in inhuman conditions. Claims for assets were also subject to a ceiling of 75 000DM. As of December 2001, the German government had paid approximately $568 million (645 million DM) in property, assets and tax claims.[25]

Compensation for damages to career or economic advancement

Self-employed and privately employed claimants (or dependent relatives) were entitled to a maximum payment of 25 000DM (approximately $6 250 at the time) for the time that persecution (firing or restriction of duties) began until 1 January 1947, the assumed date that victims could attain an adequate standard of living. The exact amount was calculated as at least two-thirds of the relevant civil servant's pay for that time period. If a victim was unable to resume his or her career, they could choose to receive their retirement pension early, calculated as two-thirds of the pension for the relevant category of civil servants. Additional provisions for victims whose careers were damaged included a loan of maximum 30 000DM to restart their businesses and reaccredidation with the relevant authorities. Victims could also claim assistance to make up their missed education, up to 5 000DM. This sum was later raised to 10 000DM (then approximately $1 250) in the 1965 revision.[26] Compensation for persecuted public officials was governed by a separate law already passed in 1951.[27]

In 1956, regulations were eased for privately- and self-employed claimants to choose a pension instead of the one-time capital payment.[28] The monthly maximum was raised from 500DM to 600DM. Eligibility for career compensation was quantified as a reduction in earning capacity of at least 25% for privately and self-employed claimants. The ceiling on claims for education was raised to 10 000DM (then approximately $1 250).[29] As of December 2001, the German government had paid approximately $8.8 billion (9.9 billion DM) in claims for damages to careers or economic advancement.[30]

The 1965 Final Law also created a *hardship fund* of 1.2 billion DM ($300 million at the time) to support refugees from Eastern Europe who were previously ineligible for compensation under the *Bündesentschädigungsgesetz or* BEG, primarily emigrants from 1953 to 1965. The fund distributed lump sum payments beginning at 1 000–3 000DM, depending on the damage incurred.[31]

Concluding observations
The enormity of the crimes committed during the Holocaust highlights with particular clarity the absolute impossibility of achieving full compensation (*restitutio in integrum*), that is, of compensating each victim in proportion to the harm she or he suffered. None of the laws ever attempted to do so. In the absence of alternative criteria of success in reparation, these laws have been criticised for offering too little too late.

A more serious criticism has focused on the exclusions in the Final Law, which still left out of consideration large classes of victims, including all those who had been persecuted outside Germany by German killing squads who, because they remained in their native countries, did not fulfil the law's residency requirements; forced labourers; victims of forced sterilisation; the 'antisocial';[32] communists; gypsies; and homosexuals. Some of these groups have been redressed in later legislation.[33]

Despite these and other drawbacks (such as procedural and evidentiary requirements that had to be relaxed over time) the German reparation efforts are impressive for several reasons: first, for their innovative character, since there was no obvious historical precedent for them; second, for the number of beneficiaries and their geographical dispersion; and third, for the magnitude of the benefits that they distributed over time at the macro, global level, even if, at the micro level of the individual, complaints about low benefits may be justified. More than $37.5 billion dollars in individual reparations (over two million claims) had been distributed through such programmes by December 2001 to individuals in more than 70 countries.[34] These numbers still make German reparation the most ambitious ever. The fact that they were also just one part of what Germany tried to do to assume responsibility for its past helps to explain what is surely an astonishing transformation in perceptions about Germany in the international context.

Argentina[35]

Argentina's reparation efforts are perhaps best known for the magnitude of their benefits. Indeed, by international standards, these are exceptionally high. That reparation continues to be exceptionally divisive in the country establishes – as if it were necessary – that the magnitude of benefits alone does not settle all controversies regarding reparation.

The National Commission on the Disappeared (CONADEP) was established by President Raul Alfonsín on 15 December 1983, just five days after taking office.[36] As its name suggests, the Commission was formed as a reaction to the massive numbers of disappearances that had taken place in the country not just during the years of military rule but also before. Indeed, the state of siege had been enacted during the government of María Estela Martínez de Perón, on 6 November 1974, prior to the military coup of 24 March 1976.[37]

Consistent with its focus on the victims and the consequences of disappearances, CONADEP's final report recommended: 'That necessary measures be taken in order to allow the children or family members of persons disappeared during the repression to receive economic assistance: educational scholarships; social assistance; work opportunities. At the same time, appropriate measures should be taken to confront the different family and social problems emerging from the forced disappearance of persons.'[38]

Not surprisingly, given the inherent difficulties of such efforts, reparation measures for the victims of disappearances were not the first to be implemented. In fact, long before the CONADEP report was issued, and just three months after Alfonsín took office, a series of laws was passed aimed at reinstating different classes of official employees who had been fired for political reasons and compensating them for lost retirement benefits.[39]

It was only on 30 October 1986, almost three years into Alfonsin's presidency, and two years after the publication of the CONADEP report, with the enactment of Law 23.466, that widows and children of the disappeared were offered some modest support. The beneficiaries of the law were spouses of the disappeared (as long as they had been living together up to the time of the disappearance and had done so for at least five years), their children younger than 21 years of age (unless they were handicapped, in which case the pension would be life-long)[40], orphaned children who had lived regularly with the family of the victim before the disappearance and the parents and/or siblings of the victims who were unable to work and were not supported through other pensions or benefits.

The law seemed intended to respond to the plight of the widows and the children of the disappeared rather than to satisfy legal criteria such as compensation in proportion to the harm suffered. What it offered, initially, was half of a minimum salary to each of the beneficiaries. Thus, a mother and a child together would receive the equivalent of one minimum salary. The unit for calculating the benefits was subsequently changed at the beneficiaries' request and became the minimum retirement pension of a worker, around $200 per month. Beneficiaries were also granted medical and drug coverage through the Institute of Social Services for Retirees and Pensioners.

Despite the low benefits offered by this law, the issue of reparation for disappearances faded into the background for a while. These were, after all, tumultuous years in Argentina. The *junta* trials that riveted the nation came to an end[41] but so did the brief non-interventionist stance of the military, some of whose members staged four coup attempts from 1984 to 1986. This led to the issuance of the two controversial laws – 'punto final' (final stop) and 'obediencia debida' (due obedience) – which sought to limit the military's exposure to prosecutions by establishing a deadline for the initiation of new cases and by protecting from liability those who committed crimes under orders.[42] The crisis extended to the economy as well, and when it became a generalised crisis of governability, Alfonsín decided to put an early end to his mandate, ceding the way to Carlos Menem who took office on 9 July 1989.[43] While the possibility of initiating criminal trials against perpetrators of human rights abuses had already been foreclosed by the final stop and due obedience laws, one of the first things Menem did upon taking office was to grant a presidential pardon to the members of the military *juntas* who had been convicted as well as to a few high-ranking military officials who were still subject to judicial process. At the same time, Menem pardoned some of the leaders of the armed organisations who were being tried.[44]

It was in this context that discussions of reparation were resumed. They received an impetus from cases brought to Argentinean courts, and to the Inter-American Commission of Human Rights, mostly having to do with unjustified imprisonment. The results of the cases in the local jurisdiction were less than stellar, for when some of them reached the Supreme Court it agreed with lower courts that the cases were inadmissible on statute of limitations grounds.[45]

Some plaintiffs also brought their cases to the Inter-American Human Rights System.[46] Eventually, the government reached an agreement with these petitioners which involved, precisely, the presentation of the decrees leading to the establishment of reparation measures available not just to the members of this group, but to a wider – but as we will see still not wide enough – class of victims. The crucial decree was 70/91, issued on 10 January 1991.

This decree made benefits available to people who during the state of siege had been detained by the national executive authority before 10 December 1983,[47] and who satisfied the following conditions: having claimed and been denied compensation through judicial means before 10 December 1985 – on grounds of the statute of limitations – or having an ongoing complaint at the time the decree entered into force. The latter class was given the somewhat flexible option to continue with their proceedings, and if their cases were dismissed on statute of limitations grounds, they would be allowed to apply for the benefits established by the decree, or to accept the compensation granted by the decree, in which case they would have to waive their judicial complaints.

This decree also introduced one of the distinctive features of Argentinean reparations. The benefits it offered were based on the salary of the highest category of the civilian personnel of the national public administration. The motivation for this choice was to disentangle reparation from the idea of compensation, in particular of labour law compensation. As the former head of the office in charge of implementing the reparation programme explained, this choice of compensation unit 'implied breaking away from criteria applied to work-related accidents. Jail was not an accident'.

Specifically, the decree determined that beneficiaries would receive a thirtieth of the highest civilian official salary for each day the victim had remained in detention. This was equivalent to US$27 at the time. It also compensated the families of those who had died while in detention, and those who had suffered 'grave injuries' in the sense expressed by article 91 of the Argentinean Penal Code. The former would be compensated as follows: $27 per day of detention, plus the equivalent of five years of detention at the same rate (US$46 275). Those who suffered grave injuries would receive $27 per day of detention, plus 70% of the sum corresponding to five years of detention ($34 492).

Petitions were supposed to be presented to the Ministry of the Interior, whose decisions could be appealed to the National Administrative Appellate Chamber. Accepting benefits under this decree required renouncing rights to any other civilian claim.

The Under Secretary of Human Rights claims that 227 people benefited from this decree, but that there is no information concerning the sum of each indemnification paid. Article 12 of the decree stipulated that the funds necessary to comply with the norm would be obtained from the nation's general budget.

Less than a year after Decree 70/91 was issued, Congress adopted Law 24.043.[48] This law broadened access to benefits in two ways: first, it offered benefits not just to those who had been detained under the disposition of the national executive authority by virtue of the state of siege but also to those detained by military tribunals, regardless of whether they had received sentences. Second, the law did not condition access to benefits on having initiated a civil suit.[49]

The structure of the benefits offered by Law 24.043 were identical to those offered by the decree, except that the benefits under the law ended up being significantly greater; whereas Decree 70/91 offered $27 for each day of detention, the law offered $74.[50] At this rate, the five-year benefits offered to the families of those who died in detention increased from $46 275 to $136 254.50, and 70% of this sum, offered to those who endured great injury, increased from $34 492 to $94 490.10. (The new law allowed those who had received benefits under Decree 70/91 to receive the higher benefits offered by the law.)

Requests for benefits were to be presented to the Office of Human

Rights at the Ministry of the Interior. Petitioners had to declare under oath that they had been detained under the conditions established by the law somewhere between 6 November 1974 and 10 December 1983. Broad criteria of evidence were established, such that detention could be proven with habeas corpus petitions or the corresponding sentence, documents from CONADEP's files, from judicial and administrative files, and documents filed with the Inter-American Commission of Human Rights and the Inter-American Court of Human Rights. Documents found in national and international human rights organisations, journalistic materials and bibliographic material were evaluated together with the other approved evidence.

Grave injury could be proven with the clinical histories of the place of detention, a copy of the judicial sentence or the medical or clinical history dated at the time of the detention by an official health institution. If necessary, it was possible to convene a medical panel, for which purposes the Under Secretary of Human Rights could enter into agreements with public hospitals. The partial or complete denial of any benefit under the law could be appealed to the National Administrative Appellate Chamber.

The deadline for presenting files was 17 September 1998. A total of 13 600 petitions were filed, of which more than 7 800 were granted. Here again, the office of the Under Secretary of Human Rights claims that no records of the sums paid in each case are available.

In any case, the benefits were not paid in cash but in public debt bonds, another distinctive feature of Argentinean reparations – and not entirely unconnected to the first, their high magnitude. Of course, a government must make provisions for the payment of bonds. But given that the issuance of bonds does not directly impact on the current year's budget and that this particular series of bonds matured in 16 years,[51] considering the short time cycle of democratic decision–making, it is easy to see why the Menem administration might have thought it could afford to be profligate in its reparation measures.

Having provided very high benefits to the unjustly detained, it was almost inevitable that compensation for the disappeared had to be revisited. Oddly, this happened not because of pressure from the families of the disappeared or from human rights NGOs. This was a government initiative from which the potential beneficiaries initially remained at a distance or expressed outright hostility. Indeed, it was this issue that catalysed the break-up of the *Madres de la Plaza de Mayo* (The Mothers of the Plaza de

Mayo) with Hebe Bonafini's faction, the so called *Asociación Madres de la Plaza de Mayo,* arguing that accepting this form of compensation was tantamount to receiving blood money. The logic behind the initiative seemed more bureaucratic than anything else.

Be that as it may, on 7 December 1994, Law 24.411 was enacted, in the early morning, and without much congressional debate. The law authorised economic reparation for the heirs of victims of forced disappearance and assassination by the military, members of security forces or paramilitary groups. The original law contains only some minimal dispositions on which all parties had reached consensus, but left aside substantial issues in order to proceed with its application. Consequently, years later and after intense debate, a second law, Law 24.823,[52] known as the 'patch law' (*ley parche*), was adopted.

One of the issues that made necessary the passing of the 'patch law' was reluctance by family members to accept benefits if they had to be declared heirs, as stipulated by Law 24.411, since this entailed accepting the death of the victims. Law 24.823 solved this problem by specifying that the law granted benefits to the victims of forcible disappearances, but that the benefits would obtain via the victims' 'assignees' (*causa habientes*). This status, granted by a judge, has the same effects as the status of heirs, but does not involve the acceptance of death. (Incidentally, the law allowed partners in de facto marriages to become assignees, as long as the relationship had begun at least two years prior to the disappearance.)

As was the case with prior reparation laws, requests and evidence had to be filed with the Under Secretary of Human Rights at the Ministry of the Interior. Once again, broad criteria of evidence were adopted and decisions could be appealed to the National Administrative Appellate Chamber.

The law provided benefits for people who at the moment of promulgation had forcibly disappeared. This was defined as the deprivation of personal liberty, detention in a clandestine location or deprivation of the right to appear in court, followed by the disappearance of the victim. The law did not establish a time frame during which the disappearance had to have occurred; it only required that the disappearance continued at the time of the law's enactment. Thus, it excluded as beneficiaries those people who had disappeared but who subsequently had re-appeared alive, people whose corpses had been identified, and those people for whom a death certificate existed – categories that could be repaired under the unjustified detention or loss of life provisions of Law 24.043.

The benefits authorised by the law were the monthly salary for personnel at level A of the national civil service multiplied by the coefficient of 100. This amounted to US$224 000. Once again, they were paid in public debt bonds. The alleged rationale for this sum was that it corresponded to what the disappeared or assassinated person would have spent to maintain a spouse, parents and children during ten years of absence.

According to the latest numbers, by mid-2002, 6 483 applications for benefits for disappearance had been filed, of which 4 718 had been granted. Altogether 1 648 applications for deaths had been filed, of which 937 had been granted. So, in total, 5 655 had been approved. At $224 000 per case, this adds up to almost 1.3 billion dollars ($1 266 720,000).

Concluding observations
As has been pointed out, two related characteristics make the Argentinean reparations notable: first the unit selected for the calculation of benefits – not a minimum wage or even the mean national wage, not a unit of expenses that guarantees a minimum quality of life – but rather the highest salary offered by the government.[53] As a consequence, the reparation efforts can be rightly characterised by a second feature, the magnitude of their benefits. Needless to say, only in circumstances of exceptional growth could such benefits be sustained. Otherwise, creative financing mechanisms become necessary and in a sense public debt bonds satisfy this description. The problem, of course, is that public debt bonds eventually also have to be paid. The Argentinean economic crisis has put into question the viability of the whole effort.

Beyond this pragmatic consideration, there is also the question of whether, despite the stated intention to break with the idea of compensation, the Argentinean reparation efforts managed to do so. They might have if compensation is understood simply in terms of labour law. But both the magnitude of the awards and the form of their distribution invited the idea that these amounts represented the government's evaluation of what a life, or a serious injury, was worth. For victims and their families, no award is ever sufficient if this is what it is meant to represent. Although it is true that the failure or success of a reparation programme depends upon many factors, ironically high awards distributed as lump sum payments may be less effective as reparation than more modest awards distributed in the form of a monthly pension – particularly if the reparations are not part of a comprehensive transitional justice policy. In the Argentinean case, it must be remembered, most of the programmes came in the wake of the cessation of attempts to achieve criminal justice and of presidential pardons for the very few perpetrators who had been convicted. The overall combination suggested that the policy was something like 'pardon for perpetrators, money for victims', where each of the measures was itself quite controversial; the pardons were the result of politically divisive decisions and the money for reparation distributed in ways that either encouraged or allowed the wrong associations.

Chile[54]

In an effort to repair the damage done during the 17-year rule of Augusto Pinochet (1973–1990), Chile has established a variety of reparation measures. For various reasons, including internal political considerations that make the government averse to advertising the magnitude of its reparation efforts, Chile is widely believed to have a weak reparation programme. Although no one can be blamed for having this impression, in reality, it is nothing more than an impression. As we will show, in some ways Chile's is one of the most ambitious reparation programmes ever – despite its very real shortcomings.

The first democratically elected president after the dictatorship, Patricio Aylwin, took office in March 1990. Just one month later, he established the Truth and Reconciliation Commission ('CVR' by its acronym in Spanish). In February 1991, the CVR handed its report to the president, who in turn made it public. The Commission established that 2 298 people died for political reasons between 11 September 1973 and 11 March 1990. The Commission could not reach a decision concerning 634 cases. Some of these cases would be decided later by the successor entity, the Corporation for Reparation and Reconciliation ('CRR'). The CVR and the CRR together received complaints about 4 750 deaths, of which they confirmed 3 197 (2 095 executions and other deaths, 1 102 disappearances).

The CVR made recommendations concerning reparation, most of which were eventually implemented by the government. Since the mandate of the CVR empowered it to examine cases of human rights abuse leading to the death of victims, most of the initial reparation efforts concentrated on those cases.[55] Over time, however, the circle of beneficiaries and the sorts of crimes for which victims were eligible for reparation benefits expanded considerably.

In April 1991, two months after President Aylwin made the CVR's report public, he sent Congress a bill creating the CRR and charging it with, among other tasks, distributing reparation to the family members of those who had been executed or had disappeared as a result of the state security forces, and of civilians killed for political reasons by armed opposition groups. The bill, adopted on 8 February 1992 as Law 19.123, distributed the following benefits:

Reparation pensions
The CRR authorised the distribution of a monthly pension to the families of victims, taking as its basic unit the sum of US$537[56] to be divided in this form:

- 40% of the pension (US$215) to spouses;
- 30% (US$161) to the mother of the victim or, in her absence, the father;
- 15% (US$80) to each of the children of the victim up to their 25th birthday, or for life if they are handicapped;[57]
- 15% (US$80) to the common-law father or mother of any children of the victim up to their 25th birthday, or for life if the children are handicapped.[58]

Families also received a once-off bonus equivalent to one year of monthly pensions (roughly US $6,500).

At the beginning of the programme in 1991, it distributed pensions to 5 794 individuals. By 1996 it was benefiting 1 330 spouses, 1 524 mothers or fathers of victims, 1 405 children under 25, 260 common-law spouses, and 89 handicapped children, a total of 4 609 persons. At the end of 2001, 3 210 persons were still receiving benefits. The costs of this programme have been:
- US$708 280 was paid for the initial bonuses for the families;
- US$8 240 905 was paid between 1992 and 2001 in reparation pensions.[59]

Other benefits
The CRR was entrusted with finding the bodies of the disappeared, qualifying the cases left undecided by the CVR and creating a historical archive including the documents of the CVR, among other tasks. Here I will concentrate only on other reparation benefits provided by the CRR to the families of victims of execution, disappearance and political violence, besides the pensions. These include:
- Exemption from obligatory military service for the children of victims;

- Participation in a special health programme, the Programme of Reparation and Integral Health Services (PRAIS), extended not just to the victims' spouses and their children, but to their parents and the victims' siblings;[60]
- Scholarships for elementary education for the children of victims, plus a stipend consisting of 1,24 UTMs per month during the school year;[61]
- Scholarships for university and technical education for the children of victims as long as they are requested before they are 35 years old. Additionally, they receive 1,24 UTMs per month while they complete their education.

In December 1996 1 021 people (158 elementary and high school students, 863 university and technical students) were receiving the educational benefits (scholarships plus stipends). Between 1991 and 2001 the state spent US$1 149 008 on these programmes.

It might be said that these benefits are modest. A surviving mother with children is eligible for a monthly pension of US$485, which is not very high.[62] The sum seems to be dwarfed by the reparation benefits for the victims of the conflict just across Chile's border, in Argentina, as described above. On the other hand, the idea behind Chile's reparation programme never was to attempt to make victims whole, to satisfy the principle of full restitution. In the message that President Aylwin sent Congress with the draft of what would become Law 19.123, which created the CRR and established the benefits just described, he advocated conceiving reparation as 'a set of measures that express the recognition and responsibility which the State can assume in the facts and circumstances that constitute the subject matter of [the CVR] report ... The whole process ought to be oriented towards the recognition of facts in accordance with the truth, the dignification of victims, and the procurement of a better quality of life for the families most directly affected [by political violence]'.[63]

Health care
Even before the CVR came into existence, the 1989 political platform of the *Concertación*, the alliance of opposition parties that won the first election after the dictatorship, had already expressed the intention to provide health care services, in particular mental health care, to victims of human rights abuses.[64] Although the CVR, in its report, did not make recommendations about the specific shape such programmes should take, it

emphasised the importance of providing mental health services to 'victims', a category significantly broader than solely families of victims of execution, disappearances and political violence.

PRAIS, as the programme came to be known, started relatively early in the Chile reparation process (June 1990) and modestly, with operations only in the provincial city of Iquique. A year later, there were PRAIS teams in seven different cities. These teams were made up of eight professionals, a general physician, one or two psychologists, a psychiatrist, a social worker, a paramedic and a secretary. Depending on need, other practitioners were added, such as nurses or physical therapists.

Eventually, the programme became much more ambitious, both in terms of the categories of victims served and the services provided. For the former, the programme has been made available to ex-political prisoners, those who had been fired by the dictatorship from their jobs in the government, universities and other educational institutions or the firms that had been previously intervened by the government of National Unity of Salvador Allende (1970–73), returned political exiles and their families, and everyone whose human rights had been violated (a category which was broadly interpreted to include, for example, peasants who had been barred from participating in land reform programmes for political reasons). The programme also includes the family members of the executed, disappeared and those who were killed as a result of political violence. Importantly, the programme also covers victims of torture.

Since most of the beneficiaries of PRAIS are beneficiaries in other programmes as well, the problem of proof has diminished significantly. In any case an effort has been made not to reproduce humiliating procedures in determining eligibility. Patients do not need to demonstrate that their present condition was caused by their experiences of political violence.

What the programme does is provide, free of charge, participation in the national health system, which is used by 80% of Chileans. Coverage includes both physical and mental health in the form of outpatient visits, emergency and regular hospital procedures. Participating in PRAIS means not only accessing these services, but also gaining priority vis-à-vis the standard customers of the health system. Neither the coverage, nor the priority, is an insignificant benefit. Employed Chileans have to pay 7% of their wages to cover this insurance and have co-payments ranging from

25–75% of the costs of different procedures.[65] Beneficiaries of PRAIS are exempt from both requirements.

At the end of 2002 this programme had 93 272 participants. During the previous year participants made 32 640 mental health visits and 22 363 visits to different physicians. There are no known estimates of the costs of the services provided.

Pensions and retirement benefits
Two separate laws, 19.234 (1993) and 19.582 (1998), attempt to restore pension benefits lost by those who were fired for political reasons from jobs in the government, universities, educational institutions and firms that had been intervened by the Allende government. The Programme for the Recognition of the Politically Dismissed (PREP, by its Spanish acronym) is run by the ministry of the interior. The president is ultimately responsible for the qualification of cases and his decisions cannot be appealed.

Leaving aside all complications, what this programme does is offer modest pensions and/or allow for the recalculation of the pension benefits of those who were fired by adding up to 54 months to the employee's record. This not only increases pension benefits, but permits some employees to retire. In some cases, the programme pays indemnification for unjustified termination of employment as well.

Certain categories of people qualify for benefits automatically: government employees fired during the first three months of the dictatorship (the period of harshest and most arbitrary rule), those who went into exile for reasons of personal safety or under a decree of expulsion, and family members (spouses and children younger than 24 who in Chile generally continue receiving the employee's pension) of the disappeared or executed. Those fired before 9 February 1979 need to show they had been employed for 15 years prior to being fired. Those terminated between 10 February 1979 and 10 March 1990 must show they had been employed for 20 years.

The period for applying for these benefits expired in September 1999. More than 103 000 people applied. By February 2003, 71 404 applicants had received some benefits. Almost 41 000 were receiving a monthly pension of around US$112. More than 15 000 had had their pension benefits increased. The budget for PREP for the four-year period from 1999 to 2002 was close to US$2 million.

Pensions for peasants
The military government not only abruptly ended the land reform programme, in place for more than ten years when it took power, but also
removed the leaders of peasant organisations from land that they had
acquired by virtue of the reform. Furthermore, it imprisoned thousands of
agricultural workers and almost 700 of them (close to 30% of the victims
identified by the CVR) were executed or disappeared. Their surviving
family members were excluded from further land assignations.

Peasant organisations during the first democratic administrations
demanded reparation in the form of a 'land fund' but to no avail. During
the presidency of Eduardo Frei an agreement was reached, in the name of
political expediency, whereby some peasants would receive not land, but
a monthly pension.

Three categories of beneficiaries were established: (a) those who were
65 years and older who would receive US$110 per month, (b) those
between 50 and 64 years who would receive $88 per month and (c) those
younger than 49 who would receive $44 per month. In the first category
1 089 people have received the pension, 1 684 in the second and 226 in
the third, a total of 2 999 beneficiaries in 1999. These pensions are for life
but they are non-transferable and the benefits end with the death of the
recipient. It is estimated that an additional 1 600 individuals could benefit
from the programme (374 applications have been pending since 2000),
but no further action has been taken on this front.

Concluding observations
Contrary to what is commonly held, Chile's reparation efforts have been
quite ambitious. The pensions are somewhat modest, but they reach a significant number of people. Furthermore, the country has established a variety of programmes that distribute benefits to different target groups.
Especially noteworthy is the health care programme, PRAIS, which covers
as full a range of victims of abuse and their families as is imaginable. The fact
that this programme is open to victims of torture also belies the widespread
opinion that this is a group that has been completely ignored in terms of
reparation. PRAIS, with 93 000 plus beneficiaries, is one of the largest medical programmes for the victims of human rights abuse in the world.

It is still true, however, that victims of torture, who may number in the
hundreds of thousands, have received no direct economic compensation.
This lacuna is particularly hard to understand given the simultaneous exist-

ence of programmes that benefit victims of lesser crimes, such as unjustified dismissal from official jobs and land expulsions. In March 2001 the 'Ethical Commission Against Torture' was formed as a pressure group that calls for, among other things, a truth commission to investigate cases of torture in Chile and recommend reparation for its victims. The existence of such a large class of victims of a very serious crime that remains largely unaddressed practically guarantees that Chile will have to revisit the issue of reparation. The fact that the different reparation laws did not impose any conditions in exchange for receiving benefits, such as limitations on initiating civil suits, increases the odds. Up to September 2002, 140 suits against the state had been filed, with mixed results. On occasion, awards easily exceed many times over the benefits of the different reparation programmes. Since September 2002 and the final ruling on Pinochet's incompetence to stand trial, suits against the state have picked up, with 180 new cases initiated since then. A recent decision by the Supreme Court, however (April 2003), has put a damper on future prospects of high awards through civil litigation.

In May 2003 the political party aligned with Pinochet, traditionally opposed to all human rights initiatives, surprised everyone by proposing a complete overhaul of the country's reparation policies, mentioning the possibility of offering a one-time payment of $200 000 to each victim of a serious human rights abuse, including victims of torture. This would constitute a radical departure from the country's reparation practices, and some commentators attribute the proposal to the party's desire to negotiate greater reparation for victims in exchange for the suspension of the more than 300 trials against military officials that have continued despite the amnesty law. It is clear that the last chapter of the reparation story in Chile remains to be written.

Critical variables in the design of reparation programmes

The following series of categories allows for systematic comparison and classification of reparation effort:

Scope
Reparation efforts can have greater or lesser scope according to the total number of beneficiaries they cover. Using this as a classificatory criterion,

and limiting our attention to those who receive monetary compensation for loss of life, the three examples in this paper would fall in this order:[66]
- Germany: in the hundreds of thousands;[67]
- Argentina: 13 455 beneficiaries;[68]
- Chile: close to 6 000 beneficiaries.[69]

It should be obvious that understood in this manner there is no inherent merit in a programme having greater scope. The fact that one programme repairs a larger total number of people than another may simply be indicative of a very large universe of potential beneficiaries. In this respect, it is important to distinguish a programme's scope from its 'completeness'.

Completeness

This refers to the ability of a programme to cover, at the limit, the whole universe of potential beneficiaries. There is no existing programme that satisfies this standard in full, and not only due to the difficulties associated with determining, as a matter of principle, what constitutes the full set of *potential* beneficiaries of a programme of reparation. After all, whatever consensus there is in international law about reparation, it is only emerging, and the boundaries of this obligation remain porous. For instance, there seems to be emerging consensus in international law about the obligation to provide reparation for disappearance and death. But there is much weaker or no consensus on whether the obligation extends to territorial displacement. The situation is still more complicated in practice for, just to mention an example, 'really existing' reparation programmes notoriously under-represent the international law consensus on the obligation to repair cases of torture. More generally, practical problems which limit the reach of programmes in a way that they end up not serving all of those who in fact have been stipulated as potential beneficiaries should be added to the conceptual, principled difficulties mentioned before, and make the possibility of a given programme actually serving *all* potential beneficiaries even slimmer. Be that as it may, obvious exclusions of various sorts impinge on the reparation efforts' completeness. In a context in which distinct forms of violence were perpetrated against multiple groups, excluding from benefits either some of the worst forms of violence or some of the targeted groups automatically diminishes the reparation's completeness. Chile's exclusion of victims of torture from programmes that provide material compensation is a notorious example of how a reparation programme is not as complete as it could be.

Comprehensiveness

A not unrelated category is the effort's comprehensiveness, which relates to the distinct types of crimes or harms it tries to redress. Using this as the ordering criterion, the three cases under analysis here would fall in the following ascending range: Argentina's reparation laws, covering illegal detention (plus death and serious injury during detention) and disappearance, would lie at the lower end of the spectrum. Chile's reparation efforts, which try to redress death and disappearance, political dismissals, exclusions from land reform programmes and, through the provisions of health care, attempt to redress some of the consequences of these crimes and of illegal detention, political exile and torture are still more comprehensive in their coverage of types of crime. Finally, the very broad categories used by the German reparation laws, namely (1) harm to life, body and health, (2) harm to freedom, (3) harm to possessions and assets, and (4) harm to career and economic advancement, make this the most comprehensive programme in our sample. All things considered, comprehensiveness is a desirable characteristic. It is better, both morally and practically, to repair as many categories of crime as feasible.[70]

Complexity

Whereas comprehensiveness relates to the types of crimes reparation efforts seek to redress, complexity refers to the ways in which the efforts attempt to do so. Thus, rather than focusing on the motivating factors, complexity measures the character of the reactions themselves. A reparation programme is more complex if it distributes benefits of more distinct types, and in more distinct ways, than its alternatives. Thus, at one end of the spectrum lie very simple programmes that distribute, say, money exclusively and in one payment, as in Argentina.[71] Monetary compensation, health care services, educational support, business loans and pension reform, as in Germany and Chile, increase the complexity of the reparation efforts still more. In general, since there are certain things that money cannot buy, complexity brings with it the possibility of targeting benefits flexibly so as to respond to victims' needs more closely. All other things being equal, this is a desirable characteristic. Of course, in most cases not all things remain equal. There are some costs to increased complexity that may make it undesirable beyond a certain threshold.

Integrity or coherence

Reparation programmes should, ideally, display what I call integrity or coherence, which can be analysed in two different dimensions, internal and external. *Internal* coherence refers to the relationship between the different types of benefits a reparation programme distributes. Most reparation programmes deliver more than one kind of benefit. These may include symbolic as well as material reparation, and each of these categories may include different measures and be distributed individually or collectively. Obviously, in order to reach the desired aims, it is important that benefits internally support one another.

External coherence expresses the requirement that the reparation efforts be designed in such a way as to bear a close relationship with other transitional mechanisms, that is, minimally, with criminal justice, truth telling and institutional reform. This requirement is both pragmatic and conceptual. The relationship increases the likelihood that each of these mechanisms be perceived as successful (despite the inevitable limitations that accompany each of them) and, more importantly, that the transitional efforts, on the whole, satisfy the expectations of citizens. But beyond this pragmatic advantage, it may be argued that the requirement flows from the relations of complementarity between the different transitional justice mechanisms. Here I can only sketch the basic argument. For example, it is not just that truth-telling in the absence of reparation efforts can be seen by victims as an empty gesture. The opposite holds true as well, since efforts to repair in the absence of truth-telling could be seen by beneficiaries as the state's attempt to buy victims' and their families' silence or acquiescence. The same tight and bi-directional relationship may be observed between reparation and institutional reform, since a democratic reform that is not accompanied by any attempt to dignify citizens that were victimised can hardly be understood. By the same token, reparative benefits in the absence of reforms that diminish the probability of the repetition of violence are nothing more than payments whose utility and, furthermore, legitimacy are questionable. Finally, the same bi-directional relationship links criminal justice and reparation. In this sense, from the standpoint of victims, especially once a possible moment of satisfaction derived from the punishment of perpetrators has passed, the condemnation of a few perpetrators, without any effective effort to redress positively victims, could be easily seen by victims as a form of more or less inconsequential revanchism. Reparation without any effort to achieve criminal justice may seem to them as nothing more than blood money. (These complex relations obtain not only between reparation and each of the other components of transitional justice but rather among all of them. That is, parallel arguments may be constructed to describe the relation between criminal justice and truth-telling and between each of these and institutional reform.)

Needless to say, both internal and external coherence are easier to achieve if reparations are designed as a programme, and if this programme is part of a transitional justice policy. Since this is rarely the case, I have for the most part referred to the cases under review here not as reparation 'programmes' but 'efforts'. Although the Argentinean and Chilean cases were developed in temporal proximity to other transitional mechanisms, and in the case of Chile as part of the political platform of the *Concertación*, none of the cases reviewed here were really designed programmatically, either in an internal sense – i.e. in a way that co-ordinates benefits for distinct crimes in a systematic way – or in an external sense – i.e. so as to co-ordinate the reparation programme with prosecutorial, truth-telling and institutional reform policies.

Finality

By the 'finality' of a reparation programme I refer to whether the programme stipulates that receiving its benefits forecloses other avenues of civil redress or not. Not all reparation efforts are final in this sense. In particular, among our samples, Germany's, and one of Argentina's laws are final, whereas Chile's are not. It is difficult to decide, in the abstract, whether it is desirable, in general, for reparation programmes to be final. On the one hand, finality means that courts have been made inaccessible to citizens. On the other, once a government has made a good faith effort to create an administrative system that facilitates access to benefits, for reasons mentioned above, allowing beneficiaries to initiate civil litigation poses not just the danger of obtaining double benefits for the same harm, but, worse, of destabilising the whole reparation programme. This is likely to take place, for the benefits obtained through the courts typically surpass the benefits offered by a massive programme, which can lead to a significant shift in expectations and to a generalised sense of disappointment with the programme's benefits. Moreover, the shift may be motivated by cases that probably are unrepresentative of the whole universe of victims.[72]

Munificence[73]

This is the characteristic of reparation programmes that relates to the magnitude of their benefits (from the individual beneficiary's perspective).[74] Needless to say, there is no absolutely reliable way to measure the absolute *worth* of the benefits, and the difficulties only increase if one aspires to do a cross-country analysis of their comparative worth. Nevertheless, abstracting from other complications, it is clear that if one simply compares the dollar value of material benefits directly distributed to victims in the three cases reviewed here, the cases would fall in the following *rough* ascending order of munificence: Chile, Germany, and Argentina.[75] As this ordering makes clear, it is obvious that munificence, by itself, is not a criterion of success in reparation. By most standards, US reparation efforts for Japanese-Americans has been more successful than the Argentinean reparation efforts.

Reflections on the notion of justice

The question of what makes a reparation programme successful or not is to a large extent a normative question, for what is at issue is not simply the satisfaction of the de facto expectations of citizens, but rather the satisfaction of their *legitimate* expectations, and this is inseparable from the satisfaction of standards of justice.

The most general aim of a programme of reparation, then, is to do justice to victims. The crucial question, however, is: What does justice require in the area of reparation? Here I can only sketch an argument I have developed at greater length elsewhere.[76] In an isolated case of a human rights violation, complete reparation (*restitutio in integrum*) is an unimpeachable ideal. The ideal of complete reparation consists of restoring the status quo ante or in compensating in proportion to the harm suffered.

As we have seen, however, although international law persists in offering full restitution as *the* standard of justice in reparation, there is no programme that has ever attempted to satisfy this criterion. The underlying reasons are complex, but they include real scarcity of resources that make it unfeasible to satisfy, simultaneously, the claims of victims and of other sectors of society that in fairness also require the attention of the state.

In such a case the state cannot simply ignore the claims of victims by arguing that there are no resources to cover the corresponding costs. This would be tantamount to acknowledging that the state is not in a position to sustain a fair regime. Having said this, I think it is important to keep in mind that full restitution may be unimpeachable as an ideal of reparative justice in the individual case, but that it may offer either little guidance or even outright misguidance in the case of massive and systematic violations. In response to the latter case, the state's responsibility is to design a programme of reparation which might be said to satisfy conditions of justice, even though its benefits are not the same as those that would be determined by a court resolving infrequent or at least isolated suits. But what is involved in 'satisfying conditions of justice'?[77]

Before attempting to sketch an answer, a comment about the intended domain of my argument is called for. A programme of reparation of the sort we are concerned with is typically designed in the context of a transition to democracy. The importance of this observation is that, independently of the precise content that might be given to the notion of justice (and any definition will be essentially contestable), in a period of transition the search for justice will involve some effort to punish perpetrators of the worst human rights abuses; efforts to understand and clarify both the structures of violence and the fate of victims; efforts to reform institutions so as to neutralise the causes which might have contributed to the violence; and, finally, efforts to repair victims. These are four basic elements of transitional justice (their precise balance is to a high degree a contextual matter). Two conclusions follow from the observation that reparation is an element of transitional justice; first, as just one element among others, reparation need not be conceived of as if it carried the burden of restoring justice on its own. As explained in the section on integrity or coherence above, the transitional justice policy ought to be designed in such a way that each of its elements supports the others – and helps to make up for the inevitable deficiencies in each. Second, as is obvious, as part of a transitional justice policy, reparation ought to serve the general aims of a transition however these are specified concretely.

There are three specific aims – whose relationship with justice is quite close – that may be served by reparation programmes. These aims are simultaneously necessary conditions and consequences of justice.

Recognition

One of the main aims of transitional justice is to return (or in some cases to establish for the very first time) the status of citizens to individuals. To the extent that a reparation programme aims to contribute to the achievement of justice, and that recognition is both a condition and a consequence of justice, this links reparation and recognition. In order to recognise individuals as citizens it is necessary to recognise them as individuals first. That is to say, it is necessary to recognise them not only as members of groups (as important as this might be), but also as irreplaceable and unsubstitutable human beings. Citizenship in a constitutional democracy is a condition that individuals grant to one another, each one of whom is conceived as having value on his or her own.

One of the ways of recognising another person, in addition to recognising the peculiarities of his or her form of life (which is to recognise the person's *agency*), is to recognise the ways in which the person is affected by the environment, that is to recognise that the person is not only the subject of his or her own actions but the object of the actions of others. In other words, there is a form of injustice that consists not in the illegitimate deprivation of liberty, but of the absence of the sort of consideration which is owed to whoever is negatively and severely affected by the actions of others. It is difficult to conceive of a regime that aspires to justice that does not involve the mutual recognition of its members. In this sense it can be argued that recognition is a condition of justice.

As if this were not enough, in a constitutional democracy it matters that members recognise one another not only as individuals but also as citizens. To withhold from victims the type of consideration we are talking about makes the mutual attribution of this status impossible. In a democracy, citizenship is a condition that rests upon the equality of rights of those who enjoy such status. And this equality of rights determines that those whose rights have been violated deserve special treatment, treatment that tends towards the re-establishment of the conditions of equality.

In my opinion, a well-designed reparation programme contributes to justice precisely because reparation constitutes a form of recognition. Reparations are the materialisation of the recognition that citizens owe to those whose fundamental rights have been violated. Although there will surely be some contextual factors that establish a link between a quantum of benefits and the achievement of recognition (links that may be easier to see in the breach[78]), arguably successful reparation programmes owe some of their success to the fact that they make beneficiaries and others experience that, despite the impossibility of compensating in proportion to harm, the benefits contribute to the acknowledgement of the victims as *individuals* and, most importantly, as *citizens*. Using the categories introduced in the last section, a programme need not be maximally munificent in order to provide recognition. Completeness – not leaving out whole categories of victims unaddressed – in this sense may be more important. There is no question that independently of how meagre the benefits of the German reparation programme were in comparison to full restitution, beneficiaries and others thought that they successfully transmitted a general social message of recognition.

Civic trust

Another legitimate aim of a programme of reparation as an instrument of justice is the formation or the restoration of trust among citizens. This form of trust is very different from trust among intimates. Civic trust is an attitude that may develop among members of a political community who will remain, nevertheless, strangers to one another.

Like recognition, civic trust is at one and the same time a condition and a consequence of justice. There are many ways to observe how a legal system depends upon the trust of citizens. At the most general level, a legal system functions only by assuming a high level of voluntary compliance with its basic norms. In other words, the majority of social interactions are mediated not by law but, to some degree, by trust among citizens.

Even more important, all legal systems rest upon not only the trust that citizens may have in one another, but the trust that they have in the system itself. To begin with, in the absence of total(itarian) surveillance, the criminal justice system relies on the willingness of citizens to report the crimes of which they are either witnesses or victims.

On the other hand, a legal system not only rests upon the trust that citizens have in one another and in the system itself, but rather, if it functions correctly, the system catalyses both types of trust. To the extent that the system helps to stabilise expectations and therefore to diminish the *risks* of trusting others, it contributes to the generation of trust among citizens. To the extent that the institutions are reliable they will give citizens reasons to trust them with the resolution of their conflicts.

The fundamental point is to clarify the relationship between reparation and civic trust. Again, for victims, reparation constitutes a manifestation of the seriousness of the state and of their fellow citizens in their efforts to re-establish relations of equality and respect. In the absence of reparation, victims will always have reasons to suspect that even if the other transitional mechanisms are applied with some degree of sincerity, the 'new' democratic society is one that is being constructed on their shoulders, ignoring their justified claims. Reparation, in summary, can be seen as a method to achieve one of the aims of a just state, namely inclusiveness, in the sense that all citizens are equal participants in a common political project. However, given the holistic nature of transitional justice, this also means that no matter how munificent a reparation programme may be, if it gives beneficiaries and others reasons to think that the benefits are an attempt to buy acquiescence with a system that remains fundamentally unfair (a problem which may be described in terms of the absence of 'external coherence'), rather than promoting mutual trust and trust in institutions, a reparation programme may do just the opposite, as some have argued happened in Argentina.

Solidarity

Finally, another legitimate aim of a programme of reparation, considered once again as one of the forms of promoting justice, is the strengthening or the generation of social solidarity, which – like recognition and civic trust – is also a condition and a consequence of justice.

Like civil trust, solidarity also comes in different types and degrees. Social solidarity is the type of empathy characteristic of those who have the disposition and the willingness to put themselves in the place of others. That this attitude is a condition of justice may be seen in the following way: an impartial perspective, an indispensable requisite of justice, is not achievable unless the person who judges is prepared to assume the place of the contesting parties. Moreover, in a democratic system, which distinguishes legitimacy from mere balances of power, the only way to assure that the legitimacy of a law has been attained is by making sure that the law incorporates the interests of all who are affected by it. And this implies having an interest in the interests of others. This is, precisely, what constitutes social solidarity.

Reparation can be seen as an expression of this type of interest and, at the same time, as generators of this form of solidarity. In societies divided and stratified by the differences between the urban and the rural, by ethnic, cultural, class and gender factors, reparation manifests the interest of the traditionally most advantaged in the interests of the least favoured. Although it cannot be assumed that the former will immediately support a reparation programme, this is a point at which the relations between reparation and other transitional mechanisms, especially truth-telling, may play an important role since historical clarification can awaken empathy with victims. On the other hand, to the extent that victims feel that a new 'social contract' in which their dignity and their interests are amply recognised is being offered, they will have reasons to take an interest in common interests, contributing in this way to strengthening the basis of a just society.

Conclusion

The first section of this essay sketched the reparation efforts undertaken by three different countries in response to a variety of human rights violations. The second section attempted to establish some of the categories around which reparation programmes may be classified. In addition to its descriptive nature, the analysis identifies potentially desirable features. The final section, although primarily normative in character, draws on empirical fact to reconstruct aims that reparation programmes arguably serve. One of the fundamental motivations for engaging in this normative-reconstructive argument is to respond to a huge normative gap in this field. Recognising that the ideal of full restitution has never been satisfied by an existing programme and that in some cases such an ideal may thwart the success of feasible reparation programmes makes it imperative to attempt to articulate criteria of fairness. This section provides a sketch of one such attempt.

Taking the promotion of recognition, civic trust and social solidarity as the main goal of a reparation programme gives it a beneficial forward-looking character. One of the main sources of dissatisfaction with most reparation awards is the fact that beneficiaries frequently consider them insufficient compensation. In this, they are usually correct, independently of the programme's munificence, for reasons that have to do with the difficulty – and ultimately the impossibility – of quantifying great harm; there is no amount of money that can make up for the loss of a parent, a child, a spouse. There is no amount of money that can adequately compensate for the nightmare and the trauma of torture. In my view, reparation programmes, not least because of the financial difficulties involved in cases of massive numbers of claimants, should not even try, and should always avoid using the vocabulary of proportional compensation. There should never be anything in a reparation programme that invites either their designers or their beneficiaries to interpret them as an effort to put a price on the life of victims or on the experiences of horror. Rather, they should be interpreted as making a contribution to the quality of life of survivors. Thinking about reparation in terms of recognition and of the promotion of civic trust and social solidarity invites the assumption of this forward-looking perspective.

Another advantage of taking these as the goals of the programme is that it allows for a healthy form of contextualism: for instance, what in a given society is sufficient to provide adequate recognition to victims is largely a matter of context. What citizens in one country expect by way of recognition may differ widely from what the potential beneficiaries in different countries may expect. And satisfying those different expectations, despite their differences, is obviously not a bad thing.

Reparation programmes, then, may be said to make a contribution to the achievement of a modest and imperfect form of justice by virtue of their fostering the quality of life of survivors, the achievement of recognition, the formation of civic trust and the development of social solidarity. None of this is tantamount to the re-establishment of the status quo ante or constitutes compensation in proportion to the harm suffered. And yet this is not merely a consolation but the grounds upon which fair civic relations may be established perhaps for the first time in countries emerging from conflict or authoritarian rule.

Notes

My gratitude to Andrea Armstrong and Anthony Triolo who read earlier versions of this paper.

1   This project will be published under the title *Repairing the Past*. It will include 12 case studies, basic documents and systematic papers.
2   I am very grateful to Anthony Triolo for tireless assistance with the overall project.
3   However, the move is not through derivation. There is no naturalistic fallacy here, no attempt to derive an 'ought' from an 'is'. The move is rather reconstructive; it constitutes an effort to reconstruct the aims that actual reparation programmes may be said to pursue. More on this below.
4   This section is based on a paper entitled 'German Reparation to Victims of the Holocaust', prepared by Ariel Colonomos, and finished by ICTJ staff including Andrea Armstrong, Pablo de Greiff and Anthony Triolo. I am grateful to Andrea Armstrong for assistance in elaborating this summary.
5   German Consulate, New York, 'Leistungen der öffentlichen Hand auf dem Gebiet der Wiedergutmachung: Stand 31.Dezember 2001', received via fax. Figures were calculated using December 2001 exchange rates of 1 Euro=.8813 USD.

6   The Conference on Jewish Material Claims Against Germany, the 'Claims Conference', is an umbrella organisation of 51 organisations formed in 1951 to represent the needs of survivors of the Holocaust and their survivors. For more information about the organisation, see www.claimscon.org

7   Ronald Zweig, *German Reparation and the Jewish World* (London, UK: Frank Cass Publishers, 2001), 112.

8   *Bündesergänzungs-gesetz zur Entschädigung für Opfer der national-sozialistischen Verfolgung,* 21 September 1953.

9   *Bündesentschädigungsgesetz* (BEG), 29 June 1956.

10 *Bündesentschädigungsgesetz Schlussgesetz,* 18 September 1965.

11 For example, it is difficult to prove that the suicide of a relative was due to official policy, even though official policy is likely to have created the context that made life unbearable.

12 *Bündesergänzungs-gesetz zur Entschädigung, 1953, Vierter Abschnitt, Zweiter Titel §85.*

13 Civil servants were divided into four earning categories (junior, middle-level, upper-level, senior). §14.9

14 Schwerin points out that refugees and stateless people were only able to claim compensation for loss of life if it fulfilled the criteria in the 1953 law, while other eligible claimants were allowed to claim compensation for loss of life either under §15 in the 1953 law (wrongful death as a result of persecution) or §41 (death as a result of injury to body or health). Kurt Schwerin, 'German Compensation for Victims of Nazi Persecution', in *Transitional Justice,* Volume II, ed. Neil Kritz (Washington, DC: USIP, 1995), 51.

15 See German Consulate New York, 2001.

16 In §15.1 of the 1953 law, 'insignificant applies to those harms that diminished neither the spiritual nor physical productivity of the persecuted and are not anticipated to do so'.

17 Christian Pross, *Paying for the Past* (Baltimore, MD: Johns Hopkins University Press, 1998), 72.

18 The benefits to compensate harm to life or health were based on the average income of the persecuted, either three years *before their death* or three years before persecution *against them* began. Claimants may have experienced a reduction in income prior to these two events because of more general occurrences (xenophobia, etc.). Thus, the basis for benefit calculations is most likely lower than if the three-year average of income *prior to the rise of the Nazi regime* had been used. (1956 BEG, §31, 40, 41.)

19 See German Consulate New York, 2001.

20 United States Court for the Eastern District of New York, Special Master's Proposal, In Re Holocaust Victim Assets Litigation (Swiss Banks), 11 September 2000. Accessed online: http://www.nyed.uscourts.gov/pub/rulings/cv/1996/665994.pdf

21 See German Consulate New York, 2001.

22 Assets, or possessions, were not defined within the compensation laws of 1953, 1956 or 1965. German case law has interpreted 'assets' (as distinct from property) as including 'inventions, patents, goodwill, business connections, and reversionary interests'. See United States Court for the Eastern District of New York, 2000, p.E-26.

23 The Reich Flight Tax or *Reichfluectsteuer* was a tax for those seeking to emigrate from Germany.

24 United States Court for the Eastern District of New York, 2000, p.E-26.

25 See German Consulate New York, 2001.

26 United States District Court, 2000, p.E-27. Art 1, 69, 70, 71.

27 This law, the 'Law to Settle Reparation for Members of the Public Service' (*Gesetz zur Regelung der Wiedergutmachung für Angehörige des Öffentlichen Dienstes vom 11 Mai 1951*), is described by Pross as 'far more generous' than for non-civil servants (i.e. no deadlines to fulfil). Also known as the '131' Law, after Article 131 of the Basic Law of Germany (the constitution), this law was passed before any nationwide law on reparation to Jewish victims of the Nazi regime. Pross, *Paying for the Past,* 21–22, 228. Kurt Schwerin notes that former civil servants, including former officers, judges, teachers, and professors, were either reinstated to their 'position, salary, or pension group which the claimant would have reached had the persecution not taken place'. Schwerin, 'German Compensation', 60.

28 In the 1953 law, claimants had to prove that they were no longer capable of their earlier occupation. In the 1956 law, they only had to show that at the time of application, the claimant was not working enough for an adequate standard of living and that attaining such a standard of living was not to be expected. (§33, 1953 and §82, 1956.)

29 United States District Court, p.E-27.

30 See German Consulate New York, 2001.

31 Artikel V, BEG Schlussgesetz. For individual suffering beyond six months of detainment or an 80% reduction in earning capacity, the 1965 law includes provisions for doubling, tripling, etc. the minimum award based on years of incarceration, etc.

32 Including those 'who were thrown into workhouses after 1933 and concentration camps after 1938, following many major campaigns against the so called "work-shy, prostitutes, vagabonds, and beggars"'. They were denied compensation under BEG since they did not fulfil the requirement of having suffered persecution 'on the grounds of race, religion, or political convictions'. See Pross, *Paying for the Past,* 53.

33 For example, as was seen above, the Final Law gave benefits to forced labourers only to the extent that they lived in 'jail-like' conditions. But this did not describe the living conditions of all forced labourers, nor did it compensate them for their work, whether in concentration camps or for private German companies. This exclusion led to the reopening of the reparation issue in Germany starting in the late eighties and running through the mid-nineties, to the conclusion of the now famous slave and forced labour reparation negotiated, at least in part, to avoid litigation against German companies in the US. This new programme not only recognised forced and slave labour, but was also open to some of those who had been excluded by the Final Law's residency requirements. See the study by John Authers in *Repairing the Past.*

34 $37.5 billion as of December 2001 and two million awards out of a total of 4 384 138 applications by December 1987; see German Consulate New York, 2001.

35 See María José Guembe, 'Economic Reparation for Grave Human Rights Abuses. The Argentine Experience', in *Repairing the Past.*

36 Alfonsín's term began on 10 December 1983. The executive decree establishing CONADEP (national executive authority decree No.157) was issued on 15 December 1983.

37 In the very same decree the government declared the state of siege and ordered the 'elimination of subversion' in Argentina, paving the way for state terrorism in the

country. The fact that systematic violence against the opposition was used during the presidency of Perón's widow generated some difficulties for Peronistas when it came to decide which crimes would be redressed. Some Peronistas opposed compensating crimes committed before the military coup of March 1976.

38 CONADEP, *Nunca Más* 2a. edición (Buenos Aires: Editorial Eudeba, 1984), 477.

39 Law 23.053 (22 February 1984); Law 23.117 (30 September 1984); Law 23.238 (10 September 1985); 23.278 (September 1985); Law 23.523 (June 1988).

40 Later on, the benefit for non-handicapped children was extended until they turned 25 or finished university education.

41 The national executive authority decided by decree to prosecute the members of the first three military *juntas*. The *Cámara Federal en lo Criminal y Correccional* of the federal capital passed judgement on 9 December 1985, convicting five *junta* leaders of homicide, illegal deprivation of liberty and torture, among other crimes. These crimes, the court held, were the manifestation of a concerted policy of terror, the main tool used by the *juntas* to eliminate subversion. Four of the *comandantes* were acquitted because of insufficient or inconclusive evidence against them.

42 The 'punto' or final law, Law 23.492 (1986), stipulated that any new charges against the military had to be filed by February 1987, not long after the enactment of the law and with the January court recess in between. The government expected that courts would not have time to conduct investigations. However, seven federal courts suspended their recess, and before the deadline 300 high-ranking officers had been indicted. The 'obediencia debida' or due obedience law, Law 23.521 (1987), limited the liability of chief, junior, or non-commissioned officers, soldiers of the armed forces, or police and penitentiary personnel, as long as it could be established that they acted in obedience to the authorities above them. See Carlos H. Acuña and Catalina Smulovitz, 'Guarding the Guardians in Argentina', in *Transitional Justice and the Rule of Law in New Democracies*, ed. A. James McAdams (Notre Dame: University of Notre Dame Press, 1997), 93–122. Acuña and Smulovitz argue that these laws were not the result of pressure stemming from the coup attempts, but were the product of agreements between the Alfonsín administration and the military which predated the military insurrections.

43 Alfonsín's term legally lasted until 10 December 1989.

44 Decrees No. 1,002; 1,003; 1,004; and 1,005 published in the Official Bulletin on 10 October 1989, and decrees No. 2,741 to 2,746 of 29 December 1990.

45 According to article 4037 of the Civil Code, the statute of limitation's term for civil actions regarding non-contractual responsibilities is two years. The court was not swayed by plaintiffs' arguments to the effect that the statute of limitation's term should be counted starting on 10 December 1983, the date of the return of democracy, since prior to that date the state did not offer sufficient safeguards for anyone to initiate a civil suit, nor were the results of the *juntas* trial available, which established state responsibility for a policy of terror. The court upheld that the term of the statute of limitations was to be counted from the day the person was freed.

46 The first Argentinean case was presented on 15 February 1989, before the Supreme Court passed judgement. Other cases were presented afterwards.

47 N.b. the absence of a starting date for the period of violence that would receive compensation.

48 Adopted on 27 November 1991.
49 In fact, those who had already received indemnification as the result of judicial sentence for the same facts were barred by the law from requesting benefits. Decree 1313/94 of 1 August 1994 would change this as well, further extending the class of beneficiaries of the law. This decree made benefits available to those who through judicial action had received awards, but lower than those offered by Decree 70/91 or Law 24.043. This category of claimants could apply for benefits and receive the difference.
50 The law followed Decree 70/91 in taking a thirtieth of the monthly wages of the highest-level personnel in the civil service as the basic unit to calculate benefits. But, in between the issuance of the decree, the enactment of the law and, most importantly, the beginning of payments, which took place only in 1994 (i.e., three years after the decree was issued), the civil service was reorganised (through Decree 993/91), and the salaries of the highest level personnel increased significantly. See resolution 352/94 from the Ministry of Economy and Pubic Works March 1994.
51 The bonds had the following characteristics in addition to their 16-year maturity: they had a grace period of 72 months, during which interest (at the average rate published by the Central Bank) would be capitalised. After these five years, 120 monthly payments would be made, the first 119 equivalent to 0.84% and the last to 0.04% of the amount issued plus the interest capitalised during the grace period. The first instalment then was paid in January 2001, just when the economic crisis was hitting hard.
52 Adopted on 7 May 1997.
53 The German reparation laws, as seen above, also used the civil service pay and benefit scales, but in a completely different way; the full range of the scales was used, not just the upper limit. Indeed, former civil servants received better compensation than other victims did.
54 See the very thorough paper by Elizabeth Lira, 'The Policies of Reparation for Human Rights Violations in Chile 1990–2002', in *Repairing the Past*.
55 CVR Mandate.
56 Expressed in 1996 dollars.
57 Since this sum ($80) is given per child, the total pension per family could exceed the $537 unit.
58 The existence of a common-law partner and children could also make the total pension exceed the basic measurement unit of $537.
59 The yearly breakdown for these pensions during the four years of existence of the CRR was: US$2 582 370 in 1992; $1 711 327 in 1993; $1 719 415 in 1994, and $1 458 263 in 1995.
60 This programme will be described in some detail below.
61 A UTM is a 'monthly tributary unit' which fluctuates in value. In April 2003 a UTM was equivalent to somewhere between US $42 and $45. Thus the stipend ranged from $52 to $55 per child per month.
62 This is the total of the pensions for her and her two children ($215 plus $160) and the educational stipends ($110).
63 *Diputados* (sesión 41a, 3 abril 1991), p. 4865.
64 Different Chilean groups had been providing mental health services to victims from

early on during the dictatorship; Vicaría de la Solidaridad since 1975, Fasic since 1977, Pidee since 1979 and Codepu since 1980. Two groups specialising in mental health, Cintras (International Center for the Treatment of Stress) and Ilas (Latin American Institute of Mental Health and Human Rights), were established in 1985 and 1988 respectively. Members of these different groups participated in drafting the platform of the Concertación, and later on advised the CVR on its mental health recommendations.

65 The 7% fee entitles regular beneficiaries of the system to choose their physicians. The co-payments are means-tested progressively, that is, higher income regular beneficiaries pay a higher percentage of the costs of treatment.

66 The numbers of beneficiaries need not correspond to the number of victims of human rights abuses.

67 As was reported above, the German individual compensation efforts have benefited more than two million people. But this figure includes recipients of the different benefits reviewed above, and here I am concentrating on monetary benefits for loss of life alone. Germany had spent $3,5 billion as of December 2001 on loss of life compensation. But I have no precise figures on the number of beneficiaries.

68 This figure includes 7 800 beneficiaries under Law 24.043 (illegal detention, death and grave injury) and 5 655 under Law 24.411 (disappearance and death). It is therefore an upper limit, for Law 24.043 gave benefits for cases other than loss of life.

69 This figure includes only the beneficiaries of the pension programme started in 1991 by the CRR and represents the programme's highest number, at its inception, since some of the benefits terminated when children of the victims turned 25 or finished university education. By the end of 2001, as reported, the number of beneficiaries had declined to 3 210. The number, therefore, does not include the many thousands of beneficiaries of the health programme or of pensions for the politically dismissed, etc.

70 While the moral advantages may be obvious, the pragmatic advantages may not be so clear, so a few words about this may be in order; leaving important categories of victims unaddressed virtually guarantees that the issue of reparation will continue to be on the political agenda, which means it will remain available as the target of legislative or bureaucratic give and take. This may undermine the stability and reliability of reparation agreements, as the Chilean case exemplifies.

71 This, of course, simplifies reality. It abstracts from the complexities introduced by the fact that the payments were made in bonds, and from other features of the general context like the vagaries of the prosecutorial efforts, the significant amount of information about the past that became available through 'truth trials' and other means and from institutional reforms that were taking place in Argentina as the reparation laws were being enacted and implemented.

72 Civil litigation thus raises the risk of entrenching prevalent social biases. Wealthier, more educated, more urban victims usually have a higher chance of successfully pursuing reparation litigation in civil courts than poorer, less educated, more rural individuals, who may also happen to belong to less favoured ethnic, racial or religious groups.

73 I have chosen this old-fashioned term because I do not want to talk about the 'generosity' of reparation programmes. I see reparation as a matter of right, not generosity. Nevertheless, it is clear that even if one considers this an issue of right, there is a large range of options concerning what it takes to satisfy that right.

74 The caveat is important, for in the aggregate programmes may end up distributing large amounts of money if the number of victims is significant – each victim, of course, receiving a small amount.

75 I emphasise the roughness of the ordering. Part of it is due to the fact that one of the programmes gave benefits in a lump sum (Argentina) and the other two in the form of pensions (Chile and Germany). Establishing the total value of a pension is always a difficult exercise.

76 See my 'Justice and Reparation' (forthcoming).

77 Mere disparities in the awards distributed by courts and by mass programmes do not necessarily manifest that the latter are unfair. In this sense, reparation programmes ought not to be considered simply as second best alternatives to judicial procedures. Reparation programmes at their best are administrative procedures that obviate some of the difficulties and costs associated with litigation. These include long delays, high costs, the need to gather evidence that might withstand close scrutiny (which in some cases may be simply unavailable), the pain associated with cross examination and with reliving sorrowful events, and, finally, the risk of a contrary decision which may prove to be devastating, adding insult to injury. A well-designed reparation programme may distribute awards which are lower in absolute terms, but comparatively higher than those granted by courts, especially if the comparison factors in the short delays, low costs, relaxed standards of evidence, non-adversarial procedures and virtual certainty that accompanies the administrative nature of a reparation programme.

78 This is likely to involve complicated comparative judgements. Whether a given quantum of benefits is appropriate or not is a function of, among other things, the relative socio-economic standing of victims, their perception of the government's efforts on their behalf and other government expenditures at the time.

20

On Monuments, Memorials and Memory:
Some Precedent Towards a South African Option

Neville Dubow

Nothing beside remains. Round the decay
Of that colossal wreck, boundless and bare
The lone and level sands stretch far away.
— from Shelley's 'Ozymandias'

1

The chain around the neck of the statue tightens as the crane on the military vehicle takes up the slack. The chain tautens. The statue yields. It describes a 90 degree arc as it falls forward. Its outstretched exhortatory arm now points to the ground as the body comes to a temporary horizontal arrest. It is still attached at the ankles to its pedestal. The chain tightens further as the vehicle pulls back. The body literally deconstructs — as if the tubes of a telescope have been pulled beyond their natural extension and, sliding apart, weighed by the outstretched arm, it bounces on the ground. All that is left on the high pedestal are the twisted reinforcing rods protruding through their boots. The head of the statue is hammered off its body by the onlookers, citizens all, and rolled away in triumph and derision.

Millions of television watchers around the world will have no difficulty in placing this sequence in time and in place: April 2003, Baghdad. We had watched a pivotal moment in the fall of Saddam Hussein. Perhaps the poets really are the unacknowleged legislators, and Shelley among the most prescient.

We had witnessed an Ozymandias moment.

It was a sequence that would be repeated in the media, time and time again. No one, whatever their views on the Iraq war, could doubt that the public monument, as symbol of tyranny, has still the power to arouse strong emotion. The iconoclastic impulse is testimony to the fact that falling icons have more grip on our memory than standing ones.

2

'Away with monuments', railed Nietzsche, contemptuously dismissing any version of history cast in stone (or bronze, for that matter).[1] But this does not mean that we cannot learn from historical precedent. Away with monuments does not mean away with memory. As Andreas Huyssen continues to remind us:

> *Remembrance as a vital human activity shapes our links to the past, and the ways we remember define us in the present. As individuals and societies, we need the past to construct and anchor our identities and to nurture a vision of the future. As readers of Freud and Nietzsche, however, we know how slippery and unreliable personal memory can be, always affected by forgetting and denial, repression and trauma, and, more often than not, serving the need to rationalise and to maintain power.*

> *But a society's collective memory is no less contingent, no less unstable, its shape by no means permanent and always subject to subtle and not so subtle reconstruction.*[2]

This reconstruction of memory finds expression in many ways: in conventional terms we expect to find it in the form of built structures – monuments, memorials and public statuary. What is the difference between a monument and a memorial?

Conventional wisdom tends to confine the concept of monument to a static object, a memorialising *thing*; whereas memorial implies a process by which memory is kept alive. Thus a standard definition, such as that given in the *Shorter Oxford English Dictionary*, gives *monument* as 'a structure intended to commemorate'.

Memorial is given as 'a sign, a token of remembrance'.

Memorials can in fact take forms other than those which are architecturally structured: there are memorial lectures and memorial publications.

There may even be art interventions that perform a memorial function in a way that might be called 'Counter-monuments'. I will describe a notable example of this later.

It is something of a cynical truism that history's victors erect monuments to their triumphs and that history's victims might have to await memorials to their suffering. However true this might be, it is nevertheless a limited view. In fact the two terms have come to be used almost interchangeably. Think of this in a local context. We have a *Voortrekker Monument* and a *Taal Monument:* this is consistent with the note of triumphalism which 'monument' often implies. But to be absolutely consistent, we should refer to that monument to Imperial vision, that monumental grouping of stairway, statuary and classical temple on the slopes of the mountain, as the Rhodes *Monument*. But we don't. We know it as the Rhodes *Memorial*. Conversely the focal building in Grahamstown that commemorates the cultural achievements of the descendants of the 1820 Settlers is referred to as the *Monument* and not the Memorial: if it is a monument to anything, it is to the survival of the English language.

Thus the interchangeabilty of usages of memorial and monument will always occur and on occasion may allow for simultaneity. Take the case of Robben Island, which in a post-apartheid era functions as a national and indeed international icon. It can be seen both as a memorial to the struggle for a democratic dispensation as well as a monument to the futility of trying to incarcerate an idea. As to its iconicity one only has to look to the burgeoning picture postcard industry. Whereas Table Mountain has traditionally been photographed from Robben Island, the current popular and commercially successful view foregrounds the Island against the back-drop of the mountain.[3]

For my part I prefer the term 'monument' when its usage is celebratory or designating a historical marker (as in historical monument); and 'memorial' for those structures and institutions whose essence is more reflective and contemplative. Monuments outwardly proclaim something. Memorials invite introspection and interpretation. Monuments tend to foreclose on further thought. The prime function of the memorial or the provocative counter-monument is precisely the opposite – to prod memory and stimulate it as an active process.

Perhaps modern sensibility can embrace the concept of memorial more readily than it can that of monument. 'What is the use to modern man of this monumental contemplation of the past?' asked Nietzsche, for whom monumental was a 'disdainful epithet for any version of history calling itself permanent and everlasting, a petrified history that buried the living'.[4]

This concept of a petrified history burying the living is a critical factor in considering the challenges we have to face in memorialising our own past. No one would argue for a 'petrified history'. There is, however, every reason for a continued examination of the past – not to monumentalise or bury it, but to remember it and gain insight from it.

As we enter the new millennium there is a continued, even a heightened interest in the defining event of the 20th century's ignominy. We know it as the Holocaust. It is the fault line that runs through our claim to civilised behaviour, the long moment of calculated genocide that continues to haunt our collective memory.

How then do we find a language to do justice to this? My recent research has taken me to Berlin, a city in the process of reinventing itself in which memory and memorials have become ideologically contested ground. There are lessons that we can learn here. I want to present two case studies. The first is the official state-sponsored Holocaust memorial in central Berlin, south of the Brandenburg gate, designated as the Memorial to the Murdered Jews of Europe.

3

The Berlin Holocaust Memorial

The Memorial was the subject of two competitions, the first, held in 1994/1995, was abortive. But it generated vast controversy and intensive public debate. The second, in 1997, run as a limited competition, was no less controversial, but at least yielded a result. The winning entry was a joint submission by Peter Eisenman, a New York-based architect and theorist, and Richard Serra, a celebrated American sculptor.

The Eisenman/Serra proposal visualised a vast uneven undulating surface on which is placed a grid of vertical, rectangularly shaped shafts or stelae (the German term *Stelenwald* – literally a forest of columns – is apt). These columns were to be placed 92 cm apart making it uncomfortable for more than one person to pass – thus inducing a feeling of isolation and alienation for those passing through.

The scale of these columns, initially set at 6 metres high, was later to be reduced to a maximum of 4 metres. No text or contextualising information was envisaged: no names – not on the columns nor anywhere else.

The scheme met with a mixed reception, much of it highly critical – it was seen as being too vast, too impersonal, too abstract, too alienating, its meaning too elusive. The latter, of course, was exactly what Eisenman intended – he wanted to have its meaning open-ended, a rift in the fabric of the city, an unimaginable chasm that would be consistent with the rupture in the city's history.

The *Bundestag,* which had earlier been negative about the *Stelenwald,* finally agreed to take responsibility for it, but in the light of continuing criticism, Chancellor Helmut Kohl asked for modifications to the Eisenman/Serra proposal. Eisenman was asked to present a scaled-down version of the original, with a clearly defined border of trees. He agreed to make modifications, but Serra, as co-author, was not happy about this. In June 1998 Serra bowed out of the partnership, citing personal reasons and declining to elaborate. It appears that Eisenman, as architect, was accustomed to compromising with his client's wishes. Serra, as artist, was not.

The results of the competition as a whole, including the winning scheme, were greeted with mostly negative reactions, ranging from indifference to hostility. As a typical example, the *London Independent* of 12 March 1998 carried a report under a heading that played (with astonishing insensitivity) on the theme of the Final Solution – 'Germans seek Atonement, but Final Solution eludes them'.

The Berlin mayor was quoted as saying that the scheme had 'more to say about the inner conflicts of today's generation in relation to that of their parents than about Nazi crimes'.

Berlin's Jewry was reported as unable to decide 'whether they should be flattered or repelled by such grandiose schemes, not dissimilar in scale from that of the Third Reich'. The report ended 'Whether the Jews were able to live without it was never in doubt. The real question is: can the Germans?'

In July 1998, Eisenman, who had agreed to Kohl's request for a compromise, presented his modified scheme in which he scaled down the height of the columns as well as reducing their number from 4 000 to 2 900. Most significantly, the proportions of the stelae were changed to a horizontal rather than a vertical emphasis. They now read more like tombs than stelae. No supporting text was proposed.

In my view this was a disastrous compromise. As an abstract statement it was not strong enough to invite contemplation without contextualisation. As a symbolic statement its evocation of the tomb association was too literal.

After all the debate, the agonising, the two competitions, one would have liked the final outcome to have produced more than a field of pillars metamorphosed into tombs 'waiting for references to be projected onto them by visitors'. And so the debate continued. Of the many questions asked, the most pertinent was: how can this memorial help in understanding the lessons of the Holocaust? It remains unanswered.[5]

The politics of memory
With the critics of the Eisenman proposal still unconvinced, the controversy now took an overtly political direction. In the summer of 1998. Helmut Kohl, publically identified with the Memorial, faced a strong challenge from Gerhard Schröder, leader of the Social Democrats. In September 1998 Schröder won the elections and entered into a coalition with the Green Party who were in favour of the Memorial.

Schröder had appointed as Minister of Culture the writer and publisher Michael Naumann, who took on the role of the City's cultural spokesman as well as heading the Memorial project development. Naumann insisted on a contextualising centre for information. He asked for a revision to the scheme. In effect he proposed a museum – a centre for historical instruction – as part of the memorial (much to the dismay of other Berlin centres for research and warnings from intellectuals of the calibre of Jurgen Habermas that an information centre could be abused by a subsequent regime to promote its own version of the truth). Nonetheless the idea of an information centre was incorporated as a series of underground spaces but reservations about the proposal persisted. The general feeling remained that the legislators in the Bundestag – those driving the scheme – were themselves driven less by conviction about proceeding with the project and more by a fear of what organs of opinion like the *New York Times* would say if they did not proceed.

On 20 April 1999 (co-incidentally, Hitler's birthday), the matter entered a final series of debates in the *Bundestag* with both proponents and opponents of the scheme allowed to make their cases. After heated argument the following resolution was reached on 25 June 1999. Eisenman's modified scheme was voted in, by 314 to 209 with 14 abstentions. The resolutions read:
1. The Federal Republic of Germany will erect in Berlin a Memorial for the Murdered Jews of Europe on the site of the former Ministerial Gardens in the middle of Berlin.

2. The design of Peter Eisenman's field of pillars will be realised, as well as a small place of information that will detail the fate of the victims and the authentic sites of destruction.
3. A public foundation will be established to oversee the completion of the memorial. The new target date for the work to commence is to be the year 2000.

Of course, this did not happen. The excavations for the planned archive and research centre ran into complications caused by the underground bunker systems from the Nazi period. There is no end, it would seem, to the ironies of the politics of memory.

4

I revisited Berlin in 2002 after a three year absence. I was curious to see how much progress had been made on the official state memorial. The answer, I found, was that progress was very slow – for various reasons, the chief of which appears to be the cumbersome workings of the bureaucratic machinery responsible for getting the project under way, as well as complications arising out of the fact that underground accomodation for the documentation centre was entangled with the remains of wartime bunkers.

The site was deserted apart from some trial blocks that had been put into place to establish scale. I felt that my fears about the compromise on the proportion of the blocks had been well founded. They indeed resembled nothing so much as monumental tombstones. There have been disagreements about their surface finish. Eisenman wanted them faced in slate. The authorities wanted a less costly finish.

The controversy goes on. I found myself wondering about the alternatives to a huge, static, centralised memorial.

What about lower profile site specific markers that attested to what had happened to Berlin's Jews in the Nazi period – signposts to what had happened, that pointed to the Where and the When, designed to cause people to ask themselves the aching question – Why?

Counter-monument
I wanted to investigate other examples of what I had earlier termed 'counter-monuments'. By this I mean unconventional interventions that do not operate on a monumental scale and do not abide by conventional

notions of what a monument or memorial should be, but jab at memory in ways that might be seen as subversive. I found what I was looking for by taking an S bahn ride westwards to the Bavarian quarter of Berlin – to Bayerischer Platz, a site where memory has been prodded and stirred in a memorable way. Bayerischer Platz in the Schoneberg district of Berlin has undergone several demographic changes. Before the war it had become a solid middle class area, home to a professional class which included many Jews. At various times the quarter was home to the likes of Hanna Arendt and Albert Einstein.

It is deceptively tranquil now when you walk through the square with its tree-lined streets that radiate out from it. When you look at its restored modestly genteel 19th century buildings you would not immediately recognise anything in the way of a Holocaust memorial.

Yet there is something to be seen. An information sign in the form of a map in the central square close to the station might give you a clue. It indicates diagrammatically that there are a series of art interventions in the form of signs to be found in the precinct. This map gives the location of some 80 works which form a collection under the rubric *Orte des Erinnerns* – places of memory.

In order to see them you have to raise your eyes and look at the lamp-posts that line the square and the streets leading from it. These seemingly mundane posts have been transformed into signposts of memory. The signs they support are at first glance, innocuous, bland. They hold simpli-fied emblematic depictions: a park bench, a child's hopscotch pattern, a bathing costume, a dog, a cat. It is their very ordinariness, the very banal-ity of the imagery employed, that sets you up for the punch they deliver. On the reverse side you find they support a text: an edict from the anti-Jewish legislation of the Nazi period together with its date. Put the two together, image and text, and you realise that they act as markers of the erosion and destruction of civil rights of a community that once lived here. Thus a sign of a seemingly ordinary park bench, painted red (fig.1), when read from the other side carries the edict: *Jews may sit only on park benches marked yellow.* (fig.1a) I need hardly comment on the echoes this evokes of our own past in this country.

Fig. 1

A smaller pendant below every sign tells you that this place of memory marks the curtailing and deprivation of rights, the discrimination against, the de-humanisation, expulsion and deportation and, finally, the murder of Berlin Jewry.

Fig. 1a

The others follow a similar pattern: a depiction of a child's hopscotch diagram drawn in chalk on a pavement (fig. 2), carries on its reverse the edict: *Aryan and non-Aryan children forbidden to play together, 1938.*

Fig. 2

A depiction of a bathing costume (fig. 3) reveals on the reverse: *Berlin swimming baths: forbidden entry to Jews, 1938*.

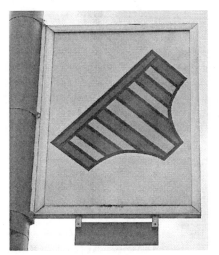

Berliner Bade-
anstalten und
Schwimmbäder
dürfen von Juden
nicht betreten
werden.

3.12.1938

Fig. 3

What lay behind the genesis of these signs? Relatively intact, with bomb damage restored after the war's end, there was nothing to indicate who had once lived in this sedate district of Berlin, no evidence of those whose rights had been systematically restricted and eroded, and whose lives for the most part had ended in the extermination camps. The Berlin Senate agreed to respond to this lacuna and in 1993 sponsored a competition for a memorial.

Enter the Berlin artists Renata Stih and Frieder Schnock with a proposal that was (perhaps surprisingly) accepted, the erection of the signs we have been discussing. Stih and Schnock are conceptual artists; they are sceptical of the grandstanding made by conventional centralised monuments. They believe instead in the quietly subversive approach: localised, site-specific statements, connecting memory with place.

It is of interest to note that Stih and Schnock were to be unsuccessful entrants for the competition for the official Memorial to the Murdered Jews of Europe in 1995. Their entry was among the more pointed examples of anti-establishment proposals which might generically be grouped under the concept of counter-monument or anti-monument. These activist proposals argue for site-specific intervention rather than monumental symbolism on a static central site. In the 1995 competition Stih and Schnock submitted a proposal for a fleet of buses to use the designated memorial site (which would have no building on it) as a terminal for taking people out to visit the actual sites of the death camps. This reflects a perfectly valid concern that while millions would be spent on a central expiatory memorial, actual on-site memorials such as that at the nearby Sachsenhausen camp were decaying through lack of funding for their upkeep.

Back in Bayerischer Platz they had shown what could be achieved with site-specific challenges to selective amnesia. Quietly, without announcement or publicity, they, the artists, had put up their signs. When the current post-war and post cold-war neighbourhood (no longer Jewish) began to take note of what was happening there was an angry reaction. Complaints were made to the police that neo-Nazis were invading the neighbourhood with anti-Semitic signs. Which of course allowed the artists to counter by making their point: when the anti-Jewish laws were promulgated and posted in the 1930s and 1940s, no less publically, there had been no complaints from Aryan Germans at the time. As James Young has commented, the anti-Jewish laws were no less public *then* than the memory of them was *now*.[6]

It is important to remember the cynicism and expedience that characterised the whole Nazi enterprise. This is commemorated in Bayerischer Platz by a sign carrying the image of a box file. The accompanying edict decrees: *All files dealing with anti-Semitic activities are to be destroyed.* The date of that edict is 16 February 1945. And there is an earlier example of self-serving duplicity: one of the signs depicts the well-known Olympic symbol of interlocking rings. This carries on its reverse the edict published just before the 1936 Olympiad: *anti-Semitic signs in Berlin are to be removed for the duration of the Olympic Games.*

So here we have a new slant on the phenomenon of presence through absence. As Young notes 'for the artists, even the absence of signs was an extension of the crime itself. [They] recognise here that the Nazi persecution of the Jews was designed to be, after all, a self-consuming Holocaust, a self-effacing crime'.[7] Thus the only signs of Jewish life in the Bayerischer Platz today are these signposts that record the steady erosion of civic rights, down to the pettiest detail, that led inevitably to the process of dehumanisation, deportation and murder.

Here are a random selection: examples of the images and backing texts that constitute the signs of the places of remembrance. I will group them roughly under generic themes, although this is not neccessarily the order in which one would encounter them. I will restrict myself to mentioning only one or two examples in each case. A brief description of the visual image will be accompanied by a summary translation of the relevant edict and its date, carried on its reverse.

The first theme is that of Proscription on Professional Activities:

A sign carrying a depiction of a thermometer – *Jewish doctors prohibited from practising. 25 7 1938*

A simplified image of a baby's dummy or comforter (fig. 4) – *Ban on Jewish midwives. 21 12 1938*

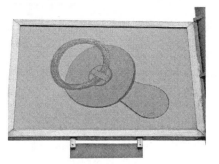

Fig. 4

A realist, friendly depiction of an Alsatian dog (fig. 5) – *Proscription on establishment of Jewish veterinary surgeons. 3 04 1936. Total professional ban on vets. 17 01 1939*

Fig. 5

Sport

A diagrammatic football pitch (fig. 6) – *Ban on Jewish membership of sports and gymnastic clubs. 25 04 1933*

Fig. 6

Education

A child's blonde braided plaits (fig. 7) – *Heredity and Racial Science to be made examination subjects. 13 09 1933*

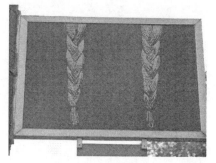 

Fig. 7

A child's school slate – *Ban on Jewish entry to public schools. 15 11 1938*

Restriction of Freedom of Movement

A country path – *Jewish rambling groups restricted to not more than 20 people. 10 07 1935*

A no-entry symbol – *Jews prohibited from entering certain areas of Berlin. 3 12 1938*

A totally blackened sign – *Total proscription on Jewish movement. 23 10 1941*

Property

An entry door – *Jewish households must be identified by a yellow star. 16 03 1942* and, devastating in its encompassing of the trivial, a depiction of a cat (fig. 8) – *Prohibition on Jewish households having domestic pets. 15 05 1942*

Fig. 8

Depersonalisation/Reinforcing of Identity

A sign carrying a selection of 'typical' German first names (fig. 9) – Peter, Paul, Renata, Frieder – these last two are the names of the artists – *Jews to be identified with additional name; males to be known as Israel, females as Sarah. 17 08 1938*

Fig. 9

Deportation

A sign carrying the DR logo of the Deutsche Reichsbahn, the Nazi state railway system – *First deportation of Berlin Jews. 18 10 1941; First direct deportations to extermination camp Auschwitz. 11 7 42*

The artists, who, for the record, are not Jewish, expressed the hope that these images and texts as part of the Berlin Cityscape would 'infiltrate the daily lives of Berliners, no less than the publicly posted laws curtailed the daily lives of Jews between 1933 and 1945'. They would show how Jews were incrementally removed from the protection of the law. These signs, these places of remembrance, would thus remind local citizens that the murder of the neighbourhood's Jews did not happen overnight, or in one fell swoop, but incrementally, over time – and with the tacit acknowledgement of their neighbours: 'Where past citizens once navigated their lives according to these laws, present citizens would now navigate their lives according to the memory of such laws.'[8]

At the time of my first encounter with the signs I wondered about this. The audience for conceptual art seldom responds in the way in which its authors would have it do. I spent a morning in the area, photographing and trying to gauge the reactions of the passers-by. It was a cold and blustery day. The few passers-by that I encountered seemed to be incurious of the fact that I was photographing something above their eyelines. Heads down, they battled against the wind. Maybe they had seen it all before. Maybe they did not care, no longer cared. How was one to know?

I have since learnt that the signs have had a considerable impact. It was originally envisaged that they would be there on a temporary basis, for a limited period. But such was the interest they generated that they were retained on a permanent basis. They are now used as a teaching tool by the local authority (Kunstampt Schoneburg).

The demographics of the neighbouring areas have changed; they are home to a mainly Turkish ethnic minority. It is significant to note that in a culture where the graffiti sprayers have left their protest marks all over the depressed areas of Berlin, these signs have not been defaced. Young children are now brought into the project to learn the consequences of racial prejudice.

5

Towards a South African Option

There can of course be no simplistic equation between the Holocaust and Apartheid. We should resist facile attempts to apportion moral equivalence. Yet it seems to me that there are lessons to be learnt from the Berlin precedent. To put it succinctly: what we need in South Africa are not monuments but memorials. Not monumental self-aggrandising triumphalism but site- specific memorials that provoke memory and challenge anamnesis. We should recognise the truth in the argument of Christa Wolf that 'memory is not an organ but an activity.' Memory is not a function that sits conveniently and dutifully in our brain, but is a repeated moral act.[9]

As to the erection of gigantic statues in honour of our Struggle heroes, we should pause for very careful thought. Nelson Mandela would be at the top of the wish list of most people who want to honour him in conventional terms. This is understandable. But it is also important to understand that this does not always happen for the purest of motives. There have been several proposals of dubious provenance and dumb aesthetics. The first goes back to 1996. It was touted by the Krok brothers, enterprising developers of a skin lightening formula in the apartheid years, who with Pik Botha as mediator, employed the kitsch talents of the sculptor Danie de Jager (the author of the rearing horses of Pretoria's erstwhile Strijdom Square) to promote a self-styled Freedom Monument to Mandela. The central feature was a giant arm, 33 metres high, bursting through prison bars. I wrote about it at the time, both in sorrow and in anger, invoking the lines of Stevie Smith – 'Not waving but drowning'.[10]

People who care about the level of public symbolism in the new South Africa obviously shared that sinking feeling: a mixture of incredulity and despair at the crudity and crassness of its central feature. That monumental arm that is supposed to symbolise freedom, bursting through prison bars, is it waving or drowning? In its gross, overblown, vein-bulging literalism, it is an echo of all that is bad in the discredited rhetoric of totalitarian art. It is blatantly the wrong image for the nation we are trying to build.

As a concept it belongs to the order of dumb, numbing gigantism that has appealed to the totalitarian mind, down the ages. It is the language of dictators, not liberators. In its 20th century incarnations it has appeared in various guises, in Mussolini's Italy, Hitler's Germany and Stalin's Russia. In the Paris Universal Exposition of 1937, when the muscle-flexing ideologies of Fascism and Communism contested the propagandist high ground, two variations on the theme of gigantism faced each other across the main axis of the Eiffel Tower. On the left, the heroic peasant and worker group by Vera Mukhina, hammer and sickle intertwined, dominated the Soviet pavilion. On the right, a riposte by Hitler's architect, Albert Speer: a giant eagle atop a tower, and huge Aryan übermenschen on either side of the entrance to the German pavilion. This debased rhetoric has appeared with local variations in Mao's China, in North Korea and closer to home, in the Heroes' Acre monument in Zimbabwe, executed by North Korean artists in the style of their Pyong Yang war memorial.

As to the dominant concept behind the Mandela memorial – the arm of the leader cast large in bronze – there is precedent for that too. And it's pretty chilling stuff. I am thinking of the Victory monument in Baghdad, commemorating the 'victory' of Iraq over Iran, in which a pair of giant forearms spring from concrete masses representing exploding earth and rise to terminal height in a triumphal arch of crossed swords 40 metres above ground. The arms are enlarged bronze casts of the arm of Saddam Hussein.[11]

The De Jager camp and its promoters would argue that this is not at all the kind of statement they have in mind. That they are celebrating freedom, not conquest. But even if the Mandela monument is meant to be saying something else, a different victory over a different enemy, the point is that the language it speaks is a tainted one, and ludicrously inappropriate for its purpose.

Instead it is entirely consistent with De Jager's work for his patrons of the apartheid era. He is, after all, the man who conceived the rearing horses in Strijdom Square in Pretoria, and the rampaging elephant at the Lost City. In short, his track record is expressed in the language of kitsch. It is the language of the instant sell; the language of the theme park. It is precisely the language of the backers of the project, the brothers Krok, who talk in terms of the largest cast bronze sculpture in the world and the Guiness Book of Records, and how many tourists it will attract.

Is this what we want? Is this what we hold as our paradigm? Is this the kind of process we should be going through in choosing our monuments, and in particular our first freedom monument?

Mercifully, sanity has prevailed. At a meeting between Government and what was initially described as the 'stake holders' in the project, the project was put on ice.

In fairness to the Krok brothers it should be noted that their undiminished entrepreneurial energy has since led to an unlikely but successful outcome in a related area. In pursuit of a gaming licence for their Gold Reef City theme park they have been the movers and shakers behind the founding of Johannesburg's new (and the country's first) apartheid museum. Against the odds, a creditable institution has emerged. The architecture is tough enough, and the installation of exhibits (which incorporate ideas borrowed from the US Holocaust Memorial Museum in Washington DC) is good enough to survive the incongruity of its cheek-by-jowl juxtaposition to a theme park. The genesis of the museum is a convoluted one. There's a PhD waiting to be written about an emerging pattern in the new South Africa: the thesis is that good works tend to happen more quickly, or happen only, if the pursuit of a gaming licence is involved.

But in the matter of monumental statuary it appears that sanity has not endured for long. Recently there have been more proposals for a Mandela monument. The most egregious of these has been proposed for the harbour at Port Elizabeth by a consortium of businessmen who have the co-operation of the Provincial government and the National Ports Authority. Sketches of how the promoters envisage the scheme are dispiriting. They show, in cloying folksy realism, a giant figure of the great man with obligatory arm outstretched, leaning on the shoulders of a child. The height given is of the order of 65 metres – that's twice the size of the De Jager proposal which rated only a modest 33 metres. If you add on the height of the plinth of the PE proposal – 45 metres – that gives a vertical dominance, as its backers love to point out, over the Statue of Liberty which clocks in at 93 metres. The plinth is intended to house a 'Museum of Freedom' and will be approached by a 600 metre causeway, to be known, inevitably, as the 'long walk to freedom'. It sounds like an adman's dream, and it comes as no surprise that the mover behind the Port Elizabeth consortium is indeed in the advertising business. The consortium has announced that feasibility studies and business plans are under way. The choice of artist is yet to be decided. This says something about priorities. It makes no bones about the fact that this represents a commercial opportunity with an eye firmly fixed on the hagiographic tourist market.

It was unfortunate, to say the least, that Mr Mandela was seen as having associated himself with the first (De Jager) proposal by being photographed with the maquette. One gains the impression that he has attempted to distance himself from the Port Elizabeth proposal. But not as firmly as one would wish. Part of the problem with being an icon in your own lifetime is that you get identified with the choice of your own iconography. The deeper trouble is when such a choice is seen to be beyond criticism. Thankfully, we appear not to be in that position. Yet.

Nelson Mandela deserves a better memorial. Schools, libraries, hospitals – and other facilities that we desperately need – can all serve memorial functions. The country needs to find a better process than that which produces not meaningful memorials but monuments to the marketing of hagio-tourism. We need to think beyond the dumbing clichés of gigantism if the imaging of honoured memory is to have any relevance to reconstruction in South Africa.

NOTES

1   Friederich Nietzsche, *The Use and Abuse of History* (New York: McMillan, 1885), quoted in Neville Dubow, *Imaging the Unimaginable: Holocaust Memory in Art and Architecture* (Cape Town: Isaac and Jessie Kaplan Centre for Jewish Studies and Research, UCT, 2001). Other extracts from the introduction to that volume are reproduced here with modifications. The author gratefully acknowledges permission for this.

2   Andreas Huyssen, 'Monuments and Memory in a Postmodern Age', in J. E. Young (ed.) *The Art of Memory, Holocaust Memorials in History* (Prestel: Verlag 1994).

3   For a discussion of this see N. Vergunst, *Hoerikwaggo, Images of Table Mountain* (Cape Town: South African National Gallery, 2000).

4   Quoted in J. E.Young, *The Texture of Memory: Holocaust Memorials in History* (New Haven and London: Yale University Press, 1993).

5   For a full discussion of the development of the Berlin Holocaust memorial see Neville Dubow, *Imaging the Unimaginable*.

6   J. E.Young, *At Memory's Edge* (New Haven and London: Yale University Press, 2000).

7   Ibid.

8   Ibid.

9   Christa Wolf, in her novel *Kindheitsmuster*, quoted by Peter Horn in a paper entitled 'Anti-fascism in GDR literature', Cape Town Holocaust Centre colloquium, June 2003.

10 Neville Dubow, *Arms and the Man, Mail and Guardian*, April 12–18, 1996.

11 Curiously, among all the extensive Iraq war media footage of toppling monuments to Saddam Hussein, the Victory Arch remained unscathed and unrecorded.

21

Ritual, Reparation and Reintegration:

The Challenge of Reconciliation in Post-Conflict African Societies

Tyrone Savage and Zola Sonkosi

Post-conflict societies throughout Africa are faced with the challenge of reconciliation in the aftermath of internecine violence. Amid the fragile interruption in the fighting that sometimes emerges as a ceasefire, as talks about talks or as the result of international intervention, societies are faced with a historical interval, 'determined by things which are no longer and which are not yet'.[1] It is a moment, sometimes little more than a flicker in time, in which survivors and perpetrators of extreme violations are asked to forget the ways of war, come to terms with the effect that it has had on their lives and work towards a productive, peaceful co-existence. Nations faced with this challenge generally have only a delicate interval of peace in which to tackle the cycle of violence begetting violence, treat the deeply entrenched effects of the conflict and provide transformative options for transition.

A few examples may suffice to make manifest the scale and depth of the challenge in Africa's post-conflict societies. A fragile peace has emerged in Sierra Leone. It comes against the historical backdrop of a decade-long brutal war in which civilians were not incidental victims but the targets of a campaign of terror. In a country of 4.5 million people, over 1.5 million have been displaced and the capital has been sacked twice. Physical mutilation, as a terror tactic, has become a glaring feature of everyday life. Survivors of gross human rights violations show signs of physical mutilation such as amputations by machete of one or both hands, legs, breasts or fingers. An estimated 15 000 women have been raped by marauding militia. The rebels also psychologically terrorised victims by forcing them to participate in their own mutilation, making them decide which arm or leg they wanted amputated or whether they wanted a 'short-sleeve' or 'long-sleeve' amputation (above or below the elbow). What reparation is possible in the aftermath of such atrocity?

In Sierra Leone's neighbour, Liberia, it is estimated that one in ten children was abducted and forced to join the forces fighting the civil war. Reports too have emerged of ritual mutilation of the bodies of enemies killed in battle, including eating an enemy's heart. During the violence the population of Liberia's capital, Monrovia, was swollen by the arrival of hundreds of thousands of rural Liberians, many of them women and children, preferring to take their chances in a city besieged, short of supplies and shelled daily than to face the threat of abduction at the hands of the rebels. What institutional mechanisms can be established to facilitate the transition out of Liberia's cycle of violence begetting violence? What reconstruction – material, psychological, social – will be possible for the one million shell-shocked people of Monrovia?

The delicate peace spreading through the welter of wars that run from Angola through the Great Lakes region to Sudan poses similar, daunting challenges. Most of the continent's estimated 120 000 child-soldiers are to be found in the jungles of central Africa.[2] Angola has known four decades of war, resulting in 140 000 former combatants and 3.5 million people – fully one third of the population – internally displaced.[3] Unofficial sources put the number of Angolans with limbs lost to landmines at about 80 000. Not without controversy, Rwanda is tackling the challenge posed by 120 000 alleged perpetrators of the 1994 genocide that left almost a million Rwandans dead in 100 days. Over three and a half million people are estimated to have died in the various, inter-connected conflicts that have proliferated in the Great Lakes region in the aftermath of the genocide.[4] Southern Sudan continues to be the arena to Africa's most intractable conflict, with agreement after agreement broken and whole communities internally displaced by a war notorious for brutality on a vast scale.

Such is the challenge of conflict – and the effects of conflict – in Africa. In each of these contexts, a fragile somewhat chequered peace has emerged in which hopes are growing for transition to a future that is unlike the past. But before forward-looking processes can begin, questions about the past and the ways it carries through into the present need to be asked. Of pressing concern in all such societies are the needs of demobilising combatants.

How are reprisals to be prevented between members of various military organisations previously engaged in conflict? How does a society provide for the particular needs of those former combatants wanting to return to civilian life? Most soldiers joined a war because they believed in something and were prepared to fight, kill and even die for it; they therefore return expecting recognition – not hardship. Former combatants often find that they battle to make a living. They are not seen as local heroes. The only bond they have left is with each other. What threat do the special needs of demobilising soldiers pose to transitional processes?

Less of a political threat but no less a humanitarian concern are the needs of those who have survived violation and victimisation in the course of war. What reparation may be made to those who have been violated repeatedly by marauding militia? Is reconciliation possible between an amputee and the perpetrator of the amputation? When that perpetrator was a child abducted, drugged and made to commit such acts in his home community, what hope can he have of ever returning? And when peace comes, what prospects does it hold for survivors who are rendered vulnerable by the return to everyday life of the soldier or soldiers that 'visited' their community? How do people – victims, perpetrators, and the many who are both victims *and* perpetrators – endeavour to demobilise psychologically from the ravages of coercion and militarism?

This chapter is set in the context of such immense questions and the variety of literature mounting international concern with the problems of demobilisation and reintegration has produced. The work of Kees Kingma and the Bonn International Center for Conversion around the challenges of disarmament and demobilisation has been formative. In southern Africa, Mafole Mokalobe has produced extensive studies of the challenges facing cadres of the military wings of liberation movements as they seek either to integrate into a single national military force or to demobilise and return to civilian life.[5] Numerous international organisations engaged in post-conflict reconstruction have highlighted the special needs of children and women. Debate around demobilisation and reintegration has grown significantly in recent years in the United Nations. In 2000, UN Secretary-General Kofi Annan appointed a peace operations panel that provided a candid review and analysis of past peace operations undertaken by the UN, highlighting problems and areas for innovation.[6] One of the points to emerge from the Brahimi Report, as it became known, was that peace operations should be designed to carry through into comprehensive demobilisation and reintegration. The view continues to grow within the UN, contributing to reshaping the concept and projected outcomes of interventions.[7] Most recently, Virginia Gamba of SaferAfrica has developed perspectives that advance a balancing of disarmament, demobilisation and reintegration with other elements of post-conflict reconstruction, drawing on this broad-based understanding of such process to develop strategies capable of redressing failed demobilisation processes.[8]

International concern that peacemaking carry through to demobilisation has spurred questions about how to prevent a fragile peace from collapsing into familiar patterns of conflict. It is, however, in the area of reintegration that the debate has remained somewhat inchoate. The very texture of the topic renders it somewhat unwieldy. It is about the hazy area of inter-personal relations that emerge in the aftermath of violation. Reintegration is therefore more difficult to measure quantitatively than, say, the number of automatic weapons handed in or the number of soldiers who have been formally decamped. Reintegration is about soldiers returning to the ways of peace and the ambivalence – the welcome, the dread and, sometimes, even indifference – that civilians and receiving communities feel at this prospect. It is about survivors of extreme violations choosing to face their perpetrators on a day-to-day basis or demanding some sort of protection from them. Reintegration, in short, is about the often messy but generally much needed process that is reconciliation.

This chapter will endeavour to forge groundwork for a wider debate that places the demobilisation of former combatants in the design of a much larger reconciliation framework in which ritual, restitution, reintegration and reparation also play a part. The material is provided by the successes and failures of various post-conflict efforts throughout Africa. Specifically, this chapter will draw on the example tragically provided by two failed peace processes in Angola, where demobilisation without reintegration re-awakened the ghosts of war. The chapter will also draw on the innovative, informal reintegration processes undertaken by communities in Mozambique as an illustration of the social complexity of reintegration as well as the role ritual and reparation can play in forging reintegration and reconciliation. In this regard, we are indebted to the fieldwork and notes of Alcinda Honwana. Following this discussion of post-conflict processes in Mozambique, we turn to contemporary Zimbabwe, where traditional rituals and rites are being deployed to help rehabilitate communities impacted by government repression. Finally, we will outline a groundbreaking initiative under way in South Africa that links the notions of reconciliation, reparation and reintegration. These initiatives reflect the overall argument made in this chapter, namely that thoroughgoing demobilisation – of the mind, of a community and of a nation – needs to be situated within a larger reconciliation framework, in which reintegration and reparation are an integral part.

Angola has been at war for 41 years. After 14 years of struggle by several armed movements for national liberation from colonial rule, Angola achieved independence in 1975. In the aftermath, sectors of the resistance to colonialism, aggrieved at their position in the new regime, returned to war. The result was a post-colonial struggle that raged, with occasional intervals of peace, for 28 years. Following the death in 2002 of Jonas Savimbi, the leader of the National Union for the Total Independence of Angola (Unita), the country is now officially at peace. Demobilisation processes intended to return approximately 80 000 Unita soldiers and their estimated 360 000 family members to civilian life have officially been completed.[9]

Yet despite the official closure to this process, vast numbers of ex-combatants and their families continue to remain in and around most of the 39 camps set up around the country by the Angolan government. Clearly, much more is expected in terms of reintegration. At the same time, post-war humanitarian assistance by international and local organisations is occurring on a vast scale. Ten UN agencies, 100 international non-governmental organisations and over 420 local organisations are involved in on-the-ground activities. The government's commitment has been to 'normalisation', a term much used by political and military elites in the capital, which has come to mean little more than 'the extension of state administration throughout the national territory ... in particular in areas previously controlled by Unita'.[10]

Much could be said of the priorities being pursued by the Popular Movement for the Liberation of Angola (MPLA) government in the wake of Unita's demise as a military threat. Suffice it here to note that for any social development or extension of state administration throughout the country to be sustainable, the reintegration of close on half a million people, historically dependent on Unita for survival, will be necessary. A whole generation in Angola has known only war; reintegration will be crucial in preventing a reversion to deeply ingrained coercive ways of pursuing change. And, as a leading Unita official recently observed, although the fighting may have stopped, the war and all that provoked people to fight for change is still there: the underdeveloped hinterland, poverty, political elitism.[11]

The current demobilisation and reintegration process is the third in 12 years. In 1991, the Bicesse Peace Accords raised hopes of an end to three decades of civil war. The Accords addressed the general issue of disarmament, demobilisation and reintegration by planning to encamp both Unita and government troops within 60 days, create armed forces comprising 50 000 personnel and demobilise the surplus Unita soldiers. The Accords, moreover, stipulated the formation of the integrated Angolan Armed Forces (FAA) as a precondition to multi-party elections, separating off the more daunting challenge of disarming, demobilising, and reintegrating 135 000 soldiers. The UN presence in the country was expanded under a renewed mandate – twice – in response to the challenge. The UN deployment was grossly under-resourced, however. Whereas in Namibia several years earlier, the ratio of UN personnel to local population had been 1:150, in Angola it was 1:16 000. The UN Special Representative to the Bicesse Process, Margaret Anstee, famously observed, '... adopting a myopic approach to UN peacekeeping, the Security Council gave [the UN Angolan Verification Mission] UNAVEM II a mandate and resources that absurdly underestimated the enormity and complexity of the tasks that lay ahead ... UNAVEM II was a misguided exercise in peacekeeping minimalism'.[12]

By the time the 1992 elections were held in Angola, only 37% of the government troops and 85% of Unita's were encamped. Amid this flailing process, the government openly established a paramilitary police force, weapons began to proliferate among the civilian population, law and order declined and the sluggishness of the integration process led to an impression among Angolans that several armies – not one – were present during the run-up to the elections. Formal integration into a national army was announced two days before the elections, creating an ominous scenario: Unita, the guerrilla movement turned political party, waited for the election outcome. When the results ran against it, it simply reverted to the bush war. In short, prioritising an electoral process over processes to reintegrate demobilising soldiers into civilian life proved disastrous.

A second demobilisation process was instituted following the Peace Accord signed in Lusaka in 1994. More progress was made this time – at least on the level of formal demobilisation. In four years of 'no peace, no war', almost 50 000 soldiers were formally demobilised. Moreover, the timetable for elections was designed with enough flexibility to ensure that demobilisation processes could fully take hold ahead of elections. Unita's participation in the quartering and registration processes – and commitment to any real demobilisation – was very mixed, however. João Gomes Porto and Imogen Parsons, among others, have noted that many of the Unita fighters who were formally demobilised may have been merely hired as substitutes for the real forces. A total of 78 886 Unita personnel were registered, of whom 8 607 were underage and 11 051 disabled. Moreover, 26 000 deserted before they had been fully demobilised.[13] As low-intensity conflict grew in the aftermath of the elections it became clear that many units had remained within their command structure, even while quartered in the camps. By 1999, the demobilisation process was formally abandoned, with full-scale war being waged on all sides.

On 4 April 2002, a 'Memorandum of Understanding for the Cessation of Hostilities and the Resolution of the Outstanding Military Issues under the Lusaka Protocol' was signed between the FAA and Unita, signalling an end to Angola's lengthy civil war. The agreement came in the immediate aftermath of the death in combat of Unita leader, Jonas Savimbi, after three years of government advances in Unita-held territory. The military triumph of the government forces was an integral factor in the resolution that emerged after decades of internecine conflict. This altered balance of power is proving a significant factor in the demobilisation and reintegration processes presently occurring in Angola. In a country desperately in need of development, will the reintegration of half a million people associated with an age-old enemy, vanquished at last, be a priority? Are the political will and the economic capacity on the part of government present to carry disarmament and demobilisation through into thoroughgoing reintegration? What would it look like? Is peace even possible among people who have never known it, cannot remember times when they had it and are now asked to reconcile and press forward? Creating such peace is a challenge that still awaits Angolans. To even embark on the journey is to engage in uncharted territory. Such is the challenge of transition in Angola.

Like Angola, Mozambique fought a lengthy war of independence from Portugal. It succeeded in 1975 and then plunged into civil war shortly afterwards. The rebel Mozambique National Resistance movement (Renamo) was initially supported by the Rhodesian regime as a means of curbing guerrilla incursions from bases in Mozambique. Following the demise of Rhodesia, the apartheid regime backed Renamo as a way of destabilising the Front for the Liberation of Mozambique (Frelimo) government in Mozambique, which was strongly aligned with the ANC. Renamo used brutal methods to recruit its rebel forces. Coercive membership was drawn from children and youth of both sexes. Children were abducted from primary schools, which were afterwards burnt down. Renamo also recruited older people to provide food for its rebels. With the support of the South African apartheid regime, Renamo planted nearly one million anti-personnel mines throughout Mozambique, resulting in over 10 000 casualties, according to Human Rights Watch.[14] Mozambican family life was devastated by the conflict, along with traditional structures and administrative infrastructure.

The conflict ended in 1992 when Frelimo and Renamo signed the Rome Peace Accord. The Accord enabled Mozambique to carry out a programme for the demobilisation of the armed forces, the formation of a new integrated army and social and economic reintegration of demobilised soldiers from both Frelimo and Renamo. One of the main purposes of reintegration was to guarantee that peace and social harmony would become a reality; people feared that if nothing was done to assist the demobilised soldiers there was a great risk of a return to violence. Complicating the reintegration of the soldiers was the fact that, given the social upheaval caused by the war, 4.5 million internally displaced people were now seeking to return home. Establishing conditions conducive to reconciliation and reconstruction was a priority for Mozambicans from all walks of life.

Formal and informal initiatives were developed by the government, non-governmental organisations, community-based organisations and the international community. The formal reintegration process received financial support from the government and the international community, enabling it to provide technical, professional and vocational training mainly in urban centres. The formal processes enjoyed some successes, not least because it worked hand-in-hand with associations of war veterans composed of Frelimo and Renamo demobilised soldiers. Yet in many cases the vocational training provided did not link up to actual demand for skills. Some veterans received training as electricians – and then returned home to areas that had no electricity. Others received training as businessmen and businesswomen where there was no business to run or no start-up capital provided.

The innovation of Mozambique's transition from war to peace occurred at the community level. Ritual, and in particular ritual cleansings, formed an integral part of the reintegration process, incorporating traditional methods of healing, reconciliation and restoring into the demobilisation and reintegration process. Specifically, it was widely believed that people who had engaged in the wrongdoings of war had experienced what was described as 'soul pollution'. It was feared that reintegration would bring the threat of disruption and contamination to the receiving community. In response, traditional leaders developed rituals known as 'soul cleansing'. The rituals generally entailed demobilised soldiers confessing to community assemblies about the gross misdeeds they had committed during the civil war. Moreover, they would agree to pay/make reparations to their victims or to render community service in cases where they had no material means with which to pay/make reparations. Symbolism also played a significant part in the process, as the following account from Alcinda Honwana's field notes makes manifest:

Samuel was only nine years old when he was abducted by Renamo rebels during a military attack on his village. He was told to carry a bag of maize meal and had to walk for four days to the Renamo military camp. Three months later he had one month of military training and was forced to serve as soldier for more than two years. After the cease-fire, Samuel was reunited with some of his relatives ...

He was not shown affection or hugged. ... Samuel was first taken to his family ndumba (the house of the spirits) where he was presented to the ancestral spirits of the family. The boy's grandfather addressed the spirits informing them that his grandchild had returned and thanked them for protecting his grandson and enabling him to return alive. The family elders then talked to Samuel to find out how he was and what had happened while he was away. A few days later a traditional healer was called to perform the cleansing ritual. The practitioner took the boy to the bush where a small hut covered with dry grass was built. The boy, dressed in the dirty clothes he brought from the Renamo camp, entered the hut and undressed himself. The hut was then set on fire, and an adult relative helped the boy out. The hut, the clothes and everything else that the boy brought from the camp had to be burned. This symbolised the rupture with the past. A chicken was sacrificed for the spirits of the dead and the blood spread around the ritual place. The chicken was then cooked and offered to the spirits as a sacrificial meal.

After that the boy had to inhale the smoke of the herbal remedies and bath himself – in the presence of the entire family – with water treated with medicine. In this way his body was cleansed both internally and externally. Finally the [practitioner] made some incisions in the boy's body and filled them with a paste made from the herbal remedies, a practice called ku thlavela. *The purpose of this procedure is to give the boy strength. Relatives and neighbours were present at this ritual and helped the practitioner by performing specific roles, or just by observing, singing and clapping.*

Only after the ritual was the boy free to interact and be integrated with the rest of the community. This is a ritual affecting an individual. At the same time it touches many others in this process. The individual and community are one. The isolation of the individual disrupts the community. The individual, in turn, cannot be healed without appeasing the community.[15]

Such 'soul cleansing' rituals were widespread and played a crucial role in developing reconciliation and reintegration 'from below' – processes at grassroots level – in ways that addressed the needs of the individual, the family and the wider community. A climate of relative peace and reconciliation was created. In this context, demobilising soldiers were also encouraged to use the formal support they received to engage in community building exercises, such as constructing houses and roads. In short, the material benefits many received were used to help make reparation to the war-impacted communities to which they returned.

Traditional ritual has also begun to play a role in contemporary Zimbabwe, as communities seek out options for redress, reconciliation and rehabilitation following – and in the midst of – government repression. These endeavours have emerged both as a response to the impact on community life of the Matabeleland massacres perpetrated during the 'Dissidents War' (1983–1987), as well as a strategy of non-violent resistance amid ongoing prolific political violence at the grassroots level. According to Shari Eppel of the human rights group, Amani Trust, the destruction of the healthy functioning of community life has been a crucial component in the efforts of Robert Mugabe's government to exert control throughout the country. Attempts to develop political compliance at grassroots level have found form in the deliberate desecration of customary rites, rituals and social needs associated with death in the community. A particular focus has been on preventing public honouring of deceased loved ones and, with that, any public discourse about the causes of death.

During the Matabeleland massacres, the notorious Fifth Brigade '... made a point of forbidding mourning, and on occasion forced people to take part in grossly disrespectful behaviour, such as dancing and singing on the graves of the newly murdered. In other cases people were threatened with death and were in fact killed, if they cried for the dead. Others were forced to leave bodies where 5 Brigade chose to leave them, on pain of death. This could include in ant bear holes, anthills, rubbish dumps and any other handy hole in the ground'.[16] In communities where the spirits of the deceased traditionally play a vital role in daily life, such desecration of funereal ritual has produced the problem of aggrieved spirits, whose discontent is felt among the community, not least through the daily reminder of the improper graves. This in turn has left mourning suspended and a lack of closure with regard both to the fact that the person has now departed this life, as well as the way in which he or she was degraded and humiliated in death.

The work of Eppel and the now banned Amani Trust focused on exhumation, not in order to investigate what happened so much as to facilitate proper burial. This in turn has allowed surviving family and community members an opportunity to acknowledge the loved one no longer present, discuss the causes of death and finally enact the symbolic inauguration of the deceased as an honoured ancestor in the community. The ceremony, known as 'umbuyiso', is conducted some time after the funeral, after an interval of waiting, and must be held during late winter, ahead of the first signs of springtime. At nightfall, the spirit of the deceased is brought back to the homestead in symbolic form as a goat. At the threshold, a ritual introduction of the deceased to the living is made, and the deceased is welcomed as an ancestor. In Eppels's words, 'This process brings the person's soul out of the wilderness and into the home to rest, and watch over the living.'[17] The following day, the ceremony widens to encompass the entire community. Everyone in the village now visits and pays their respects to the family. The goat is then ritually slaughtered to honour the dead person and the meal is shared by all.

Such ritual provides communities the means of together witnessing the truth about the past, together mourning with dignity and then finally laying their beloved to rest in ways that restore moral order and social cohesion in the community. This in turn allows the community to find healing for dysfunctional behaviours resulting from the ungrieved loss and answers to questions about why the death occurred. Derek

Summerfield notes: 'Those abusing power typically refuse to acknow-ledge their dead victims, as if they had never existed and were mere wraiths in the memories of those left behind. This denial, and the impunity of those who maintain it, must be challenged if survivors are to make sense of their losses and the social fabric is to mend.'[18] Amid the resurgence of repression that has marked Zimbabwe since April 2000, exhumation and re-burial ritual have thus become a means of addressing the past, a source of restorative justice within communities and a counter-strategy against the deliberate weakening of community life in the latter days of the Mugabe regime.

Restorative justice measures have also begun to play a significant role in non-governmental demobilisation and reintegration efforts in South Africa. In keeping with South Africa's commitment to developing struc-tures of unity in the aftermath of apartheid's divisions, initial efforts went into integrating the seven armies active in the country into a national defence force. This resulted in 50 000 personnel in excess of South Africa's defence needs.[19] Only 7 238 ex-combatants were formally demo-bilised, leaving tens of thousands of war veterans either discharged or simply to their own devices. Among various responses to this national problem, the South African government, a formerly white commercial farmers organisation called Agri South Africa and some 7 000 demobilised soldiers from Umkhonto we Sizwe and the Azanian People's Liberation Army together developed a collaborative commercial farming project, the basis of which is restitution of land rights, agricultural training and co-operatives that link the project's produce to markets.

The project makes manifest a number of reintegration 'best practices'. It acknowledges demobilising combatants as a special group, facing partic-ular challenges – such as lack of resources and skills – as they endeavour to return to civilian life. Rather than denying the past, the project affords veterans of the liberation war preferential treatment and places upon them the particular responsibility of learning to live and work with their former enemies. As such, it bestows on the demobilising soldiers a special status as leaders in grassroots processes of dialogue, reconciliation and transition. Having fought for a new order, veterans are now asked to help shape and construct it. In turn, the initiative gives a community much privileged under apartheid, namely the agricultural sector, an opportunity to be con-fronted by the views and needs of people disenfranchised under the system from which they drew their benefits. And above all, through its commitment to land restitution and re-distribution, the arrangement is grounded in the wider transitional mechanism of reparations.

In conclusion, southern Africa provides a kaleidoscope of ritual, reparations and reintegration strategies integral to tackling the challenge of reconciliation in post-conflict African societies: ritual that allows for perpetrators to acknowledge their role in past atrocities and return to community; exhumation, re-burial and ancestor rites of passage that promote restorative justice in community in the midst of repression; reparation and economic re-distribution as integral components in reintegration and post-conflict reconciliation. The southern African experience also makes manifest many errors, above all that to hold winner-takes-all elections ahead of dismantling heavily armed military formations is to invite a return to violent conflict. Above all, the post-conflict processes in southern Africa reveal that thoroughgoing demobilisation needs to go beyond the simple dismantling of military units to develop military, political, social and psychological components. Demobilisation, in short, needs to be situated and framed within a larger commitment to establishing peace through reintegration processes linked to economic development, political transition, community healing and social transformation. Although fully repairing the fabric of a war-torn society may be impossible, learning to live together in the aftermath of war is to weave anew the social threads of our shared humanity.

Notes

1 Hannah Arendt, *Between Past and Future, Six Exercises in Political Thought* (New York: Viking Press, 1961), 9.

2 International Labour Office, *Wounded Children: The Use of Children in Armed Conflict in Central Africa* (International Labour Office, 2003), 1.

3 Kees Kingma, Bonn International Center for Conversion (BICC), *Demobilisation and Reintegration of Ex-combatants in Post-war and Transition Countries: Trends and Challenges of External Support* (Bonn: Deutsche Gesellschaft für Technische Zusammenarbeit [GTZ], 2001), 20.

4 International Rescue Committee, *Mortality in the Democratic Republic of Congo: Results from a Nationwide Survey* (2003), 18. Reprinted at http://intranet.theirc.org/docs/drc_mortality_iii_full.pdf (accessed 6 August 2003).

5 See for example Mafole Mokalobe, *Rationalisation in the SANDF: Issues and Challenges* (Cape Town: Centre for Conflict Resolution, June 2001).

6   United Nations, *Report of the Panel of Peacekeeping Operations* (2000). Reprinted at http://www.un.org/peace/reports/peace_operations/ (accessed 6 August 2003).

7   United Nations, Security Council, *Report of the Secretary-General on Children and Armed Conflict*. 26 November 2002. S.2002/1299.

8   Virginia Gamba, *Post-agreement Demobilization, Disarmament and Reconstruction: Towards a New Approach*. Paper delivered at the Peacebuilding and Peace Accords conference, Joan B. Kroc Institute for International Peace Studies, Notre Dame, 11 September 2003.

9   The figures are taken from João Gomes Porto and Imogen Parsons, *Sustaining the Peace in Angola: An Overview of Current Demobilization, Disarmament and Reintegration* (Pretoria: Institute for Security Studies Monograph 83, 2003), 5. Reports emerged during a recent visit by Institute for Justice and Reconciliation staff to Angola indicating that the figures may be even higher.

10 Porto and Parsons, *Sustaining the Peace in Angola*, 6.

11 Interview with Paulo Gato, the immediate successor to Jonas Savimbi and the Unita leader tasked with transforming Unita from a guerrilla movement into a political party.

12 M. Joan Anstee, *Orphan of the Cold War. The Inside Story of the Collapse of the Angolan Peace Process, 1992–93* (London: Macmillan, 1996), 13.

13 Porto and Parsons, *Sustaining the Peace in Angola*, 25.

14 Human Rights Watch. *Landmines in Mozambique* (New York: Human Rights Watch, Arms Project Report, 1994), 214.

15 Charles Villa-Vicencio (ed.), *Transcending a Century of Injustice* (Cape Town: Idasa, 2000), 103 and 107–8.

16 Shari Eppel, *Healing the Dead: Exhumations and Re-burial as a Tool to Truth-Telling in Rural Zimbabwe*. Work in Progress, 8.

17 Shari Eppel, *Healing the Dead*. Work in Progress, 7.

18 Derek Summerfield, 'Raising the dead; war, reparation and the politics of memory', in *British Medical Journal*, Vol. 311, August 1995, 495.

19 The seven armies comprised the armed wings of the African National Congress, Umkhonto we Sizwe and the Pan Africanist Congress's Azanian People's Liberation Army (APLA), the military apparatus of the apartheid regime, the South African Defence Force (SADF), and the armies of four former homelands, Bophuthatswana, Ciskei, Transkei and Venda.

22

A Plan of Integral Reparations

Truth and Reconciliation Commission of Peru

The mandate of the Peruvian Truth and Reconciliation Commission (TRC) calls for the clarification of acts related to, and the conditions that caused, Peru's internal armed conflict between the state's armed forces and insurgent groups from 1980 to 2000. To fulfil its obligations, the TRC has been collecting testimonies from victims, witnesses and perpetrators of the violence as well as conducting related studies since June 2001, all of which will form the basis for its final official report.

In addition, the TRC will make recommendations intended to promote national reconciliation, the aim being to ensure that the past never repeats itself. Recognising that the prerequisites of reconciliation include the promotion of justice, the TRC will submit to the Public Ministry those cases that require further criminal investigation of alleged perpetrators of human rights violations as well as propose an integral plan of reparations intended to respond to the pain, suffering and damage caused by these violations.

Why reparations? The ethical and legal dimensions

The acts of violence over 20 years caused grave harm to the dignity and integrity of Peruvian citizens, the majority of whom came from the poorer and more marginalised sectors of society. Keeping in mind the immeasurable damage caused by the armed conflict, reparations are considered to be an act of recognition and affirmation of those affected by the conflict. In addition, reparations seek to mend something that has been broken not only in the material sense, such as lost property, but also in the moral sense, such as lost hope in the future, the 'proyecto de vida',[1] and civic trust in democratic institutions.

The state's obligation to provide adequate reparations for human rights violations caused by the conflict arises out of both domestic and international law. It includes the guarantee to prevent such violations or, when not possible, to investigate diligently those responsible and impose the appropriate sanctions as well as provide reparations to the victims. The state's duty to provide reparations extends to violations caused by private actors. Therefore the Plan of Integral Reparations (PIR) includes victims not only of acts caused by state agents but also by insurgent groups. The incumbent government must assume this responsibility even if the illicit acts occurred under the leadership of the preceding governments.

The limits of juridical venue and the political dimension of reparations

Traditional legal recourse fails to address effectively systematic and gross violations of human rights in that a competent court awards reparations only to those individuals who bring an original complaint. Thus, similarly situated victims who are not a part of the original litigation, who cannot successfully invoke the jurisdiction of the courts or who lack resources to pursue legal recourse are denied their right to a remedy. This patent inequality among victims demands the development of other methods of redress that depend more on politics and less on the courts. An alternative political approach that includes individual, collective, symbolic and material reparations also helps to overcome institutional prejudices that have historically denied justice to indigent, ethnic and racial minorities. The PIR may be considered part of a larger political project of consolidating democracy for ethical reasons, not just legal and juridical ones.

Theoretical framework

The general objective of the PIR is to 'repair and compensate the victims of human rights violations as well as the social, moral and material losses or damages suffered by victims as a result of the conflict'. To accomplish this goal, the PIR aims to offer an integral approach to reparations that includes complementary programmes that are individual and collective as well as symbolic and material in nature. Moreover, the PIR is designed to complement other recommendations made by the TRC on clarifying the truth, reconstructing Peru's historic memory, seeking criminal justice and reforming democratic institutions. While some of these reparation programmes may improve the quality of life of victims and their families, the central goal is the reparation and recognition of victims as human beings whose fundamental rights were violated.

Beneficiaries of the PIR

The TRC considers 'victims' to include 'all those persons or groups of persons who, as a result of the armed internal conflict from 1980 until 2000, have suffered acts or omissions that violated international human rights norms'. Beneficiaries of reparations will include these victims or the families (spouse or common-law partner, children and parents) of those killed or those who disappeared during the conflict. It also includes certain collectives, including native and rural communities, other populations affected by the conflict in provinces where the conflict was more intense, and groups of displaced people who have not returned to their place of origin but stayed where they settled during the conflict. Those victims who have already received reparations from the state through other political acts or judicial decisions will not be included in the PIR to avoid being indemnified twice.

Cross-sectional focus

In order to best serve the population intended to benefit from the reparations plan, the PIR advises that all reparation programmes include five distinct dimensions: a psycho-social focus; an emphasis on participatory decision-making; sensitivity to intercultural needs; promotion of gender equality; and emphasis on the inherent symbolic nature of all reparations.

The programmes of the PIR

Symbolic reparations

Symbolic reparations, consisting of certain public acts and civic rituals, seek to restore social ties between citizens and between citizens and the state that were broken during the conflict. In particular, certain acts and civic rituals will be used to demonstrate the government's recognition of the damage caused by the conflict. Included among the proposals are:

- Public gestures such as the president fully endorsing the PIR as well as offering public apologies to victims;
- Acts of recognition such as establishing a national holiday in memory of victims, personal letters recognising the innocence of those unjustly imprisoned and naming certain schools after victims of the conflict;

- Memorials, such as monuments or plaques at the entrance to cemeteries, as well as legal and administrative protection of mass graves still not exhumed;
- Acts of reconciliation, such as closing certain prisons and military bases closely associated with the conflict.

Health reparations

This programme seeks to help populations affected by the conflict regain their mental and physical health to enable them to pursue their personal and social development and reconstruct their individual and community life projects truncated by the conflict. The components of this programme include:

- Capacitation. Given how few qualified personnel there are to provide mental health care to human rights victims, especially in the Andean and Amazon regions, this programme would prepare professionals to return to their communities to train their colleagues (professionals in public and private institutions, community leaders and traditional healers) to apply special methods used for treating populations affected by political violence, while keeping in mind the special needs of their community;
- Community intervention. External facilitators will help repair the social fabric of communities by reconstructing support networks, providing conflict resolution and helping members reintegrate into their communities. This component will be implemented within the plan for collective reparations, first being applied in selected zones and then later expanded to include other affected communities;
- Clinical intervention. This programme recommends designing therapeutic modalities that can provide individual, family and group therapy that takes a holistic approach, with psychological, physical, family, work and social dimensions. The module would be applied by multidisciplinary teams that include professionals from existing local health providers who would adjust the treatment to the needs of the particular individuals and communities being treated;
- Promotion and prevention. This component will help disseminate information and develop educational programmes to sensitise people about the physical and psychological effects of the conflict.

Educational reparations

The general objective of this programme is to provide access to educational opportunities for people who, as a result of the conflict, missed the opportunity to receive an adequate education or complete their studies. This programme would include:

- Exoneration of costs. This component would require primary and secondary schools, universities, institutions of higher learning, Centres of Occupational Education (COE) and other relevant educational institutions to waive the costs of all applicable entrance exams, tuition and board, and fees for transcripts, certificates of graduation and diplomas;
- Scholarship programme. This consists of a competitive scholarship programme (with quotas for regions and types of career tracks) for all types of higher educational programmes, both national and international. In cases where a beneficiary does not have adequate preparation to compete equally with other students, the programme would include free access to pre-university programmes to make up for this inequality;
- Adult education. In co-ordination with local educational institutions with experience in adult education, this component will develop methods specifically geared towards affected populations, keeping in mind cultural and linguistic differences as well as the mental health status of its students. It will include flexible programmes allowing beneficiaries to complete primary and secondary studies at a distance or during hours that accommodate their work schedule.

Restitution of citizens' rights

This programme seeks to re-establish full political and civil rights to people affected by the actions or omissions of the state during the conflict. Such measures include:

- Normalising the juridical status of the disappeared. The TRC recommends the revision of the civil code to establish a special legal category that recognises 'absence because of forced disappearance' of people who disappeared between 1980 and 2000 whose whereabouts have never been confirmed and who therefore cannot be 'presumed dead'. This new legal category should be summarily declared by a judge, free of charge, for all people who voluntarily opt for this benefit.
- Normalising the juridical status of outstanding arrest warrants. The TRC recommends arrest warrants for terrorism and sedition that lack sufficient

and reasonable basis to link the accused person to the imputed acts be speedily annulled. In addition, a statute of limitations is recommended for orders of detention for terrorism so that they automatically expire after six months if not renewed. It is also recommended that the plan modernises information systems shared between the offices of the Ministry of the Interior (national/internal affairs) and the national police.

- Annulment of criminal, legal and police antecedents. The TRC recommends that the judicial powers comply with the order to annul the criminal, legal and police antecedents of all innocent people unjustly imprisoned who have been absolved, freed for having completed their sentences, pardoned or given presidential grace. This recommendation applies to those whose cases are linked to cases still being processed. This should be communicated automatically to the national police.
- Normalisation of documentation. The TRC recommends the establishment of a large-scale documentation programme run by civil registration offices and the municipalities of affected zones to reissue identity documents that were destroyed or lost as a result of the internal conflict, with minimum standards of proof. This programme would also grant amnesty to those who failed to fulfil their military duty or enlist in these services. The programme should inform all displaced populations of the benefits of this programme.
- Free legal services. The TRC recommends that special legal assistance be provided through the Ministry of Justice free of charge to help beneficiaries access the above programmes. The TRC also recommends that the ombudsman amplify its Protection Programme of Populations Affected by Political Violence.
- Exoneration of all costs. All costs associated with the programmes recommended above will be waived.

Economic reparations

The object of this programme is to provide economic compensation for moral and material damages suffered by victims and their families to contribute to their recuperation and improve their life expectancy in conditions of dignity and wellbeing. Specifically, pensions and indemnification will be provided to the families of people who disappeared and who were extrajudicially killed during the conflict, as well as for people partially or entirely incapacitated physically and mentally, people imprisoned although innocent, and victims of rape and the children of rape victims until they are 18 years old. It is recommended that all beneficiaries of the PIR will receive preferential access to national housing and employment programmes.

Collective reparations

The objective of this programme is to contribute to the reconstruction and consolidation of collective institutions in affected communities that were partially or totally destroyed by providing the necessary capital and technical help. Given the diversity of realities faced by affected populations, it is recommended that the content of each programme be designed through the participation of the beneficiaries who will diagnose the particular needs of the community. This programme has the following components:

- Institutional consolidation. This component seeks to return respect to the institutions, authorities and leadership of traditional organisations of governance in rural and native populations in the Andean and Amazon regions. Strengthening technical capacities and management skills of all relevant organisations, this process will resolve internal conflicts, reform the legal system and reinstate authorities in their designated roles.
- Recuperation and reconstruction of production infrastructure. The aim would be to improve the resources and capacity for production in the community, and thereby increase employment and other income-generating opportunities in a dynamic market.
- Recuperation and amplification of basic services. This programme responds to an urgent need to rebuild basic public services like health and education. This may include strengthening or replacing the infrastructure and equipment needed for the provision of these services.
- Employment and the generation of income. This component provides technical assistance in developing businesses, including access to credit from private lenders and non-profit programmes designed to assist micro businesses.

Institutionalisation

The TRC recommends the creation of a national entity to assume the co-ordination and global supervision of the implementation of the PIR. It is also recommended that this entity be based in Lima with regional offices that can work with regional and local governments as well as all other relevant institutions involved in the implementation of the PIR recommendations. Co-ordination should also be established with the judicial powers, the ombudsman's office and other ministries.

Funding

The TRC recommends the formation of a National Fund for Reparations to fund the programmes outlined by the PIR. This fund should be supported by the public budget to reflect the commitment of the government and to ensure the viability of the PIR. However, complementary funds may come from international sources such as the conversion of external debt for projects related to reparations.

Conclusion

Recognising that some violations cannot be repaired, such as the death of a loved one, the PIR intends to provide the closest approximation to remedying the damage suffered by victims of the conflict with an eye towards national recognition. While these recommendations resulted from a process of dialogue and negotiation between the TRC, NGOs and organisations representing victims, the next stage of implementation must consist of a full dialogue among political and social actors from both national and international settings.

Notes

1   As established by the Inter-American Court of Human Rights to signify the principle of the applicant's reasonable expectations for the future.

23

Reparation Policy in Nigeria

Sonny C. Onyegbula

The prolonged period of military rule in Nigeria was characterised by gross violations of human rights in the country.[1] Respect for the rule of law and due process was abandoned in the pursuit of naked abuse of power. The press reported people being harassed, detained without trial, tortured, extra-judicially executed, murdered, discriminated against and sometimes forcibly displaced from their homes. Environmental pollution, degradation and destruction of the ecology resulted from oil exploration activities in the oil-rich Niger Delta.[2] Successive military governments enacted decrees aimed at curtailing fundamental rights and liberties. The military regime's arrogation of judicial power and prohibition of court review of its action significantly impaired the authority and independence of the judiciary.

The regime of the late General Sani Abacha was probably the worst. It carried out widespread repression of human rights advocates, pro-democracy activists, journalists and critics of his government. Extra-judicial killings, torture, assassinations, imprisonment and general harassment of critics and opponents were the hallmark of his administration.[3] These ugly events of the past left many victims of gross violations of human rights, many of whom still seek redress for the abuses that they suffered.

Nigeria's domestic law, as well as international human rights instruments, both at the United Nations and regional levels, recognises the rights of victims to compensation, restitution and rehabilitation for gross violations of human rights.[4] The words compensation, restitution and rehabilitation are interchangeable with the term reparation. The reparation that we refer to here may take many forms and go beyond the payment of cash to victims. In general, reparation includes a variety of types of redress such as restitution, compensation, rehabilitation, satisfaction and guarantees of non-repetition. Restitution aims to re-establish to the extent that it is possible the situation that existed before the violation took place;

compensation relates to any economically assessable damage resulting from the violations; rehabilitation includes legal, medical, psychological and other care; satisfaction and guarantees of non-repetition relate to measures to acknowledge the violations and prevent their recurrence in the future.

It is frequently difficult for governments, including that of Nigeria, to provide direct financial compensation to every victim or survivor commensurate or proportional to the loss they suffered. Governments that have very limited resources and competing demands for them are reluctant to fulfil the obligations they owe the victims. In Nigeria, the Human Rights Violations Investigations Commission (HRVIC), popularly known as the Oputa Commission, was mandated to recommend measures that would redress the abuses of the past. Most citizens believed the Commission could fashion a full reparation package for victims. Some victims who testified at the Commission's public hearings stressed the fact that reparation was a key to healing the wounds that had been inflicted on them. Most victims believed that the duty of the Commission itself was to grant them some form of reparation. For some very poor victims, the possibility of receiving financial assistance was paramount, and was often a motive for their testifying before the Commission in the first place. They came with great expectations of how the Commission would help them financially. It did not seem to matter to them that the Commission had no powers to assist them financially directly.

This chapter will examine the way the question of reparation for victims of gross violations of human rights in Nigeria is being discussed. I start by reviewing the Nigerian domestic law on reparation as well as international law that is applicable in Nigeria. I then look at the perspective of major stakeholders on how reparation should be addressed. These stakeholders are the Nigerian government, the victims of past abuse, and the HRVIC or Oputa Commission.

Nigerian law and practice with regard to reparation

Nigeria's domestic law recognises the right of victims of gross violations of human rights to reparation. The 1999 Constitution of the Federal Republic of Nigeria contains a comprehensive bill of rights which provides for the protection of rights to life, dignity of human person, personal liberty, fair hearing, private and family life, thought, conscience and religion, expression and the press, peaceful assembly and association, freedom of movement, freedom from discrimination, and the right to acquire and own immovable property anywhere in Nigeria.[5] When any of these rights are violated, the Constitution raises the possibility of compensation. The Constitution provides that if any person alleges that any of his/her rights covered by the bill of rights have been or are likely to be violated, that person may apply to the high court for redress.[6]

Under the common law of torts, which is applicable in Nigeria, any person or group of people whose rights have been violated is entitled to initiate legal proceedings to recover damages or to prevent the violation. The basic type of compensation for violated human rights is monetary awards or damages.[7] The categories of damages include general damage, special damages, and exemplary or punitive damages. An analysis of a number of Nigerian cases on damages reveals a few significant features. First, an action for damages will cover bodily harm, which includes battery, assault, false imprisonment, physical injuries and death. In case of assault, battery and false imprisonment, the damages largely represent a solarium for the mental pain, distress, indignity, loss of liberty and death. General damages will be awarded in recognition that a right has been violated. Special damages are awarded to compensate the victim for expenses or costs arising directly out of the violation, including medical expenses, transport expenses and loss of income. The court may award exemplary or punitive damages to a victim in cases in which agents of the state have conducted themselves in an oppressive, arbitrary and unconstitutional manner.

The other type of compensation is the restitution or restoration of property wrongfully seized and in violation of human rights. Further decisions of the high court show that it considers a number of factors in determining the nature and amount of compensation payable. These factors include actual injury (physical or mental) to the victim, prospective injury to the complainant based on prediction of future aggravation of damages, consequential injury or damage to third parties and, in particular, loss of financial and emotional support. Though these measures of redress were available in Nigeria during the periods of military rule the government usually ignored court orders that went against them.[8]

How international law on reparation is applicable in Nigeria

The right to a remedy for victims of violations of international human rights and humanitarian law is recognised in numerous international instruments such as Article 8 of the Universal Declaration of Human Rights, Article 2 of the International Covenant on Civil and Political Rights, Article 6 of the International Convention on the Elimination of all Forms of Racial Discrimination, Article 11 of the Convention against Torture and other Cruel, Inhuman or Degrading Treatment or Punishment and Article 39 of the Convention on the Rights of the Child. Nigeria has ratified all of the above instruments except for the Convention against Torture, which the country has signed but not ratified. At the regional level, Article 7 of the African Charter on Human and Peoples' Rights recognises the rights of victims of gross violations of human rights to compensation for the violations that they have suffered.

Apart from the international instruments that are binding on Nigeria, there are soft laws under the auspices of the United Nations of which Nigeria is a bound member. With resolution 40/34 of 29 November 1985, the United Nations General Assembly adopted the Declaration of Basic Principles of Justice for Victims of Crime and Abuse of Power. This Declaration, apart from defining who can be classified as a victim of a crime, enumerates principles that provide for access to justice and fair treatment. It also provides for restitution, compensation and assistance for victims of crime and abuse of power. The principles called on states to establish, strengthen and expand national funds for compensation to victims. Further, the Economic and Social Council of the United Nations, in its resolution 1989/57 of 24 May 1989, called for the implementation of the Declaration of Basic Principles of Justice for Victims of Crime and Abuse of Power. To add further impetus to the recognition of the right to remedy for victims of human rights abuses, the Rome Statute of the International Criminal Court adopted on 17 July 1998 obliges the court to 'establish principles relating to reparations to, or in respect of, victims, including restitution, compensation and rehabilitation' and obliges party states to establish a trust fund for the benefit of victims of crimes within the jurisdiction of the courts and mandates the court to protect the safety, physical and psychological wellbeing, dignity and privacy of victims and to permit the participation of victims at all stages of the proceeding determined to be appropriate by the court. Nigeria ratified the Rome Statute in 2001.[9]

The Nigerian government's perspectives on reparation

It was clear from the beginning of the work of the Oputa Commission that the question of reparation for victims of gross violation of human rights was not top of the government's agenda. In his address at the inauguration of the Oputa Commission, President Olusegun Obasanjo's emphasis was on reconciliation. At the occasion he talked of, '… our determination to heal the wounds of the past and quickly put the ugly past behind us so as to continue to stretch our hands of fellowship and friendship to all Nigerians for complete reconciliation based on the truth and knowledge in our land'.[10] Further, he added: 'We want to reconcile all those who feel alienated by past political events, heal wounds inflicted on our people and restore harmony in our country.'

Throughout the address, President Obasanjo made no reference to reparation for the victims or the thinking of the government on this issue. However, on other occasions he made his views on reparation for gross violations of human rights clear; he appears to believe that no amount of money can compensate for the loss of life or other serious violations of human rights, that it would be insulting to the victims or their families to be offered money for the abuses that they suffered. At the 2001 World Conference on Racism in Durban, South Africa from 31 August to 8 September 2001 President Obasanjo was a key opponent of the demands by the people of African descent for payment of monetary compensation for centuries of colonialism and slavery. He has maintained this position in most public speeches and press interviews. In his statement at the Conference, the president had this to say about the demand for monetary compensation:

I must, however, disabuse the minds of those who believe that every apology must be followed with monetary compensation for the victims. For us in Africa, an apology is a deep feeling of remorse, expressed with the avowed commitment that never again will an individual who offered the apology have recourse to such a reprehensible act. And the recipient of the apology forgives … The issue of reparation then ceases to be a rational option. In any case we must not forget that monetary compensation, as being proposed, may further hurt the dignity of Africans and exacerbate the divisions between Africans on the continent and Africans in Diaspora.[11]

The views of President Obasanjo are hardly representative of those of other Africans and people of African descent who are still suffering the effects of colonialism and slavery. His position is in direct contradiction with those held by Lord Anthony Gifford who established the legal basis of the claim for reparation and further argued that there is no legal barrier to those who still suffer the consequences of crimes against humanity from claiming reparation.[12]

While giving evidence at the public hearing of the Oputa Commission for his unlawful trial and detention by the regime of General Sani Abacha for the so-called '1995 phantom coup',[13] the president declined to ask for any compensation for what he suffered during his three years of detention by the Abacha regime. According to President Obasanjo, 'God and Nigerians have compensated [me] enough by making [me] President of Nigeria'.[14]

Apart from the statements by the president opposing the payment of monetary compensations to victims of human rights abuses, no official government policy on the issue of reparation is known. It is clear that the form of reparation that the president seems to be opposed to is financial compensation, which he feels is insulting to the victims – even though this line of thinking denies the very serious needs that confront some victims of human rights abuses. Instead, the president proclaimed May 29 – the date set for the handover of power to the new civilian government in 1999 – as Democracy Day in Nigeria. He called on all Nigerians to celebrate that day as the day they regained control of their democratic destiny and ended many years of oppressive and corrupt military rule. Other states in Nigeria, notably Lagos and Ogun, have taken certain symbolic actions in remembrance of victims of human rights abuses during the regime of General Abacha, for example, by renaming streets and public buildings in honour of some of the victims. The governments of all the states in the southwest have proclaimed June 12 as their own version of Democracy Day in remembrance of the 12 June 1993 presidential election, which Chief M. K. O. Abiola won but which was annulled by General Ibrahim Babangida's regime. The election was acclaimed as the freest and fairest election since independence. According to these states, June 12 has more significance for the struggle for democracy and human rights than May 29.

The calls for the recognition of June 12 as Democracy Day in Nigeria continue to reverberate.

Perspective of the victims

The majority of those who submitted petitions to the Oputa Commission and actually testified at its public hearings were quite clear that they needed and wanted reparation for the abuses that they suffered. The victims suffered untold hardship from unlawful detention and torture as well as other unjustified violations of their human rights by state agents. Some of the victims lost their economic base and source of livelihood while in prison. There is no doubt that these victims are legally justified in their demands.

Victims expressed similar sentiments at the Seminar on the Right to Compensation, Rehabilitation and Restitution for Victims of Gross Violations of Human Rights organised jointly by the HRVIC, the Centre for Democracy and Development and the Legal Resources Consortium from 31 July to 3 August 2001. The seminar was organised to give voice to the various perspectives on the issue of reparation for victims. Some of the victims who attended the seminar to give their perspectives included Colonel R. S. Bello-Fadile and Chris Anyanwu who were jailed with President Obasanjo for the 1995 alleged coup plot against the Abacha regime, and Professor Femi Odekunle who was jailed for the 1997 alleged coup plot against General Abacha.[15] The victims who participated in the seminar were unanimous in their demand for reparation. Nothing short of justice, financial compensation and a public apology for the gross violations of human rights that they suffered could start a healing process for them.[16] In his response, the then Minister of Justice, Chief Bola Ige, who was present at the seminar, said: 'The Oputa Commission was not an *ad hoc* Committee but a full fledged Commission ... It will work as long as it is necessary to work. It is like the Bishop Tutu's Commission. [W]hatever it will take for government to make the Commission work like the Tutu Commission this government will make it work.' Yet, despite these lofty statements from the then Minister of Justice the government has neither published nor implemented the Commission's report, which it received on 28 May 2002.

In a survey carried out by a human rights organisation, Media Rights Agenda, in Lagos, a small majority of respondents said that they doubted the ability of the Commission to achieve meaningful reconciliation and insisted that reconciliation was insufficient if it did not include 'justice' and 'adequate' compensation for victims. According to Lagosians, genuine reconciliation is not possible in an atmosphere of lies and an unremorseful and unrepentant attitude by witnesses towards those who suffered rights abuses. They said that people's rights have been violently and blatantly violated and that genuine reconciliation must involve some form of restitution. They therefore cautioned that for the Commission to be relevant and credible, its terms of reference should be stretched to include justice and adequate compensation for victims. Lagosians also said that the government must ensure that the Commission's findings and recommendations are not swept under the carpet, as has commonly occurred with similar past investigation commissions, nor should the Commission's report be tampered with before being made public.

Asked whether respondents think reconciliation of victims and their tormentors is sufficient, 80 respondents representing 11.3% said 'yes' while 622 respondents representing 88.7% said 'no'. All of the respondents who answered 'no' recommended 'justice' and 'adequate' compensations for victims.[17] The result of this survey is a clear testimony of the feelings of the people towards the issue of reparation. Unfortunately the Nigerian government has not really brought the issue of reparation into the public domain for a comprehensive debate on the issue. However, what could be discerned from gathering various views on the issue is that most victims and the public at large favour the payment of monetary compensation and other forms of reparation as a starting step towards a healing process. Mere apology would in no way suffice.

Perspective of the Oputa Commission

The issue of reparation was always present during the sittings of the Oputa Commission. The Commission spent considerable time shaping its views on this very important issue. Though the mandate of the Commission did not specifically mention the issue of reparation, it did include recommending measures that could be used to redress the injustices of the past. The Commission was also aware of the legal obligation that the Nigerian state owed victims of human rights abuses both under domestic and international law.

However, a review of the Oputa Commission shows that it approached reparation with utmost caution. It could be that the caution was in deference to the opposition of President Obasanjo to monetary compensation to victims. In any case, throughout the sitting of the Commission, it tried to de-emphasise the issue of monetary compensation while emphasising symbolic forms of reparation. In its report to President Obasanjo, the Commission made a number of recommendations:

1. Institutional transformation
(a) Training and sensitisation on human rights principles:
Victims have been subjected to abuses by several state security institutions, in particular the police. A number of problems still exist within the police service. There is a need for the police to transform their role as instruments of terror into protectors of human rights. The police officers who appeared before the HRVIC did not accept responsibility for committing gross violations of human rights. There is need for a complete transformation of the Nigerian police force to one that is human rights oriented. The culture and method of policing have to change. The changes in the structure and operations of the police should be holistic rather than superficial. The training and orientation of the police should de-emphasise the continued use of torture by the police, the ill treatment of suspects and corruption by police officers.

Other institutions that need reforms are the state security services, the military and the prison service. Officers of these institutions need to be taught the principles of human rights and the need to desist from torture and inhumane and degrading treatment.

(b) An end to impunity:
There is need for the government to discipline identified and named perpetrators of human rights abuses whether they are still in service or retired. If no visible action is taken against them, victims will perceive it as a denial of their sufferings. This would institutionalise impunity. We cannot argue that we have guaranteed non-repetition of those violations in future if identifiable perpetrators are not prosecuted.

Doing justice implies that the perpetrators be prosecuted. In this connection, laws providing impunity constitute by themselves a violation of human rights and must be rejected. Creating immunity for those responsible for violations is not only highly unsatisfactory for victims, but it also makes it virtually impossible to obtain reparation since it reduces and limits all kinds of legal rights and responsibilities.

(c) Respect for the rule of law:
To prevent the recurrence of the abuse, the government should adopt or strengthen measures designed to re-establish the rule of law, permit the full functioning of all state institutions and bring the police force under effective civilian control. This could be achieved by appointing civilian officials with oversight and authority over security and criminal justice agents. The independence of the judiciary must be ensured and respect for the rule of law to be guaranteed.

(d) Discontinuing of military involvement on non-defence from foreign invasion related activities:
Military involvement on non-defence matters must discontinue. It is important to take away from the armed forces all law enforcement and domestic intelligence capabilities so that they redirect their efforts to preparing for the defence of the country against foreign invasion.

(e) Military courts restricted to hearing only military offences and actions of members of the armed forces:
Military jurisdiction should be restricted to disciplinary offences and crimes that are military in nature. Violations by members of the armed forces against civilians should be heard in the appropriate civilian courts. Military courts should under no circumstance have jurisdiction to try offences committed by civilians.

2. Symbolic reparation
The following are some of the symbolic reparation that can be put in place by the government:

(a) Public holidays:
The government could recognise the sufferings of victims, especially those who paid the ultimate price with their lives, by recognising their birthdays or the day they died as national holidays.

(b) National monuments:
The government could also recognise the pain of victims by establishing national monuments in recognition of past injustices.

3. Material and monetary assistance
Material assistance and compensation, in the form of monetary payments, will not in any way compensate for the loss of loved ones. However, it is also necessary for the government to consider the creation of a fund to which the state as well as individuals, including perpetrators and the

international community, could make contributions. The argument for this is compelling. There are many victims as well as survivors who are in dire need of financial assistance to make ends meet or even to seek medical treatment for the injuries sustained while in custody.

The Commission suggested that the president must as a matter of urgency establish a National Human Rights Trust Fund to provide for the claims of victims.[18] Money from this fund should not only be used to pay monetary claims but also to support the capacity of appropriate institutions whose activities contribute to democratic consolidation, especially building a culture of human rights in our society.[19] Contributions from the fund can be obtained from the national budget, international donor community, local and multinational businesses and monies recovered from corrupt public officials.

On the issues of monetary compensation, there is the temptation to dismiss claims by victims as unrealistic given the huge sums involved. While the criteria for determining the amount of compensation need to be carefully addressed, this should not diminish the intrinsic value of the principle itself – stated in the Universal Declaration of Human Rights – that everyone has the right to an effective remedy.[20] Justice has to be done to the victims of violations of human rights irrespective of concerns about resources.

Decisions relating to reparation for identified victims should be implemented in a diligent and prompt manner. Specifically, the disbursement of the funds may include but not be limited to the following:

(a) Emergency compensation to victims:
    This involves small grants to victims in need of urgent assistance to cover medical expenses, educational requirements, rents, etc.

(b) Individual reparation:
    This grant is for individuals (if deceased, their families). It includes a determined amount to acknowledge suffering and/or to subsidise daily living costs, taking into account current economic conditions. In this case an attempt should be made to ensure that the victim is at least returned to the status quo ante.

(c) Community reparation:
    This may include the resettlement of displaced people, infrastructure investment in the community, etc.

4. Acknowledge that reconciliation has not been achieved
The HRVIC has started a process that, if followed by a holistic govern-

mental programme, may in future achieve reconciliation. It is not possible for the Commission to achieve reconciliation within its short life span. The government should, however, follow up on the efforts the Commission has made to reconcile Nigerians who have been deeply affected by past government policies or gross abuse of their human rights.

5. Access to psychological/medical services
Victims and survivors of gross abuse of human rights should be given free access to psychological and medical services. The money for such services should be paid by the state. A proper referral system should also be set up so that psychological services are accessible to victims in rural areas.

6. Removal from public office
To allow named and identified perpetrators of gross violations of human rights to remain in office, either as security officials or in the public service, is insensitive to the pain and suffering of the victims of gross violations of human rights. The government should as a matter of urgency remove from office those who have been indicted by the Commission who are still holding important security positions or top government posts and disqualify them from holding public office for a number of years.

Conclusion

In accordance with its mandate, the Oputa Commission focused particularly on the many years of military rule that generated numerous innocent victims of torture, maiming, ill-treatment and murder. Many witnessed the destruction of their families and communities. Given the fact that the Commission interpreted its mandate in a manner that promotes national unity and reconciliation, it is imperative that those whose rights were violated are acknowledged through access to reparation. Although reparation can never fully compensate for the suffering of the victims, it can nonetheless improve the quality of lives of the victims. Without reparation there can never be real healing or reconciliation. In our view, the main purpose of reparation is that we as a nation are saying sorry to the victims over the human rights abuses that they suffered: 'Reparation is not just about money, it is not even mostly about money. Reparation is mostly about making repairs; self made repairs, on ourselves – mental repairs, psychological repairs, cultural repairs, organisational repairs, social repairs, institutional repairs, technological repairs, economic repairs, political repairs, educational repairs, repairs of every type.'[21]

Though no amount of money can compensate for the death or disappearance of a loved one, in some cases even a modest payment can act as an acknowledgement of the wrongs of the past and an official, symbolic apology. It is also widely recognised that establishing the truth about gross human rights violations that have occurred in the past, offering an apology and respecting the memory of victims through memorials or other official forms of acknowledgement are one aspect of reparation. Thus the work of a truth commission can be one important part of a full reparation package. Other forms of reparation could be a recommendation for the reform of state institutions and efforts by the state to provide a suitable environment for victims to testify in dignity about the abuses they suffered. A majority of victims who testified before the Oputa Commission asked for monetary compensation. Some of these people, as well as the relatives of those who died, could be in dire need of financial help either for medical attention or other form of emergency care. A number of these victims even thought that the Oputa Commission was in a position to give them money directly. Experiences from other countries have revealed that the records of the truth commission are an obvious source on which to build a reparation programme. However, it should be remembered that in most cases the commission is able to document the testimonies of only a small portion of the total number of victims and can hardly even corroborate their stories. In view of these obvious shortcomings it is generally better for the commission to make general recommendations and an overall assessment of need, which can serve as a beginning point for the development of a substantial reparation programme for victims of violations of human rights.

In South Africa a strong case for reparation for victims of gross violation of human rights was made by the Truth and Reconciliation Commission (TRC) in its Report. The TRC said: 'Victims of human rights abuses have suffered a multiplicity of losses and therefore have the right to reparation. Without adequate reparation and rehabilitation measures, there can be no healing or reconciliation.'[22]

The victims of gross violations of human rights in Nigeria cannot be different from those of South Africa. In some cases the needs of the victims may clearly indicate a dependency on monetary compensations, especially in cases where the victims require medical treatment for the injuries they have suffered. Victims' pleas for compensation usually come up when the commission's staff take their testimony or during public hearings and often the seriousness of the situation of the victims justifies the demand. Sometimes, as was the case at the Oputa Commission's public hearings, the victims are of the opinion that it is the duty of the commission itself to grant them some form of reparation for the injuries they suffered. For some very poor victims what is paramount to them is the possibility of receiving financial assistance and this is usually the driving force that brings them to the commission. They come with great expectations of how the commission can help them financially. It does not seem to matter to them that the commission has no powers to assist them financially directly.

In Nigeria, the lack of consensus on how to disassociate oneself from the past, a fear of creating new divisions, the massive nature of the problem and the perceived financial inability to cope with such a massive problem will undoubtedly remain a challenge. Nevertheless while the process of healing and reconciliation may be important to Nigeria, such a process must not be seen to work to the detriment of the victims.

Finally, it is important to appreciate the fact that although there are a number of Nigerians who personally suffered violations of their rights, it is useful to recognise that a substantial number of violations that occurred had an impact beyond the individual. The majority of Nigerians suffered human rights violations during the period under review. The many years of military rule ensured that Nigerians were denied the right to vote. A number of organisations, especially media houses that campaigned for a return to civilian rule and good governance, were harassed and several were shut down. Therefore, in developing an appropriate policy of reparation, in addition to taking cognisance of the rights of individuals, there is also the need to adopt a community-based and development-centred approach to reparation. In addition to individual means of reparation, adequate provision should also be made to entitle groups of victims or victimised communities to receive collective reparation.

In conclusion, the HRVIC recommended that the president and the commander-in-chief of the armed forces of the Federal Republic of Nigeria adopt the most practical measures to facilitate granting reparation which would, at the very least, restore the dignity of individuals and communities designated as victims of human rights violations within the period of the Commission's mandate.[23] Procedures relating to the settlement of claims should be made expeditious and effective, respecting the needs of the victim and in accordance with basic principles of fairness and justice.[24]

As a first step, it was recommended that the government should set up a post-Oputa Commission body to assess and execute the reparation package. The package should extend to all those who suffered from gross violations and not merely be restricted to those who brought their petition before the Commission. Apparently, the president adopted this recommendation only to the extent of setting up a committee headed by Elizabeth Pam, one of the commissioners, to implement the recommendations. More than 12 months later, the report is yet to be officially released, even though the president had given his word that the Oputa report would not go the way of past reports. It appears that the report has been read by an inner circle within the presidency, analysed for political gains or damage, and then discarded. Perceptions are that the need of the incumbent regime to negotiate its way to a second term with the very same people indicted in the report may mean the suspension of the Oputa report until a time when it may be used as a suitable political pawn.

Notes

1 Prior to the inauguration of the democratically elected government of President Olusegun Obasanjo on 29 May 1999, Nigeria had been ruled by the military for all but ten years since independence in 1960.

2 Ike Okonta and Oronto Douglas, *Where Vultures Feast: Shell, Human Rights and Oil in the Niger Delta* (San Francisco: Sierra Club Books, 2001).

3 Constitutional Rights Project, *Annual Report Human Rights Practices in Nigeria July 1997,* September 1998; for further reading see US Department of State, *Nigeria Country Report on Human Rights Practices for 1997* (US: Bureau for Democracy, Human Rights and Labor, 1998).

4 Section 35(6) of the 1999 Constitution of the Federal Republic of Nigeria and the international bills on human rights.

5 Sections 30–39 of the 1999 Constitution of the Federal Republic of Nigeria.

6 Section 46 (1) of the Fundamental Human Rights Enforcement Procedure Rules states the procedure for initiating legal proceedings on human rights issues. See V. Bello, Attorney-General of Oyo State (1986) 5NWLR 828, citing with approval the dictum of Holt, C. J. in Ashby V. White (1703) 2Ld.Raym.938. 'If the plaintiff has a right, he must have the means to vindicate it, and a remedy, if he is injured in the enjoyment

or exercise of it: and it is a vain thing to imagine a right without a remedy: for want of right and want of remedy are reciprocal.'

7 Section 35(6) of the 1999 Constitution of the Federal Republic of Nigeria. 'Any person who is unlawfully arrested or detained shall be entitled to compensation and public apology from the appropriate authority or person.'

8 Femi Falana, 'Origin and History of Detention Law in Nigeria', a paper presented at the Nigeria Bar Association Conference, 1 September 1989, 6.

9 Presently the position of the United Nations on the issue of the right to restitution, compensation and rehabilitation for victims of gross violations of human rights and fundamental freedoms is contained in the Basic Principles and Guidelines on the Right to a Remedy and Reparation for Victims of Violations of International Human Rights and Humanitarian Law. The Commission on Human Rights at its 56th session adopted the principles. E/CN. 4/2000/62 of 18 January 2000.

10 Address by President Obasanjo at the inauguration of the Human Rights Violation Investigation Panel, Monday 14 June 1999 at State House, Abuja, Nigeria, 1–2.

11 Statement by President Obasanjo at the World Conference Against Racism, Racial Discrimination, Xenophobia and Related Intolerance, Durban, August 31 to 8 September 2001.

12 Anthony Gifford, 'The Legal Basis of the Claim for Reparation', a paper presented at the first Pan-African Congress on Reparation, Abuja, Nigeria, April 27–29, 1993.

13 The Nigerian press tagged the 1995 coup the 'phantom coup' based on its belief that the coup only existed in the imagination of the Abacha regime, which cooked up the coup plot to punish its critics and perceived enemies.

14 President Obasanjo while testifying at the Oputa Commission in October 2001.

15 Eze Anaba, 'Why Oputa Commission Has Been Inactive,' *Vanguard*, August 8, 2001 and August 15, 2001.

16 Eze Anaba, 'Why Oputa Commission Has Been Inactive', *Vanguard*, 15 August 2001.

17 The survey was conducted between 9 and 18 December 2000 and published in *Media Right Monitor*, 2001. See http://www.internews.org/mra/mrm/newsletter.htm

18 There will also be a need for an independent body of recognised competence to oversee the activities of the fund.

19 For example, the National Human Rights Commission, the Legal Aid Council and other human rights non-governmental organisations.

20 Article 8 of the Universal Declaration of Human Rights.

21 Professor Chinweizu, 'Reparation and a New Global Order: A Comparative Overview,' A paper presented at the first Pan-African Congress on Reparation, Abuja, Nigeria, April 27–29, 1993.

22 TRC, Final Report (Pretoria: RSA, 1998), 170.

23 The definition of a victim is defined by the Declaration of Basic Principles of Justice for Victims of Crime and Abuse of Power (GA Res.40/34 of 29/11/1985).

24 Final draft of the recommendations of the Oputa Commission's report, which the writer participated in writing.

Index

Page references in italics indicate tables and illustrations.

A

Abacha, Sani 401, 406, 407
Abiola, Moshood 278, 406
Abuja Declaration 278
accountability 271–274
acknowledgement 3, 67, 72, 242–244, 248, 272
Adler v. *Federal Republic of Nigeria* 287
affirmative action 190, 191
African Bill of Rights 163n13
African Charter on Human and Peoples' Rights 404
African Charter on the Rights and Welfare of the Child 219, 220
African Union (AU) 76
Aleut Indians 279
Alexander, Neville xiii–xiv
Alfonsín, Raul 328, 329
Alien Torts Claims Act (ATCA) 91, 273, 283, 284–288, 300
Allende, Salvador 338, 339
Aloeboetoe v. *Suriname* 94
amnesty
    see also *Azapo* v. *The President of South Africa and Others*
    blanket amnesty 23, 73
    Interim Constitution 120, 128, 149, 157, 158
    legislation 103n15
    legitimacy of 71–72
    Mbeki's views on TRC's recommendations 22–23
    opposition by human rights groups 149, 150–153
    process 225–229, 237–238, 239

purpose of testimonies 108
    reparation as counterbalance 6, 33, 73, 124, 162n3, 164n21, 179, 233
    role in restorative justice 166–167
Amnesty Committee 40, 225–227, 228, 229
Amnesty International 149, 150–152, 157
ANC (African National Congress) 46, 52, 58
anger 69–73
Angola 380, 382, 383–385
Annan, Kofi 381
Apartheid Debt & Reparations Campaign 301
apartheid lawsuits 41, 117, 154, 162n9, 190, 300–302
    see also foreign litigation
apology
    for abuses during colonialism 271–275
    by F.W.de Klerk 251–253
    individual and institutional apologies 247–250
    moral and practical amends 244–247
    promise of 243–244, 253–254
    as term 242–243
Argentina 97
    equitable tolling 289
    reparation efforts 42, 96, 277, 328–335, 342, 343, 345, 346, 350
    role of truth commission 238
armed combatants, status of 36
Armenian genocide 281
Asmal, Kader 126, 146n51, 157
Australia 291
Aylwin, Patricio 335, 336
Azapo v. *The President of South Africa and Others* 33–34, 64n60, 71, 121, 145n47 & 48, 157–159

B

Babangida, Ibrahim 406
banks
    apartheid claims 300–302
    role in apartheid 297–298
Basic Income Grant 42
Bassiouni, Cherif 91, 278
Beanal v. *Freeport-McMoran, Inc.* 287,
    307n19
Belgium 294
beneficiaries of reparation 93–95, 100,
    129, 137, 232
    see also victims
Benjamin, Walter 133, 145n48
Berlin Conference (1884–85) 282, 306n12
Berlin Holocaust Memorial 362–364
Biko, Steve 16, 157
Black Economic Empowerment 25
black empowerment 78
black labour 198, 199–200
Bonn International Center for Conversion
    381
Bosnia-Herzegovina 285, 313n96
Botha, P.W. 252–253, 258
Brahimi Report 381
Brazil 78, 100
Broken Hill Proprietary 291
Burma 285–286, 289
business community
    see also apartheid lawsuits
    as beneficiaries of apartheid 203–204
    levels of culpability 295–299
    responsibility towards society's recon-
        struction 25, 41, 73, 78, 137
    role in financial reparations 188–190
Business Trust 25
Bussineau v. *President & Dirs. of Georgetown
    College* 288

C

Calata, Fort 66
Cape plc 291
Chad 304n4

Chikane, Frank 19
Child Justice Bill 215–218, 220–221
    see also juvenile justice
Chile 97, 153
    demand for Pinochet's trial 69
    reparation efforts 42, 93–94, 100, 277,
        290, 335–341, 342, 343, 345, 346
    role of truth commission 238
Claims Conference (Jewish) 278, 323
cleansing rituals
    in Mozambique 387–388
    value in healing 262–264, 269–270
    in Zimbabwe 388–390
Colombia 82
colonialism
    see also foreign litigation
    accountability for abuses 271–273
community
    family structures 218
    reconciliation within communities
        230–231
    rehabilitation programmes 4–5, 37
    role in reparation 172
    versus individual 73–78, 79–80, 95–96,
        98, 219–220
compensation *see* material compensation
CONADEP (National Commission on
    the Disappeared) 328, 329
Conference of Jewish Material Claims
    (1952) 278, 323
Constitution of Republic of South Africa
    (Act 108 of 1996) 46–47, 48, 49, 50,
    51, 55, 56
Constitution of Republic of South Africa
    (Act 200 of 1993)(Interim Constitution)
    on amnesty 120, 128, 149, 157, 158
    legitimacy 62n27
    on need for ubuntu 155, 203, 214, 225
    on reconciliation 126–127, 203
    on reparations 7–8
corporations *see* business community; for-
    eign litigation; multinational corpora-
    tions

Council of South African Banks (COSAB)
297, 298
Cradock Four 66
crimes against humanity (term) 305n7
criminal justice system *see* justice

D
Darwin, Charles 213
De Klerk, F.W. 251–253, 302
De Kock, Eugene 164n25
De Lange, Johnny 126
demobilisation
    challenges in Angola 382, 383–385
    cleansing rituals in Mozambique
        385–388
    cleansing rituals in Zimbabwe
        388–390
    needs of combatants 36, 380–382
    in South Africa 390–391
Democratic Alliance (DA) 58, 63n48
Didcott, Justice 33–34, 86n26, 121
Didiza, Thoko 200
Doe v. *Unocal* 285–286

E
Eastman Kodak Co. v. *Kavlin* 309n34
economic growth 74–79
Ecuador 82
educational reparations (Peru) 397
Eisenman, Peter 362–363, 364, 365
El Salvador 100
employment 192–193
    exploitation of black labour 198,
        199–200
Estate of Cabello v. *Fernandez-Larios* 290

F
Fagan, Ed 300, 318n202
farmers
    see also land issue
    as benefactors 188
    project for reintegration 390–391
    role in healing process 205–207

whites as major land owners 199–202,
    203–204
farm workers 199–200
Filartiga v. *Pena-Irala* 279, 283, 284
financial compensation *see* material com-
    pensation
Fishel v. *BASF Group* 290
foreign investment 76, 276–277
foreign litigation
    see also German Holocaust
    apartheid claims 295–302
    criticism 41, 117, 190
    development of reparation as concept
        277–283
    Herero claim 291–295
    Nigerian lawsuit 286–287, 307n20
    in non-US courts 290–291
    possible destabilising impact 154
    reasons 272–273
    role of multinationals in human rights
        abuses 275–277
    statute of limitations 288–290, 311n70
    in US courts 283–288, 303–304
Foreign Sovereign Immunities Act (FSIA)
    287, 309n30
forgiveness 69, 71, 108, 143n26, 230
Forti v. *Suarez-Mason* 289
France 294
Freedom Charter 163n13
Freedom Park 26, 83–84, 265–270
Frei, Eduardo 340
funding
    concept of wealth tax 11, 25, 41, 78,
        188
    President's Fund 25, 26, 39, 41
    sources viii, 75, 92

G
genocide (term) 306n9 & 10
German Herero claim 91, 273, 291–295,
    306n10, 308n25
German Holocaust
    Berlin Holocaust Memorial 362–365

counter-monuments in Berlin
365–366, *367, 368,* 369–371, *369,*
371–373, 374
lawsuit 286, 289–290
reparations 273, 278, 279–281,
322–328, 334n53, 342, 343, 345,
346, 349,
Gerwel, Jakes 123
Gifford, Lord Anthony 406
Goldstone, Richard 67–68
Goniwe, Matthew 66
Goniwe, Nyameka 66
Guatemala 82, 98, 100
Gugeletu Seven 66, 156

H
Hani, Chris 16, 17
healing
psychological 260–264
recovery of everyday life 112–113
value of testimonies 106–112
health reparations
Chile 337–339
Germany 325
Nigeria 412
Peru 396
hearings *see* testimonies
Herero claim 91, 273, 291–295, 306n10,
308n25
Hilao ruling 289
Holocaust *see* German Holocaust
homelands 208n3
Honduras 100
human rights
differing interpretations 149, 150–154
insights from TRC process 159–162
role of corporations 275–277
TRC as one interpretation 154–159
human rights groups 149, 150–154
Human Rights Violations Committee
34–35, 37, 39, 41, 228, 229

I
individual compensation 4
versus communal 73–78, 79–80,
95–96, 98, 219–220
Indonesia 287
*In re Austrian and German Bank Holocaust
Litigation* 280
In re Holocaust Victim Assets Litigation 280
institutional apologies 247–250
institutional reform
in Nigeria 409–410
RRC recommendations 5
Inter-American Commission of Human
Rights 98, 330, 332
Inter-American Convention on Human
Rights 35
Inter-American Court of Human Rights
94, 279, 307n16, 332
Inter-American Human Rights System
330
Interim Constitution *see* Constitution of
Republic of South Africa (Act 200 of
1993)
International Center for Transitional
Justice 321
International Convention on the
Elimination of all Forms of Racial
Discrimination 404
International Covenant on Civil and
Political Rights 34, 404
International Criminal Court 81, 90, 271,
278, 404
International Criminal Tribunal 271,
309n37
international litigation *see* foreign litigation
Iraq 95
Ireland 93
Israel *see* German Holocaust
Iwanova v. *Ford Motor Co.* 286, 289–290

J
Jane Doe I v. *Karadic* 290
Japan 96, 97, 279, 280, 281, 288

Japanese-Americans 278–279, 346
job creation 75, 76
justice
   see also juvenile justice; prosecution;
    restorative justice; retributive justice;
    transitional justice
   achievement within reparation pro-
    grammes 346–351
   as concept in South Africa 66–69
   indigenous models 212–213
juvenile justice
   children's rights 218–220
   new approach from Africa 213–215
   reponse based on restorative justice
    211–213
   restorative justice in criminal justice
    system 215–218

K
Kadic v. *Karadzic* 285
Kairos Document (1985) 125
Kalmich v. *Bruno* 290
Khulumani et al v. *Barclays et al.* 300–302
Kingma, Kees 381
Kohl, Helmut 363, 364
Krog, Antjie 117, 144n38, 155

L
Land Claims Commission and Court 56,
  95
land issue
   see also farmers
   discontent leading to illegal land grabs
    193
   dispossession during colonialism and
    apartheid 198–200
   lack of progress of land reform pro-
    gramme 201–202
   land reform programme (post 1994)
    200–201
   redistribution 200–201
   restitution 200, 201
   role of land in healing process 205–207

   white landowners 203–204
Latin America 81–82, 100
law, domestic 7–8
law, international
   see also foreign litigation
   reparation as principle 88–102
Legacy Project 265
legitimate expectation 8, 346
Leon, Tony 117, 148n67
Liberia 380
Locke, John 213
Luxembourg Agreement (1952) 278, 322,
  323

M
Maduna, Penuell 55–57, 195n15, 302
Mahomed, Ismail
   on amnesty and reparation 34,
    158–159
   on need for redress and reconciliation
    68
   on restoration for victims 71
Malan, Magnus 164n25
Mandela, Nelson xiii, 50, 123, 190
   monuments 375–378
Manuel, Trevor 302
Marcos, Ferdinand 91
Marootian v. *New York Life Insurance*
  Company 281
material compensation
   amounts and resources 101–102
   Argentina 96, 329, 330–334
   Chile 336, 337, 339–340
   Germany 323–325, 326–327
   importance 135–136, 172–173,
    244–247
   individual grants 4
   Japan 96
   Nigeria 410–411
   as one focus of reparation 175–176
   Peru 398–399
   public opinion 184–194, *186, 189,*
    191

Rwanda 90
materialist history theory 133
Mbeki, Thabo
    acceptance of TRC Final Report 203
    criticism of foreign litigation 41, 117
    on Freedom Park 266, 270
    government's response to TRC Final
        Report 41–42, 181
    politics of race and opposition 148n67
    response to tabling of TRC Final
        Report 15–28
    TRC Final Report debate 52, 54–55
Medical Association of South Africa
    (MASA) 248–249
memorials *see* symbolic reparation
memory 110, 112, 127, 132–134
    see also symbolic reparation
Menem, Carlos 329–330
Mhlauli, Sicelo 66
migrant labour 198, 218
Mkhatshwa, Smangaliso 127
Mkhize, Hlengiwe 40
Mkonto, Sparrow 66
monuments *see* symbolic reparation
Mozambique 382, 385–388
Mugabe, Robert 307n20, 388
multinational corporations
    see also foreign litigation
    claims 299–302
    role in human rights abuses 275–277,
        302–303
multi-party negotiations 116, 121
Mxenge, Griffiths 157

N

Namibia, Herero claim 91, 273, 291–295,
    306n10, 308n25
*National Coalition Government of Union of
    Burma v. Unocal, Inc.* 289
National Heritage Resources Act (Act 25
    of 1999) 265, 266
National Institute for Crime Prevention
    and Reintegration (Nicro) 217

Natives Land Act (1913) 198
Natives Trust Act (1936) 198–199
ndugu 214
necklace murders 114n16, 256–264
Nepad (New Partnership for Africa's
    Development) 76
New Partnership for Africa's
    Development (Nepad) 76
Ngewu, Cynthia 66, 156, 245
Nicro (National Institute for Crime
    Prevention and Reintegration) 217
Nigeria
    applicability of international law
        404–405
    government's perspective on repara-
        tions 405–407
    human rights violations 401–402
    initiatives towards reparation in Africa
        278
    lawsuit 286–287, 307n20
    legal right to reparation 402–403
    Oputa Commission's perspective
        408–412
    recommendations for future 414–415
    victims' perspective on reparations
        407–408, 413–414
non-repetition (term) 96, 97, 102
Ntsebeza, Dumisa 203
Nuremberg trials 275
Nyerere, Julius 214

O

Obasanjo, Olusegun 405–406, 407
Omar, Dullah 67, 125–126, 145n47, 216
Oputa Commission 402, 405, 406, 407,
    408–412, 413
Organisation of African Unity (OAU)
    Group of Eminent Persons for
    Reparation 278
Orr, Wendy 31, 40
Osbourne v. United States 288

P

Perón, María Estela Martinez de 328

perpetrators

see also amnesty; victims

experience of public exposure 234

reconciliation with victims 230

responsibility for reparations 188

TRC definition 203

Peru 82, 92

Plan of Integral Reparations 393–400

Philippines 91, 280, 281

Piet, Christopher 66, 156

Pinochet, Augusto 69, 238, 335, 341

Pollack v. *Siemens* 314n131

poverty 74, 75–76, 77, 78

increasing discontent 193–194

President's Fund 25, 26, 39, 41

Pretoria Bar 246

Promotion of National Unity and

Reconciliation Act (No. 34 of 1995)

1960 cut-off date 134

objectives of TRC 20, 224–225

Parliamentary debate (May 1995)

125–126

on reparation 1–3, 7, 32–34, 70–71

prosecution

evidence inadmissible after refusal of

amnesty 233

justice after TRC process 235

position of Amnesty International

150–151

possible indemnity 72

in retributive justice 71, 170

role of National Directorate of Public

Prosecutions 23–24

psychological reparation 260–264

public attitudes 184–194, *186, 189, 191*

punishment *see* prosecution; retributive

justice

R

RDP (Reconstruction and Development

Programme) 200

recognition 347–349

reconciliation

as concept 66, 116–117, 121–123, 124,

229–232

as element of TRC ethos 225

national vision 79–84, 231

post-conflict challenges 379–391

potential of relationship with repara-

tion 131–138

public opinion 185–187, *186*

relationship with reparation 79,

118–119, 121–128, 138–140, 239

reparation as priority before reconcilia-

tion 128–131

reconstruction (term) 121

rehabilitation

community programmes 4–5, 37

as element of reparation 96, 97, 172

necessity for 32–33

reintegration

challenges in Angola 382, 383–385

cleansing rituals in Mozambique

385–388

cleansing rituals in Zimbabwe 388–390

of combatants 381–382

efforts in South Africa 390–391

relationship-building *see* restorative justice

reparation

see also material compensation; repara-

tion policy; reparation programmes;

symbolic reparation

claims 295–302

as concept 66–68, 117, 121, 123–125

delays in implementation 5–6, 37–40,

167, 174, 177–182, 233–234

development of concept 277–283

enforcement and delivery 97–99

forms 95–97

guidelines from domestic and interna-

tional law 6–8

as human rights obligation 88–90

importance of restoring dignity 3, 4,

32, 70, 72

individual versus collective reparation
73–79, 95–96, 98
Mbeki's views on TRC recommendations (April 2003) vii, 18–22
moral versus material amends 244–247
potential of relationship with reconciliation 131–138
as priority before reconciliation
128–131
psychological 260–264
purposes 70–71, 73, 272, 412–413\
relationship with reconciliation
117–119, 121–128, 138–140
requirement after amnesty process 6,
33, 73, 124, 162n3, 164n21, 179,
233
role in restorative justice 171–177
significance of process during transition
99–102
as voluntary process 233
reparation policy
arguments 31–35
development 29–31
final proposals 37, 38–39
TRC views 35–36
reparation programmes
Argentina 42, 96, 277, 328–335, 342,
343, 345, 346, 350
Chile 42, 93–94, 100, 277, 290,
335–341, 342, 343, 345, 346
critical variables in design 341–346
German Holocaust reparations 273,
278, 279–281, 322–328, 334n53,
342, 343, 345, 346, 349
Nigeria 402–412
Peru's Plan of Integral Reparations
393–400
requirements for transitional justice
346–351
Reparation and Rehabilitation Committee
(RRC)
see also reparations policy
implications of report 8–13

insights from victims and community
180
mandate 1–3
policy 3–5
resentment 244
responsibility 90–92, 94, 187–188
restitution vi, 3, 95–96, 176
restorative justice
as approach in juvenile justice 211–213
extent within criminal justice system
215–218
implications for South Africa 177–182
importance of role of reparation
171–174
role of amnesty 166–167
role and function within reparation
174–177
as theory of justice 67, 167–171
retributive justice 67, 69–73, 170, 215
see also prosecution
revenge 69–73, 100
rhetoric
levels of rhetoric and TRC Report
52–57
rhetorical presidency 48–52
rhetorical situation and homonymy
57–59
rhetorical traditions 45–48
Ribeiro, Christopher 66
Ribeiro, Churchill 157
Ribeiro, Florence and Fabian 66
Rome Statute 278, 404
RTZ 291
Russia 281
Rwanda 90, 91, 92, 95, 271, 278, 380

S
Sampson v. *Federal Republic of Germany* 290
satisfaction (term) 96, 97
Saudi Arabia v. *Nelson* 287
Savimbi, Jonas 383, 385
Schnock, Frieder 369–370
Schröder, Gerhard 364

Serote, Mongane Wally 19, 26, 266, 268
Serra, Richard 362–363
Sierra Leone 92, 379–380
silence of victims 109, 110, 261
Skills Training Levy 25
slavery 143n30, 144n31
   see also foreign litigation
   claims 280, 282–283
   need for apology and reparation
     271–272, 273, 278
   WCAR declaration 273, 308n24
Smith, Adam 213
Sobukwe, Robert 16
social collectivism 213–214, 220
social solidarity 350–351
Sooka, Yasmin 39, 40, 204
Stih, Renata 369–370
Sudan 380
Suriname 94, 100
symbolic reparation
   Berlin Holocaust Memorial 362–365
   counter-monuments in Berlin
     365–366, *367, 368*, 369–371, *369,*
     371–373, 374
   as element of reparation policy 31, 37
   Freedom Park 26, 83–84, 265–270
   importance 4, 12, 82–84, 173
   monuments and memorials 4, 12, 26,
     360–362
   Nigeria 406, 410
   Peru 395–396
   relationship with material compensa-
     tion 116, 125, 130–131
   South African options 375–378

T
Tambo, Oliver 16
tenure reform 200, 201
testimonies
   amnesty hearings 226–229
   implications of 106–108, 235–237
   purposes of listening 108–110
   role in healing 110–112, 231

Thor Chemical Holdings Ltd 291
Torture Victim Protection Act (TVPA)
   288–290, 307n19, 314n116
transitional justice
   achievement within reparation pro-
     grammes 346–351
   objectives 66–67
   as term 128
transnational corporations 275, 276, 296
trauma 260–264
TRC (Truth and Reconciliation
   Commission)
   see also amnesty
   benefits 238–239
   Final Report 40–43, 123, 157, 166
   Final Report debate 41, 44–59
   insights for modern human rights
     159–162
   Mbeki's address on tabling of Final
     Report 15–28
   objectives 20, 224–225, 254n2
   as one interpretation of human rights
     154–159
   opposition by human rights groups
     149, 150–154
   providing terms of transition 119–125,
     135
   recommendations on reparation vi,
     vii–viii, 40–41, 177–182, 413
   Report of Reparation and
     Rehabilitation Committee 1–13
   as restorative justice process 166–167,
     179–180, 214–215
   on role of business 203–204, 296–299
Truche, Pierre 44
trust 349–350
truth 229–230, 231, 237–238
Tutu, Desmond 19, 37
   reaction to De Klerk's apology 251,
     252
   on reconciliation 81, 229
   on restorative justice 215
   on role of business 188

U
ubuntu
    interpretation of human rights 160, 161
    role in reconciliation 231
    as term 146n51, 155–157, 214, 220
    within child justice system 216, 221
UDF (United Democratic Front) 258
ujamaa 214
UN Basic Principles and Guidelines
    on the Right to a Remedy and
    Reparation for Victims of Violations
    of International Human Rights
    and Humanitarian Law 95–97,
    277–278
UN Commission on Human Rights 91,
    278, 296
UN Commission of Human Security,
    Africa Report 76
UN Convention against Torture and
    Other Cruel, Inhuman or Degrading
    Treatment or Punishment 35, 89, 404
UN Convention on the Rights of the
    Child (CRC) 219, 220, 404
UN Declaration of Basic Principles of
    Justice for Victims of Crime and Abuse
    of Power 404
United Democratic Front (UDF) 258
United Nations Compensation
    Commission 95
United States
    litigation 273, 274–275
    reparations payments 278–279
Universal Declaration of Human Rights
    (1948) 34, 158, 160, 163n11, 276, 404
universal jurisdiction 272–273
    see also foreign litigation
Urgent Interim Reparation 3, 31, 32, 37,
    38, 39, 40, 41, 177

V
Van Boven, Theo 277, 316n150
victims
    see also testimonies

effects of TRC process 234–235,
    237–238
implications of telling stories 106–113
in post-transition 102
recognition and selection 9–10, 93–95,
    100, 129, 136–138, 203
reconciliation with perpetrators 230
victim competition 101
victim (term) 13n7, 14n11, 93

W
wealth tax 11, 25, 41, 78, 188
white community
    attitudes re reparation 184, 187
    as benefactors of apartheid 191–193
    reponsibility for reparations 188, 190,
    194
Wiwa v. *Royal Dutch Petroleum Co.*
    286–287, 307n20
World Conference against Racism, Racial
    Discrimination, Xenophobia and
    Related Intolerance (WCAR) (2001)
    82, 273, 306n11, 405

X
Xuncax v. *Gramajo* 288

Y
Yugoslavia 90, 271, 278, 309n37

Z
Zalaquett, Jose 153, 161
Zamela, Nosipho 256–260, 263
Zimbabwe
    cleansing rituals 382, 388–390
    land issue 205–206, 206–207